NO CONSTITUTIONAL RIGHT

TO BE LADIES

ALSO BY LINDA K. KERBER

Federalists in Dissent: Imagery and Ideology in Jeffersonian America

Women of the Republic: Intellect and Ideology in Revolutionary America

Women's America: Refocusing the Past (edited with Jane Sherron De Hart)

U.S. History as Women's History: New Feminist Essays
(edited with Alice Kessler-Harris and Kathryn Kish Sklar)

Toward an Intellectual History of Women

NO CONSTITUTIONAL RIGHT
TO BE LADIES

Women and the Obligations of Citizenship

LINDA K. KERBER

 HILL AND WANG

A division of Farrar, Straus and Giroux • New York

Hill and Wang
A division of Farrar, Straus and Giroux
19 Union Square West, New York 10003

Distributed in Canada by Douglas & McIntyre Ltd.
Printed in the United States of America
Designed by Abby Kagan
First edition, 1998

Library of Congress Cataloging-in-Publication Data
Kerber, Linda K.
No constitutional right to be ladies : women and the obligations
of citizenship / Linda K. Kerber. — 1st Hill and Wang ed.
p.   cm.
Includes bibliographical references (p.   ) and index.
ISBN 0-8090-7383-8 (alk. paper)
1. Women and democracy—United States—History.   2. Women—Legal
status, laws, etc.—United States—History.   3. Citizenship—United
States.   4. Political obligation.   5. Civics.   I. Title.
HQ1236.5.U6K47   1998
305.42'0973—dc21   98-21393

Grateful acknowledgment is made to those who gave permission for the reproduction of
illustrations. Individual credits appear in the list of illustrations.

CONTENTS

ILLUSTRATIONS

1. Old Suffolk Court House by Frederic C. Detwiller, copyright © 1997 by Frederic C. Detwiller, reprinted by permission of Frederic C. Detwiller. This material was revised from a drawing by Detwiller published in *Mass. Law Review*, Vol. 74, December 1989.   21

2. Portrait of James Sullivan by Gilbert Stuart, 1807, reprinted by permission of the Massachusetts Historical Society.   22

3. Drawing of Ethel Mackenzie, from the San Francisco *Chronicle*, reprinted with permission.   40

4. Streets in Houston, Texas. Courtesy Houston Metropolitan Research Center, Houston Public Library.   48

5. Houston city map, 1869. Courtesy Houston Metropolitan Research Center, Houston Public Library.   61

6. Julia and Abby Smith, early 1870s. Courtesy The Historical Society of Glastonbury, Inc.   82

7. Painting of Kimberly Mansion by Laurilla Smith. Courtesy the Connecticut Historical Society, Hartford.   84

8. Woodcut of Abby Smith, 1877. Courtesy The Historical Society of Glastonbury, Inc.   91

9. Gwendolyn Hoyt, 1957. Reprinted by permission of the Tampa *Tribune*. This material originally appeared in the Tampa *Daily Times*, Dec. 19, 1957.   126

10. Clarence Hoyt, 1957. Reprinted by permission of the Tampa *Tribune*. This material originally appeared in the Tampa *Tribune*, Sept. 21, 1957.   127

11. "What We May Confidently Look For," cartoon reprinted by permission of the Alice Marshall Women's History Collection, Pennsylvania State University, Harrisburg. This material originally appeared in *Punchinello*, June 4, 1870.   132

12. "Woman Suffrage in Action," 1920, reprinted by permission of Alice Marshall Women's History Collection, Pennsylvania State University, Harrisburg. This material originally appeared in a widely distributed broadside.   138

ACKNOWLEDGMENTS

 s participants told me their stories of how they had come
to be part of the history of women's civic obligation, I found
myself thinking, more than once, of Dickens' novels, which
I had once scorned for what I thought were heavy-handed plot devices that leaned on chance encounters, on luck that draws precisely
the right people together. The stories in this book are full of coin-
cidences worthy of Dickens. And in ways of which they were only
dimly aware, these people were linked to me by lively networks that
could have come straight out of a nineteenth-century novel: networks
of committed and generous historians, lawyers, judges, archivists, and
private citizens—some in Civil Liberties Unions, many in universities, some in public life—who remembered the stories, who saved the
documents, who made time in their lives for an inquiring stranger.
And so I came to encounter dozens of people who have been trying,
some at enormous psychological sacrifices, to retain the memories of
these events so that they will have meaning for future generations.

I am humbled by the knowledge that the meaning of these stories
(or, at least, my understanding of their meaning) would have been
hidden thirty years ago, twenty years ago, even ten years ago. To take

these men and women seriously has required first that the work of feminist and social historians of the last quarter century be done; that the traditional narrative of the American past—often readable, generally instructive, sometimes comforting, but all too often told primarily from the perspective of elected officials and military leaders— be reconfigured, reimagined, rethought by thirty years of criticism. Each of the stories in this book, standing alone, once looked like nothing more than an anecdote. Together, we can see them as successive acts in a grand narrative that reveals the way in which American society has been constructed through successive readjustments of the relationship between men and women.

I am especially grateful to the people who patiently submitted to a historian's questions about their lives: Dallas Albritten, Richard Christie, Rhonda Copelon, Richard Danzig, Raya Dreben, Carl and Jeannette Durrance, Timothy Dyk, Helen Feeney, Ruth Bader Ginsburg, Betty Gittes, Robert Goldberg, Patricia Hardee, Charles Hardee III, Leland Hawes, Gwendolyn Hoyt, Paul Hunt, Paul Johnson, Robin Pirie, Bernard Rostker, Stuart Savett, David Sitman, Richard Ward, and Joanna Weinberg. I am grateful to Marvin Sparrow for permission to quote from administrative material in the files of Goulston & Storrs.

Many lawyers and judges whom I interviewed not only generously described their own activities but patiently constituted themselves as my teachers. I am especially grateful to Judge Shirley Abrahamson of the Wisconsin Supreme Court, Rhonda Copelon of the City University School of Law at Queens College, John Reinstein of the Civil Liberties Union of Massachusetts, Sylvia Law of New York University School of Law and Elizabeth Schneider of Brooklyn Law School. Martha Minow of Harvard Law School patiently demystified the workings of the U.S. Supreme Court; Bruce Mann of the University of Pennsylvania Law School made time to conduct an elementary tutorial on pleadings. Aviam Soifer of Boston College Law School, Joseph Singer of Harvard Law School, Hendrik Hartog of Princeton University, and Bill Turnier of the University of North Carolina School of Law exchanged work in progress and paid me the compliment of treating me as a colleague. Mary Becker of the University of Chicago Law School and Elizabeth Rapaport, now of the University of New Mexico School of Law, read portions in progress and offered important advice.

Colleagues at the University of Iowa College of Law welcomed my questions, early and late. Martha Chamallas, now of the University of Pittsburgh School of Law, drew me into feminist legal argument and law school teaching. It was Mary Dudziak's idea that Helen Feeney's case would answer some questions I was raising. Martha and Mary generously tutored me in a wide range of legal complexities, gradually widening my scope. H. Jefferson Powell, now of Duke University School of Law, included me in his seminar a long time ago and for years he patiently answered questions about the intricacies of eighteenth-century law. Herbert Hovenkamp and Arthur Bonfield helped me think about citizenship and obligation. Patricia M. Cain answered tax questions and has welcomed me to the classroom we now share.

A happy chance brought me to a month's residency at the Rockefeller Foundation's Villa Serbelloni in Bellagio, Italy, when Jack Greenberg of the Columbia University School of Law, Albert A. Alschuler of the University of Chicago Law School, and Jerome Skolnick of the University of California–Boalt Hall School of Law were in residence; they suffered my questions cheerfully, shared their knowledge and wide experience enthusiastically and generously. It is particularly important to add here the standard warning that none of these generous colleagues should be held responsible for any lapses of my own.

This book began as the Jefferson Memorial Lectures at the University of California–Berkeley in 1989; when it was nearly complete extended portions were offered as the 1997 Merle Curti Lectures at the University of Wisconsin. An early version of Chapter 5 was presented as the Abraham Baldwin Lecture at the University of Georgia and published in the *University of Chicago Law School Roundtable*, vol. 1993, pp. 95–128. Chapter 3 was offered as the Milton Klein Lecture at the University of Tennessee; an early version of Chapter 1 was offered as the Ernst Fraenkel Lecture at the Free University of Berlin and appeared in the *American Historical Review*, vol. 97 (1992), pp. 349–78.

By inviting me to spend a semester in the Philadelphia Center for

Early American Studies at the University of Pennsylvania, Michael Zuckerman made sure I began this work surrounded by encouraging colleagues. Substantial portions of the manuscript were read in various stages by Willi Paul Adams, Tim Breen, Connie Brothers, Fumiko Fujita, Robert Gross, Hendrik Hartog, DeAnna Heindel, Thomas Holt, the late Sydney V. James, Alice Kessler-Harris, Masako Notoji, Katherine Preyer, Dorothy Ross, Leslie Schwalm, Carroll Smith-Rosenberg, and Alfred F. Young. Conversations with Leora Auslander, Lauren Berlant, and William McFeely sharpened my arguments. At the end, Michael Grossberg made time to read the entire next-to-last draft; that I did not take all his advice is not his fault.

My work has benefited from challenging questions posed at seminars at Harvard Law School, the University of North Carolina School of Law, the University of Chicago Law School, Georgetown University Law Centre, the University of Iowa College of Law, the University of Pennsylvania, the Newberry Library and the American Bar Foundation. I am grateful for the responses of audiences at meetings of the Organization of American Historians, the American Studies Association, the American Historical Association, the Berkshire Conference of Women Historians, and the Japanese Association for American Studies.

I could not have written this book without the generous support I was given by the National Endowment for the Humanities, the John Simon Guggenheim Memorial Foundation, the Rockefeller Foundation, and the National Humanities Center. I have learned more than I can fully acknowledge from the rich scholarship of others whose work these foundations also sustain. I could not have found my way in dense and often confusing archives without the generous guidance of many documentary editors, curators, and archivists, especially Leslie Rowland of the Freedmen and Southern Society Project at the University of Maryland–College Park, Mary Wolfskill at the Library of Congress; Stanley Toszeki at the Federal Records Center, Waltham, Massachusetts; Wendy Chmielewski at the Swarthmore College Peace Collection; Eva Moseley at the Schlesinger Library, Radcliffe College; Amy Hague and her colleagues at the Sophia Smith Collection, Smith College; Martha Sachs at the Alice M. Marshall Women's History Collection, Pennsylvania State University, Harrisburg; and Ben Primer at the Seeley G. Mudd Manuscript Library, Princeton University. By their energy and enthusiasm, Charles Hawley of Iowa City, Naomi Ben-Shahar of New York City, Marilyn Wandrus and Michael Campbell of Washington, D.C., made it possible to include many of the illustrations that are in this volume.

Over the years I have benefited from research assistants who threw themselves into the project with unusual energy and devotion. At the University of Iowa there have been Randall Tosh, Leslie Taylor, David Manderscheid, Charles Hawley, Rachel Bohlmann, and Kevin Gao; at the University of Chicago, Alexandra Gillen; in North Carolina, Katherine Hermes and Lori Gudeman; in Houston, Angela Boswell; in Florida, Ellen Babb and Tim Huebner; in St. Louis, Karen Meacham; in Glastonbury, Ann Morrisey; in Boston, Ruth Dearden and Julia Soyer.

Jane De Hart and Dick Kerber have commented on more drafts than any of us can count. The Serendipity group has sustained my spirits. At the University of Iowa, a department of colleagues and a sequence of deans, provosts, and presidents have supported this research by their interest, their good questions, and their patience. The May Brodbeck Chair in the Liberal Arts offers precious gifts of time and research funds. Jay Semel and Lorna Olson make the Obermann Center for Advanced Studies a congenial and supportive retreat.

Near the end, good fortune brought me to Georges Borchardt, and he, in turn, brought me to Lauren Osborne. Each has taught me by example to read prose with an intensity I once thought was reserved for poetry. Lauren has been the editor of whom I had only dared to dream; a colleague who reads line by line, with a pencil, and then muses creatively on how well the structure of the chapters may be serving the argument of the book. It has been invigorating to be accompanied, as this book moves into press, by colleagues who still believe that precision of language can make a difference in our lives.

My family waited for this book for a long time. Dick Kerber was certain, early on, that I should undertake the entire project rather than publish one of the chapters standing alone; if this book has merit, much is due to his insistence that it was worth waiting to see the entire picture whole. My parents always believed that their daughter could grow up to be a writer. I mourn that my father did not live to see this book. He was a poet who loved the playfulness of words, and as I write I keep his thesaurus close at hand. My mother, Dorothy Haber Kaufman, a woman of spirit and determination, receives this book on her ninetieth birthday. I once promised our sons, Ross and Justin, that my next book would have boys in it; since they themselves are now adults, I trust they will accept the men in this book in fulfillment of my promise. It is a great pleasure to me that it is published just as we happily welcome two daughters, Nancy Clapp and Hope Goldberg, to our circle.

PREFACE

It is often hard for an author to gauge what semiconscious need has inspired a particular book. Why this project, with its specific set of questions? Sometimes I reply—and it is a true response —that when I stumbled upon an occasion, shortly after the American Revolution, when the highest court of Massachusetts ruled that a married woman's loyalty to her husband took precedence over her loyalty to the state, I recognized an intriguing story. Sometimes I reply—and this is also true—that when the University of California at Berkeley asked me to offer the three Jefferson Memorial Lectures in 1989, I thought I would base them all on that lawsuit, until I realized that only a fool could expect a substantial audience to materialize on three successive afternoons to hear about a legal skirmish in a state court nearly two hundred years ago. The prospect of humiliation concentrates the mind. I searched for other cases that raised similar issues of obligation and state power, and when the Jefferson Memorial Lectures were over, I had the outline of a book.

But in my heart I know this book began early on a misty morning in Oakland, California, in June 1967, when my husband, whose sociological profile is virtually the same as mine—we were born within

nine months of each other, to families similar in religion and ethnicity, to mothers who were teachers in the same public school system
and to fathers who had roughly congruent professional aspirations;
we attended the same high school, the same university, we have
roughly the same amount of graduate training—when Dick, his hair
cut so short his scalp showed, his body covered in olive drab, boarded
a bus that would take him into the center of a war we both believed
to be immoral, and I, not weeping, dressed carefully in case this would
be our last memory of each other, entered the taxi that would take
me to an airport, and home, where I would wait out the war in physical if not emotional safety, not ever understanding enough even to
ask how it happened that the same state power that was propelling
him on that bus was not also dressing me in olive drab, cutting my
hair, and forcing me on that bus. Sometime that morning my need
to write this book was born.

It was as a citizen that Dick went to Vietnam. And it was as a citizen
that I struggled to comprehend his vulnerability and my own simultaneous invulnerability. "Citizen" is an equalizing word. It carries
with it the activism of Aristotle's definition—a citizen is one who
rules and is ruled in turn. Modern citizenship was created as part of
the new political order courageously constructed in the era of the
American Revolution. Reaching back to the Greeks and reinventing
what they discovered, the founding generation produced a new and
reciprocal relationship between state and citizen. They used a capacious rhetoric that ignores differences of gender, race and ethnicity,
religion and class; any free person who had not fled with the British
or explicitly denounced the patriots was a citizen. After the Civil War,
the Fourteenth Amendment permitted no formal categories of first-
and second-class citizens. Philosophically, all persons (whether or not
they are citizens) are entitled to equal protection of the laws, and all
citizens are bound equally to the state in a web of rights and obligations.

Women have been citizens of the United States as long as the
republic has existed. Passports were issued to them. They could be
naturalized; they could claim the protection of the courts. They were
subject to the laws and were obliged to pay taxes. But from the be-

ginning American women's relationship to the state has been different in substantial and important respects from that of men. The struggles over women's suffrage between 1848 and 1920, and, in recent years, over the Equal Rights Amendment and the meaning of the "equal protection of the laws" guaranteed in the Fourteenth Amendment, have publicized the extent to which the meaning of *rights* has been linked to gender. That there is a history of gendered *obligation* is less well understood.

American political theory has traditionally had much to say about rights and little about obligation. This tendency is wholesome; emphasis on rights is the most progressive characteristic of American legal traditions, the aspect of American law and social practice that is most admired abroad and best understood at home. People unversed in legal complexity do understand that they are entitled to the right of free speech, to a right against self-incrimination, to the right of religious freedom, to the right to a jury trial, to the right to vote. The Tenth Amendment is crucial: rights not granted to the state are *reserved* to the people. It is not a bad thing to live in a system in which we have so many rights we do not list them all.

In the liberal tradition, rights are implicitly paired with obligation. The right to enjoy a trial by jury is mirrored by an obligation to serve on juries if called upon. The right to enjoy the protection of the state against disorder is linked to an obligation to bear arms in its defense. The right to enjoy the benefits of government is linked to an obligation to be loyal to it and to pay taxes to support it.

Obligation is the means by which the state can use its power to constrain the freedoms of individual citizens. Our civic obligations are usually duties to which most of us would gladly consent in principle; we understand that the stability of our society rests on willingness to bear the burdens of citizenship. In common speech we often use the word "obligation" to mean a voluntary undertaking; we may refer to our obligation to vote, our obligation to be responsible parents. But in this book I use it only in its primary sense—to be bound, to be constrained, to be under compulsion. I treat as obligations only those duties that invite state punishment if they are not performed. (If the obligation to defend the nation were not in some measure distasteful, there would never be a need for a draft.) It has been a struggle to ensure that the burdens are fairly distributed; controversies have cropped up throughout our history and continue today. As we exercise the rights and bear the obligations of citizenship, we need to know what we are accepting, what burdens we are bearing, and in what ways rights and obligations define individual citizens' relationships to each other and to the society within which we live.

If we were to construct a "Bill of Obligations," what would it look like? Some obligations are wide-ranging, applying not only to citizens and resident aliens but to anyone on U.S. territory. Among these are the general obligation not to violate criminal laws and the obligation to observe legislative and administrative requirements (such as paying the minimum wage or not discriminating on the basis of race). In this book I treat five distinct obligations that rest on American citizens. Two are shared with all inhabitants: the obligations to pay taxes and to avoid vagrancy (that is, to appear to be a respectable working person). Two are occasionally also imposed on resident aliens: the obligation to serve on juries and the obligation to risk one's life in military service, to submit to being placed in harm's way when the state chooses. (This obligation has slipped out of common conversation since the advent of the All-Volunteer Force in 1975, but it is a real one, and when we consider the meanings of citizenship we ignore it at our peril.) Only citizens bear the obligation to refrain from treason.

Two of these obligations are negative ones. We do not try to measure the loyalty of citizens, but we think we can know when they are traitors. Instead of an enforceable obligation to be loyal—we have no legal obligation to say the Pledge of Allegiance, for example, nor does the state normally seek to measure degrees of loyalty—we have a negative obligation to refrain from treason. Similarly, as a society we have valued work but have never insisted that every person must work. Nor can we define clearly what work is. But occasionally we declare that an individual has failed a test of appearances, and we arrest for vagrancy a person who does not appear to be working. The obligation to refrain from vagrancy is rarely noticed, for it is usually greatly outweighed by other needs that impose on us the duty of waged labor or its substitutes—the need to feed and clothe ourselves and our families, for example. Vagrancy was often invoked just after the Civil War, when emancipation altered the relationship between work and the economy. Vagrancy has been used capriciously as a device to assure a cheap labor supply or to control the most impoverished, and as a result its burdens have weighed heavily on African-American women.

If concepts of rights and obligations are to be meaningful, they must have about them the quality of solidity and fixedness. But historically they have been also fluid and negotiated. In each of these five modes, a general obligation that appears at first glance to weigh on all individuals equally turns out in practice to have been experienced differently, over the years, by men and by women. Although the founding generation brilliantly revised the definition of citizenship for their new country, they did not have the heart or the energy to reconstruct the entire legal system. Even after the Declaration of Independence, the forms and procedures of American law—the understanding of what a contract means, the manner of probating a will, the very concept of phenomena like juries or sheriffs—all had their bases in English practice. Thirteen state constitutions, the Northwest Ordinance, and the Constitution of 1787 radically changed the relationship of state and citizen. But the United States absorbed, virtually unrevised, the traditional English system of law governing the relationship between husbands and wives.

The old law of domestic relations began from the principle that at marriage the husband controlled the physical body of the wife. (There was no concept of marital rape in American statutes until the mid-1970s.) There followed from this premise the elaborate system of *coverture*. By treating married women as "covered" by their husbands' civic identity, by placing sharp constraints on the extent to which married women controlled their bodies and their property, the old law of domestic relations ensured that—with few exceptions, like the obligation to refrain from treason—married women's obligations to their husbands and families overrode their obligations to the state.

Coverture originally encompassed relations between parents (especially father) and children and between masters and servants. The early republic did away with many of those elements, but the asymmetrical relationship outlined in "the law of baron and feme" (master and woman, or lord and lady) remained. The assumption that married women owe their primary civic obligation to their husbands persisted long after the Revolution. It continued to define relationships among men, women, and the state. It lurks behind what many people take to be the common sense of the matter in our own time.

The right to be treated like "ladies," observed Kathleen Teague in 1980, is a right "which every American woman has enjoyed since our country was born." Teague was representing the Eagle Forum, a conservative women's organization whose president was Phyllis Schlafly, at a hearing held by the Armed Services Committee of the House of Representatives. A few months before, the Soviet Union had invaded Afghanistan and President Jimmy Carter had proposed that all men and women eighteen years of age be obliged to register for a future draft. Teague was shocked; women had never been drafted. Teague believed that the absence of an obligation to military service was tantamount to the presence of a right. Women, she said, had never been required to fight.

Do women have "a constitutional right to be treated like American ladies"? Should a woman have a freedom from civic obligation that men must fulfill? For Kathleen Teague, the right to be a lady was clearly more than a rhetorical flourish; she called upon it as a shelter from state power. She recognized that the principles of coverture were still recognizable in American law and social practice. One by one, the people we will meet in this book challenged these principles, questioning the unequal burdens placed on men and women in the practice of citizenship. They all lost their lawsuits. But one by one they revealed the hollowness of claims that coverture protected women; one by one they revealed, I believe, that the allegation that coverture shielded women from certain public burdens was likely to camouflage practices that made them more vulnerable to other forms of public and private power. One by one they revealed what the obligations of citizenship have been. This book is their story.

NO CONSTITUTIONAL RIGHT

TO BE LADIES

1

"NO POLITICAL RELATION TO THE STATE" CONFLICTING OBLIGATIONS IN THE REVOLUTIONARY ERA

"She must take her fate with him for better for worse"

In February 1801, James Martin submitted a complaint to the Supreme Judicial Court of Massachusetts, the state's highest court of appeals. He demanded that the state return land and houses confiscated from his mother twenty years before, toward the close of the American Revolution. The case forced leading lawyers and judges to put into words their understanding—normally implicit—of the obligations that married women citizens owe to the state.[1]

James Martin won his case. The outcome was doubly ironic. One irony was that the decision forced the state to reclaim property it had already sold to loyal citizens and restore it to heirs of Tory supporters of the Revolution's enemies. The other irony is that through the recognition of the claim of Anna Gordon Martin's son, her family saved her property at the price of simultaneously denying that she was an autonomous citizen with her own civic responsibilities. Deep into the twentieth century, long after new legislation had confirmed married women's power to manage real estate and personal property, the citizenship of an American woman who, like Anna Martin, had married a foreign man continued to be problematic. Aspects of married women's citizenship continued to be filtered through their husbands' civic identity.

James Martin's family had rejected the American Revolution. From the depositions filed with the Loyalist Claims Commission after the Revolution, from a handful of letters gathered by an antiquarian at the beginning of the twentieth century, and from scattered court papers in scattered archives, it is possible to piece together some of the family's history. James's father, William Martin, was born in England. In 1742, as a young man, William joined the Royal Regiment of Artillery, the one regiment in which careers were open to talented men without wealth. Artillery officers tended to have a high sense of themselves because of their technical expertise, but their often humble origins gave the regiment low social status. Sometime during the French and Indian War, William Martin was sent to the American colonies, where he made an upwardly mobile marriage to Anna Gordon, the daughter of James Gordon, a wealthy Boston merchant and landholder who was an active member of the Anglican Church. But the demands of the service pulled Martin away, and in 1752 we find him in Halifax, Nova Scotia, having left his wife and at least one child with her parents in Boston.[2]

William Martin was torn between the Gordons' desire to keep their family close and his own ambitions for rank and economic success. His correspondence with James Gordon suggests the real difficulties of the ambitious young man in need of patronage in the eighteenth-century British Empire. The only way to maintain his army career was to serve where he was sent. Anna Gordon Martin was evidently of another opinion, and William tried to persuade her through a message to her father: "[Were I to quit the service,] I must thro' away a growing certainty and loose a good prospect, with the advantages I may in time derive from a few chosen friends; so that I would recommend it to Mrs. Martin to think of those things and consider she is married to a man whose bread and interest may very soon lead him out of America (and in case she should have occasion) win herselfe from these childish attachments which ought to be laid asside after marriage."[3]

A year later there was a new baby, Jamie (who would ultimately bring suit against the state of Massachusetts). Anna apparently left the children with her parents and joined William in Halifax. Her father tried to make the best of it: "As to advising Anne about staying or returning, tho thers none of my children nearer or dearer to me, I darst not determine as she was of age before she married & knows her engagment. As she has now a husband, she must take her fate with him for better for worse, & must be determind by him where his business leads. You must share each others fate. Its Gods holy ordinance."[4] James Gordon and his wife continued to raise Jamie and his sister Betty, sweating through the smallpox epidemic and their inoculation in 1763, worrying about the impossibility of keeping children focused on their studies during the Stamp Act riots, when they kept wanting to join the excitement in the streets—"As for James, wee cannot keep him from amongst the hurly burrly without I would chain him"—conscious always of the expense and work, especially by their grandmother, who was "allwaise minding [sic] & and repairing & making their cloaths, linnens, hose, &c to make them last."[5]

By 1765, William Martin was the captain of his battalion. Sometime between then and the outbreak of the Revolution, perhaps when James Gordon died in 1770, William and Anna Martin returned to Boston. When the British evacuated the city in 1776, the Martins fled. "William Martin, Esq." was significant enough to be mentioned by name when the Massachusetts legislature passed a statute permanently banishing "persons . . . [who] have left this State . . . and joined the Enemies thereof . . . thereby . . . depriving the States of their personal services, at a time when they ought to have afforded their utmost aid in defending the said States, against the invasions of a cruel enemy."[6] They went first to Halifax and then to New York City, where William Martin remained throughout the war on the staff of Brigadier General James Pattison. When Pattison went home on sick leave in 1780, Martin took his place as commander of artillery. In that role, William Martin conducted the formal inquiry into the causes of the great fire that destroyed much of New York City in 1776. By the time the war was over, having benefited from a flurry of wartime promotions, Martin had achieved the rank of brigadier general. When the British evacuated New York in 1783, the Martin family left for England.[7]

What wealth William Martin had seems to have come largely from his marriage, and his relationship to that wealth was precarious. The letters from James Gordon in the 1750s and 1760s are sprinkled with reminders of the extent to which he was supporting the Martin family. Indeed, when Gordon died in 1770, his son William Gordon, who was also the administrator of James Gordon's estate, actually brought suit against William Martin, claiming that he owed Gordon all the money that had been laid out for the family's support over eighteen years since 1752. The expenses were itemized in excruciating detail, beginning with the costs of a nurse and midwife in March, 1752, £1.18.8, and ranging from substantial sums of cash advanced for William Martin over the years to "Pair of shoes for his son, £0.1.6, Oct. 1754"; "Galoshes, Hatts, Gloves, Ribbens &c for his Daughter, £0.14.11, 1763"; and the funeral of his child Christiana, Sept. 1769, £1.14.5. There were schoolbooks for young James: Ovid, Caesar, Virgil, Terence, Greek grammar, Greek lexicon; expenses for smallpox inoculation; "a parrot Cage and Tub of Butter sent to Halifax"; and monthly provisions for the children, usually amounting to £4 or so.[8]

After James Gordon's death in 1770, Anna Gordon Martin inherited one-third of his estate, which amounted to at least 844 acres of land, improved and unimproved, in New Hampshire and central Massachusetts, at least one farm in Braintree on the outskirts of Boston, and a house on Boston Harbor, with a wharf and stables for ten or twelve horses. The house was a spacious one, and the Martins were able to rent it to a British general during the war for £30 a year, a substantial sum.[9]

When William and Anna Martin had fled with the British, all this property was left behind. In 1778 the Boston house was destroyed by the British in order to build a fort on the site. When the patriots were again in control of Boston, the Massachusetts property was seized according to the Massachusetts Confiscation Act of April 30, 1779. It was sold at auction in 1781 to five different purchasers. It was this property for which their son James sued in 1801.[10]

James seems to have accompanied his parents briefly to New York City.[11] By that time, however, Jamie was no longer a child. He appears to have studied law in England, and returned to Boston in 1773, where he was admitted to practice in the Court of Common Pleas of Suffolk County. By the beginning of 1774 he was practicing law in the British West Indies, and he remained there in safety for the rest of the war. By 1791 he was back in Boston, assuming he could resume his legal practice there.

James Martin's position was ambiguous. On the one hand, he had not taken an aggressive, public position against the Revolution. The Boston bar supported Martin's wish to rejoin the community; indeed, said the bar, "he has uniformly been from conviction of the justice of his country's cause attach'd to its interests."[12] But Martin's situation was different from that of other colleagues whose practices had been interrupted by the war, for his relationships to émigrés and his own emigration placed him under suspicion. When the Supreme Judicial Court of Massachusetts insisted that he "become naturalized agreeably to law," including taking an oath to support the Constitution of the United States, Martin refused. The court defined James Martin as a person born under the British flag, an alien in the new nation. He understood himself to be a person born on the soil of Massachusetts who had never explicitly been disloyal. The difference was important. If he submitted to the naturalization process, he could easily take up the practice of law. But if he already had in mind the reclaiming of the property that had been confiscated from his mother, then his claim to be a citizen by birthright weighed heavily. Under the common law, only citizens could own or inherit land. Even if Martin had been naturalized, it remained an open question whether the courts would treat his citizenship retroactively, especially taking into account his long absence from the republic and the sale of the confiscated property to other citizens.[13] Judge Francis Dana, who had been a member of the Sons of Liberty and a delegate to the Continental Congress in 1776 and was now a member of the Supreme Judicial Court, refused to let Martin have it both ways. James Martin lost his temper and came close to threatening a duel; Dana refused to answer Martin's angry note.[14]

Twenty years later, when James Martin's suit appeared before the court, Dana still sat on it. This time Dana would be more sympathetic to Martin's position.

Rights and Obligations

American constitutional theory, like liberal political theory in general, has usually emphasized rights rather than obligations. It has rested on the confidence that individuals can be authentically bound only by rules that they themselves have chosen and that authentic government is shaped by freely chosen agreements among the ruled. Obligation in some way should be an obligation to oneself, "there being," Thomas Hobbes wrote in the seventeenth century, "no obligation on any man, which ariseth not from some act of his own."[15] Much American constitutional talk proceeds as though the Revolution had created a state of nature and as though the Constitution were a social contract; the governed having consented to the political order, all obligations are ones that have been chosen.

But as historian Edmund S. Morgan has poignantly argued, "government requires make-believe." It requires that an imagined community be called into being, personified "as though it were a single body . . . superior to government, and able to alter or remove a government at will."[16] When the Continental Congress of 1776 issued a decree "on the authority of the people," and—especially—when the Federal Convention of 1787, exceeding its mandate to revise the Articles of Confederation, issued its Constitution in the name of "We the People," they were calling an imagined community into being.

"We the People" achieves much of its power by its egalitarian spirit. It makes no traditional hierarchical and patriarchal claims. It does not say, "We the Founding Fathers." It does not say, "We the politically active men who have been sent to Philadelphia by our colleagues in the states but who do not represent a majority of the adult male population." It is rather a wonderfully dynamic fiction. Except for naturalized citizens, there is no particular moment when most individuals can be said to assume obligations to the state. Instead we take consent as implied by our failure to refuse (to pay taxes, for example, or to pledge the flag) and by continued acceptance of services the state provides.

"We the People" provided the mythic space for later entry into the active citizenry of those whose membership had been ignored or explicitly denied by legislators of the founding generation. The classic statement of entry into the civic order and consequent obligation was that of John Winthrop, governor of the Massachusetts Bay Colony in the 1630s: "The woman's own choice makes such a man her husband; yet being so chosen, he is her lord, and she is to be subject to him, yet in a way of liberty, not of bondage; and a true wife accounts her subjection her honor and freedom. . . . so brethren it shall be between yourselves and your magistrates."[17] In the revolutionary era, American men rejected this formulation for themselves. They entered the liberal republic as individuals. They insisted on periodically choosing and rechoosing obligation; as they voted they would sign the social contract afresh. In our own time we have witnessed fresh installations of the social contract: in the reconstruction of the Soviet Union into fifteen republics, in the reconfiguration of a unified Germany, and, notably, in the first free elections in South Africa.

But male members of the American founding generation generally refused to address freshly the question of the extent to which women were members of the social compact, bound by their own free choice. Historian Gerda Lerner has recently reminded us that compact or covenant is one of the oldest ideas in the Judeo-Christian tradition —and that the sign of the covenant God made with Abraham (circumcision) is impossible for women.[18] But one need not go so far back. The revolutionary generation of men who so radically transgressed inherited understandings of the relationship between kings and men, fathers and sons, nevertheless refused to revise inherited understandings of the relationship between men and women, husbands and wives, mothers and children. They continued to assert patriarchal privilege as heads of households and as civic actors. They explicitly denied married women entry into the new political regime.

It is not anachronistic to raise this point. It *was* possible in the mid-eighteenth century to conceive of alternatives. "If . . . all were reduced to a state of nature," asked James Otis, one of the most important lawyers in colonial Massachusetts, in 1764, "had not apple women and orange girls as good a right to give their respectable suffrages for a new King as the philosopher, courtier . . . and politician? Were these and ten millions of others such . . . consulted?"[19] Women merchants had long established themselves in town commercial life. They owned stores and traded goods; a few ran newspapers. Writing as "Sally Tickle" in 1773, a pseudonymous columnist for the New York *Journal and General Advertiser* urged women to value and to exert themselves: "Consider yourselves as *intitled* to a Suffrage, and possessed of Influence, in the Administration of the great Family of the Publick—Take a Part in the momentous Affairs of the Community, which Providence by the liberal Endowments he has granted you in Mind and Person, manifestly intended for you."[20] Were women—even Otis' apple women and orange girls—part of the new social compact? Or did they remain in a patriarchal social order in which their only freely chosen obligation was to their husbands?

Toward the end of the American Revolution, Abigail Adams tactfully observed that Otis' question remained unanswered. "Even in the freest countrys our property is subject to the controul and disposal of our partners, to whom the Laws have given a sovereign Authority. Deprived of a voice in Legislation, obliged to submit to those Laws which are imposed upon us, is it not sufficient to make us indifferent to the publick Welfare?" Women were "excluded from honours and from offices"; their patriotism must then be "the most disinterested of all virtues." One of the few issues on which patriot and loyalist men agreed was their belief that the only service to the state of which women were capable was a financial one, and therefore women owed few obligations—notably the obligation of single women to pay taxes.[21]

Men took pride in qualities that distinguished them from women. "Luxury, effeminacy and corruption" was as much a revolutionary-era refrain as "life, liberty and the pursuit of happiness."[22] Republican ideology was antipatriarchal in the sense that it voiced, as Tom Paine had accurately sensed, the claim of adult men to be freed from the control of male governors who had defined themselves as rulers and political "fathers" in an antique monarchical system. "Is it in the interest of a man to be a boy all his life?" Paine asked in *Common Sense*.[23]

But republican ideology did not eliminate the political father immediately and completely. It was simultaneously patriarchal and antipatriarchal, holding a liberal ideology of individualism in ambivalent tension with the old ideology of patriarchy. Thus George Washington quickly became the "father of his country"; at the Governor's

Palace in Williamsburg, Virginia, the life-size portrait of George III was quickly replaced by a life-size portrait of Washington in the same pose.[24] The men who remodeled the American polity after the war remodeled it in their own image. Their anxieties for the stability of their construction led them, in emphasizing its reasonableness, its solidity, its link to classical models, also to emphasize its manliness and to equate unreliability, unpredictability, and lust with effeminacy. Women's weakness became a rhetorical foil for republican manliness.[25]

When the Eagle Forum's Kathleen Teague claimed that American women have "the right to be . . . ladies" she was—more precisely than she was perhaps aware—squarely in the middle of an antique legal tradition that substituted married women's obligations to their husbands for obligations to the state. This tradition had largely eroded when she spoke, but her ability to articulate it meant it was not yet dead. From the era of the American Revolution until deep into the present, the substitution of married women's obligations to their husbands and families for their obligations to the state has been a central element in the way Americans have thought about the relation of all women, including unmarried women, to state power. One by one, most of these substitutions have come to seem inappropriate and have been abandoned, but in each case only after a long and complicated struggle.

When American revolutionaries challenged laws governing the relations between male subjects and the king, reconstituting men as individuals free of patriarchal constraint, they left intact the system of the old English law of domestic relations. This system of law was among the many elements of English common law that were quietly absorbed into American legal practice in order to save the trouble of restating what seemed obvious. Some of this system was written into statutes, some kept alive as unwritten precedent that courts respected and could be counted upon to sustain.

Long before constitutions were constructed as new social contracts, there were marriage contracts and the complex system of subordination and authority which they were understood to embody.[26] The practice of coverture, which transferred a woman's civic identity to her husband at marriage, giving him use and direction of her property throughout the marriage, was central to the old law of domestic relations. The republic promised to protect "life, liberty and property" but under the old law a married woman was deprived of her property and had none to protect. Coverture was theoretically incompatible with revolutionary ideology and with the newly developing liberal commercial society. But patriot men carefully sustained it. They even continued to refer to the body of law of domestic relations by its traditional name, "the law of baron et feme"—not "husband and wife" or "man and woman," but "lord and woman." The same treatises that described the law of baron and feme invariably went on to laws of parent and child, master and servant.

If ever there was a site to examine the personal as the political, it is here. The American Revolution was preeminently a crisis of authority; a democratizing society was rebelling against the authority claimed by Parliament and king. The challenge that the Revolution posed to patriarchal relationships was dramatically expressed in attacks on the father figure of King George III, especially in the violent pulling down and melting of his statues in the streets. But anxiety combined with self-interest to restrain male legislators from changing the inherited system of coverture. In stabilizing the Revolution, founding-era legislators minimized differences between white men in comparison to what they had been before the war—all were theoretically equal, a shoemaker was as good a man as John Hancock.[27] But at the same time the founders maintained in place a legal system which heightened differences between free women and men, especially between married women and men. As the suffrage was expanded to embrace more and more white men, the difference between them and their wives, who could neither vote, nor hold office, nor serve on juries, expanded. As white men increasingly freed themselves from the constraints of public patriarchy, they sustained a fully developed, complex system of law that maintained the private privileges of patriarchy.[28] "Do not put such unlimited power into the hands of the Husbands," Abigail Adams urged in 1776. "Remember all Men would be tyrants if they could."[29] But her own husband laughed at this remark, and male rebels against royal tyranny resisted acknowledging their own all too human capacity for it. The legal treatises of the early republic describe American households as hierarchical as if

Locke had never written, as if the Revolution, and all the radical political change associated with it, had never taken place.

Yet the new nation made women citizens. The fact of women's citizenship contained deep within it an implicit challenge to coverture. Patriot men rarely spoke about this issue, but their actions speak for them. In England, the killing of a husband by a wife was *petit treason*, analogous to regicide, although the killing of a wife by a husband was murder. The penalties for petit treason were worse than those for murder. The concept was not much enforced in colonial America, but it remained in the statutes. It was the only element of the old law of domestic relations which legislators of the early republic eliminated. Legislators were conscious of what they intended; they carefully retained the concept of petit treason for the killing of the master by a slave. With that single exception, neither the revolutionary government under the Articles of Confederation nor the federal government of the Constitution directly challenged the legal system of coverture.[30] Every free man, rich or poor, white or black, gained something from the system of domestic relations already in place; they had no need to renegotiate it.

The best introduction to the old system of thinking about relations between women and men is to read the treatises on which judges and lawyers relied. In an era before law schools were attached to universities, and when prospective lawyers "read law" as apprentices in the offices of practitioners, Tapping Reeve conducted perhaps the most respected legal training in the nation. Students came from all over the country to study in his Litchfield, Connecticut, home; among them were Reeve's own brother-in-law Aaron Burr and, years later, John C. Calhoun from South Carolina. There were also future U.S. congressmen and senators, judges and Supreme Court justices. Reeve's treatise on the law of baron and feme, first published in 1816, was reprinted with up-to-date annotations in 1846, a testament to its continued vitality. Reeve offers us pithy accounts of what the early generations of American jurists took to be the common understanding of the matter of relations between men and women. Nothing that he wrote would have surprised his contemporaries.

To follow the law of domestic relations, as Reeve delicately spun out its implications, is to watch the playing out of a stacked deck. Reeve began his book with the forthright statement that "the husband, by marriage, acquires an absolute title to all the personal property of the wife." Husbands also gained extensive power over her real estate; wives gained no advantages "in point of property" from marriage.

Once these asymmetrical property relations were established, personal implications wound their way throughout the law. The husband's control of all property gave him such coercive power over the wife that she could not defy him. Instead of revising the law to remove its coercive elements, jurists simply ensured that the coerced voices would not speak. Husbands were responsible for crimes committed by their wives in their presence or with their approval—except in the case of treason, a crime so severe that responsibility for it overrode obligation to the husband, or in the event that a wife kept a brothel with the husband's knowledge, since keeping a brothel "is an offense of which the wife is supposed to have the principal management."[31] Before married women signed away their right to dower property, judges were supposed to question them privately about whether their husbands had coerced them, although the law offered no protection against continued coercion. A wife could not normally make contracts in her own name; if she did, her husband was bound "to fulfil the contract of his wife, when it is such an one as wives in her rank of life usually purchase. . . . If, however, she were to purchase a ship or yoke of oxen, no such presumption would arise, for wives do not usually purchase ships or oxen."[32]

This system of domestic relations presupposed the husband's right to sexual access to the wife's body. When Reeve explained why it was logical that wives could not enter into contracts, his reason was not only that wives did not control property that could serve as a guarantee; it was also that wives could not enter into contracts involving their own labor. "The right of the husband to the person of his wife," Reeve observed, ". . . is a right guarded by the law with the utmost solicitude; if she could bind herself by her contracts, she would be liable to be arrested, taken in execution, and confined in a prison; and then the husband would be deprived of the company of his wife, which the law will not suffer." If a husband were banished from the realm, however, then his wife "could contract, could sue and be sued in her own name; for, in this case, . . . he was already deprived of the company of his wife, and her confinement in prison would not deprive him of his wife to any greater extent than was already the case."[33]

Under the old law of domestic relations, a woman's only freely chosen obligation was to her husband. Once she made that choice, he controlled her body and her property; there were relatively few constraints on what he could do with either, though she was nearly always guaranteed the use of one-third their combined property during her widowhood. Recognizing that husbands could easily pressure the electoral choices of married women, legislators concluded not that husbands should be controlled, but that women—unmarried as well as married—should not vote.

For families with a substantial amount of property to protect against dissolute sons-in-law, real estate law offered some devices which ensured that land and buildings could be passed down through the generations despite coverture. The real estate that came to Anna Martin by bequest was marked off to her directly, thus keeping it in the Gordon line. William Martin had control of it only once they had children, and only during his lifetime. Technically Anna Martin had a "right of remainder" in it; when William Martin died the property would pass not directly to his heirs, but to hers. Normally these heirs would have also been his. But since he had been targeted as a loyalist and his property confiscated, her ultimate claim on the property, and the claim of her heirs, was crucial to the outcome of James Martin's lawsuit.[34]

In effect the law of domestic relations came down to the husband's property rights in his wife's body and his position as barrier between her and public obligation.[35] If she could not make a private contract, how could she enter the social contract? Rhetorically, however, the system was generally described as privileging women rather than oppressing them. Married women were understood to be shielded from the stresses of public life, from the need to risk property and reputation in political encounter. In his classic treatise on the common law of England, which American jurists revered, William Blackstone concluded that woman was a great "favorite of the law of England." Against that system of law there would be hurled, throughout the nineteenth and twentieth centuries, the complex ideologies of individual rights, fueling a political women's rights movement from the founding generation of the republic to the present.

"Her dower shall be set off to her"

Confiscation of loyalists' property was one among many ways in which patriots defined theirs as an authentically new social order. Virtually every state gave force to this demand for loyalty by means of a trio of statutes, solidly in place by 1778, that linked treason, oaths of allegiance, and the establishment of a system of confiscation. Together, the three were demands for commitment to the Revolution; the penalties could not be easily undone or forgiven. Treason—the act of aiding the enemy—and misprision of treason—the knowledge of and concealment of an enemy plot—could be punished with death, banishment, or enforced service on a naval vessel (from which escape was virtually impossible). Oaths were a commitment to be loyal to the new political order. In the eighteenth-century religious system, oaths were understood to be existentially binding, the punishment for violations to be experienced in the next world. And the confiscation of property was the punishment for disloyalty. The state of Massachusetts was unusual in the care it took to include women in each aspect of the triad.

Treason and misprision of treason were understood throughout the nation to be crimes that either sex might commit. Generally the statutes were written in terms of "persons," or substituted the explicit "he or she" for a generic male pronoun. The New Jersey statute provided that the person condemned for treason might receive a pardon if he enlisted in the Continental Navy. Since women were not welcome in the navy, an alternative punishment was provided for them: a fine up to three hundred pounds and imprisonment for up to one year.[36]

Massachusetts' 1777 treason statute made an even more explicit claim to women's allegiance. The statute applied to all "Members" of the state, who were defined as "all persons abiding within . . . and deriving protection from the laws." When the General Court defined the punishments for treason, it made sure that the implication of "all persons" was clear: "every person who shall be attainted of treason within this State, whether male or female, shall be punished by being hanged by the neck until they are dead."[37] Although the statutes explicitly applied to women, and women were accused of misprision of treason, it was exceedingly rare for a woman to be accused of treason. No person was executed for treason in Massachusetts in the course of the Revolution.[38]

Although occasionally framed in terms of all residents, oaths of allegiance seem almost always to have been selectively imposed on men. The strategy of requiring oaths assumed a community of Christians who truly believed their immortal souls to be at risk should they break their oaths. When tension built between the colonies and the empire in the 1770s, tests of loyalty were instituted, among them the boycott of British imports. Throughout the colonies, women were encouraged to support boycotts by changed patterns of consumption. Only in Massachusetts, where the Assembly drew up a Solemn League and Covenant as evidence of commitment, were women explicitly included. Contemporaries report "every adult of both sexes putting their names to it, saving a very few."[39]

Those who refused to swear loyalty when it was demanded of them faced physical and financial punishment, primarily in the form of confiscation. Even the most primitive government oversees the orderly transmission of property—by exchange, sale, or inheritance—and the patriots were no exception, for their understanding of a new political order rested solidly on the guarantee of the security of property. Indeed, the patriots required that the active citizen have sufficient property to assure that he acknowledged no one as master. But patriots felt no obligation to oversee the inheritance of *loyalist* property. The explicit refusal to do so was one of the ways in which patriots defined their Rubicon as one which could not be recrossed.[40]

To confiscate a loyalist's property required that the property could be identified with precision. As we have seen, in English law coverture ensured that the property which a married man held was almost never fully his, free and clear; one-third of his real estate was always reserved to his wife for her use during her widowhood—that is, until she remarried or died. This dower property—the "widow's thirds" —was understood to be an equitable recompense for the woman who had given up control of her property at marriage, and British law treated her rights to it with great care. The dower property even of widows whose husbands had been hanged, drawn, and quartered for treason was carefully preserved. In confiscating loyalist property, most patriot legislatures left dower as a recognized claim on the estate.

They did so partly because of long-established tradition, partly on the practical grounds that to assign dower would prevent the wives and children of absentees from becoming a burden on public charity (although their standard of living would obviously drop precipitously).[41]

Confiscation statutes varied widely in their treatment of dower right. Most simply assumed that there would be no change in the practice of treating dower as among the "just debts" that were to be satisfied before confiscated property was transferred or sold.[42] A few states—Pennsylvania, New Hampshire—explicitly provided for the support of absentees' families out of confiscated estates.[43] In Georgia, a Board of Commissioners in each county might, if the estate was very small, allocate it entirely to the support of wives and children left behind.[44] Only a few states—Virginia, North Carolina, and Massachusetts—specified that dower would be recognized if the woman claimant had stayed in America.[45]

The Massachusetts legislation was "ardent," writes one of its historians, and did not leave dower claims to implication.[46] The statute passed in 1779, after several drafts, provided

> That where the wife, or widow, of any of the [loyalists] aforenamed and described, shall have remained within the jurisdiction of any of the said United States, and in parts under the actual authority thereof, she shall be [e]ntitled to the improvement and income of one third part of her husband's real and personal estate (after payment of debts) during her life, and continuance within the said United States; and her dower therein shall be set off to her by the judges of probate of wills, in like manner as it might have been if her husband had died intestate and a liege subject of this state.[47]

The explicit requirement that she remain in the state implied that wives of absentees who fled with their husbands could not claim dower in confiscated property. An early draft was even stronger; it had a revolutionary preface explicitly attacking the king, it provided that debts owed to Americans were the first lien on the estates, and also required that proceeds from the sale of loyalist estates be used to relieve inhabitants who had suffered in the war and the wives and children of dead American soldiers.[48] There is no parallel to this last clause in the confiscation legislation of any other state.

By spelling out what was probably the usual expectation through-out the United States, Massachusetts made the expectation of the usual into a self-limiting proposition: not that most cases would relate to wives who stayed on, but that all cases should. By doing so, Mas-sachusetts enacted a statute that bore within it a deeply radical and broader set of claims for a revolutionary relationship between the married woman and the state. Anna Martin's heir did not claim her dower property; he claimed property that she had held in her own right. Yet because she had fled the Revolution, the state of Massa-chusetts did not think the property should be returned to her.

"Cannot a feme-covert *levy war?"*

James Martin was forty-eight years old, and the twenty-year statute of limitations was about to run out when the Supreme Judicial Court of Massachusetts heard his case. He had been angry since 1792, when he had discovered, through Francis Dana's denial of his petition to practice law in Boston, that he was being treated as an alien. Martin believed he had been "very materially injured in being obliged to give up engagements he had entered into for the purchase of lands . . . and prevented from taking and keeping possession of lands belonging to [him] in right of his mother Mrs. Ann Martin."[49] On February 4, 1793, Martin turned to the United States Supreme Court, then sitting in Philadelphia, asking for a writ of error which would direct the Supreme Judicial Court of Massachusetts to reconsider his case; the justices had no trouble reading between the lines of Martin's appeal, and refused to consider it "until certain expressions . . . imputing corrupt motives to the Judges of the said Supreme Court of Massa-chusetts be expunged." Although he swore that he had been admitted to practice in New York, the Supreme Court turned down Martin's demand. But James Martin somehow managed to establish his cre-dentials in New York; he was admitted to the bar of the New York Supreme Court on August 4, 1792.[50] His citizenship thus established, Martin could appear before the Supreme Judicial Court of Massa-chusetts to demand the return of his mother's property—the same

Massachusetts court that had once denied him the right to practice before it.

Francis Dana had risen to Chief Justice of the Supreme Judicial Court by the time it heard James Martin's case in 1805. Dana had served in the Governor's Council when the confiscation legislation had been passed in 1779. He had already denied James Martin's plea for special treatment; it may be that Dana's refusal engendered Martin's lawsuit. Dana and the other members of the four-judge panel were Federalist by political conviction and deeply conservative by temperament.[51] In the party politics of Thomas Jefferson's presidential years, during which time Martin fought his lawsuit, Federalists attracted merchants, creditors, and some exporters. Jefferson's Democratic-Republican Party was a complex coalition of southern tobacco planters, subsistence farmers, mechanics and artisans in seaport towns. Federalists included some who distrusted Jefferson and his allies for their hypocrisy: slave owners who claimed to be democrats. Party affiliations were not always good indicators of political positions—the opposing pairs of lawyers had a Democratic-Republican and a Federalist on each team. The often overlapping political positions in the early republic meant that the judges and both sets of lawyers in the Martin case had decades of extensive and sometimes tense rivalry with one another.[52]

Martin's case was presented by George Blake, a well-established Boston lawyer who had been appointed to the lucrative office of Federal District Attorney by the Jeffersonians in 1801.[53] Blake situated himself on the conservative edge of the Democratic-Republican Party; it was often difficult to tell him apart from a Federalist.[54] Blake's colleague in Martin's defense was Theophilus Parsons, a prominent Federalist with whom the future President John Quincy Adams had studied law, and who would, the following year, be elevated to the post of Chief Justice in the court in which he now appeared as attorney. Parsons had close Tory connections, and was a leader of the most conservative wing of the Massachusetts Federalists, among whom Tory sympathies were common.[55]

The state's lawyers also came from both parties. Daniel Davis, the Solicitor General for the Commonwealth of Massachusetts, was a moderate Federalist who had built his career on the Maine frontier; he was a solid, if uninspired, trial lawyer.[56] Davis' colleague was the

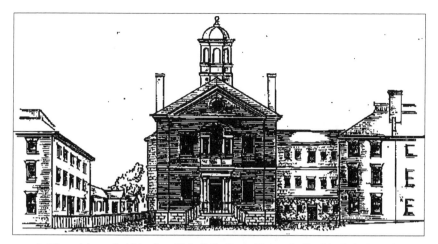

1. The trial was held in the old Suffolk Court House, built shortly before the Revolution. This image has been reconstructed by architectural historian Frederic C. Detwiller. The brick building was attached to the stone jail. The courtroom, probably thirty-five feet wide, was on the second floor. The judges sat behind a long table (not a raised bench); the lawyers faced them. Any spectators stood at the back of the room.

state's Attorney General, James Sullivan, who at the time of the trial was the Republican candidate for governor. Sullivan was a man of the center, but he consistently took some positions that were more progressive than any articulated by John Adams, Thomas Jefferson, and many other contemporaries more famous than he. Sullivan's role in the Martin case was congruent with the unusually consistent liberalism which he displayed throughout his career. Believing that society was composed of equal individuals, he spun out the implications of that belief in a wide range of issues as they presented themselves—banking and the economy, religious freedom, an end to slavery, and, most unusually, gender relations.[57]

Born the son of an Irish immigrant in Berwick, Maine, in 1744, Sullivan was sixty-one at the time of the Martin trial. He lacked, in John Adams' words, an "Accademical Education," and had begun "with neither Learning, Books, Estate or any Thing, but his Head and Hands." He also suffered from epilepsy and was badly lame as a result of a boyhood accident. But in spite of these handicaps Sullivan moved quickly to claim a legal education, make an upwardly mobile marriage, and enter public service.[58] From the mid-1770s on he could be found on one revolutionary committee or another, in the General

2. This portrait of James Sullivan was painted by
Gilbert Stuart in 1807, only two years after he argued
the Martin case.

Court, in the Provincial Congress, or as Attorney General; he was a
member of the legislature when it passed the confiscation laws of
1779.[59] During the revolutionary era he endorsed strong, even punitive confiscation law, and after the war he was often found on the
side of those who were making it difficult for Tories to return, but
he also assisted some returning Tories whom he knew personally.[60]
Although as Attorney General Sullivan aggressively prosecuted the
state's interest against the proprietors of large speculative endeavors,
he had also been a lawyer for the largest of Maine's land speculators.[61]

Sullivan was committed to the democratic promises that the Revolution had made. He worried about the future of civil liberties under
the new Federal Constitution until the Bill of Rights was added.[62]
When the French Revolution broke out, Sullivan wrote at least one
pamphlet supporting it and emphasizing its parallels with the American experience.[63] He was serving as a judge when the first in the

series of Quock Walker cases made slavery illegal in Massachusetts in 1781; he believed that the nation as a whole should adopt a long-range program of gradual emancipation coupled with equal education for black and white children.[64] Sullivan was skeptical of capital punishment.[65] An ardent advocate of religious liberty, Sullivan defended the Universalists—a high proportion of whom were women—both in court and in print at a time when they were very unpopular.[66] He was, in short, a moderate Jeffersonian and a classical liberal, and, most importantly for our purposes, Sullivan was willing to follow the principle of government by the consent of the governed where it led; certainly as far as the elimination of property requirements for voting, and, long before the Martin case, up to the boundaries of gender.

In the spring of 1776 Sullivan wrote to Elbridge Gerry:

> Every member of Society has a Right to give his Consent to the Laws of the Community or he owes no Obedience to them. This proposition will never be denied by him who has the least acquaintance with true republican principles. And yet a very great number of the people of this Colony have at all times been bound by Laws to which they never were in a Capacity to Consent not having estate worth 40/ per annum &c. . . . Why a man is supposed to consent to the acts of a Society of which in this respect he is absolutely an Excommunicate, none but a Lawyer well dabled in the feudal Sistem can tell.

Sullivan distrusted the rich as well as the poor—"Stupid Souls . . . are as often found on the throne as on the Dunghill"—and urged that voting for legislation that did not involve new taxes should involve "every person out of wardship that is bound thereby."[67]

Gerry sent Sullivan's long letter on to John Adams, who was representing Massachusetts at the Continental Congress in Philadelphia and dealing daily with the problem of how to turn the principle of the consent of the governed into practical devices for a new political order. Sullivan's letter came hard on the heels of Adams' own correspondence with his wife on this point. "In your new code of laws," Abigail Adams had written, "I pray you remember the Ladies." Together Abigail Adams and James Sullivan forced him to a consideration of the composition of "the public." In response to Sullivan, John

Adams wrote the powerful and now well-known letter of May 26, 1776, in which he contemplated the question "Whence arises the Right of the Men to govern Women, without their Consent?" Sullivan had said that "every person out of wardship" should participate in legislation in some way, and Adams might well have responded that coverture placed married women in "wardship" to their husbands. But Adams construed Sullivan's letter to imply that women and children were governed without their consent, and he could see that the logic of liberalism, pressed as extensively as Sullivan was willing to press it, led inexorably to a challenge to coverture. "Depend upon it, sir," Adams warned, "it is dangerous to open So fruitfull a Source of Controversy and Altercation, as would be opened by attempting to alter the Qualifications of Voters. There will be no End of it. New Claims will arise. Women will demand a Vote."[68]

Sullivan continued to align himself with those who supported various challenges to women's subordination; in 1792 he could be found working as state Attorney General, persuading a jury "that girls had equal rights under the constitution and could not be expelled from school" when the selectmen of the town of Northampton refused to allocate funds for the schooling of girls.[69]

In short, though Sullivan was a clever lawyer, and quite capable of constructing arguments to fit the case at hand, on this occasion the arguments he offered were rooted deeply in his understanding of the meaning of the Revolution and his own belief in what the outcome of the Revolution should be. His commitment to principle may well have been heightened by his political experience; a year after the trial, Sullivan would describe the Supreme Judicial Court as "artful, malignant and cruel."[70]

The attorneys who spoke for Martin strove to confine the case to narrow grounds. Had the Court of Common Pleas had appropriate jurisdiction? Had there been procedural due process? Was William Martin's title clear? The two opposing lawyers, by contrast, explicitly located the case in its revolutionary context. They focused on the question of married women's obligations to the state, and urged the court to sustain the radical implications of the choices made by the revolutionary era legislature.

As the case developed in court, the arguments were aligned along two strands. One line of argument stressed due process: Martin claimed that his property had been seized without proper legal procedure. James Sullivan introduced a political dimension. Arguing for the state of Massachusetts, he claimed that in time of war a loose interpretation of statutes was permissible, indeed inevitable.

The other line of reasoning challenged the relationship of married women to the state. No one denied that the state had a right to seize any property belonging to William Martin. Martin had met virtually all the requirements of the confiscation statute. As an officer in the Royal Regiment of Artillery, he had levied war against the government and people of the United States; he had withdrawn from Massachusetts to a place "under the power of the fleets or armies of the . . . king," and he had not taken "an oath of allegiance to [the United] . . . states." But what about Anna Martin? No one denied that she had property, and she, too, met some of the explicit conditions of the statute: she had absented herself from Massachusetts after April 19, 1775. Did she have an obligation to make clear her own loyalty to the revolutionary state?

The answer would be found, George Blake argued in his opening statements, in a close reading of the statute. The Confiscation Act addressed itself to "every *inhabitant* and *member* of the state." Women were inhabitants of the state; were they also *members*? Blake thought not. His assertion is worth reading at length:

> ' Upon the strict principles of law, a *feme covert* is not a member; has no *political relation* to the *state* any more than an *alien*. . . . The legislature *intended* to exclude *femes-covert* and infants from the operation of the act; otherwise the word *inhabitant* would have been used alone, and not coupled with the word *member*.[71]

As we have seen, confiscation had been linked legislatively with oaths of allegiance and with definitions of treason. Now Blake drew on those links to maintain his point: "A *feme-covert* was never holden to take an oath of allegiance." Like treason statutes, he went on, the confiscation "statute is highly penal" and therefore demanded very narrow interpretation. Blake construed the preamble in gender-specific terms:

The object [of the statute] was not to punish, but to retain the physical force of the state. . . . How much physical force is retained by retaining married women? What are the *personal services* they are to render in opposing *by force* an actual invasion? What *aid* can they give to an enemy? So far are women from being of service in the defence of a country against the attacks of an enemy, that it is frequently thought expedient to send them out of the way, lest they impede the operations of their own party.[72]

Blake proceeded to run through a long list of British precedents, easily found, for the common-law rule *"as a woman is supposed to have acted under the coercion of the husband,"* she is regularly excused for acts, otherwise illegal, done with him. "And can it be supposed"— one imagines him thundering—"in the case before the Court, that the legislature contemplated the case of a wife withdrawing with her husband? It ought not to be, and surely was not intended that she should be exposed to the loss of all her property for withdrawing from the government with her husband. If he commanded it, she was bound to obey him, by a law paramount to all other laws—the law of God."[73]

Blake's voice reaches across the centuries to spell out, in politically intense and loaded language, what his contemporaries took to be the political implications of the concept of the *feme covert*. Women were merely residents. Only men were active members of the commonwealth; indeed, the eighteenth-century slang for penis underscored the extent to which the concept of the citizen was not truly universal; at some level, to be a *member* was necessarily masculine and generative. Implicit in this understanding was the antique definition of *citizen*, a definition as old as the Roman republic: the citizen was the man who is prepared to take up arms to defend the republic, and so, in reciprocal relationship, had a right to claim a voice in the decision to resort to arms.[74] Thus Blake could speak in terms of *"personal services"* and the right of the state "to retain the physical force of the state." Once this was established, then much else followed; at its extreme, the *feme covert* "has no *political* relation to the *state* any more than an alien." It would be hard to be more unambivalent than this. Many years later, claiming a political voice for women, the abolitionist Sarah Grimké would ask plaintively, "Are we aliens because we are women?" Blake's answer, obviously, was an unequivocal yes.

In a striking example of how contemporary usage shapes the thoughts that it is possible to think, no one in the courtroom was able to separate women from infants. Blake could not imagine that by "inhabitant and member" a state might have wished to identify adults who were competent to make judgments of their own; that infants might be inhabitants but not members; that married women might be both. Blake elided the issue by simple assertion: "The legislature *intended* to exclude *feme covert* and infants . . . otherwise the word inhabitant would have been used alone."[75] Even in his own terms, this was not an accurate assertion, for earlier in his argument Blake had given the treason statute of 1777 a close reading for other purposes, and surely had cast his eyes on the opening words of that document, which began by saying that every *person* was an "inhabitant and member" of the commonwealth. If women could not be separated from infants, neither could women and infants be separated from men in the revolutionary definition of "inhabitant and member." But Blake was speaking a quarter century after the revolutionary statute, and it was becoming possible to construe it in ways that elided the initial understanding.

In an argument that, as far as I can tell, was unprecedented, the Attorney General and the Solicitor General undertook to challenge what Blake had offered as the common sense of the matter. They insisted that Anna Martin met the clear terms of the law; she had *withdrawn* from the state. Was she excused because she was *feme covert*? The statute said "any person." The provisions that confiscated dower had provided that dower would not be confiscated for women who stayed; this suggested that married women had the "power of remaining or withdrawing, as they pleased." This element of choice, of course, had traditionally been absent from the repertory of the married woman; to introduce it was a challenge to traditional practice.

James Sullivan attacked Blake's assertion that women were not included in clauses that were phrased with masculine pronouns; that is, Blake's denial of the generic *he*. On this point, Sullivan was outraged:

The same reasoning would go to prove that the *constitution* of the commonwealth does not extend to women—secures them no rights, no privileges; for it has no words in the feminine gender; it would prove that a great variety of crimes . . . could not be committed by women, because the statutes had used only the words *him* and *his.* . . . Who are members of the body politic? are not all the *citizens,* members: infants, idiots, insane, or whatever may be their *relative* situations in society? Cannot a *feme-covert* levy war and conspire to levy war? She certainly can commit treason; and if so, there is no one act mentioned in the statute which she is not capable of performing.[76]

Together, Davis and Sullivan articulated a case for the politicized married woman. Shaking loose from traditional assumptions about women's vulnerability, their incompetence, their distance from issues of concern to the commonwealth, Davis and Sullivan offered the court a woman who had been redefined as competent citizen by revolutionary legislation and who had been challenged to make her own political choices in the crucible of revolution.[77]

Throughout the trial Sullivan raised the level of intensity, using politicized words that others carefully avoided: *enemy, war, sovereignty.* "Both . . . the *absentee* and the *conspirator* act . . . were made for getting hold of the property of an enemy. . . . The statutes were a sort of declaration of war, and the measures then adopted . . . were grounded on a state of war."[78] He accused the other side of being unfaithful to the intent of revolutionary legislation: "If all the decisions which were had during war . . . are, in time of peace, liable to be reversed, there would be instant cause of war, and there would be no end of war."[79] For Sullivan and Davis the Revolution had claimed the loyalty of all *persons*—not only physical service but emotional and mental allegiance as well.[80] Women could share this sort of citizenship, and, they concluded, women could also share in its obligations. As the Declaration of Independence had done, their understanding leaned on general principles of natural law more than the English tradition of common law; indeed, they abandoned the common-law principle of "unity of person" accomplished by marriage and substituted natural-law understanding of the possibilities of reason to shape political behavior.[81] It may be that the woman they envisaged bore some debt to the radical British author Mary Wollstonecraft, who had offered competence and capability as preconditions of citizenship. "How can a being be generous who has nothing of its own? or virtuous who is not free?" Wollstonecraft had asked. If Anna Martin were to be a member of the commonwealth, she would have to be defined as a being who had something of her own.

"Was she . . . criminal because . . . she did not . . . rebel against the will of her husband?"

The end of the story is quickly told. The politics of the courtroom pitted the republican candidate for governor against a panel of judges who were committed to his political defeat. The two days of argument took place before a bench composed of men in late middle age—George Thatcher, the youngest, was fifty-one; Francis Dana the eldest, sixty-two—who had moved in and out of elective politics throughout their careers. All four judges voted to support James Martin's claim to his mother's property, thus reversing the lower court's decision. Three of the judges addressed in their opinion the issue of the nature of female citizenship in a republic; the most extensive of these opinions was offered by Theodore Sedgwick.

Sedgwick had been a cautious supporter of the Revolution and now was a conservative Federalist.[82] As a member of the state legislature, the Continental Congress, and then the Federal Congress, Sedgwick had voted against harsh treatment for returning Tories. He had been energetic in helping friends he considered conscientious and honest loyalists to recover their confiscated property after the war. In writing his opinion, Sedgwick began with the Revolution, offering a curiously *apolitical* interpretation of what it had been, stressing its elite origins, and respecting those who from "principles of duty and conscience" could not support it. Rereading the charges, Sedgwick emphasized that William and Anna Martin had been *jointly* charged with levying war, adhering to the king of Britain, and withdrawing themselves. "[W]e are called upon . . . to say whether a *feme-covert*, for *any* of these acts, *performed with her husband*, is within the intention of the statute; and I think that she is not." The common law, Sedgwick emphasized, exempts a married woman from punishment for most crime when performed with her husband because of the strength of his "authority" and "her duty of obedience." How can we have a situation, Sedgwick asked, in which women are not held responsible for independent judgment on straightforward ethical matters like theft, and yet held to independent judgment on political matters in which even "men of great powers and equal integrity, as is said by the *Attorney-General*, divided [?]"

> Can we believe that a wife . . . should lose her own property, and forfeit the inheritance of her children . . . [and] be considered as criminal because she permitted her husband to elect his own and her place of residence? Because she did not, in violation of her marriage vows, rebel against the will of her husband?[83]

In this way, Sedgwick came to articulate the issue of the relationship of women to rebellion and disorder. Was it possible to imagine that the revolutionary coalition in Massachusetts had intended to call upon married women to rebel against husbands? It had certainly called upon sons to rebel against fathers. But, Sedgwick thought, the state could not possibly have tried to recruit women; there was nothing they could contribute to the rebellion.

> A *wife* who left the country in the company of her husband did not *withdraw* herself; but was, if I may so express it, withdrawn by him. She did not deprive the government of the benefit of her personal services; she had none to render; none were exacted of her. . . . Can it be believed that a humane and just legislature ever intended that wives should be subjected to the horrid alternative of, either, on the one hand, separating from their husbands and disobeying them, or, on the other, of sacrificing their property?

In the end all the judges chose common law over natural law, English precedent over republican potential, narrow interpretation over loose construction. They chose James Martin's private claim over the Commonwealth of Massachusetts' public claim. The judges spoke in terms of deference, of obligation, of what women *owed* to their husbands, what men had a right to demand of their wives. Dana spoke of the "duty, which, by the laws of their country and the law of God, [women] . . . owed to their husbands"; Sedgwick spoke of the propriety of a woman's submission to her husband's opinions and judgments, even when they were evil; Simeon Strong observed that the married woman "is bound to obey his commands . . . except *perhaps* in treason and murder . . ." (emphasis mine).

The marriages these men describe are not companionate marriages.[84] Blackstone had defended coverture as protective; the woman, he had said, was a "favourite" of the laws of England. But there is little in the language of the judges or of the plaintiff's attorneys that suggests favoritism and protection: all is force, violence, constraint. In odd juxtaposition, the Federalists spoke of the Revolution itself in mild terms. They referred to the Revolution primarily in connection with giving extended time for loyalists to make up their minds about allegiance, in referring to the persistence of English common law despite the revolutionary fault line. To define the married woman this way in the context of the Martin case was to deny the claims of the American citizens—the purchasers of the confiscated property, as well as the state of Massachusetts—and to privilege the claims of the alien and Tory; yet all the judges reached this conclusion. The paradox was that in order to sustain the state's claim that Anna Martin had been a "member" of the Commonwealth, she and her heirs would have had to forfeit their property.[85]

Federalist judges ruled on behalf of the Tory claimant as they had often done in the past.[86] The significance of the Martin case lies not so much with the substance of the decision, which was congruent with long-term trends in Massachusetts and elsewhere, but in the texture of the argument. The Federalist jurists rallied around a traditional, corporate vision of society in which the family was still, as it had been for the Puritans, a "little commonwealth" headed by a benevolent patriarch. Ironically they may well have been blinded from understanding how retrograde their decision was precisely because they understood themselves to be personally generous, even indulgent, toward the women of their own families. Sedgwick himself took enormous pride in having freed the family's slave, "Mumbet," who took the name Elizabeth Freeman, and in nurturing his own daughter's love of reading—Catharine Maria Sedgwick, who was fifteen years old in 1805, would grow up to be a leading novelist of her generation. Yet personal generosity left patriarchal relations intact; the father who *chose* to be indulgent toward his dependents had the option of choosing otherwise.[87]

That conservative public politics should be thus linked with patriarchal private politics comes as no surprise, except insofar as these Federalist judges and lawyers are unusually explicit in their denial of the civic capacity of women. They were voicing an interpretation of marital relations that we now understand to be anachronistic in light of what would follow. What is more intriguing is that the state should have taken on the defense in the case, and that James Sullivan and Daniel Davis should have offered the arguments they did in favor of the civic capacity of women. For Sullivan and Davis moved far past the claim of mutuality in marriage to a vision of marriage in which the partners were independent moral actors. Theirs was a vision of family life in which wives as well as husbands were challenged to evaluate the Revolution, take a position, and risk their property and prosperity on the choice they made. Sullivan and Davis were arguing that if patriarchy in politics is rejected, so too must be patriarchy in marriage. The Federalist judges wanted it both ways: to abandon patriarchy in politics but maintain it, albeit in sentimental form, in their private lives. "Judicial patriarchy" would persist for the rest of the nineteenth century.[88]

Sullivan's comments in the Martin case suggest the outer limits of how far it was possible to go on the woman question, and seizing a married woman's property because she had not made her own political commitment was going very far. In Sullivan's language, the insistence that married women had the power to make choices was associated with a vision of the Revolution as violent. It was congruent with other positions which Sullivan took throughout his career, and with positions that others articulated—briefly—in the radical spaces of the Revolution. Sullivan was consistent in his liberalism, supporting a free market not only in the economy but in ideas, and not flinching when that position suggested that women were necessarily part of the polity. No one joined Sullivan and Davis out on their limb, and they would not venture out there again.[89]

In 1809, the Supreme Judicial Court of Massachusetts, now with Theophilus Parsons as Chief Justice, sustained the dower right of loyalist wives who had fled with their husbands by upholding the claims of the widow of the colonial Solicitor General to dower in a confiscated estate.[90] In the same year another legally astute woman, Grace Tabor Kempe, the widow of the king's Attorney General for New York City, challenged the wartime confiscation laws that had taken New Jersey property that she, like Anna Martin, had brought into her marriage. Her attorney, Richard Stockton, a conservative supporter of the Revolution, echoed Blake and Parsons in his arguments before the U.S. Supreme Court. "Here then is a *feme covert* charged . . . for accompanying her baron," observed Stockton. "A woman cannot commit . . . this species of treason, by obeying her husband. . . . Receiving her husband, knowing him to be a traitor, is not treason." Stockton could not have said it more strongly; until the traitor was convicted, his wife could not even deny him access to her bed and her body. It did not matter to the married woman that the state was disrupted; she remained under the power of her husband. In New Jersey single women voted in 1809, "because the law supposes them to have wills of their own." But in a married couple, only the husband was the inhabitant; "the wife cannot properly be called an inhabitant." For technical reasons, Justice John Marshall upheld the claims of those to whom the New Jersey lands had been transferred, but he made it clear that his sympathies were with Stockton and Kempe.[91]

"*Marriage . . . with a foreigner is as voluntary . . . as expatriation*"

At the height of the French Revolution, an anonymous contributor to a conservative Boston newspaper expressed confusion about women's claim to citizenship. " 'No cit[izen]ess to my name, I'll have,' says Katey, '[it] means, A woman of the town.' " "Katey" dismisses the potential of female citizenship, literally linking—as the ancient Greeks had done—the woman of the *polis* to woman of the streets. To make no distinction between the woman who participates in public life and the woman who makes herself sexually available in public has for millennia been a conservative political device. The story of *Martin v. Commonwealth of Massachusetts* emphasizes the conservative outcome of the American Revolution, as men who had supported independence nevertheless undertook in its aftermath to defuse the memories of revolutionary violence and upheaval, to constrain the renegotiation of gender roles, and to limit the political responsibilities of married—by which they actually meant adult—women. They found it impossible to imagine respectable adult women as anything other than wives. They could not separate the sexual monopoly which a man exercised over his wife in marriage from the political monopoly which he exercised over her property. They could not imagine the adult woman with her own obligation to the state.

But the story of *Martin v. Commonwealth* also contains within it evidence that there existed another scenario. This alternative acknowledged the authenticity of the revolutionary break with the past, pointed the way to a reconstruction of the relationship of women to real property, and explicitly claimed for women the responsibility of assuming the obligations of citizenship. The important point is *not* that this path proved too rocky for the revolutionary generation. The important point is that, for a brief moment, it was glimpsed. The issues raised in 1805 were not fully settled; indeed, they would linger on, in various forms, into our own time.

A quarter century after the decision in *Martin*, Joseph Story—the vivacious youngest justice ever appointed to the Supreme Court—brought them to one kind of closure, in his thoughtful opinion for the majority in *Shanks v. Dupont*, decided in 1830. Story had known many of the principals in the Martin case during his years practicing and teaching law in Massachusetts.[92] The Martin case lurked behind *Shanks*. Although the issue was inheritance rather than confiscation, the case turned on the question of the allegiance of Ann Scott Shanks, who, like Anna Gordon Martin, had been born in the colonies, a subject of the king. Ann married a British officer in 1781 (that is, before the war's end, and while American claims to independence were still in some doubt), and like Anna Martin, had returned with him to England. Her sister Sarah married an American. Their father died just before the end of the Revolution, leaving his property to his two daughters; years later, when both Sarah and Ann were dead, Sarah's children sued to recover the lands that Ann's children claimed. Was Ann Scott Shanks a British subject? If she was, the United States was bound by the terms of the peace treaty that ended the Revolution to protect her claims to property lost in the war. Was she an American citizen who had renounced her allegiance? What choices did she, as a *feme covert*, have the capacity to make?

Coverture was still the rule in the United States, and Story did not try to undermine it explicitly. He acknowledged that the act of marriage was "the only free act of her life." But in keeping with his already well-established sensitivity to questions of women's social situation, Story did widen the range of choices available to the married woman. Story credited his experience in country schooling. Boys and girls "studied the same books," Story observed years later; "we recited our lessons in the presence of each other. . . . I was early struck with the flexibility, activity, and power of the female mind. Girls of the same age were . . . quite our equals in their studies and acquirements."[93]

In 1830, Story argued that "marriage with an alien, whether a friend or an enemy, produces no dissolution of the native allegiance of the wife. It may change her civil rights, but it does not affect her political rights or privileges." Ann Scott had not lost her American citizenship simply by marrying Joseph Shanks. But, Story argued, she *did* intentionally dissolve her allegiance by going "voluntarily under British protection, and adhering to the British side, by her removal with her husband." Two nations—Britain and America—claimed her allegiance, "but they virtually allowed her the benefit of her choice." Story explicitly denied that "her situation as a feme covert disabled her from a change of allegiance." He pointed out that the United States had treated as citizens "British femes covert, residing here with their husbands at the time of our independence, and adhering to our side until the close of the war." The Supreme Court concluded that Ann Shanks, whom the British government had never ceased to treat as a British subject, *was* a British subject, and that her heirs could claim her property under the terms of the Treaty of 1783.

Story made a distinction between the "incapacities . . . provided by the common law, [that] apply to [married women's] . . . civil rights, and are for their protection and interest" and married women's "political rights, [which] . . . stand upon the general principles of the law of nations." These political rights, he argued, are not undermined by coverture, nor do they prevent married women from "acquiring or losing a national character." In this way Story's decision in *Shanks v. Dupont* opened the door toward a broader conceptualization of the

political capacity of married women. The woman with political capacity was a woman who could choose not only her husband but also
her political allegiance.[94]

Citizenship is basic to all other claims which individuals make on
the state, or the state makes upon them. At its founding, the American
government assumed that any free person who had not fled with the
British or explicitly denounced the patriots was a citizen. It established no formal categories of first- and second-class citizens or of
active and passive. Most people who become citizens do so by being
born on American soil; they claim *jus soli*, the common-law right of
the land. Others, born to U.S. citizens in other parts of the globe,
claim citizenship by descent, by *jus sanguinis*, the right of the blood.
And U.S. citizenship can be acquired by naturalization. The citizenship acquired in each of these three ways is essentially the same.[95]

The Naturalization Act of 1790 was generous in the welcome it
offered any "free white person." A new citizen needed only to reside
for two years in the United States (and one year in any one state), to
prove his or her "good character," and to take an oath to "support
the constitution of the United States." But by racializing the qualifications for newcomers, this first naturalization statute used blood-
lines for the transmission of citizenship, recalibrating the relationship
to the political order of resident free blacks and free whites and setting strict limits for the future. (Only after 1870 could people of
African birth or descent be naturalized.[96]) Naturalized parents automatically conveyed citizenship to their children under twenty-one. All
children of citizens were citizens wherever they were born, but "the
right of citizenship shall not descend to persons whose fathers have
never been resident in the United States."[97] Thus the first statute
situated blacks differently than whites, and mothers differently than
fathers. Subsequent variations on naturalization law strengthened the
skewing toward fathers. Until 1934 a legitimate child born abroad
was a birthright citizen only if its father was a citizen who had resided
in the United States before the child's birth. (The residency requirement was intended to protect against the development of a category
of legal citizens who had no experience of life in the United States
generation after generation but who could still claim its protection.)
Nothing was said about citizen mothers.

The first naturalization law was written in terms of "persons," but naturalization records show that virtually all naturalizations were of adult men. It is generally thought that the desire of immigrants to purchase property in the United States, rather than the desire to vote, drove the decision to naturalize; it was the rare single woman with property to protect who was most likely to take her own oath of naturalization during the years of the early republic.

When Ann Shanks's niece and nephew sued for property that they thought she had lost title to by her marriage to an alien man, they may have had in mind the practice in France, where the Code Napoléon of 1804 had made a Frenchwoman an alien upon her marriage to a foreigner. Americans were rarely consistent in what they meant when they said a woman was a citizen of the United States, and even less consistent when they said a married woman was a citizen. For example, in 1822 a Kentucky judge expressed a capacious definition of citizenship which included married women in its boundaries: "A citizen," Benjamin Mills wrote, ". . . is one who owes to the government, allegiance, service, and money by way of taxation, and to whom the government in turn, grants and guarantees liberty of person and of conscience, the right of acquiring and possessing property, or marriage and the social relations, of suit and defence, and security in person, estate and reputation." But he was outvoted; the majority, in a judgment that echoed the decision in *Martin*, ruled that women and infants "are generally dependent upon adult males, *through whom* they enjoy the benefits of those rights and privileges."[98] It was thus an easy step when in 1855 Congress extended the principle of marital unity to provide that "any woman who might lawfully be naturalized under the existing laws, married, or shall be married to a citizen of the United States shall be deemed and taken to be a citizen."[99] That is, foreign women who married male citizens did not need to go through a naturalization process or even take an oath of allegiance, because they absorbed citizenship through their husbands' identities.

The 1855 law made U.S. practice congruent with that of major European powers. It also protected many women—whose native countries treated them as aliens when they married American men—from statelessness. It protected such women from legal challenges to their ability to inherit real property when widowed.[100] The law, however, made no comment about American women who might marry alien men; Story's position that they retained their citizenship prevailed. By pulling the concept of political rights out from under coverture, Story's decision helped markedly in the redefinitions that would have to occur before Benjamin Mills's minority position prevailed, and it was possible to establish the full political identity of American women.

Story's decision in *Shanks* was one of many developments which transformed the inherited law of domestic relations during the first century of American national life. The appropriate marriage for a postrevolutionary republic was one that emphasized the contractual nature of marriage—a civil contract between equals who are bound by love—and that understood the household to be, as historian Michael Grossberg has phrased it, "a voluntary collection of separate individuals."[101] But until the full emancipation of the Thirteenth Amendment in 1866, the law of domestic relations continued to treat the relations of husband and wife, parent and child, master and servant as part of a single continuum. The civil contract was not between individuals of equal civil capacities; the obligations of wife to husband continued to be considerably more severe than the obligations of husband to wife.

What had been virtually unquestioned at the beginning of the century was, over the course of it, subjected to heavy attack—the law of master and servant by people opposed to slavery and to indentured servitude; the law of husband and wife by women's rights advocates. Often these were the same people. The Declaration of Sentiments drafted by Elizabeth Cady Stanton for the Seneca Falls Convention of 1848 made legal demands for women's rights, attacking the rules and assumptions of coverture. These demands led to married women's property acts in many states; most were developed after the Civil War. The Thirteenth Amendment made slavery illegal and the Fourteenth Amendment's guarantee of citizenship to "all persons born or naturalized in the United States" made the word "white" in the naturalization legislation of 1790 and thereafter unconstitutional. (However, state and federal laws excluded Asians from citizenship. In 1870 California required "Mongolian, Chinese or Japanese females" to convince the Commissioner of Immigration that they came voluntarily and were not prostitutes; in 1875 federal law placed a similar burden on all women immigrants from Asia.[102]) Although no single statute ended coverture as a system, each rubbed away at one or another raw edge. By 1870 a new, magisterial treatise on the law of domestic relations by James Schouler spoke of "confusion and uncertainty."[103]

Schouler is a good guide to locating the moderate position on these matters in the Gilded Age. Instead of defending coverture for making woman "a favourite of the law," as Blackstone had done a century before, Schouler was apologetic. Coverture, he said forthrightly, was no friend to the wife: "it sacrifices her property interests, and places her almost absolutely within her husband's keeping, so far as her civil rights are concerned . . . The husband . . . is permitted to lord it over the wife with a somewhat despotic sway." Schouler contrasted common-law practice with the civil-law tradition descended from Rome, where the property rights of husband and wife were independently protected. "The wife was comparatively free from all civil disabilities. She was alone responsible for her own debts; she was competent to sue." Schouler shrewdly interpreted the drift toward married women's property laws as a movement to make common law more like civil law.[104]

But Schouler quickly fled from the implications of his own insights. Despite the inequalities of the common-law tradition, the Anglo-Saxon "race" cherished "justice and independence." Identity of interests, Schouler thought, "is essential to domestic happiness." In the United States, the laws were contradictory. Some—like married women's property acts—encouraged women's independence; others, which preserved special protections like homestead exemptions for widows, rested on the assumption of the wife's subordination. Schouler knew where he stood; the example set by Rome, where the interests of husband and wife had diverged, was not a good model. "Wide-spread incestuous intercourse, licentiousness most loathsome and unnatural, followed in the wake of marital independence. When Rome sank into utter dissolution, woman possessed a large share of cultivation and personal freedom; yet she had touched the lowest depths of social degradation."[105] The message was clear: American women scorned common-law traditions at their peril.

Meanwhile there was little consistency in how courts dealt with the cases that came before them. It frequently happened that foreign-born women married American men who worked abroad. These women gained derivative citizenship during their marriage, but they

3. The San Francisco *Chronicle*'s coverage of Ethel Mackenzie's lawsuit in 1915 emphasized her physical beauty and elite social status.

often found that if they were widowed, they could not count on being issued American passports.[106] When women of American birth moved abroad with their foreign-born husbands, sometimes American courts followed Story's lead and sustained the women's claim to their birth-right citizenship. Since the Shanks case was embedded in the turmoil of the revolutionary era, however, not all judges agreed that its precedents were permanent, and many were prepared to argue that a married woman's citizenship "naturally" followed that of her alien husband. They treated such women as having "suspended" their citizenship. What "suspended" citizenship meant was not always clear, but in accordance with the principle of "marital unity," it was common that citizen women who moved abroad actually lost their citizenship until they returned to the United States.

Expatriation—the loss of citizenship—traditionally has been a severe punishment, usually reserved for cases of treason. Indeed, sympathy for foreign women who faced it lay behind the derivative citizenship offered to women by the law of 1855. If an American-born woman had to assume the nationality of her husband when she married she might become the subject of a king or tsar in a political system that offered her even less protection than did the United States. She might even become stateless. In time of war, the American woman who married, say, a German man, could overnight change her status from a citizen to an alien enemy. If Americans claimed to base their political system on the "consent of the governed," could women's "consent" be arbitrarily denied? Joseph Story had thought not, but in the second half of the nineteenth century xenophobia strengthened, and what had seemed self-evident in 1830 was less so in 1900. When President Ulysses S. Grant's daughter married an Englishman in 1874 and went to live with him in England, she lost her citizenship, which had to be reinstated by a special act of Congress in 1898.[107] In 1907, Congress passed a statute which explicitly provided that American women who married aliens actually lost their citizenship, even if they continued to reside in the United States.

Ethel Mackenzie, who had been born in California, married Gordon Mackenzie, a British subject, in 1909—two years after the passage of the Expatriation Act of 1907. Mackenzie was active in the woman suffrage movement in California, and when it was successful in 1911 she worked in the San Francisco voter registration drive. It is not surprising that she herself should try to register to vote. When the Board of Election Commissioners denied her application, holding that upon her marriage to a British subject she had "ceased to be a citizen of the United States," she refused to let her husband apply for citizenship and instead challenged the law, claiming that Congress had exceeded its authority. She could not believe that Congress had actually *intended* to deprive her of the citizenship she understood to be her birthright. But the Supreme Court ruled that she had "ceased to be a citizen by her marriage," grounding its decision on what it called the "ancient principle of our jurisprudence": the "identity of husband and wife."

Ethel Mackenzie had claimed that citizenship was a right, a "privilege and immunity which could not be taken away from her except as a punishment for crime or by her voluntary expatriation." But Justice Joseph McKenna observed that the "marriage of an American woman with a foreigner . . . *is as voluntary and distinctive as expatriation* and its consequence must be considered as elected."[108] (emphasis mine)

The decision in *Mackenzie* angered and energized suffragists. American women needed suffrage to protect themselves against involuntary expatriation and statelessness. During World War I hundreds of native-born women were required to register as alien enemies because of the status of the men they had married. The Alien Property Custodian confiscated millions of dollars of property from native-born women married to alien enemy husbands.[109] The repeal of the Expatriation Act of 1907 was high on the suffragists' agenda, and they turned to it as soon as suffrage was accomplished. The Cable Act of 1922 provided that "the right of a person to become a naturalized citizen shall not be denied to a person on account of sex or because she is a married woman." But the decision in *Mackenzie* has never been expressly overruled, and the Cable Act had severe limitations. It permitted American women who married foreigners to retain their citizenship only if they married men from countries whose subjects were eligible for U.S. citizenship—that is, not from China or Japan. American-born women who married Chinese or Japanese men still lost their citizenship; American women who married men who were eligible to apply for citizenship were themselves treated as naturalized citizens who lost their citizenship if they resided abroad for two years. The Cable Act was extended by amendments well into the 1930s, but loopholes remained, and not all of it was made retroactive. Japanese women were not eligible to marry American men until the cautiously worded Soldier Brides Act of 1947. As late as the 1950s, some American-born women were denied passports because they had married aliens before 1922. The heritage of coverture, though submerged, remained in place.[110]

At the turn of the twenty-first century, traditional marriage relations continue to play a significant role in the ability of citizens to transmit birthright citizenship to their children, the eligibility of foreign individuals for sanctuary from political persecution, and the ability of foreign nationals to take advantage of American laws encouraging family reconstitution. Although the word "coverture" is no longer used, immigration law retains elements of the old system. Courts have held that there is no implicit constitutional right to transmit citizenship to one's children; the transmission is guided by specific legislation.

For example, not until 1934 was naturalization law revised to make it possible for *either* citizen parent to transmit birthright citizenship to a legitimate child if the parent could show some prior residence in the United States. The basic legislation has been revised over the years, and the amount of prior residence required has varied. (For births after 1986 it has been five years of prior physical presence, at least two of which were after age fourteen.) But none of these statutes was retroactive, and an adult legitimately born abroad in 1933 or earlier who wishes to claim birthright citizenship has had difficulty claiming it through a mother. In 1971 a federal court held that the pre-1934 practice of making a distinction between fathers and mothers was not discriminatory because citizenship is "a privilege conferred as a matter of grace."[111] Not until 1989 did a federal court affirm maternal birthright citizenship for a woman born abroad before 1934. When Martha Elias' Nebraska-born mother married a Canadian in 1910, she lost her U.S. citizenship; only if she divorced her husband and registered as a U.S. citizen with a U.S. consul or returned to live in the United States could she reclaim it. Martha Elias argued that her mother had never intended to give up her U.S. citizenship; that men who were born in the United States could move and marry abroad without putting their citizenship status in jeopardy. The federal court for the Northern District of California upheld the dead mother's right, as a matter of equal protection under the law, to transmit citizenship to her child. But the suit was not filed as a class action, and the court did not issue a nationwide injunction that would bar the State Department from denying passports in similar cases; at this writing, the question remains unsettled.[112]

If the status of the legitimate child born before 1934 to a nonresident woman citizen remains in doubt, the status of the out-of-wedlock child born to an alien father and a citizen mother is somewhat more clear. Until 1941, if the out-of-wedlock child was legitimated by the alien father its citizenship followed that of the father. For the out-of-wedlock child, it was the alien father's choice to legitimate (or not to legitimate) the child that determined the child's ability to claim U.S. citizenship. For refugees in the late 1930s, these limitations could have grave consequences. Not until 1941 was the line of descent also threaded through the mother.

A complex series of statutes have continued to monitor the terms by which an illegitimate child born abroad with only one citizen parent can claim citizenship. There is no question that U.S. citizen mothers can transmit their citizenship to their children born abroad, whether legitimate or illegitimate, as long as the mother had lived in the United States for at least five years, two of which were after she reached the age of fourteen.[113] But U.S. citizen fathers have had to meet those requirements and also establish their paternity and financial support before the child reaches the age of eighteen. In 1998 the U.S. Supreme Court decided that the unequal burdens on citizen fathers and mothers were constitutional, because parents were differently situated: as Justice John Paul Stevens wrote: "The child's blood relationship to its birth mother is immediately obvious . . . [but] an unmarried father may not even know that his child exists." But Justice Ruth Bader Ginsburg, who, as we shall see later in this book, had spent much of her career considering questions of equal rights and equal obligations, attacked the practice as dependent on stereotypes of what was likely to be "obvious" and as "one of the few provisions remaining in the United States Code that uses sex as a criterion in delineating citizen's rights." That the imbalances were now reversed, and it was the unmarried citizen father who could only transmit birthright citizenship with difficulty, did not seem to her to establish impartiality or equal application of the law. It continues to matter to a child born abroad of unmarried parents, only one of whom is a citizen, whether that parent is the father or the mother.[114]

Gender has been a significant, though underestimated, factor in

U.S. refugee policy; most recently it has affected the issue of whether fear of genital mutilation is reasonable grounds for asylum. Nearly half the world's refugees are women; they constitute a majority of refugees from Africa.[115] In U.S. law, in order to qualify as a refugee and apply for asylum, an alien must be unable or unwilling to return to his or her country of nationality because he or she has a well-founded fear of persecution on account of race, religion, nationality, political opinion, or "membership in a particular social group." Most claims for asylum have been made on the basis of persecution for political opinion or social group. (Jews in the Soviet Union were one large "social group.") Although genital mutilation has been outlawed in the United States, women who face genital mutilation have not clearly been defined as such a social group, nor has female genital mutilation clearly been defined as persecution.[116] Although they are receiving increasingly sympathetic public attention, those who make that claim, either as refugees themselves or as legal visitors whose visas have expired, cannot predict the outcome. The hesitant response of the U.S. legal system to claims women make on it as a social group independent of and indeed, in the case of genital mutilation, in resistance to men as a social group, suggest how troubling American courts still find this concept to be.

A third mode in which considerations of gender continue to shape the solutions to questions of national allegiance is immigration law. Since the War Brides Act of 1948, American immigration law has aided the divided family and especially heterosexual spouses by offering preferences to aliens with family relationships in the United States. Married women whose green cards have been issued primarily as a matter of family unification, to join their legal resident husbands, find themselves in vulnerable positions should domestic violence lead them to flee their households. In these cases, the husband no longer plays the role of protector between wife and the state, which the old law of domestic relations envisioned.[117]

Embedded in the concept of same-sex marriage—which would assure the legal advantages of marriage to spouses of any gender—is a deep challenge to traditional immigration law. In 1975, Anthony Corbett Sullivan, who was an Australian citizen, came to Boulder, Colorado, where he and Richard Frank Adams obtained a marriage license and were married by a minister. Adams then applied for a visa for Sullivan, claiming him as his spouse and "immediate relative." When Joseph D. Howerton, acting district director for the Immigration and Naturalization Service, refused to process the application, Adams appealed. Adams claimed that he had been denied equal protection of the laws; but the U.S. Court of Appeals for the Ninth Circuit held that Congress "has almost plenary power to admit or exclude aliens" and also power to decide to confer "spouse status . . . only upon parties to heterosexual marriages." As Americans continue to debate the legitimacy of same-sex marriage, sexuality is treated as a measure of political legitimacy.[118]

At the end of the twentieth century, the old practices of filtering civic identity through husbands are eroding, but glimpses of a world in which women's citizenship was dependent on that of their husbands can still be discerned. Birthright citizenship can generally be claimed by children born abroad to citizen mothers, although there are still some small categories (people born before 1934, for example) that remain to be brought into compliance with general practice. Unmarried male citizens face barriers to transmitting birthright citizenship to children born abroad that unmarried women citizens do not face. Gendered threats to women's bodily and mental integrity are not quickly responded to when the claims have to be filtered through husbands who insist that genital mutilation is a reasonable practice, not the persecution of a "particular social group"; the definition of what counts as persecution is still debated. The most basic challenge to the concept of coverture has come with the claims of same-sex partners to marry and to transmit to each other the privileges of the married citizen—including immigration preference—that is, the making of new citizens who are spouses, but fully independent of the rules that once governed the powers of the husband over the wife.[119]

2

"I AM JUST AS FREE AND
JUST AS GOOD AS YOU ARE"
THE OBLIGATION NOT TO BE A VAGRANT

"The women will of course provide for themselves by a life of prostitution"

We don't know much about Harriet Anthony. We do know that she was "Col[ore]d," that she was pregnant, and that in late October 1866 she was forced to perform heavy labor on the streets of Houston, Texas, a punishment normally reserved for those who were vagrant and disorderly.

Houston was not a pleasant place for black people in the aftermath of the Civil War. Union troops had never invaded Texas, and so the state did not experience the gradual destabilization of slavery that developed elsewhere during the war as slaves took refuge behind Union lines. Indeed, the slave population of Texas nearly doubled as planters from Louisiana and neighboring states fled west, taking their slaves with them and prospering by selling food and raw material to the Confederate Army. "[N]obody thunk dey'd have to free de slaves in Texas," one slave recalled many years later.[1] "[M]assa . . . say in Texas dere never be no freedom," said another. Even after the war many former masters still spoke of "gradual emancipation." The pro-

4. Unpaved, muddy streets in Houston at the end of the Civil War.

visional governor of Texas reported to President Andrew Johnson
that "slavery virtually exists the same as though the old system of
oppression was still in force."[2] In the days after Appomattox Confederate troops rioted in the streets of Houston; "the last convulsions
are the most dangerous," observed a young Texas Confederate soldier.[3]

Throughout the former Confederacy, the creative energy that masters had once dedicated to defending slavery was quickly refocused
on creating a labor system that would continue to guarantee docile
and intimidated workers. In response, Congress established the Bureau of Refugees, Freedmen, and Abandoned Lands, locating it within
the War Department and charging it with protecting the rights of
former slaves and assisting their transition to a market economy. The
Freedmen's Bureau, as it came to be known, had agents in every state
of the former Confederacy during 1865–68. Once the national government established a military presence in the region, freedpeople
found that they could turn to Bureau agents for good counsel, assistance, and protection in their struggles to sustain independence and
integrity. The Bureau had a National Commissioner, supported by
Assistant Commissioners in each state—in Texas he was Henry A.

Ellis, based in Galveston—to whom reported Subassistant Commissioners based in counties throughout the state.

The Freedmen's Bureau was an enormous and complicated affair, and its agents held varying ideas of what independence and ultimately citizenship ought to mean for freedpeople. Agents generally came to believe in the principle that freedpeople ought to have a relationship to the state similar to that whites enjoyed. The men who served as the Bureau's agents were often former Union officers; many had strong convictions about stabilizing the end of slavery.

In Houston, the Subassistant Commissioner for the Freedmen's Bureau was Jacob C. De Gress, an immigrant from Germany who had spent the war years in the Sixth Missouri Cavalry. De Gress, writes William Richter, who has carefully studied the Bureau's operations in Texas, "had a Prussian stubbornness and penchant for detail that made him well hated by the Texans who ran afoul of him. He also had the courage to ride alone through the counties around the city, and the bravado to pull off his patrols without incident. He . . . had a tendency to believe the blacks' version of disputes that dismayed former slaveholders."[4] Shortly after he arrived in Houston, for example, De Gress intervened to protect a freedwoman from her former master, who had kept the freedwoman's daughter as an unpaid house servant and was threatening to move her three hundred miles away. De Gress arrested the man we know only as Mr. Bennett for assault and battery with intent to kill and also fined him heavily; when Bennett pleaded that he was old and frail, De Gress sneered, "If he considers himself an old man he had better commence to make reparation for past acts of cruelty."[5]

When De Gress arrived in Texas in the fall of 1865, he confirmed freedpeople's complaints that planters in the region north of Houston were regularly defrauding their farmhands; "a great many of the planters are treacherous and will bear watching," he warned. When planters did not pay their hands, Richter reports, De Gress "seized up to half the crops in some counties, and threatened to chase down those whites who sold out and fled the state without paying their black fieldhands."[6]

A year later, De Gress still faced the same problem. The Houston *Telegraph* complained: "A great number of negroes are daily making their appearance in our city. . . . They are almost all ragged and dirty, and ill fitted to stand the cold of winter. The women will of course provide for themselves by a life of prostitution, but the men will not work at anything, and can be seen any day squatted around the corners and lanes and back streets of the city. We think our authorities should . . . arrest all those who have no visible means of support, and put them at something that will benefit both them and the city."[7]

This article, which took barely two column inches in the Houston *Telegraph*, was exaggerated by resentment. Blacks had left town in the spring, when work became available on outlying plantations. But in the fall, when plantation owners refused to pay the wages promised, freedpeople crowded back into city, demanding help from the police and the Bureau in collecting back wages.

A tense drama was enacted on the streets of Houston throughout the fall of 1866. Recognizing that freedpeople's "lives were threatened when they applied to their employers for their pay," De Gress froze the sale of plantation produce, holding the harvest hostage until the "chivalry of Texas" paid the workers what was owed. Simultaneously, the Houston police rounded up the "ragged and dirty" and, just as the *Telegraph* had counseled, put them to work "at something that will benefit . . . the city"—often heavy labor on road gangs, cleaning streets.

The scornful dismissal of freedwomen as "of course" being able to "provide for themselves by a life of prostitution" did not protect them from the sweeps. And when Harriet Anthony suffered a miscarriage after working at hard labor on the streets, she complained to the Freedmen's Bureau. De Gress sent a doctor to examine her.

What Counts As Work?

The only official records of Harriet Anthony's life that have yet been found are the brief, evocative notations in the Freedmen's Bureau files. The police records for the city of Houston for the Reconstruction years have long been lost. We would like to know much more about Harriet Anthony: how old she was, whether she was married, whether this was her first pregnancy, what her experience of slavery had been, what her experience of freedom had been. We would like to know more about her encounter with the law: the circumstances of her arraignment, the management of the jail, the logic by which the City Recorder used his authority to send her there.

But historians cannot always be fussy. The contrast between Harriet Anthony and the Martin family is great. In the Martin case there was a substantial amount of property at stake; the decision was made by the highest court in the state. The lawyers and judges left an extended paper trail. Even though we have no words from Anna Martin's pen, we can at least try to understand her family and community. Harriet Anthony came from a different stratum of society. Her case was handled by a municipal court whose records did not have to be archived and have long since been lost. Yet Harriet Anthony's story is important. It is a telling example of the obligation not to be a vagrant, one that weighed particularly heavily on African-American women in the late nineteenth century. The Freedmen's Bureau and its successors were especially vigilant in imposing this obligation, and their story, however poorly documented, encourages us to search for similar stories in subsequent generations. If we contented ourselves with the experiences of those who left extensive documents we would have a very skewed understanding of the past.

Like the obligation to be loyal, which as we have seen is legally framed as an obligation to refrain from treason, the obligation to work is a civic obligation legally framed in negative terms; an obligation not to be *perceived* as idle and vulnerable to punishment for vagrancy. It is not surprising to find that an obligation so fluid has been erratically enforced. Harriet Anthony was one among hundreds of thousands of freedwomen. With little property to manage and with few sophisticated legal skills, marked as dependent by their class, their race, and their sex, impoverished black women found themselves especially vulnerable in their dealings with state authority. Because American society rarely expected women of European descent to be working in public, if we are to understand the distinctive ways in which American women have experienced the obligation not to be a vagrant we are more likely to find them in the experiences of African-American women. And we will have to be content to scrutinize the scraps of evidence left by people of modest status, like Harriet Anthony and Jacob De Gress.

The term "vagrant" can be a simple descriptor for wandering or digressing, as in the phrase "vagrant fancies" or "vagrant thoughts." But as early as fourteenth-century England, it was already loaded with pejorative implications; vagrants were those who, as the Oxford English Dictionary puts it, "having no settled home or regular work wander from place to place, and maintain themselves by begging or in some other disreputable or dishonest way; an itinerant beggar, idle loafer, or tramp." Not having "regular work" was a bad thing in a society which, as Robert Steinfeld has written of early modern England, viewed labor "as a common resource to which the community had rights, and laborers and artificers had legal obligations to make that resource available to community members on terms and conditions the community prescribed." These assumptions were codified in the English Statute of Artificers, which dates to the reign of Queen Elizabeth, and which provided that "every Person" between the ages of twelve and sixty who did not have a visible means of livelihood could be "compelled to be retained to serve in Husbandry by the Year"; if the skills of an unmarried person under thirty were demanded by a master of their trade, the artisan "shall not refuse to serve."[8]

The Statute of Artificers marks an important moment in the history of Anglo-American labor relations. It assumed that able-bodied adults—adulthood generously defined as beginning with puberty—might be compelled to work, on extended contracts "by the Year." Wanderers were singled out for special attention. Vagrants included itinerants who sought to appear to be not what they were: unlicensed peddlers, fortune tellers, sturdy beggars, those who, without license, represent "any tragedy . . . comedy, farce." Long after the Elizabethan statute had been revised out of recognition in law and in practice in England and in the United States, its assumptions and, indeed, many of its specific provisions would be revived, marking the boundaries of a new, racially tainted labor system after the Civil War. The Houston ordinance under which Harriet Anthony seems to have been arrested had elements which Elizabethans would have recognized. It defined as vagrants "idle persons . . . without any visible means of support and making no exertion to obtain a livelihood by any honest employment . . . all persons who may be found begging; and all persons found loitering or strolling about the streets, and having no fixed abode . . . sleeping in the public places of the city."[9] Indeed, many of these provisions remained in statutes throughout the United States deep into the twentieth century. Examining vagrancy laws of the 1950s, Arthur H. Sherry cited phrases paraphrased from fourteenth-century English law; the laws of Florida and Illinois, he remarked, "are distinctly Elizabethan."[10]

If everyone in the laboring classes was supposed to be at work, then not to work was an offense against the Statute of Artificers. In England distinctive prisons known as bridewells—the name of the first abandoned palace to be renovated into such an institution—were developed in the sixteenth century as sites of punishment for the status offenses of the poor and to keep the streets clear of beggars, homeless, vagrants, petty thieves, common prostitutes. Together, the law of vagrancy and the institution of bridewells closed off alternatives to supervised wage or contract labor. The boundaries were never clear—nor were they intended to be. "What constituted an unjustifiable refusal to work?" asks a historian of early modern British practice. "How much carousing in taverns and consorting with the opposite sex might one indulge in before being exposed to judgment as lewd, idle, and disorderly?"[11]

English colonists thus brought with them to America a set of understandings of the relationship between work and freedom already more than a century old, understandings in which even "free" individuals could be obliged to work. "Free" laborers were often strictly bound by contracts which specified not only certain kinds and amounts of work but also constraints about where they lived, what was available for them to eat and wear, and what they might do during their limited leisure time. These contracts were enforceable in the criminal courts and violations were punishable by imprisonment. Indentured servitude was not an outcropping on the landscape, but the landscape itself.

The same law of domestic relations that defined the authority of husbands over wives and parents over children established the authority of master over servant.[12] In that system, wives owed work to husbands and children owed work to parents. (Until the child labor laws of the twentieth century there were few limits on parents'—especially fathers'—authority to indenture their children to work.) Until the expanded Married Women's Property Acts toward the end of the nineteenth century, husbands controlled all the wages earned by their wives.[13] A married woman's vulnerability to identification as a vagrant was controlled by her husband's economic status. In early America, where an individual's eligibility for poor relief was related to whether he or she had been born in a town or owned property in it, the claims of a married woman to charity were based not on whether she had "a settlement"—that is, had established residency in a town by birth or property—but on the claims her husband could make. If she married a man from another town or state, "she shall follow her husband, tho she has never been there." Moreover, observed Zephaniah Swift, the erudite author of the first major treatise on the law of a state, "if a woman having a settlement marries a man that is a foreigner . . . her settlement is suspended during coverture." If she were "reduced to want" during the marriage she could not return to the community of her birth and claim her settlement because—it was a Catch-22—"as it is not the settlement of the husband, he cannot be sent with her, and the law will not admit of the separation of husband and wife." The result was harsh: "They must both be considered as vagrants wherever they are."[14]

It is not easy to follow the history of Americans' changing understanding of women's obligation not to be a vagrant. In part this is because vagrancy is a status offense; the crime is not what a person has done but what the person *appears* to be. The faults generally specified in vagrancy statutes—living idly, loitering, not having a steady, wage-earning job, strolling about in idleness, leading a profligate life—are all perfectly legal for people of property.[15] "[If] it is a criminal offense not to work," mused a twentieth-century judge, ". . . every unemployed person, every housewife and every retired person conceivably could be arrested for vagrancy."[16] Moreover, for much of the history of the United States there has been general agreement that middle-class married white women should *not* work at income-generating or physically demanding tasks outside their own homes; that is, middle-class married white women—and those who wished to be taken as such—had an informal civic duty to appear *not* to be working.[17] That they actually did sweat over the hard work of child rearing, housecleaning, food preparation; that their piecework or the products of their domestic labor like jams or butter often brought in cash, everyone knew. But this work was performed within the household in service of their white husbands who controlled their work and their earnings and whose prosperity and sense of manhood was thereby enhanced.

Impoverished white women, by contrast, have been expected to labor in public: as indentured servants, as peddlers, in factories. They and their children could be sent to the workhouse. In the years of the early republic, men like Alexander Hamilton, the first Secretary of the Treasury who conceptualized a new mercantile and manufacturing economy, had no hesitation about mobilizing female and child labor to staff the new factories. For African-Americans, male and female, the legacy of slavery merged with the legacy of medieval England to create a heightened obligation to appear to be working, a special vulnerability to punishment as vagrants *even when* they were working, even when they appeared to be law-abiding. In a society dedicated to the denigration of the masculinity of black men, the black woman who conducted her work in private, in the service of her husband, was in a more ambivalent position than her white counterpart. As Alice Kessler-Harris has observed, such a woman disrupted "an emerging social order in which black men are expected by whites to continue to serve, not to *be* served."[18] If Americans have had a civic obligation to *appear* to be self-supporting, what counts as appearance of self-support has varied by race as well as by gender. If we wish to trace changing understanding of the obligation to work we will find it most clearly in the history of the claims that the state has made on the duties of African-American women.

The Civil War was about many things, but most obviously it was about work. At its base the war was a clash of labor systems, and when it was over one of those systems had been eliminated by blood. Certain kinds of work—slavery and involuntary servitude—were absolutely prohibited "except as a punishment for crime whereof the party shall have been duly convicted" and the prohibition was embedded in the Constitution as the Thirteenth Amendment. But the elimination of slavery as a form of work did not automatically eliminate an obligation to work.

After "slavery"—the legal equivalence of people and chattels, the explicit purchase of bodies at auction—had been eliminated by the

Civil War, constitutional change, and military Reconstruction, there remained considerable room for debate about whether the formerly enslaved still bore an obligation to engage visibly in labor. The understanding that the willingness of the poor to work is a resource on which the whole community can draw had been the principle behind the Elizabethan Statute of Artificers, and it remained alive in post-Civil War America, helping, as historian Michael B. Katz has phrased it, to "ensure the supply of cheap labor in a market economy increasingly based on unbound wage labor."[19] Much of the energy that had once been applied to defending the slave society was subsequently applied to constructing systems of labor that stopped just short of slavery and in which a common controlling device was the threat of being defined as a vagrant.[20] The system of slave law may have been erased, but the understanding of the obligation to work was recodified in accordance with long-standing beliefs about race.

All southern whites had been raised in a society in which it was assumed that black men and women were normally kept at heavy labor, at work that it was possible to *observe*. Even Freedmen's Bureau agents often brought with them assumptions that black people were destined for poverty, destined to work that was visible and measurable to outsiders, that wandering was vagrancy, and that women who moved about in public were sexually accessible. Slave women had been sexually accessible to their masters; formerly enslaved women were often still perceived as sexually accessible as prostitutes. These assumptions drew life not only from their roots in the now-defunct system of slavery but also from ancient Anglo-American understandings of how to police the poor which only a generation before had been lively in the North.

Conservatives everywhere sought an oxymoron: in historian Eric Foner's words, "a compulsory system of free labor."[21] We do not have to look very far to find the perception that freedpeople were idle; even their white allies warned that former slaves would have to be constrained to avoid vagrancy and idleness and transformed into reliable, steady workers. The concept of compulsory "free" labor ironically was reinvigorated by Union forces during the war. When they occupied Louisiana in 1863, General Nathaniel Banks issued what came to be the infamous General Order No. 23. The occupying Union troops protected freedpeople's wages by making them a first lien on the crop, but they also enforced a ten-hour working day and in-sisted upon "voluntary" labor contracts that could extend as long as a year. These contracts were racialized: blacks who refused to enter into them were regarded as unemployed, although white farmers in the Midwest who also depended on hired, seasonal workers of Eu-ropean descent rarely insisted on annual contracts. After the war, the Freedmen's Bureau continued to encourage contract labor systems, and the "Black Codes" of the states of the former Confederacy de-ployed similar language and requirements. Mississippi required all blacks to be able to show each January that they had a "lawful em-ployment or business"; lacking contracts they were defined as va-grants. South Carolina required blacks to enter contracts to work from sunrise to sundown. The Texas law of 1866 provided that "every laborer shall have full and perfect liberty to choose his or her em-ployer, but when once chosen, they shall not be allowed to leave their place of employment unless by consent of their employer, or on ac-count of harsh treatment or . . . breach of contract on the part of the employer."[22]

Historian Gerald Jaynes argues persuasively that the point of the contract system was less to keep blacks at work than it was to keep them at work on a commercial crop, which could, in predictable quantities, enter the national and international markets. Left to them-selves, freedpeople opted for subsistence farming. Plantation work, with all its associations with slavery, they avoided when they could. Whites rarely trusted freedpeople to develop an acquisitive ideology of the sort that had, in the eighteenth and early nineteenth centuries, propelled other peasant societies into commercial and industrial so-ciety.[23] Southern contracts were generally framed with the bulk of the payment at the end, after the crop was sold; in the interval the best employees could get was an advance on wages, which bound them even more tightly to the contract. Commonly workers received a share of the crop. Because they did not get paid until the end of the year, workers in effect, as historian Harold Woodman has pointed out, granted a year's credit to their employers. Meanwhile they gen-erally were charged high interest on goods they purchased on credit, while they waited to be paid themselves.[24]

Key to the struggles of freedpeople for a meaningful freedom were efforts to keep all African-American workers out of gang labor, to keep women and children from field labor, and to choose the time, place, and terms of employment. Seeking alternatives to gang labor, which, like slavery, permitted no self-direction and was intensively supervised by overseers, freedpeople found work that was no less intensive but was considerably less supervised. The work they chose was often self-employed, freelance, seasonal, odd-job, such as hauling and loading, hunting and fishing—fluid versions of work that together could well add up to subsistence or more, but are not readily observable and left room for their own fluid choices. Inadvertently freedpeople found themselves navigating not the invigorating possibilities of the meaning of free labor, but the accusation that they were not working at all; that they were, in short, vagrants.[25] Americans of European descent had long criticized Native American men for laziness because the work they did was not observable, contractual, and regular; after the Civil War the same complaints were made by whites about blacks.[26]

Throughout the former Confederacy, masters demanded—as one stipulated in writing—that a former slave "do bind herself to obey me as before." Insistence on controlling their own workdays was regarded as impudence or worse.[27] Of all the startling changes brought by the end of the war, perhaps none was so disconcerting to whites as African-Americans' assertion of their freedom to move about, to walk "on the street corners, dressed in the height of fashion," to travel long distances. Freedom to travel is not specified in the Constitution, but it is implicit in it, a necessary accompaniment to all the activities that gave meaning to an end to slavery. A slave was permanently imprisoned, moving past the boundaries of plantations only at the master's will; a free person asks no one's permission to travel. The opening of the roads at the end of the war sent hundreds of thousands of people out on them: adults hunting for each other, parents searching for children, men and women seeking work. In Texas as elsewhere, writes the most careful historian of Reconstruction there, the roads were "filled with refugees, [who] . . . wandered the roads testing their freedom. They threw parties. They danced and sang for joy. They congregated in large towns and near army posts, where freedom seemed more real to them. They sought out lost relatives. . . . [they] often went down the road to the next plantation to work, just to test their rights as free persons."[28] When freedpeople left coerced relationships, former masters were quick to charge them with the crime of "abandonment of husband or wife."[29] Women who took to the roads searching for husbands and children were labeled vagrants, and often prostitutes; the woman who wandered—especially the black woman who wandered—was assumed to be in the flesh trade.[30]

All that travel, whether joyous or worried, vocational or recreational, was quickly defined as vagrancy. "Our city is infested with freemen and women," complained the Waco, Texas, *Register* early in 1866.[31] "We know there are many honest freedmen and women in this city," conceded the Houston *Tri-Weekly Telegraph*. "But the black vagrants to be seen on the street corners, dressed in the height of fashion, and who sport their jewelry and gold watches when they have no visible means of support—these are the villains we declare war upon."[32] Throughout the South, provost marshals rounded up "vagrant" blacks. Like many other places, Galveston, Texas, established a series of ordinances that provided for the imprisonment and trial of "all idle, mischievous and disorderly negroes."[33]

In Texas and elsewhere, a cruel variation on the vagrancy concept made children especially vulnerable. Apprenticeship statutes, requiring children to work, were often framed as racially neutral but were selectively enforced. In order to leave no loopholes, special care was taken to avoid the generic "he"; the terms of apprenticeship required "the master or mistress" to "furnish said minor sufficient food and clothing—to treat said minor humanely—to teach or cause to be taught him or her some specified trade or occupation. . . . [T]he master or mistress shall have power to inflict such moderate corporeal chastisement as may be necessary and proper." In a context that permitted "any minor to be bound as an apprentice," until the age of twenty-one, "by his or her father, mother, or guardian," it became the *duty* of sheriffs and other civil officers to identify, and the *duty* of the county judge to apprentice "all indigent or vagrant minors . . . and, also, all *minors whose parent or parents have not the means, or who refuse to support said minors*" (emphasis mine). The Texas law also provided that runaway apprentices should "receive such punishment as may be provided by the vagrant laws . . . until said apprentice agrees to return to his employment."[34] The Texas code, like many others, allowed civil officers to make their own determination of whether parents could support their children, ignored the claims of a wide range of kin who generally figure into child care—grandparents, aunts and uncles, cousins—and dumped children into the category of vagrants.[35]

Nearly everywhere, failure to appear to be working on a binding contract was defined as vagrancy, and vagrancy was severely punished. Some vagrancy codes were written as though they applied to blacks and whites alike, but in fact were largely enforced against blacks and the few whites who were as desperately impoverished as most freedpeople. Historian William Cohen has pointed out that all the former Confederate states "had had adequate vagrancy laws before the war. The new statutes were not necessary except as a way of warning blacks . . . that contracts had to be made and obeyed."[36] In Florida the statute was written as though it applied to both races but was enforced only upon blacks; those convicted of vagrancy because they had "no visible means of support" were required to post bond for good behavior; if they could not post bond they could be whipped, stood in the pillory—which was still being used in Florida—imprisoned, or set to labor without pay for private individuals for up to a year.[37] In Texas, even some Freedmen's Bureau personnel began with the assumption that freedpeople had to be constrained to work; the first Assistant Commissioner for Texas "ordered that on an employer's affidavit an employee who missed two consecutive days work or five days work in a month would be considered vagrant."[38] By Texas law of 1866, a refusal to work according to the contract could be punished by deductions of double the amount of wages, and, if the "refusal to work" persisted longer than three days, "the offender shall be reported to a Justice of the Peace . . . and shall be forced to labor on roads, streets and other public works, without pay, until the offender consents to return to his labor."[39] Harriet Anthony may well have been one of these people.

"I am just as free and just as good as you are"

"It is reported to these Hd Qs," wrote Henry A. Ellis, the Acting Assistant Commissioner of the Freedmen's Bureau in Galveston, "that the City authorities of Houston are taking up freedwoman [sic]

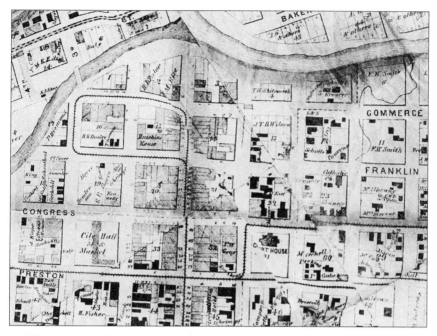

5. This 1869 map of Houston shows the City Hall, the courthouse, and the jail where Harriet Anthony was imprisoned.

as vagrants and compelling them to work on the streets of the City."[40] Dismayed, he ordered De Gress to investigate.

Houston had its own vagrancy ordinances, enforced by the City Recorder, a position equivalent to a Justice of the Peace. Elected by the City Council, he was the lowest-paid city official. In 1866 the Recorder was Judge T. B. Hadley, a deacon in the Baptist Church, who, as a member of the Mississippi legislature before moving to Houston in the 1840s, had strongly supported Mississippi's path-breaking 1838 Married Women's Property Act.[41] Hadley's liberalism did not cross the color line; the Mississippi statute had emphasized the protection of slave property that married women inherited from their natal families.

The Recorder had the power to require vagrants to post bond "not less than one hundred nor more than five hundred dollars" to keep the peace and not become a charge upon the city for a year.[42] Hadley regularly fined those found guilty of disorderly conduct $13. Even in inflated postwar currency these were prohibitive fines; monthly wages for farm contract workers in Texas were in the neighborhood of $8 to $10 for men and $5 to $7 for women.[43] The enforcement provisions of the civic ordinance on vagrancy made clear gender distinctions: able-bodied men who could not give bond were to "labor on the public works for not less than six nor more than eighteen days"; able-bodied women were to be "imprisoned in the city jail not less than three or more than fifteen days."[44]

At first, Houston vagrants unable to pay their fine were simply imprisoned. All year long the *Telegraph* called for them to "have the pleasure of cleaning our long neglected streets and gutters."[45] By late March men who could not pay were put to work in the streets, and by late spring Judge Hadley began to send black women into the streets.[46] The Houston *Telegraph* was pleased; in June it published the names of women of color who were convicted of disorderly and riotous conduct, and were "sent to the gutters" because they lacked money to pay their fines. "These ladies are all stout and muscular, and capable of achieving great good for the city in the work to which they have been ordered. They labor under the supervision of an overseer, as in the old days that are past."[47] Hadley did not send white women to the gutters, even when they were arrested "in a state of beastly intoxication" and presented "a loathsome picture of depravity."[48] Judge Hadley, the *Telegraph* observed, "is the most powerful individual for good in this city."[49]

How could black women fulfill their obligation not to be a vagrant? Black women carried into freedom their racial identity as former slaves and an obligation to work that could be traced back not only to the dim memories of the Elizabethan Statute of Artificers but to the vibrant knowledge of the system of slavery. Enslaved women were only several generations removed from sub-Saharan cultures in which women did the farming, and often understood themselves—and were understood by whites—to be skilled agriculturalists. As early as the mid-seventeenth century, black women were put to work in the fields though white indentured servant women rarely were. The freedwoman carried with her the obligation to work and simultaneously the obligation to display deference. "We ladies are in great trouble," wrote a white woman, imagining herself speaking for "the wives and mothers of the country," to the Houston *Telegraph*. The close of the war found her at the head of a large plantation and a large family, "but with all of my well-trained, attentive, respectful and affectionate servants . . . scattered to the four winds and replaced by one-fourth their number of idle, impudent, worthless, dirty wenches . . . what have I in return? Unwilling service constantly accompanied by an air which says, 'I am assured that I am just as free and just as good as you are; that you cannot do without me, and should make you feel that I know it'. . . . 'Dismiss her at once' say you Mr. Editor! And how am I to have my family's clothes washed!"[50]

The belief that free black women had no option to be "idle" was turned into practice repeatedly long before the war's end, when occupying Union troops established de facto freedom and simultaneously accompanied it by an insistence that physical labor continue. The Union Army had required black soldiers' wives to work. When the Union Army occupied Vicksburg, Mississippi, in 1863, able-bodied freedmen were sent to join the troops, but women, children, and men not fit to be soldiers were required to labor in army staff departments or on plantations within the army lines.[51] In May 1865 in Manchester, Virginia, "idle" black men were set to work on the streets and "idle" black women were "packed off to Belle Isle to wash for the soldiers." Although the Bureau insisted that "the whites must work as well as the idle blacks," we have no evidence that "idle" white women were "packed off" to do a regiment's laundry.[52] When the Bureau sent an agent to take a census of the freedpeople of Jacksonville, Florida and to put the unemployed to work, it was very specific: "*No discrimination will be made between males and females; all who are able to work on a plantation & their families will be included*" (emphasis mine).[53]

The old law of domestic relations was—as we noted in Chapter 1—gradually destabilized over the course of the nineteenth century, but that destabilization had only just begun when enslaved women emerged into freedom. Married women everywhere largely lacked independent civil status and husbands still controlled their wives' property and the money wives earned by taking in boarders, doing laundry, and working at odd jobs. Husbands' control of their wives extended to the concept of vagrancy, particularly for African-

Americans. Black men had their own obligation to work. But they also had an obligation to see to it that the women and children for whom they were responsible also worked. Black families came under suspicion if the work of women and children was conducted privately, in their own households, in the service of the male heads of those households. In the revised race and class relations of the postbellum South, black men did not become more "manly" when they protected their wives and children from the workforce. In the emerging postwar social order, whites expected black men to serve, not to *be* served. As individuals freedwomen shared with white women an obligation to work; as wives they were similarly obligated to their husbands, who stood between them and the state. "All labor contracts shall be made with the heads of families," provided the Texas statute; "they shall embrace the labor of all the members of the family."[54] The Bureau —that is, the community of whites most sympathetic to the situation of blacks—generally assumed this was a reasonable practice. Contracts in which the male head of the household committed the labor of other family members had been common in the North only a generation or two before, among native-born shoemakers in Lynn, Massachusetts, for example, and the immigrant workers in New England mills in the 1840s.[55]

Throughout the former Confederacy, Freedmen's Bureau agents respected the authority of husbands over wives' labor and earnings. Acting on what was to them the common sense of the matter, they often inadvertently but emphatically denied freedwomen's civil identity, agency, and, indeed, their freedom. One Bureau agent in Arkansas ascribed the lack of "harmony" between employers and employees to "the negro women [who] have failed to perform their part of their contracts."[56] When the Freedmen's Bureau Assistant Commissioner for Texas, Edgar M. Gregory, addressed a gathering of freedpeople in January 1866, he emphasized that "the freedmen could purchase and own any kind of property that a white man could—his wife, his children, a horse, a cow or lands."[57] In a careful study for one region in Georgia, Susan E. O'Donovan has found that one measure of the independent manhood of a former slave was his control of his wife. Thus one freedman demanded that the Freedmen's Bureau restore his runaway abused wife; she was, he told the agent, "the only nigger he had." In that context, it is not surprising to find that when a woman married in the middle of the contract year, an argument was likely to ensue over who was entitled to her wages—her father or her husband. No one considered that she might be entitled to them in her own name.[58]

Freedwomen whose marriages had been the result of pressure from their former masters had particular reasons to resent the old law of domestic relations and the subordination it enforced. For every once happily married woman who searched to reconstruct her family there was likely to be another woman who had been "married" under duress and for whom "freedom" meant she could now resist the claims of the husband assigned to her by a master. Desperate to sustain plantation labor in 1865, a year when it was widely predicted that because of the war there would be crop failures which in turn would lead to social disaster, one Bureau agent in Georgia regularly ordered married women to return to plantations to fulfill their contracts. "Kate Wade, a colored Woman who has left her husband without cause will return to him, and live with and help him support his & her children. If this order is not complied with on the part of said Kate, she will be imprisoned as a vagrant."[59] Polly Knight, who had been "compelled to live" with another slave, Ike, announced as soon as the federal troops arrived in their neighborhood "that she had been living with him . . . under compulsion, that she was then her own woman, and henceforth she would never have anything to do with him." Ike promptly signed a contract to work on the same plantation where she did, "knowing . . . that they would be thus thrown together during the remainder of the year."[60] "[M]any negro women," reported an Arkansas agent, "have failed to perform their part of the contracts . . . claiming the husband has no powers to control her labor. She being free & responsible as himself."[61]

When white men insisted that freedmen work for wages on contract they could add that white men also had an obligation to appear to be working. They could offer the inducement that in a middle-class system of values, the freedmen might enhance their own manliness by honorable work for wages. But the assumptions were gender-specific, as freedwomen were quick to see.

Unlike middle-class white women, freedwomen could not enhance their femininity by displaying the flexibility of their work lives and by removing themselves from the workforce. Like poor men, poor women were expected to display their subjectivity as workers. But unlike men, who enhanced their gender identity by their work identities, black women could not by their work enhance their identity *as women.* Indeed, to be a woman laborer—to sweat, to have work-hardened hands and sun-lined face—was for many of the middle and aspiring middle class to be perceived as *less* of a woman. When they did try to remove themselves from the workforce as respectable white women did, black women were denounced as irresponsible, outrageous, vagrant. A Georgia agent complained that freedwomen were "loitering and lounging about . . . most of them sponging upon the scanty earnings of their Fathers Husbands and friends . . . the women . . . have not earned their rations . . . they must cultivate the earth or starve in idleness . . . Next year the plantation women will nearly all be vagrants."[62] The Unionist governor of Georgia, M. Wells, complained that "there are a number of stout women here who refuse *now* to work in any way, assigning as the reason [that] white women do not work." His response was to stop their rations.[63]

Of course, many white women did work for wages; the census of 1870, which generally undercounted all women workers and seriously undercounted domestic workers, reported that nearly one out of four nonfarm wage earners was a woman. The proportion would remain relatively steady for the next fifty years. Even white women found it difficult to carry respectability with them across the lines of class if they could not show that they were provided for by husbands or fathers. Only about 7 percent of white married women worked outside the home in 1880; in sharp contrast to the 35 percent of black married women who did so.[64] Schoolteaching, for example, was respectable, but only if it did not cross the color line. When white women volunteered to teach black children, they were often welcomed by blacks but virulently abused by other whites. The usual accusation was that they were common prostitutes, superficially an irrational accusation, but one that reflected the assumption that a woman out of place has made herself sexually available.[65]

Freedwomen were not wrong to discern that white women had a differently calibrated obligation to work than did African-American women. Nowhere did white women have an obligation to enter extended work contracts. Even the most impoverished white women generally worked in the fields only sporadically, at harvest and planting time, not steadily, on yearlong contracts. In Memphis in 1865, for example, it seems to have been taken for granted that women "are unable to work on the public streets and thus [when in prison] become a dead expense to the City."[66] But when the occupying Union Army was having trouble finding enough men to build a Louisiana levee in 1864, a Bureau agent asked permission to recruit "able bodied negro women"; he had already been "using them successfully doing nearly as much work as the men."[67] In 1865 the manager of a Louisiana plantation offered the Bureau "several women well able to work but too lazy; they are a nuisance on the place & I wish to get rid of them; if you wish any one on Public works I should be pleased to have you take these persons from here."[68] And when Polly Knight, denying her "marriage" to Ike, was fined and imprisoned in a "filthy jail" on his claim that she was an adulterer, "locked in the jail yard with perhaps a dozen convicts—the object of their insults, and, at their option an unwilling sacrifice to their basest passions," she found that the only way she could get out of jail would be to work out her $100 fine "by hauling dirt in a wheelbarrow on the streets of this City."[69]

"We have to work for little or nothing"

When Henry Ellis ordered Jacob De Gress to investigate the treatment of freedwomen accused of vagrancy, it came as no surprise. "The same thing was reported to me some days since," De Gress replied quickly. "I investigated the matter at once." In his mind, however, the central comparison was race, not gender. When De Gress found that, along with Harriet Anthony and other freedwomen, white men had also been arrested for disorderly conduct and set to street labor when they could not pay the fine, he concluded there was nothing more to do. He did not consider whether any white women had been put to work at hard labor on the public streets. For black women, race trumped gender. "I would have interfered," De Gress asserted, "had the civil authorities made any difference in the punishment of freedpeople and whites."[70]

In taking this position, De Gress exemplified the restraint that was generally characteristic of Freedmen's Bureau agents. As Eric Foner has pointed out, "instead of seeing itself as the champion of one side or the other in an ongoing conflict [between former slaves and former masters, a conflict in which the Bureau would be expected to sustain the former slaves] the Bureau sought to stand between . . . [the two classes] and make both aware of the common interests they shared, if only they would recognize it." Thus De Gress comfortably concluded that since both freedpeople and whites were found working out sentences at labor on the streets, he would not, on behalf of the Bureau, inquire further into the equity of the sentences. To take this position was to ignore disparities of power between blacks and whites that persisted long after the Civil War. "Perhaps the greatest failing of the Freedmen's Bureau," writes Foner, "was that it never quite comprehended the depths of racial antagonism and class conflict in the postwar South."[71] Yet the Bureau was the only federal agency devoted to reconciliation, and when it was closed down in 1874 nothing took its place. By 1876 Reconstruction was dead, ended by the violent resistance of the Ku Klux Klan, by the revitalization of the Democratic Party, and, finally, by the settlement of the contested presidential election in favor of the Republican candidate, Rutherford B. Hayes, with the understanding that the federal government would retreat from efforts to protect fundamental rights of black citizens.

Black women like Harriet Anthony emerged from slavery into a social order which demanded of them precisely the labor by which they had already been defined: housework and field work. Not until 1970 would a majority of African-American women earn wages in other ways. In a society that is not a police state, the enforcement of civil obligations occurs informally, embedded in the cultural practices of everyday life. But under what is "natural" and "self-evident" lurk formal systems of obligation that developed differently for men and for women, and differently for white women and black women.

For roughly three-quarters of a century after Reconstruction, African-Americans in the South fulfilled their obligation of self-support in a system of segregation buttressed by forms of involuntary servitude, a fluid system in which the obligation to work for a wage was defined as an expression of freedom and in which, as historian Barbara Fields has put it, men and women were "broken" to market discipline.[72] Courts and legislatures participated in codifying the obligation to work, offering up the entire black community as ingredients of the labor force, much as the colonists had offered up "the poor" to the same purpose. The system persisted in one shape or another until it was undermined by the civil rights movement of the mid-twentieth century. It was governed by rules involving sharecropping, the crop-lien system, and peonage and guarded by enticement statutes, contract-enforcement statutes, and vagrancy laws. "Broadly drawn vagrancy statutes," writes William Cohen, "enabled police to round up idle blacks in times of labor scarcity and also gave employers a coercive tool that might be used to keep workers on the job. Those jailed on charges of vagrancy or any other petty crime were then [given the] . . . 'opportunity' to sign a voluntary labor contract with his former employer." Those who did not sign faced convict labor. Between 1890 and 1910 nearly all the former Confederate states adopted new and harsher vagrancy laws, most of which lasted well into the 1960s.[73]

In the more than a century that has passed since Reconstruction, Americans have earned wages within pervasive systems of job segregation by sex and by race. Black women have been paid between one-half and two-thirds of the wages of black men, who in turn lived within pay scales considerably lower than those governing the work of white men. White women and women of color rarely performed similar tasks or shared the same workplaces; that remains true as the twentieth century draws to a close. The structural barriers encountered by all working women have meant, as historian Joanne Goodwin has put it, that "the majority of women could not work their way out of poverty as men theoretically were able to do."[74]

As the obligation to work was reconstructed for those who had been enslaved, it was constructed distinctively for black women in ways that differentiated their obligations from those borne by white women. W. E. B. Du Bois memorably pointed out that even when white workers received low wages they were "compensated in part by a . . . public and psychological wage. They were given public deference . . . because they were white. They were admitted freely, with all classes of white people, to public functions [and] public parks."[75] What it could mean for a woman to fulfill the obligation to work without the "wage of whiteness" was memorably described in 1912, when a national magazine interviewed a forty-year-old widow, the mother of three children, who had been a domestic servant "in one capacity or another" in white families in Atlanta since she was a child of ten. A half century after the Civil War, she understood herself to be stuck in a servitude policed by vagrancy laws:

> More than two-thirds of the negro women here, whether married or single, are compelled to work for a living—as nurses, cooks, washerwomen, chambermaids, seamstresses, hucksters, janitresses, and the like. . . . Tho' today we are enjoying nominal freedom, we are literally slaves. . . .
>
> I frequently work from fourteen to sixteen hours a day. I am compelled by my contract, which is oral only, to sleep in the house. I am allowed to go home to my own children . . . only once in two weeks . . . You might as well say that I'm on duty all the time—from sunrise to sunrise, every day in the week. . . . And what do I get for this work—this lifetime bondage? The pitiful sum of ten dollars a month!
>
> We have no labor unions or organizations of any kind that could demand for us a uniform scale of wages for cooks, washerwomen, nurses, and the like; and, for another thing, if some negroes did here and there refuse to work for seven and eight and ten dollars a month, there would be hundreds of other negroes right on the spot ready to take their places and do the same work, or more, for the low wages that had been refused. So that, the truth is, we have to work for little or nothing or become vagrants! And that, of course, in this State would mean that we would be arrested, tried and despatched to the "State Farm," where we would surely have to work for nothing or be beaten with many stripes![76]

African-American women like her found themselves trapped in an ideology of work riddled with a dizzying series of contradictions, some of which applied to all women, black and white, others only to African-Americans. To the obligation to support themselves and their families that, it could be said, all citizens shared, were added the ideological legacies of slavery, which rigorously maintained the race- and gender-segregated labor market and simultaneously denied that what domestic laborers did was respectable "work." As the *Independent*'s informant said, they worked in a context in which labor organization and resistance seemed impossible. Their removal from the wage labor market by fathers and husbands—as "respectable" white women were supposed to be removed—was made impossible by a system that paid such low wages to black men that they could not protect their wives and children from the marketplace.

The very concept of the "family wage" cut fault lines between the different obligations of white men and white women to work for wages and also, it would turn out, between the different—though implicit—obligations of white men and black men to keep their wives and children out of the waged labor force. The explicit goal of defenders of the family wage has been that white men earn enough to keep their wives and daughters out of the waged workforce. Well into the late twentieth century, sociologists find that when white men call themselves "workingmen," they mean to convey not only a gendered identity as against the women in their families but also a racial identity, "an identification of whiteness and work so strong that it need not even be spoken."[77] In the hands of organized labor, the concept of a family wage offered a language of unselfishness that could be useful in gathering popular support for union mobilization. In this way of thinking, white men have an obligation to work that encompasses the obligations of their wives and shields the more vulnerable family members. In this way of thinking, white women have an obligation to *support* the work of their husbands and fathers, but neither a right nor an obligation to claim work for their own self-support.

Even white men rarely achieved stable family wages in that sense. Moreover, as skeptic after skeptic pointed out year after year from the 1880s through the 1960s, the flows of support run in reality not only from fathers to women and children but from child and women laborers back to fathers. Sophonisba Breckenridge observed in 1923, "If many fathers support wives and young children, many daughters assist their fathers in doing that very thing, while many other daughters support aged parents and young nieces and nephews as well as themselves."[78]

Skeptics might sneer, but as long as the demand for a family wage persisted—and it remains a familiar demand at the turn of the twenty-first century—it has carried with it the understanding that women do not have the same implicit obligation to support themselves with paid work that men do. Furthermore, as long as the demand for a family wage has been voiced, it has generally been articulated in contexts in which it is understood to apply only to white families. Rarely, when articulated by integrated labor unions, or more recently by the Nation of Islam in the 1995 Million Man March, has it been framed as the claim of black men to a family wage so they can keep black women out of the waged labor force. As historian David Katzman put it, "The inadequacy of the wages received by black men forced their wives to work while raising families and running their own households, and black married women in 1900 were at least ten times more likely to be gainfully employed than white married women."[79]

African-American women have been most likely to work in regions of the economy to which maximum hour, minimum wage laws have not applied. One way of thinking about this is to say that laws that were intended to shield women from waged labor have been construed racially; if they shield anyone it has rarely been women of color. When the U.S. Supreme Court upheld legislation limiting hours for working women in *Muller v. Oregon* in 1908 on the grounds that "as healthy mothers are essential to vigorous offspring, the physical well-being of woman becomes an object of public interest and care in order to preserve the strength and vigor of the race," the ruling primarily affected factory, office, and sales workers, who were likely to be white. Neither Supreme Court nor Congress extended its concern to the health of women like the domestic worker *The Independent* interviewed four years later. Historian Tera Hunter finds that during World War I, when many other cities deployed the principle of "work or fight" to push unemployed men into the draft, Atlanta municipal authorities used it to argue that uppity black domestics who quit their jobs were hindering the patriotic effort.[80] In the 1920s, when pensions were made available to single mothers by forty states and the territories of Alaska and Hawaii, benefits were allocated according to racialized rules. "Although all able-bodied women were urged to find some type of employment," writes Joanne Goodwin, "African American women were believed to be more able to find work."[81] Throughout the country, only 3 percent of the money in mothers' pensions went to black women, and some counties and some states excluded them completely.[82]

New Deal legislation expanded the boundaries of social provision in the United States, but New Deal legislation was, we can now understand, carefully crafted to exclude African-Americans in the South and women, black and white, throughout the country. The exclusion was constructed in part to respond to President Franklin Delano Roosevelt's need for the votes of segregationists if Congress was to pass any social provision legislation at all. It was also constructed in conformity with contemporary white Americans' assumptions about the proper dynamics of a respectable family and their belief that it was appropriate that black women *not* be shielded from the obligation to work. By excluding all agricultural and domestic workers, the Social Security Act of 1935 failed to cover between three-fifths and two-thirds of all black workers. By not requiring states to standardize benefits, the legislation permitted substantial differences in benefits to whites and blacks. Furthermore, as sociologist Jill Quadagno emphasizes, by excluding from the original Social Security legislation "teachers, nurses, hospital employees, librarians and social workers—all occupations heavily dominated by women," more than half of all employed women were left out.[83] The drafters of the original legislation took the position that millions of working women were not really working and therefore were not entitled to Social Security benefits of their own. Viewing the situation through the prism of rights, they did not ask whether the women were obligated to work. But of course no women denied their "rights" by the new Social Security legislation stopped working on that account.

When the Social Security law was extensively amended in 1939, drafters of the legislation continued their blissful assumption that all women were married to wage-earning men. They were untroubled by a structure that filtered women's claims through their husbands' entitlements; indeed, as historian Alice Kessler-Harris has emphasized, "the very first set of amendments . . . added Old Age Insurance benefits for wives and widows who had not paid for them."

No charitable impulse toward women motivated this act; no concern for their poverty inspired it. Rather, Congress added dependent wives and aged widows in order to shore up the legitimacy of a system in trouble. It did this by making the benefits of already-covered (mostly white) males more adequate by granting extra benefits to those who had aged wives to support and extra insurance to those with young children who survived them.

Thus, it reinforced the prerogatives and self-images of some males while reaffirming racialized conceptions of gender.[84]

The revised system of Social Security offered benefits to fatherless children. Widowed mothers received three-quarters of their husbands' pensions to enable them "to remain at home and care for the children"; these pensions were "to be reduced or eliminated if her earnings exceeded $15 a month (a tiny sum, even in 1939)."[85] The mother of children was in effect rewarded for staying out of the waged workforce. Race made a major difference; since the system covered few black men or their widows, black mothers were not rewarded for staying out. Indeed, relief practices during the Depression often had the opposite effect. In short, Social Security law continued to offer contradictory signals about the extent to which women's obligation to be self-supporting would be recognized. The new legislation penalized women who "earned their own way" and "rewarded women who remained in stable marriages and were supported by their husbands."[86] That did not remove the obligation at all, but it paradoxically rewarded the women, largely white, who did not fulfill it.

At the same time, there were women, disproportionately nonwhite, for whom the obligation to work was enforced with increasing vigor. These women were often referred to as "employable mothers," a concept which began to be used in the 1930s and persisted for decades thereafter. Oxymoronic in the social context of the 1930s, it described African-American women and Latinas who, in their character as mothers, could have been shielded from the obligation to work, but who, in their character as "employable," were not shielded. Thus social agencies often refused to pay clients' support during picking seasons for tobacco and cotton, and relief agencies commonly denied aid when it appeared that jobs as servants and field workers were locally available.[87] Even though the Federal Emergency Relief Administration (FERA) generally "supported workers' choices to refuse private sector employment when wages were too low, conditions poor, or the prospect of being paid doubtful," administrators could press the most vulnerable workers into agricultural or domestic labor. The concept of the "employable mother" made it possible for state and federal systems of relief to hold some—generally white—mothers out of the

waged labor force and simultaneously to obligate other mothers—
often women of color or of lower-status ethnicities—to enter it. WPA
and CCC programs—limiting women by statute to no more than
one-sixth of the participants and in practice to far less, justified by
the goals of putting "some brake upon women's eagerness to be the
family breadwinner, wage recipient and controller of the family
pocketbook"—offered notoriously little skilled work or job training
for women.[88] In an eerie continuation of the Freedmen's Bureau understanding of appropriate work for black women, the WPA, which
generally denied job training and outdoor parks conservation work
to any women, occasionally did put black women on beautification
projects—"a trash gang doing road work," reports historian Eileen
Boris. "These thing aint fare," a black woman wrote to President
Roosevelt, complaining that the WPA put her in the woods "with
grub hoe an pick ax" while white women got comfortable indoor
jobs.[89]

Field supervisors in the South found that local administrators "see
no reason why the employable Negro mother should not continue
her usually sketchy seasonal labor or indefinite domestic service rather
than receive a public assistance grant." Joanne Goodwin has traced a
shift that occurred between 1935 and 1960 and has continued into
the present, one that was felt first by poor black women and, eventually, by all women who sought social assistance. "Louisiana adopted
the first 'employable mother' rule in 1943. . . . all capable women
with children over the age of seven years who received public aid
could be denied assistance when field work was available. Georgia
implemented a similar rule in 1952 but lowered the children's age to
three years." The federal Bureau of Public Assistance disapproved of
the practice but was unable to control it; "by 1962," writes Goodwin,
". . . thirty-three states had work requirements in their ADC regulations."[90] Efforts to challenge the "employable mother" regulations
in the courts were unsuccessful. There is "no federally protected right
of a mother to refuse employment while receiving assistance and remaining at home with her children," observed a three-judge panel of
the U.S. District Court in Atlanta, upholding the portion of Georgia's
"employable mother" regulation which provided that "a mother must
accept suitable employment, *assuming adequate safeguards to the mother
and her children, such as the availability of adequate child care plans*" (em-

phasis mine). The court offered no comment on the extent to which the assumed "safeguards" were actually available in the state of Georgia.[91]

New Deal policies were clear on the point that mothers of children—even adolescent children—should be protected from wage labor in the interests of child nurture, but New Deal policies simultaneously offered states broad options to oblige large categories of women to do minimally paid labor. During the postwar years AFDC maintained rhetorically that the program kept women out of the workforce, but its effects were erratic and bore differently on women of different races. By 1961 twice as many African-American women who received AFDC also worked for wages as white women; in the South the disproportion was even greater.[92]

The welfare rolls grew steadily in the 1950s—increasing by 17 percent—and then by more than 100 percent in the 1960s, with a 60 percent increase in the four years between 1964 and 1968. The reasons for this explosion are still debated, although some of their ingredients are clear—the movement of many black families from the South, where they were likely to be excluded from welfare eligibility, to the North, where they were more likely to be added to the rolls; the lowering of thresholds of entitlements; and, in the late 1960s, the heightened sophistication of the poor and their increased likelihood of demanding their entitlements. The National Welfare Rights Organization, organized by the brilliant and energetic George Wiley, led by civil rights lawyers and committed social workers, and primarily composed of black women who were recipients of welfare, often adopted confrontational strategies.

The successes of NWRO triggered a backlash; a resistance that might well have come no matter what they did in the more conservative political climate of the mid-1970s.[93] It may be that the NWRO was squelched by the backlash against the urban riots of the late 1960s. In analyzing the underlying causes of these riots, white and black policymakers focused on the severe unemployment and demoralization of young black men. Nixon's Family Assistance Program was intended to stabilize families and "encourage young men to . . . form stable, male-headed households." This is not unreasonable, but the argument got vicious when analysts (most famously Daniel Patrick

Moynihan, but also African Americans like William Julius Wilson and Roy Innis) pitted the independence of black women against the stability of black men, urging that "federal policy should reinstate black men as household heads by reducing the labor-force participation of black women . . ." and simultaneously promised that welfare mothers would work more, while providing them neither job training nor child care. For the practical purposes of the Family Assistance Program, "welfare mothers . . . were not the working poor."[94] But while the Family Assistance Program scurried to find them breadwinner husbands, single mothers on welfare still could not stay home. Their obligation to work trumped their obligation to sustain stable families.

As the feminization of poverty proceeded through the last quarter of the twentieth century, poverty among younger women and their children outpaced poverty among elderly women. Poverty among women of color rose more sharply than for white women. "The public cannot seem to decide whether it expects or even wants mothers of young children to work," observed sociologist Mary Jo Bane in the mid-1980s; "the levels of support for female-headed families are stingy and the harassment great."[95] By 1996 the public had decided; the Welfare Reform Act of that year required wage labor of virtually all recipients, including mothers of preschool children.[96]

As the stresses of the welfare system exploded in the 1960s to reveal the ways in which the obligation to work was imposed on women of color in distinctive ways, so the system of vagrancy law and its complicity in sustaining race- and gender-based definitions of what counted as work also came under scrutiny and attack. Although vagrancy laws were drawn up in terms capacious enough to absorb prostitution, prostitutes had often been protected from challenge as vagrants. Although they wandered for immoral purposes and so would fit the categories of the Elizabethan statutes, they "had homes, paid rent, bought food and clothes" and otherwise contributed to local economies.[97] When Julia Custer was arrested as a vagrant in Edgecombe County, North Carolina, in 1870 on the grounds that she was "frequently seen idly sauntering about . . . and endeavoring to maintain herself by whoring," the North Carolina Supreme Court found her not guilty on the grounds that "she was *endeavoring* to do something wrong . . . not that she did it, and the thing she was endeavoring to do, was something immoral only, and not unlawful."[98]

Still, vagrancy laws retained their vitality deep into the twentieth century, especially in the South. Used selectively, they could force those out of work to choose between prison and working for a particular employer; used widely, they could reconstruct a peonage system, despite the fact that work or imprisonment for debt had been outlawed in 1867. William Cohen offers one succinct example: "In 1937, when depression-ridden Miami, Florida, could not find the funds to maintain its trash collection schedule, it began to use Negro prisoners as garbage men." The Miami *Daily News* reported that when there weren't enough Negro prisoners available, the police "promptly went out and rounded up a hatful of negro vagrants." There was no similar roundup of whites.[99] In the 1930s and 1940s, interracial organizations undertook to resist peonage. When the Farm Tenant Union tried to organize agricultural workers in the South, they found vagrancy laws a strategy used against them. For example, in 1936, Paul Peacher, city marshal and a cotton planter in Earl, Arkansas, was fined $3,500 in the first use of the civil rights law of 1866 in the state. "Peacher arrested eight Negroes for vagrancy and forced them to work for him clearing some school district property."[100] In 1948 the Workers Defense League, a nonpartisan organization founded by Norman Thomas, mobilized an International Commission of Inquiry into Forced Labor, focusing on the Soviet Union, South Africa, and the southern United States. It drew into its membership cautious men like Harry Gideonse and Arthur Schlesinger, Jr., as well as activists more usually associated with the socialist left. In the mid-1940s, staff member Morris Milgram, who would later be a leader in the development of integrated housing in New York City, investigated the arrest of dozens of black workers in Florida on the grounds of vagrancy. The League reported a victory when twelve men in Fort Lauderdale were awarded damages for involuntary servitude and illegal arrest. "The Negroes charged that they were ordered to work against their wills and jailed on vagrancy charges for refusal to do so."[101]

By the late 1950s, the reformers had succeeded in publicizing the anachronism, the arbitrariness, and indeed the internal contradictions of vagrancy law. If there is no slavery or peonage, if, that is, there is no federal obligation to be at work, how can statutes that seek to compel the poor to be at work be constitutional? Law review articles emphasized the anachronism of focusing on "sturdy beggars" and "vagabonds," and argued that vagrancy laws typically were vague and should be declared "void for vagueness." Vagrancy laws typically flaunted the appropriate use of police power by punishing vagrants not for what they had done but for what they seemed to *be*. Reformers typically called for more precision in the law or eliminating it altogether; not all wandering by the poor was appropriately marked as vagrancy. In *Edwards v. California* (1941) the U.S. Supreme Court unanimously protected the right to travel across state lines as a fundamental freedom untouched by wealth or poverty. In a powerful essay, law professor Anthony Amsterdam argued that "there is a federal constitutional right against any such compulsion [to work] . . . founded in the Thirteenth Amendment's prohibition of involuntary servitude" and predicted that vagrancy laws would be declared unconstitutional.[102] Reformers poked fun: "Luis Muñoz Marín, former Governor of Puerto Rico, commented once that 'loafing' was a national virtue in his Commonwealth and that it should be encouraged."[103]

When the vagrancy concept was finally tested in the U.S. Supreme Court it came in the form of a challenge by two interracial couples. The vagrancy ordinance of the city of Jacksonville, Florida, was traditionally worded: it began "Rogues and vagabonds, or dissolute persons who go about begging . . . persons who use juggling or unlawful games . . . persons wandering or strolling around from place to place without any lawful purpose or object." Margaret Papachristou and Betty Calloway, who were white, and Eugene Eddie Melton and Leonard Johnson, who were black, were charged with "prowling by auto."

The four of them were riding in Calloway's car on the main thoroughfare in Jacksonville. They had left a restaurant owned by Johnson's uncle . . . and were on their way to a nightclub. The arresting officers denied that the racial mixture in the car played any part in the decision to make the arrest. The arrest, they said, was made because the defendants had stopped near a used-car lot which had been broken into several times.

The Supreme Court found the Jacksonville ordinance void—for vagueness, for giving too much discretion to the police, for stretching the concept of "probable cause": "a presumption that people who might walk or loaf or loiter or stroll or frequent houses where liquor is sold, or who are supported by their wives or who look suspicious to the police are to become future criminals is too precarious for a rule of law. . . . The Jacksonville ordinance . . . is plainly unconstitutional."[104]

A vague obligation to work—or to appear to be working—has continued to permeate American systems of law and justice. In the quarter century since Papachristou's challenge, the site of definition has shifted from vagrancy law to welfare law. There remains an obligation to work, paradoxically laid out with most precision for those people for whom the need to work would seem most self-evident, suggesting that the language of obligation developed as guardian of unwelcome working *conditions* rather than the work itself.

The displacement onto black women—especially black women of childbearing age—of anxieties about the insecurity of family life has been expressed heavily in a language of obligation to work. Impoverished black women have been caught in the internal contradictions of a gendered ideology of an obligation to work that succeeded slavery. The ideology was deeply rooted in antique concepts that stressed the obligation of the poor not only to be self-supporting but also to be at work that is measurable and visible, and that envisioned black women as appropriately engaged in physical labor from which their white counterparts were more likely to be protected. When the obligation to work for self-support was loosened for the wives of the deserving poor, the wives of the manly white men who had earned their Social Security credits, it was maintained for women whose men were not covered by Social Security, and who dragged with them from the nineteenth century burdens and expectations grounded in the experience of slavery. Ironies abound; the 1996 legislation that ended federal commitments to welfare was entitled "The Personal Responsibility and Work Opportunity Act."

3

"WHEREVER YOU FIND TAXEY THERE VOTEY WILL BE ALSO" REPRESENTATION AND TAXES IN THE NINETEENTH CENTURY

"Taxation without representation is wrong"

Abby Hadassah Smith was seventy-six years old, and her sister Julia Evelina was eighty-one when they announced in person and in print that they were refusing to pay the highest property taxes in town until they could vote. "Taxation without representation is wrong," declared Abby Smith. "Is it any more just to take a woman's property without her consent, than it is to take a man's property without his consent?"[1]

Their test of the obligation to pay taxes began in 1869 and lasted for seven years. By the end of that time they had become confident and widely traveled public speakers, they had linked their names with a massive attack on taxation without representation launched by the national women's rights community, and they had become integral to an effort that dared legal theorists explicitly to acknowledge the suffragists' claim that the obligation to pay taxes rests on state force, not the consent of the governed.

Glastonbury is seven miles from Hartford. Until a decade ago farms flourished in the township; there are still apple and peach orchards in the vicinity. The Smith sisters' home on Main Street is still

6. Julia and Abby Smith, early 1870s.

a private residence; its residents today can walk the same seven-tenths of a mile to the building that was once the town hall. The neighborhood retains much of the charm of the colonial New England town on the Connecticut River. But Glastonbury was also a mill town; its earliest factories were built in the 1830s. It had only 3,000 inhabitants when the Smith sisters mounted their challenge. When Abby Smith claimed that she and her sister paid the highest taxes in town, she probably knew what she was talking about.[2]

Abby and Julia Smith were the two surviving daughters of Zephaniah Hollister Smith, born in 1758, and Hannah Hickok Smith, born in 1767. Zephaniah studied theology at Yale during the hard years of the American Revolution; when he entered, the college had just returned to New Haven from a self-imposed exile in Glastonbury because of food shortages and the dangers of British attack (an attack that actually occurred at the end of Zephaniah's first year). After graduation Smith went on to a Congregational pulpit and marriage to the daughter of another Congregational minister. With the birth of the first of his five daughters, he seemed to have settled into a permanent career. But within a few years he came to believe (with the Sande-manian sect) that no one should accept money for preaching the word of God, and after a sharp quarrel with his congregation, he left the pulpit. One local historian reports that Zephaniah Smith "excommunicated the whole congregation, and was in turn dismissed by them," perhaps establishing a family tradition in which taking a position challenging the entire community was understood to be heroic.

Liberated from the pulpit, Smith returned to Glastonbury to study law with Jonathan Brace, its leading citizen, who had confirmed his own position by marrying the widow of the previous lawyer in town and moving into the house she had inherited. Brace also represented Glastonbury in the Connecticut General Assembly. When Brace moved on to Hartford and a series of judgeships, Smith, in a nearly parodic enactment of Federalist patronage politics and kinship relations in the early republic, bought Brace's house and farm, and was in turn elected to represent the town in the General Assembly for the next nine years.[3]

A girl growing up in a household in which her father, as Justice of the Peace, tried cases and performed marriages in the living room could be pardoned if she emerged with a heightened sense that law was something that ordinary people made and manipulated and with a diminished sense of its mystery. Elizabeth Cady Stanton also grew up in a lawyer's household and explicitly credited her father's professional activities with shaping her own view of what she might do in the world; in Glastonbury it was Julia among the five sisters who seems to have been most responsive to her father's example. She read Blackstone, she considered herself well informed on matters of law, and she had a local reputation as one who could help her neighbors untangle points of law and settle their estates.

The mother of Abby and Julia was energetic and talented. Her diary offers proof of the substantial amount of spinning and other home manufactures that she and her daughters accomplished. By the second decade of the nineteenth century, as manufactured textiles became more readily available, the Smith daughters spent more time on their studies of literature, history, Latin, and Greek. Hannah

7. Laurilla Smith painted this watercolor of the family home sometime before her death in 1857. The house stands today at 1625 Main Street in Glastonbury, one of dozens of well-preserved eighteenth-century houses in the neighborhood.

Hickok Smith herself translated French and Italian; at the age of seventy she began the study of Hebrew. She had some talents in mathematics and astronomy, she wrote lively verses, and as her energetic commitment to abolition would show, had strong political skills.[4]

Town tradition remembers that the sisters were raised to be innovative, idiosyncratic, and political. They lived within walking distance of the town hall, close to the political heart of the community. They were carefully educated by tutors at home and in short terms in boarding schools. Julia Evelina would claim that she had an education as good as any offered by Yale, and for a brief period she taught French, Latin, and arithmetic at the famous Emma Willard School in Troy, New York.[5] She was fluent in Greek, Hebrew, and Latin; she doggedly retranslated the King James Bible into each language she knew.

We know less about the other sisters. Three died before the years of the tax protest, among them Laurilla Aleroyla, a painter and watercolorist, and Hancy Zephina, a "mechanical genius" whose "ox-sling, used for shoeing cattle, was such a success that every blacksmith in the neighborhood adopted the contraption."[6]

Hannah Hickok Smith engaged her daughters in charitable work, of the sort expected of the family of the "squire" but done with a vigor and energy that made it memorable. Julia's diary documents visiting the sick, Sunday-school classes, sewing societies. This work persisted all their lives, and when Julia and Abby challenged the town by refusing to pay taxes, even their critics, as a Boston reporter would write, "were careful to put themselves in a friendly position to begin with by citing the charity of these sisters, and many stories were told of the suffering that their hands and purses had alleviated."[7]

Hannah Smith pulled her daughters with her into the abolitionist movement. In the mid-1830s they joined the Hartford Anti-Slavery Society. They entertained white abolitionists; they apparently went to gatherings of black abolitionists. They are said to have collected forty signatures on the first antislavery petition in the region during the great campaign of 1839–40, when John Quincy Adams sought to stop the work of Congress by flooding it with petitions.

For the Smith women as for so many other white women, claiming rights for slaves flowed easily into claiming rights for themselves. This connection was open to alternate interpretations; one skeptic would tell the Boston *Post* that "the Misses Smith, after anti-slavery days went by, in which they were prominent actors, had watched and waited for something to take their place, and for that reason the suffrage movement was a God-send to them and eagerly embraced." But there is also Hannah Hickok Smith's report to Abby Kelley about how the Smith daughters came to understand the connection between abolition and women's rights: when they "visited almost every house in this town," she said, they found that "women have been taught to depend on the men for their opinions." The daughters had to per-suade the men, "for the women would not act contrary to the ideas of the male part of their families."[8]

The Smith sisters' challenge to the obligation to pay taxes was compounded of constitutional theory, personal pique, and delight in being deliciously outrageous, especially at their advanced age. They presented themselves publicly as a unit, though Abby tended to do the public speaking; as one journalist put it, "Miss Julia is . . . a faster talker, though both talk well, and they could hardly hold more harmonious views did the same brain do the thinking for both." They presented themselves as modest, commonsensical, even naive. Abby Smith explained to one reporter, "I am sure that I made no attempt after effects in these communications. I had a plain story to tell."[9]

As Julia Smith told it, her first direct suspicion that town taxation could not be trusted came when she was double-taxed in 1869. Having paid "about eighteen dollars" when an overseer of the highway asked for early payment in June so that he could pay the laborers, she was billed again in October.

> "I called on the overseer, but he seemed to know nothing how it happened. He was a republican and wanted to . . . show me how miserably the democrats governed the town . . . he read several items and among the rest was more than $700 for registering men's names.
>   "What's that?" said I.
>   "Why . . . some men would vote twice over if their names were not put down."
>   "But who pays this?"
>   "Why the tax payers of course."
>   "But if I wanted my name set down would they do it?"
>   "Oh no! it is the voter's names."
>   "What! and make the women pay for it? . . . If they are going on at this rate, I must go to that suffrage meeting in Hartford and see if we cannot do better, for I have no doubt one woman would write down every name in town for half that money."[10]

"That suffrage meeting" was the first convention of the Connecticut Woman Suffrage Association, held on October 28 and 29, 1869. Organized by Isabella Beecher Hooker—sister of Harriet Beecher Stowe and Catharine Beecher—it was a local meeting with national vigor, part of a regional challenge to Elizabeth Cady Stanton and Susan B. Anthony's National Woman Suffrage Association. The New England suffragists distrusted Stanton and Anthony's wide-ranging agenda, which included alliances with free love advocate Victoria

Woodhull and the mercurial and dangerous Francis Train, and efforts to get the word "sex" included in the Fifteenth Amendment. It is no surprise that the Smith sisters reported that they heard "capital speeches"; the program included some of the greatest orators of the century—Stanton and Anthony, who came to rebuild alliances, Paulina Wright Davis, Mary Shaw Livermore, William Lloyd Garrison. But in all the flood of talk, only Garrison mentioned taxes, and that briefly: "While women are taxed they ought to be represented. When they are held as criminals they ought to have a part in making criminal law. When men say women shall not be taxed or punished they will be consistent."[11]

The Smith sisters returned home to develop their skepticism.[12] For Abby and Julia Smith, claiming the right to vote was considerably more than a matter of abstract principle. No railroad reached Glastonbury until 1874; town taxes were used primarily to pay for roads. Already in 1869 the sisters had been critical of the town's choices of where new roads were laid out and which roads were marked for improvement. Their resentment built over the years. "[T]he roads make the most complaint to every woman that owns property," said Abby. People voted in person at the Glastonbury town meeting, and, critical as they already were of the way road taxes were allocated, the Smith sisters wanted above all the opportunity to appear in town meeting and attempt to persuade their fellow citizens where their taxes should be spent. Taxpaying men represented themselves in town meeting. Women were obliged to pay taxes but could not speak in town meeting. Glastonbury was a participatory democracy and the Smiths wanted to participate.[13]

In the spring of 1873, Abby and Julia Smith accompanied Rosella Buckingham, a feisty woman of forty who herself was deeply involved in the national suffrage campaign, to demand that the town registrars list them as voters.[14] This venture was the Glastonbury suffragists' part in an extensive—and now largely forgotten—national effort to test the potential of the Fourteenth Amendment. Although one of the enforcement clauses of the amendment introduced the word "male" into the Constitution for the first time, the ringing declaration of the opening section that "all persons born or naturalized in the United States are citizens of the United States and of the State wherein they reside," and are entitled to all "the privileges and immunities of citizenship," carried with it an implicit promise. Was not the right to vote a privilege of citizenship? Whether exercised in a participatory mode at town meeting or abstractly in a large election, suffragists insisted that it was. In 1872 Susan B. Anthony and approximately fifty women registered to vote in Rochester, New York. When fifteen actually did vote, the registrars were sued for malpractice and Anthony herself charged with voting fraud. Her subsequent trial in the state courts gained national attention. In St. Louis, Missouri, Virginia Minor sued the registrar for refusing to enroll her on the voting lists, claiming that she was a "tax-paying, law-abiding citizen." Her case reached the U.S. Supreme Court, where, however, she would lose.[15]

In Glastonbury, the registrars wrote the names of Abby and Julia Smith and Rosella Buckingham on their forms and promised to pass them along to the town selectmen. The Smith sisters would later amuse a Boston *Post* reporter with the tale of how they tried to discover the selectmen's secret meetings in order to force a public hearing. In October 1873, they traveled to New York City, where they were among the 1,200 people who attended the annual convention of the American Woman Suffrage Association; they heard reports from delegates from many parts of their country about efforts to vote, and a moving address by Frances Ellen Watkins Harper on the desperate need of black women for the right to vote. They joined in a memorial resolution marking John Stuart Mill's death. They returned home with deepened convictions.[16]

And when they returned home they found, as Julia Smith told it, their property taxes raised to $200 on no evidence except the judgment of the assessor. They checked the tax lists and discovered that they and two widows were the only ones on whom levies had been increased. "To be sure it increased our tax but little, but what is unjust in least is unjust in much."[17] Abby and Julia Smith refused to pay.

The Smith sisters had been listening to women's oratory since the 1830s. They knew how it was done. When Abby Smith appeared at the Glastonbury town meeting on November 5, 1873—almost surely she would have remembered it was Guy Fawkes Day, the anniversary of the thwarting of an alleged plot to blow up the Houses of Parliament in 1605, a holiday which the American patriots had revered—her speech was an impressive blend of specific claims and political theorizing. She charged the members of the town meeting with exercising an unrepublican authority over women. She echoed the arguments patriots had made against Britain in the 1760s, when they denied that Parliament had the right to tax them, and when patriots insisted that it was the principle, not the size, of the Stamp Tax and the Tea Tax that they resented. She moved easily into analogies with the abolitionist campaign—"The Southern slaveholder only possessed the same power that you have to rule over us"—and then back to the rhetoric of the Revolution:

> [T]here is always excuse enough where there is power. [The men of the town] say all the property of the town should be taxed for the expenses of the town, according to its valuation, and as taxation without representation is wrong, they give permission to a part of these owners to say what valuation shall be made, and how the money can best be applied for their benefit. They meet together to consult who among them shall have the offices of the town and what salary they will give them. All this is done without ever consulting or alluding to the other part of the owners of this property. But they tax the other owners. . . . Is it any more just to take a woman's property without her consent, than it is to take a man's property without his consent?

She concluded by insisting that the lines of gender were real: that men and women were differently situated and had different interests. When the logic of her argument drove her to the assertion that men were in fact the enemy she did not flinch: "the robber would have the whole community against him, and he would not be apt to come but once; but from the men of our town we are never safe."[18]

The next day George Andrews, the tax collector, came to see if the Smiths had changed their minds. "Our money we owned, and we were not willing, any more, to take what we owned to pay for what we did not own. Our father, when he advised us to keep the farm, said, 'You need not cultivate it, but it wont run away from you.' It did not seem to enter his mind but what we might hold it as securely as the men held theirs." The sisters announced, "If they gave us no hopes of voting, we wanted them to sell our farm for the taxes, for it was but reasonable, if they owned it, to get the taxes from it, we could not."[19]

Andrews said "he thought women that had property ought to vote. We said those that had none needed it more. If they could have the power to vote against the grog shops, their drunken husbands would never dare to abuse them as they did, but they could do it now with impunity, for the town officers would not punish a voter."[20]

The Smith sisters had believed that "we might let the tax be, as long as we pleased, by paying 12 per cent interest," while their arguments were being considered. But they were wrong. New Year's Day was not yet the public holiday it has since become; George Andrews showed up at the Smiths' household with "an attachment . . . to execute it that very day." He would begin, he said, with personal property, starting with the cows. As the Boston *Herald* would put it, "In choosing between the several horns of the dilemma he took seven pairs of horns, with cows attached."[21]

Abby and Julia Smith had a sophisticated understanding of the uses of taxes and the way in which tax policy could be used for political purposes and for the encouragement of economic expansion:

> We wanted to petition the men, we said, to let us own our land as they owned theirs. . . . The town had waited on a factory company in the north part of the place for their taxes for years, till the company failed, and they lost several thousand dollars by it. We had our share of this money to pay; a larger share, as it appeared by his books, than any other of the inhabitants, and there was no risk in waiting for us to pay. But they were men, and we are women.[22]

Announcing that prices for cows were low and he wanted to be sure he covered the taxes, George Andrews drove seven of the eight cows away. He left them in the custody of a neighbor, who found them troublesome. "These cows," said Abby later, "will sometimes be very contrary, when nobody can manage them but my sister. She will call them all by their names, and as soon as they hear, they will come to her upon the gallop. The Boston *Daily Advertiser* reported

8. This woodcut of Abby Smith and her cows was used as the frontispiece for Julia Smith's 1877 pamphlet.

that one cow "moaned all night in her loneliness. Cows are not commonly so sentimental, but these were a woman's cows."[23]

Abby Smith had a stunning sense of street theater. She understood that there was an analogy to be made between the plight of the cows and her own: the cows are female, they are penned up, they are bought and sold to satisfy men's needs.[24] Here is her report to the Springfield *Republican*, published on January 12:

> We walked, at noon, two or three houses above us to see the cattle let out of their pen. By orders of the collector, the cows —seven of them—had been huddled into a space of 15 feet by 12 (measured by my sister) and tied up for seven days and nights, together; always having had their freedom before . . . the sensitive young wife of the tobacco-shed owner declared that a drop of that milk should never come into her house, for it seemed to her just as if it was stolen. Mrs. K. said, yesterday, that the cows had failed, by two-thirds, of their milk since they were taken from our yard.[25]

As Abby Smith told it, they made a procession, led by George Andrews, who was constable as well as tax collector, "leading the best cow; the others, driven by four men with a dog and a drum; several teams; and we in the rear in a wagon with Mr. and Mrs. K. We intended to walk together alone, but Mr. K. insisted upon our riding . . . Mrs. K. remarked on the way that it appeared like a funeral." Some forty men were gathered at the crossroads "who bid so low that Mr. K. was forced to speak for the four best, below their value, which covered the tax and expenses, leaving the three smallest. All would have been sacrificed, for it was evident from the bids that they intended to get them for a song."[26] In the end, their tenant bought their cows back, probably with the sisters' own money.

Political allies like the *Republican* may have agreed with the sisters' view of what they were up to, but the crossroads crowd was a different matter. "Not a man came to speak to us. It was remarked by one who liked the business that the whole town was against us. We thought we had many friends as we have been treated with the greatest outward respect, as if we were complete, with only one failing—that of not paying our taxes, this winter."

Undaunted, Abby and Julia intended to continue the theater:

> We know not what they will do when the March tax is claimed, but must not now be surprised at anything. They say personal estate must be seized first, and we greatly fear they will ransack our house, tear up our carpets, and take ornamental things, the work of a lamented sister, and her fine paintings. . . . We are now in a lonely situation. . . . As the town now manages our property, we must soon be forced to the poor-house, and none are better acquainted with its inmates.[27]

"A permanent malcontent"

The American revolutionary struggle had been steeped in the claim that those who had obligations also had rights. The decade after the Civil War was one of intense constitutional argument. Once again, constitutional debate inexorably carried with it a set of related arguments about obligation and entitlement. Examining these arguments, we can see that gender made a difference in what obligations citizens bore.

The Thirteenth Amendment of 1865 made slavery illegal, but whether and to what extent political rights for freedpeople followed remained uncertain. The former states of the Confederacy struggled hard to carve out an intermediate and secondary form of citizenship for black people—limiting or denying their right to serve on juries, to control their own labor, and to marry whites.[28] Even the states that had remained in the Union were not uniformly enthusiastic about granting free black citizens the same rights as those claimed by whites. Against these efforts, liberals employed a rhetoric that denied that there could be an intermediate category between "slave" and "citizen."

In the era of the American Revolution, patriots had reached back to the arguments of the English Civil War to insist that the right to set limits on how much of one's property would be paid in taxes was essential to the right to property itself. That is why money bills—taxes—could be initiated only in the House of Commons, the part of the legislature elected by the people; the practice continues in the United States, where tax bills must originate in the House of Representatives. "Taxation," insisted William Pitt the Elder, "is no part of the governing or legislative power. The taxes are a voluntary gift and grant of the Commons alone."[29] If taxes were a gift, then Americans demanded to do the giving. When the British asserted that Americans should be content to be virtually represented in Parliament—that is, content with the assurance that legislators who cared about the interests of the whole imperial community would take care of Americans' specific interests, American patriots and their British allies emphatically dissented. "[N]o Power on Earth has a Right to impose Taxes upon the People or to take the smallest Portion of their Property without their Consent, given by their Representatives," asserted the Virginia House of Burgesses in 1768. In the fight over the Stamp Act, the patriots had some powerful British allies, among them Charles Pratt, Baron Camden, the future Lord Chancellor, who declared in Parliament: "taxation and representation are inseparable;—this position is founded on the laws of nature; it is more, it is itself an eternal law of nature; for whatever is a man's own, is absolutely his own; no man hath a right to take it from him without his consent, either expressed by himself or representative; whoever attempts to do it . . . throws down and destroys the distinction between liberty and slavery. Taxation and representation are coeval with and essential to this constitution."[30]

Patriots absolutely rejected the concept of virtual representation. As John Adams put it, the "representative assembly . . . should be in miniature an exact portrait of the people at large. It should think, feel, reason, and act like them."[31] A century after the Revolution, the Smith sisters and their colleagues found the analogy easy to draw. Like Parliament before the Revolution, men claimed that they "virtually" represented women, that women could trust men whom they had not elected to represent their interests, and that women taxpayers should be content to fulfill their obligations without expressing their judgments.

The logic of virtual representation ought to have forced American patriots to turn a critical eye on their own constraints on suffrage, but it rarely did. Even at the height of the Stamp Act, Massachusetts taxed unrepresented towns. "Why taxation without representation should be tyranny with respect to England but not tyranny in Massachusetts was, as one newspaper writer said, . . . 'a mighty shrewd question,'" observes historian Robert Becker.[32] If representative assemblies should be an "exact portrait" and if no individual could reasonably be said to represent anyone who had not voted in the election that chose him, then universal suffrage—including, as James Otis asserted, "apple women and orange girls"—was the only logical conclusion, but for many a frightening one. Only the state of Vermont directly linked allegiance and suffrage by "giving the vote to all adult males who would take the Freeman's Oath."[33] Only New Jersey, by phrasing its election laws in terms of "persons," made space for women to exercise the franchise.

But James Otis died before the Revolution actually broke out, Vermont had no imitators, and as soon as New Jersey women actually voted together in a way that had an impact on the outcome of an election, the state revised its statute and eliminated their vote. Other states brought into the republic the traditional English link between property holding and voting, grounded in the belief that, as John Adams put it, some were "too poor to have a will of their own." Those without independent ownership of property, the reasoning went, were too easily coerced by those who controlled their means of livelihood—employers could direct the votes of their laborers; husbands could direct the votes of their wives. If holding property, and paying taxes on that property, was linked to independence of mind and spirit, then it was an easy step to linking property to suffrage.

In the early nineteenth century, workingmen responded to the vast social and economic changes set off by the industrial revolution by demanding greater roles in determining the direction and purposes of state power. Framing their demands in the language of democratization, working inside a competitive two-party system, they were largely successful in divorcing property holding from suffrage; by the 1840s most states had moved to universal white male suffrage.

But their road to universal suffrage was rarely direct. Between a suffrage that was a right of property owners and a suffrage which was a right of all male citizens, there was an intermediate stage, in which men (often limited to white men) who paid some kind of tax could vote. Tax substituted for real estate as a proxy for class. During the Revolution, state after state offered the right to vote for members of local committees or state legislators not only to those who owned real estate, but also to those men who fulfilled their obligation to pay some level of taxes.[34] The argument shifted to whether only some taxpayers or all taxpayers should vote. In Massachusetts, militia captains protested when the new state constitution included a high taxpaying qualification.[35] One New Jersey man wrote to a newspaper to urge that "all who paid taxes but could not vote should, in fairness, either be given the vote or exempted from paying taxes."[36]

Connecticut offers a good example of the gradual path that ran from a property requirement, through taxpaying as a qualification, to universal male suffrage. During the Revolution, the state made only minor changes in its old colonial charter. Connecticut had once been the most democratic of the colonial governments, with a weak executive and a strong legislature, but by late-eighteenth-century standards it was conservative—even retrograde. The old qualifications for suffrage remained in place, translated from the forty-shilling freehold or forty-pound personal property requirements for men of twenty-one years into freeholds valued at $7 per year or $134 in personal property. As inflation lowered these thresholds, conservative Federalists raised them by adding racial and class qualifications: freemen must be white; new freemen must be approved by selectmen; the property must be free of mortgages. In the years in which Zephaniah Smith served in the legislature and his daughters were adolescents, Republicans were vigorously seeking to lower suffrage requirements. Their theme was no taxation without representation.[37] Not until 1818 did an alliance of Republicans and moderate Federalists, under the name of the Toleration Party, manage to establish a secret ballot and call a constitutional convention, which granted suffrage "to every white male citizen of the United States of good moral character, who had gained a settlement in the state, reached the age of twenty-one, and had resided in the town at least six months, providing that he possessed within the state a freehold of seven dollars a year; or had performed militia service within the past twelve-month, if not legally excused from such service; or had paid taxes during the past year." In this construction, race, age, and gender were definitive. Property holding, militia service, and taxpaying were roughly equivalent. For Connecticut, as for ten other states, taxpaying marked the boundary of the political community. Connecticut did not adopt white male suffrage until 1845, nor universal male suffrage until after the Civil War.[38]

After the Civil War, southern attacks on universal male suffrage stressed the likelihood that an unpropertied black proletariat would be positioned to enact punitive taxes: "Taxation and representation are no longer to be united. They who own no property are to levy taxes and make all appropriations. The property-holders have to pay these taxes, without having any voice in levying them!"[39] Radical Republicans, who of course strongly supported universal male suffrage, even more solidly linked the obligation to pay taxes to broad claims of citizenship. In the U.S. Senate, Charles Sumner of Massachusetts quoted Lord Coke:

> [I]n a state of nature no man can take any property from me without my consent. *If he does, he deprives me of my liberty and makes me a slave.* The very act of taxing, exercised over those who are not represented, appears to me to deprive them of one of their most essential rights as freemen, and if continued seems to be in effect an entire disfranchisement of every civil right. For what one civil right is worth a rush, after a man's property is subject to be taken from him at pleasure without his consent?

Thus Sumner challenged his colleagues; there was no space between taxing freedpeople and letting them vote. And no one was prepared not to tax them.[40]

Women's rights activists were highly attentive to these debates. Before the Civil War, there had been ample conceptual space between slave and fully active citizen to accommodate a wide variety of discriminations; free white women were located in this intermediate space. Indeed, defining the components of white women's citizenship as different from those belonging to white men confirmed the logic of defining the citizenship of black men differently from that of white men. Thus in New York, free African-American men had to meet substantial property requirements for voting long after such requirements had been abandoned for white men; property-holding single white women could not vote at all. As class became less salient in defining the rights of citizenship, race and gender became more significant. If the Civil War had indeed been about race relations, then race would also have to drop out as a marker of degrees of citizenship; that left gender.[41]

Before the Civil War, women's suffrage manifestos and petitions had often linked the obligation to pay taxes with the privilege of voting. Indeed, although voting was literally the final item on the Seneca Falls agenda, unfair taxation was among the first: "After depriving her of all rights as a married woman, if single, and the owner of property, he has taxed her to support a government which recognizes her only when her property can be made profitable to it." Suffragists noted that when the New York State constitution of 1846 removed property requirements for white men and raised them for black men, it had also eliminated property taxes for black men whose property was valued at less than the $250 threshold required for voting.[42] In the 1850s a number of suffragists had enacted their protest by refusing to pay taxes. In Claremont, New Hampshire, Mary L. Harrington refused to pay taxes for two years and actually worked on the roads in lieu of the tax until the hostility of her neighbors forced her to stop. When Lucy Stone, the great abolitionist and suffragist orator who retained her own name after her marriage, received a tax bill for her own house in 1857, she refused to pay on the grounds that she was unrepresented, "which is not only unjust to one half of the adult population, but is contrary to our theory of government."

Some of Stone's household goods were seized and auctioned off on a cold January afternoon in 1858; Thomas Wentworth Higginson, hearing that among the items sold were engraved portraits of Salmon P. Chase and William Lloyd Garrison, wrote to her: "The selection of these portraits will be so melodramatic for your biography that I suspect you of having bribed the sheriff to seize them."[43]

Accustomed to speaking—as the Declaration of Sentiments did—in the rhetoric of the American Revolution, women's rights activists continued in the postwar years to count the litany of claims made by their ancestors against George III that were still denied to them. Rights cut into obligations; but it was hard to make them reciprocal. Obligations were hard to dramatize. Women could not refuse to serve on juries, since no one asked them. Women could not refuse militia service, since no one asked them. But women could refuse to pay taxes, and voting for representatives had been linked to paying taxes ever since the tea was thrown into Boston Harbor. Taxation was an obligation they could turn into a political test.[44]

The argument gained in vitality in the erratic economy of the post-Civil War years, which deteriorated into the Panic of 1873 and the depression that followed. The National Women's Rights Convention took note of Senator Charles Sumner's argument that taxing former slaves committed the state to offering the franchise, and was appalled that Sumner did not follow his own logic:

> Woman now holds a vast amount of the property in the country, and pays her full proportion of taxes, revenue included. On what principle, then, do you deny her representation? By what process of reasoning Charles Sumner was able to stand up in the Senate, a few days after these sublime utterances, and rebuke 15,000,000 disfranchised tax-payers for the exercise of their right of petition merely, is past understanding. If he felt that this was not the time for woman to even mention her right to representation, why did he not . . . propose to release the poor shirtmakers, milliners and dressmakers, and all women of property, from the tyranny of taxation?[45]

These suffragists had been abolitionist, and after the war they supported the Reconstruction Amendments, which ended slavery and offered political rights. The Fourteenth Amendment, ratified in 1868, seemed to provide an opportunity. If, as the amendment provided, "all persons born or naturalized in the United States are citizens of the United States and of the State wherein they reside," and entitled to all the "privileges and immunities" of citizenship, then women's rights activists were prepared to see whether the Constitution meant what it said. Disappointed by the Fifteenth Amendment, which was ratified in 1870, they thought themselves to have one last narrow chance: to test the possibilities of the Fourteenth. By the late 1860s, taxpayer protests began again, and in the early 1870s, the national women's rights movement launched not only a major campaign to test the possibility of voting under the Fourteenth Amendment but also a challenge to the obligation of paying taxes if it were unaccompanied by voting rights.

The suffragists' arguments echoed congressional debates on the amendments and were grounded in the writings of traditional liberal theorists, notably those of the English politician and philosopher John Stuart Mill. At the end of her life Susan B. Anthony wrote in her copy of Mill's *The Subjection of Women*, "This book has been the law for me since 1869." Mill's writings of the 1850s and 1860s offer a view of representative government in which the health of a nation depends heavily on the extent to which all its citizens understand themselves to be part of a political community. Written at a time of his life when his secret love for Harriet Taylor could be publicly acknowledged, and when, after the death of her husband, they could marry, Mill's work in this period is suffused by joy and by his intellectual collaboration with Harriet Taylor—and then by his unquenchable sorrow after her early death. *Considerations on Representative Government*, published in 1861, spoke in terms capacious enough to admit women to the political community; *The Subjection of Women*, published in 1869, was explicit. For Mill, the *process* of participating in representative government was itself an important pedagogic device: "It is by political discussion" that each inhabitant of a state "becomes consciously a member of a great community." Mill went on: "It is from political discussion, and collective political action, that one whose daily occupations concentrate his interests in a small circle round himself, learns to feel for and with his fellow-citizens, and becomes consciously a member of a great community. But political discussions fly over the heads of those who have no votes, and are not endeavouring to acquire them. . . . Whoever, in an otherwise popular government, has no vote, and no prospect of obtaining it will either be a permanent malcontent, or will feel as one whom the general affairs of society do not concern . . . a looker-on."[46]

The suffragists were definitely "permanent malcontents"; women were "lookers-on." Frederick Douglass discerned that those deprived of the vote understood well that the government regarded them as "unfit"; he observed that he and other black men were led "to undervalue ourselves, and to feel that we have no possibilities like other men." His comments about blacks easily extended to women.[47]

John Stuart Mill also did much to reinvigorate the link between taxation and representation, which had been a slogan of American revolutionary agitation. He linked obligation to voting: "If he is compelled to pay, if he may be compelled to fight, if he is required implicitly to obey, he should be legally entitled to . . . have his consent asked."[48] Here, instead of a slogan, Mill leaned upon reason and common sense. Healthy communities do not emerge from opportunistic governments.

"The inexpressible meanness of the thing"

Abby and Julia Smith initiated their protest several weeks before Lucy Stone used the pages of the *Woman's Journal* to call upon "the women of New England" to celebrate the centennial of the Boston Tea Party by insisting on the principle of no taxation without representation. The context in which they acted had been built by others, whether the Smith sisters knew it or not. Because they presented themselves as naive and simple, it was not in their interest to stress their connections with the national community of activist women's rights advocates. We do not know what they knew and when they knew it.[49]

Taxes have long been central to public argument about the relationship between the individual citizen and the state, and they gained fresh saliency after the Civil War. When women set out to measure that relationship with precision, however, they found it hard to do. Throughout the nineteenth century federal taxes came in the form of customs duties or excise taxes, the latter largely on liquor and tobacco. They were felt by individuals only indirectly, in higher prices for imported goods and for two items of consumption in which men were more likely than women to indulge. During the Civil War a modest federal income tax had been invented but it was soon abandoned. States and municipalities relied heavily on general property taxes. Women, notably widows and single women, paid these taxes in substantial amounts. "Assessment was local, chaotic, and frequently unfair," observes Lawrence Friedman. "There were many exceptions and exemptions." One state might exempt a year's crop or family pictures; another state might not. "There was a great temptation for an assessor to undervalue property in his county: why not let the burden fall on other parts of the state?"[50] George Andrews, one of four Glastonbury tax collectors, had a range of options as he set the valuations of the Smith sisters' estate; one of their complaints was that the taxes varied erratically from district to district.[51]

American cities invested in expensive technological civic improvements during the Gilded Age. As political women increasingly defined themselves as a group engaged in "civic housekeeping," they were likely to legitimate their claims to vote not only on liberal grounds like their right to equal treatment as individuals under the law, but also by the claim that women should be able to make choices about supporting or resisting new expenditures for which their taxes had helped to pay. The new technologies were readily described in domestic terms—water supply and sewers as cleanliness, street railways as efficiency and danger, roads—as the Smith sisters maintained—as convenience. As mothers, civic-minded women could enlarge the sphere of their "housekeeping." Women paid the invisible federal tariffs, and they could reproach Charles Sumner for his failure to join in helping them achieve national suffrage. Women paid state taxes, and they could logically lobby state legislatures for a right to vote in state elections. They also paid town and municipal taxes, and so could reasonably try to persuade their neighbors to let them vote for members of school boards or on bond issues in towns and municipalities (as the Smith sisters wanted). Many suffragists proposed that if they could not accomplish full voting rights in a single step, they should be offered "municipal suffrage," enabling them to make more limited, but still very practical choices where they lived and paid taxes.

It is clear that the Smith sisters were not alone in tapping into the aquifer of the belief that taxation without representation is tyranny. In the context of the effort to include the term "sex" in the Fifteenth Amendment, the argument that taxation was linked to suffrage became a familiar one. It was made by the radical Victoria Woodhull in her widely publicized testimony before the House Judiciary Committee in 1871 and by a member of Congress who added the joke that at least widows should get to vote because the Fifteenth Amendment prohibited discrimination on the basis of "previous condition of servitude."[52] California's first woman lawyer, Clara Shortridge Foltz, led a taxpaying women's protest in San Jose in 1877.[53] In Colorado Springs, women claimed that they owned one-third of the taxable property, "and yet were obliged (at the recent spring election) to see the bonds for furnishing a supply of pure water, voted down because women had no voice in the matter."[54] In Iowa, petitions from taxpaying women persuaded three state senators to propose—unsuccessfully—that women be excused from all property taxes until they were given the vote.[55] But the arguments were most fully conceptualized by Francis and Virginia Minor of St. Louis, Missouri, in a campaign to enlarge the Fifteenth Amendment at the time of its submission to Congress in 1869.

In St. Louis, a creative group of upper-middle-class women, many of whom had come together as the Ladies' Union Aid Society to care for the wounded Union soldiers who descended on the city during the Civil War, had reorganized themselves as a woman suffrage association in 1867.[56] Highly conscious of the costs of war and the costs of government, confident that as people who had made their own sacrifices for the Union they had claims to make on it, these elite women moved fearlessly in the corridors of power. Led by Adaline and Phoebe Cousins, the wife and daughter of the police chief of St. Louis, and by Virginia Minor (she and her husband Francis—the clerk of the Missouri Supreme Court—were among the most intellectually adventurous of the Radical Republican community in St. Louis), the suffragists reached out to recruit German-speaking wage-earning women, and took as their own the fight for equal pay. Their respectability deflected the attacks of men who had no use for women who "go from State to State 'agitating' the subject, and who publish in [Stanton and Anthony's newspaper] *The Revolution* as much inspired twaddle as ever gets printed in the English language." The members of the Woman Suffrage Association of St. Louis were efficient politicians, gathering some 600 signatures on petitions to Senator Samuel Pomeroy of Kansas, one of the leading congressional supporters of the movement.[57] When they sent a delegation to lobby the Missouri legislature, they were met at the railroad station by the governor and the Speaker of the House.[58]

Early in 1868, Francis Minor sent a letter to *The Revolution*: "Taxation and Representation should go hand in hand. . . . Is it at all more indelicate for a woman to go to the polls, than it is for her to go to the court-house and pay her taxes?"[59] A year later, Virginia Minor initiated an effort to discover how much St. Louis women paid in taxes. Phoebe Cousins, a splendid public speaker who would some years later become the first woman to graduate from a major law school, Washington University, and Emma Rombauer Finkelnburg, whose husband, Gustavus, was a member of Congress and a vigorous ally of Carl Schurz and the liberal Republicans, signed a letter to the city assessor, demanding a report. When the assessor "told them he hadn't time, just yet, to make out the list," they were insistent. That the assessor, Robert J. Rombauer, was an immigrant who had fought in the Revolution of 1848, whose wife had spied for Louis Kossuth, and who may well have been related to Emma Finkelnburg could not have hurt. By the end of the month they could say that there were "2,000 tax-paying ladies" in the city, whose property was valued at $14.5 million. The information strengthened their speechmaking. "We are a part of the people of the United States; citizens subject to all its laws; taxed without representation; classed with criminals, paupers, idiots and lunatics; governed without our consent . . . deprived of trial by a jury of our peers," declaimed Phoebe Cousins a week later to the legislature.[60] Years later, when Elizabeth Cady Stanton, Susan B. Anthony, and Matilda Joslyn Gage wrote *The History of Woman Suffrage*, they commented: "Shall 2,000 men, not worth a dollar, just because they wear pantaloons go to the polls and vote taxes on us, while we are excluded from the ballot-box for no other reason than sex? . . . *No taxation without representation.*"[61] The logic of the paradox, Virginia Minor thought, was clear: "Failing before the Legislatures [to get the vote], we must then turn to the Supreme Court of our land and ask it to make us [secure] in our rights as citizens, or at least, not doing that, give us the privilege of the Indian, and exempt us from the burthen of taxation to support so unjust a government."[62]

Thus the link between taxation and representation resounded in the vigorous campaign launched by the women's rights community of St. Louis, culminating in Virginia Minor's effort to vote in 1872 —the demand that would force the Supreme Court to consider the question. Minor lost her case, and the St. Louis suffragists were left to challenge the expenditures for celebrations of the Centennial of 1876 by announcing that they saw no reason to celebrate, and certainly did not want their taxes for pay for fireworks.[63]

In Massachusetts, where suffragists had powerful allies among Republican politicians, ministers, and intellectuals, they were able to force a revealing investigation. At the time of the Smith sisters' protest, Massachusetts men qualified to vote only if they were over age twenty-one, were literate, were not receiving public assistance, had lived in the state for a year, and had paid taxes, at the very least a poll tax of two dollars. Two dollars would buy a pair of gloves or a good-quality man's dress shirt; it represented a meaningful gesture by a working-class man, and emphasized that property holding and taxpaying as the threshold of suffrage was still emphatically in place. In 1871, the Massachusetts House of Representatives ordered the state tax commissioner to report "the number of females taxed directly, those who had property taxed to husbands, guardians, or trustees, and also the corporation taxes paid by them." House report #428 was published in 1874, shortly before the Centennial celebrations at Lexington and Concord.[64]

The responsibility of turning an arcane public document into a political weapon was undertaken by William Ingersoll Bowditch. Bowditch was in his early fifties, a Harvard graduate whose work as an insurance agent and trustee of estates had instructed him in the vulnerability of women's claims to property. A committed abolitionist, Bowditch had been a speaker at the first woman's rights convention ever held in Boston, in 1854. In 1870 he was named to the largely symbolic role of vice president of the newly founded Massachusetts Woman Suffrage Association; in the 1880s he would serve as its president.[65]

In time for the Centennial, Bowditch wrote an extensive and biting analysis of the House report. He began with, and frequently recurred to, the preamble to the state constitution, which announced that it represented "a social compact, by which the whole people covenants with each citizen, and each citizen with the whole people, that all shall be governed by certain laws for the common good." It was not hard to establish that substantially more than half "the people" in the social compact were women. Anticipating the argument that perhaps "the people" meant specifically men, as in "all men are born free and equal," Bowditch pointed out that when slavery was abolished in Massachusetts all slaves, not just slave men, were freed; and that when no one was to be molested "for worshipping God in the manner and season most agreeable to the dictates of his own conscience," everyone assumed women had freedom of religion.[66]

Unlike the Smith sisters, who focused on their high property taxes, Bowditch began with indirect taxes, which had an impact on the working class as well as the elite. He estimated that over $21 million in customs duties had been collected in Massachusetts alone in the year ending June 1870. Roughly half would have been paid by women; "a taxation which the very rich are obliged to submit to, and the poor cannot escape. . . . Do not the women of the country feel the need of salt as much as men? . . . [W]omen cannot possibly escape bearing their full share of the effects of this indirect but very effective taxation."[67] Bowditch emphasized the importance of the waged work that women did. The state census of 1870 revealed that there were nearly two-thirds as many employed women as employed men. In some fields—notably the manufacture of men's clothing and the manufacturing of cotton goods—women workers outnumbered male workers by a factor of 100 percent, and they were to be found in unexpected places, including the eleven women who worked in the leather trades and the many who made ammunition cartridges. That the women were paid substantially less than men "for equally good services" was a burden to women but a benefit to the state's economy.[68]

As for the direct ownership of property, Bowditch supplemented the report with his own careful survey of individual cities and towns. Women paid, either directly or through their husbands, guardians, or trustees, nearly $2 million, almost one-twelfth of the property taxes in Massachusetts. If poll taxes were subtracted, women paid one-eleventh. "[B]eing a man, I am ashamed to point out," Bowditch observed, ". . . the inexpressible meanness of the thing. . . . [E]very man of property in the State saves more than one-eleventh of his taxes by the taxation of women." In cities and towns, the disproportion was even greater; city men saved "more than one-ninth of their taxes, by compelling the women who have no votes with which to protect themselves to pay the amount."[69]

Bowditch was a reformer, who gave extensive attention to the ways working women were invisibly taxed by tariffs they could not see, by wages that were a fraction of those paid to men, but Bowditch was also a Boston Brahmin, who could not resist invidious contrasts of the contributions to the commonwealth made by propertied women and by propertyless men who paid only a poll tax. He certainly knew how to dramatize class distinctions: "In Newton, one woman paid as much tax as 1,424 of the men." And he knew how to make numbers tell a political story:

> Only 185,990 men voted for Governor last autumn . . . 146,986 men paid only a poll tax, 66,415 of them being in Boston; and Governor Gaston's plurality in the State was 7,032. . . . On the principle that a chain is only as strong as its weakest link, it seems clear, therefore, that the last election was carried by poll-tax voters. . . . These 146,986 men paid $293,972. The 18,685 women paid more than six times as much. . . . According to the Report of 1871, the women tax-payers could have overcome Governor Gaston's plurality four times.

Bowditch's data suggested that in 158 places women taxpayers were numerous enough to have controlled elections of state representatives and of ten of the twenty-one wards of Boston. "Is it wise," he asked, "for us to rely, as we now do, for our government upon the class of voters most easily influenced or purchased, and neglect those who pay more than one-eleventh of the public burdens?[70] In this reference to the voters "most easily influenced or purchased"—Irish and other working-class men—Bowditch conveyed that propertied women could participate in buttressing the power of privileged classes in the political system, and that propertied men were shortsighted in refusing their assistance. It was clear to him that white men were preferring patriarchy to class solidarity.

Bowditch made the Smith sisters central to his most expansive images. He pointed out that soon the people of Concord would celebrate the eighteenth of April and the fight at the Old North Bridge; Ralph Waldo Emerson would read a poem and dedicate a statue of a Minuteman. "Our fathers risked death rather than pay a tax of threepence a pound on tea. We, their sons, have taxed the women of the land 25 cents for every pound of tea they consumed." The extra taxes paid by women in Concord, Lexington, and the nearby town of Acton amounted to some $7,000; more than enough to pay for the statue, he sneered. In fact, Louisa May Alcott would lead a protest of Concord women who resented their exclusion from the platform, anticipating a similar demonstration in Philadelphia the following year, when Susan B. Anthony and her colleagues actually disrupted the opening ceremonies of the Centennial by distributing a printed manifesto while speeches were going on. "Is it probable," Bowditch asked, "that Mr. Emerson, in his poem, will call to mind the fact that he and other Concord men of property and influence have been spared every year about one-fifth of their taxes. . . . We are inclined to think [no speaker] . . . will make any such allusions. It might cause confusion on the faces of the Committee of Arrangements."⁷¹ He ended by proposing a Centennial statue, with contrasting images of a revolutionary hero challenging the practice of taxing men without representation and of the sale of Abby Smith's cows.

"Wherever you find Taxey there Votey will be also"

Within a week of the seizure of the Smith cows, leading voices for the national women's rights movement grasped the way in which the Glastonbury challenge theatricalized their own linkage of taxation, representation, and participation. Arguments that assertive suffragists in St. Louis, Rochester, San Francisco, and Boston had constructed out of the rhetoric of war and constitutionalism looked more appealing when constructed out of white frame houses and Alderney cows. The tea-party analogy was run to the ground; the tea of 1873 was the milk of the Smith Alderneys. "[T]he Misses Smith affair is but a fit centennial celebration of the Boston tea party," one reader wrote to the Hartford *Times*.[72] "In refusing to continue paying heavier taxes . . . while refused a voice in assessing and spending them," wrote the editorialist for the Springfield *Republican*, twenty-five miles away up the Connecticut River, "Abby Smith and her sister as truly stand for the American principle as did the citizens who ripped open the tea-chests in Boston harbor."[73] Rosella Buckingham, constituting herself the Smith sisters' public relations office, stressed revolutionary antecedents in the letters that flowed from her desk to every newspaper within reach, and the Massachusetts Woman Suffrage Association passed a resolution asserting that "the recent seizure and public sale of the property of the Misses Smith" was "a repetition of the crime of the British government . . . with the added meanness . . . that . . . the crime [is] . . . in flagrant violation of their own avowed political principles."[74]

In arguing their own interests, the Smith sisters widened the space between men's interests and women's. "The men of Glastonbury are not worse than other men," offered Rosella Buckingham. "[B]ut the interests of the best of men are not identical with those of women. . . . the revolution which brought freedom to the men of this land, brought nothing to American women but the honor of being governed and taxed by men of all colors, races and conditions, instead of the king and nobles of the mother country."[75] *Harper's Weekly* demanded: "Does taxation without representation cease to be tyranny, and become justice, when the taxed property owner is a woman? . . . a good-natured laugh at Miss Anthony does not seem to be an entirely satisfactory answer."[76] Other observers made the point that even if married women were understood to be virtually represented by male relatives, Abby and Julia Smith, whose father was dead, who had no brothers, who had not married, who had no sons, lacked even virtual representation; "their disfranchisement has been complete and absolute."[77] When the Hartford *Times* spoke of "women who had failed to provide themselves with husbands," and proposed that "spinsters should be placed in the same category with negroes before the passage of the Fifteenth Amendment," Rosella Buckingham indignantly demanded to know why the sisters should have considered it desirable to bestow "on some man a life interest in their property," when it was clear that they would also, by the act of marriage, have made themselves vulnerable to domestic violence.[78]

Claims based on taxpaying slid invisibly into expressions of class pride. For many observers the situation was soaked with "absurdity and injustice" primarily because the Smiths paid so much money into the town treasury. The more this theme was stressed, the less the Smith sisters embodied a demand for universal suffrage and civic participation. The wealthy mill owner Amos Lawrence wrote a letter of support, appalled by the spectacle in his own town of Brookline, where "a widow pays into the town treasury $7,830 a year, while six hundred men . . . who have no property, who pay only a poll-tax, and many of whom cannot read or write have the power of voting away the property of the town, while the female owners have no power at all."[79] The argument pointed to a narrowing of suffragists' claims.[80]

But others resisted this temptation, understanding that it poisoned their case. "I do not blame any naturalized citizen for opposing Woman Suffrage if he finds it habitually urged on the ground that it will help to neutralize the foreign-born vote," observed Thomas Wentworth Higginson. "I do not blame any Roman Catholic for opposing it, if he finds it merely an added engine to strengthen the Protestant churches against his own. . . . For the sake of winning support in one direction, we forfeit support in another, besides leaving our fundamental principle to be obscured and ignored."[81] Julia Smith told a suffrage meeting in Worcester that she believed that "a great majority" of her "own townsmen" would let the sisters vote, but they claim that "the difficulty is it will let in all the Catholic women and other good for nothing working women. We say, 'do right and let the heavens fall.' . . . But no! and so they are all propping up the heavens with all their might."[82]

The Smiths did, however, make claims for women's special virtue and distinctive needs. Without representation, Abby Smith insisted, tax money was spent on men's needs and problems. "The women are more honest than the men. They are moral; better citizens. They are never seen round the grogshops, and therefore make the State very little trouble and expense in comparison to the men. . . . There are but two women in our State's Prison and 228 men. Should she, with her small earnings, be taxed for men's bad conduct . . . ?"[83]

Once again George Andrews appeared at the Smiths' home to collect taxes; once again they refused to pay, once again he announced an auction: not of cows this time but of land. Once again the sisters went out to speak. When they were refused permission to speak at town meeting they took up a position on an "old wagon" outside the build-ing. Abby read a speech, responded to hecklers, debated the ques-tioners. Reporting the experience to Lucy Stone, the sisters recounted some of the exchanges:

> "Could we shoulder the musket? Must not our property be taken to carry on the war? Could we work the highways?"
> We replied "we would work as well as those did whom we had seen in front of our house, and we would have them fixed very differently too."[84]

They wangled an invitation to the Connecticut legislature's Com-mittee on Woman Suffrage in New Haven; Abby Smith argued that without representation there were no restraints on male exploitation of women: "To the superior class the State has given permission to take our money from us, the lower order, whenever they may agree to do so, whenever they choose to take it, and as much as they choose to take. . . . If we, the owners, refuse to give it, they seize what we value the most and sell it at the public sign-post, knowing they are accountable to none for their deeds; if we desire to speak in our defence, when they assembled together, we are at once denied the privilege, even in a house for the erection of which they had taken more money from us than from any of the men assembled in it."[85]

Once again a public auction was staged; this time there was only one bid, from a neighbor who had been trying for years to get more of the land contiguous to his own. He won it for $78, which was considerably below the market value of the property, which the Smiths claimed was nearer to $2,000; they charged Andrews with trespass. The scene, reported the sympathetic Springfield *Republican*, was "worthy the brush of a Hogarth." The trial was held in the home of the local Justice of the Peace, into which crowded the attorneys, the tax collector, the town surveyor, witnesses, and some twenty male spectators—farmers in their shirtsleeves, "the miller well powdered with flour."

> [D]ressed in prim but genteel black . . . Abby . . . thin and straight as a lath . . . sits erect in her cane-bottomed chair through the tedious hours with less signs of weariness than a modern girl in her teens would show. Julia . . . entered into the occasional humors of the affair more heartily than Abby. . . . a couple of young ladies . . . furtively listened to proceedings through the open door of an adjoining parlor.[86]

The Smiths believed that any taxes levied on them were illegal because they were unrepresented. But in court they made the technical point that the law provided that when property was seized for nonpayment of taxes, movable property must be seized first, and that the collector had been wrong to auction the land when the sisters held a considerable amount of personal property. The Justice of the Peace ruled for the Smiths, and charged the tax collector costs and $10 damages. The town appealed; it won a reversal in the Court of Common Pleas in February 1875, but the reversal was in its turn set aside by the Connecticut Supreme Court, in an equity hearing in Hartford in 1876. In the course of these rearguments, the Smiths added the complaint that the original tax had been set improperly in 1873: the four town assessors had divided the town into districts and each set his own assessments, but the assessments had not been equalized as between districts or properly filed. Elements of the lawsuit persisted until 1880 through more than eleven continuations. In the end, the courts decided for the Smiths for technical reasons; the principle for which they struggled went unrecognized by the courts.[87]

Abby Smith died in 1878, aged eighty-one, two years before the ending of the suit. It was left to Julia to bring their campaign to closure. The following year Julia married for the first time; her husband was an elderly lawyer, Amos Parker, whom friends suspected of marrying for her property. He moved into the Glastonbury home and "dutifully," says Julia's biographer, paid the taxes; rumors persisted that she reimbursed him.[88] Shortly after Abby's death, suffragists who had gathered in Washington, D.C., to attend congressional hearings and their own annual convention held a reception in Julia's honor. Julia, who had always insisted that Abby do the public speaking, rose to the occasion:

> There are but two of our cows left at present, Taxey and Votey. It is something a little peculiar that Taxey is very obtrusive; why, I can scarcely step out of doors without being confronted by her, while Votey is quiet and shy, but . . . it is my opinion that in a very short time, wherever you find Taxey there Votey will be also.[89]

The tax protesters had hoped to use the association of taxation with representation to construct a female suffrage. In failing they had tested the resilience of national metaphor and revealed the sharp edge of civic obligation. Taxation was obligation. Its reciprocal was not representation.

"The power of taxation is an incident of sovereignty"

As long as women conceded that their own civic identity was absorbed by husbands and fathers, they simultaneously conceded that husbands and fathers virtually represented their interests in the civic sphere. As long as widows and spinsters conceded that they were in effect noncivic beings, neither sheltered by men who enacted their similar interests nor claiming the right to speak on their own, they too were virtually represented by male members of the community. But as the century wore on, fewer women were willing to make either concession. Once women had decided—as Abby and Julia Smith decided in 1873—that it was possible to have interests, as women, that were different from the interests of men of their own class and even their own family, then virtual representation would no longer do. Once they reached that point, the language of the revolutionary era rang freshly in their ears, and the promise that the destructive force of the obligation to pay taxes would be softened by the opportunities of representation grew in significance.

Popular political understanding and professional legal understanding are not always congruent. When taxation and representation were linked in the writings of the theorists of the founding generation the reference was normally to the representation of towns in state legislatures or of states in Congress, not of individuals by their representatives.[90] A generation after the Revolution, in his magisterial treatise on the Constitution, Justice Joseph Story devoted most of a lengthy chapter on taxation to reflections on how a general, substantive power to tax could be made congruent with a limited government. He found the answer not in representation, but in the words of the Constitution which gave Congress the power to tax in the same sentence that it was charged with providing for the *common* defense and the *general* welfare. The italics are implicitly Story's; the taxes levied by Congress must benefit the entire community.[91]

All that was left, it seemed to many suffragists, was to establish that women were part of the community. Suffragists welcomed the task; it seemed an easy one, especially after the passage of the Fourteenth Amendment. If all "persons" were citizens, and entitled to the privileges and immunities of citizenship, all one had to ask was whether women were persons.[92] But just what element of personhood and citizenship undergirded voting? Was voting reciprocity for taxpaying, or reciprocity for physical protection? Was it both? Neither?

Popular narratives, valuing as they did the Boston Tea Party, continued to convey that civic authority was related to democratic control of taxation. Resistance to England had been built out of the argument that even a little bit of misused authority to tax could quickly become the power to destroy; that those who were taxed had a reciprocal right to name the representatives who would do the taxing. Suffragists believed this argument and sought to use it for their own purposes.

But there were other ways of understanding the obligation to pay taxes, alternatives implicit even in Story's own interpretation. If the key justification of the power to tax was the common defense and the general welfare, then it was an easy step to the argument that the reciprocal of taxpaying was not suffrage but the enjoyment of the protections government offered. This latter argument was articulated forcefully in the 1870s. Henry Bowditch's keen eye noticed that theories of taxation linked payment as frequently to protection as to representation. "The King and Parliament also proposed to tax the colonists for their own protection," observed Bowditch, "but the colonists wholly failed to see that this made any difference, or that the tax was any less tyrannical in consequence. They preferred to determine for themselves exactly how, when, and where such protection should be exerted." In this mode women were like aliens who were taxed without representation, and for whom the reciprocal of taxation was protection. Bowditch cited the Massachusetts Supreme Judicial Court at the beginning of the nineteenth century: "It may possibly be urged . . . that whoever is . . . protected may be taxed, whether a voter or not; in other words, that taxation and protection—not taxation and representation—go together. And it is true that aliens who are not allowed to vote are, nevertheless, sometimes said to be taxed on the ground of this very protection which they receive."[93]

It is hard to avoid the suspicion that the women's protest had something to do with the salience of the denial of a link between taxpaying and representation—between "Taxey" and "Votey"—in legal treatises published in the era. In legal theory, taxation was an expression of state power, not a reciprocal of representation. For example, Thomas M. Cooley, who had a long career as professor of law at the University of Michigan, an associate justice on the Michigan Supreme Court, and a member of the first Interstate Commerce Commission, wrote the classic nineteenth-century legal defenses of laissez-faire principles and voiced an expansive understanding of the taxing power. It was, he held, one of the "essential powers of sovereignty, which the State must exercise again and again, as its needs or its interests may require. . . . [it cannot be] crippled or abridged."[94]

Cooley's *Treatise on the Law of Taxation* was published in time for the Centennial of 1876, in the midst of women suffragists' political tax protests. Although Cooley did not respond to them by name, he responded to them in substance.[95]

Taxes are . . . the enforced proportional contribution of persons and property, levied by the authority of the state for the support of the government, and for all public needs. . . . The justification of the demand is to be found in the reciprocal duties of protection and support between the state and its citizens, and the exclusive sovereignty and jurisdiction of the state over the persons and property within its territory. The citizen and the property owner owes to the government the duty to pay taxes, that the government may be enabled to perform its functions, and he is supposed to receive his proper and full compensation in the protection which the government affords to his life, liberty and property. . . . Taxes differ from . . . the forced contributions, loans and benevolences of arbitary and tyrannical periods, in that they are levied by authority of law, and by some rule of proportion which is intended to insure . . . a just apportionment of the burdens of government.[96]

Nowhere did Cooley mention representation. Taxation was "an incident of sovereignty." The authority was extreme: "*All subjects*, therefore, over which the sovereign power of the state extends are, in its discretion, legitimate subjects of taxation; and this may be carried to *any extent to which the government may choose to carry it*" (emphasis mine). Cooley acknowledged that the power to tax could be abused. He opposed the use of taxes to support religious instruction and private business enterprises because they were not levied for the benefit of the entire public. But the "only security against abuse" which he recognized was the "responsibility of the legislature which imposes the tax to the constituency who are to pay it."[97]

Cooley's contemporary John Dillon, who sat on the Eighth U.S. Circuit Court, was the author of another classic text on taxation. Dillon's understanding of the meaning of taxes was similar to Cooley's: "Theoretically, the tax-payer is compensated for the taxes he pays in the protection afforded to him and his property by the government which exacts the tax."[98] Neither he nor Cooley inquired into the appropriate composition of the "classes of persons" who ought to bear taxes, even though, as the suffragists were insisting, many who paid taxes were not part of a constituency.

Cooley was focusing on making a case against progressive and redistributive taxation systems; he wished to distinguish directly between "taxation" and "confiscation." Suffragists like Bowditch insisted that a system in which the unrepresented 50 percent of the population paid more than 11 percent of the taxes *was* redistributive. Cooley did not address this point.

Thus even as the Smith sisters and suffragists around the nation developed their protest, the relationship between taxation and representation was being leached out of American political and legal theory, leaving the payment of taxes an obligation without a reciprocal. If it had a reciprocal, it was the enjoyment of public services, like waterworks and policing.

This line of reasoning was well established by the end of the century. When Edwin R. A. Seligman, professor of economics at Columbia University, came to write his magisterial *Essays in Taxation*, published in 1895, he began with the assertion that until recently it had been "deemed necessary to base the theoretical justification of taxation on fanciful doctrines of contract, of protection and the like." Seligman's was a brilliant and wide-ranging mind; he acknowledged, as historian Dorothy Ross has put it, "that capitalist development necessarily involved class conflict and international contest" but he also thought that capitalism was "the motor of economic progress . . . creating greater means and wider equality among the mass of people."[99] Seligman shrugged off the mythologies; taxation rests on power. But power could permit itself to be constrained by a social ethic, by the desire to contribute to a share of the "common burden." Even the use of direct taxation could mean "a highly developed political consciousness. The method of taxing every one according to his property is the first rough attempt of a property-owning community . . . to assess each member according to his relative ability. The introduction of the direct property tax is a vast step forward in the development of social ethics. . . . It needs a far greater sense of civic obligation to submit cheerfully to direct property taxation than was necessary in primitive times."[100]

Seligman concluded that the property tax was a failure. It had no way of offsetting debts against property; it did not take personal property into account. Seligman's task was to kill the concept of general property tax; "the state," he wrote, "has direct relations not with property, but with persons." But for Seligman, those relations were not the pair taxation-representation, but protection-support. "It is the individual who, from the very fact of his existence within the state, is under definite obligations toward the state, of which the very first is to protect and support it. The state, indeed, can exist without the particular individual, but the individual cannot exist without the state."[101] Reciprocity, as the suffragists understood it, disappeared. Paying taxes is the reciprocal of living inside the state, not of being represented within it.

Between them, Cooley and Seligman rejected the tax protesters' vision of a direct link between taxation and representation. But what they did at the level of high theory failed to silence the rank-and-file suffragists. As long as the power to initiate tax bills was located in the House of Representatives, efforts to unlink taxation and representation would never be fully convincing. If suffragists could not get Congress to act, they had some success with state legislatures, especially if they could frame their demands so that legislators' own seats were not at stake.

In the 1880s and 1890s suffragists had a considerable degree of success establishing taxpayer suffrage in local settings: often school boards, sometimes town councils. They described limited taxpayer suffrage as a step in the direction of universal suffrage, basing their arguments in part on their claims as mothers and in part on their claims as taxpayers. Elizabeth Cady Stanton reminded them, whenever she had a chance, that in 1846 New York State had conceded the principle when black men who were excluded from voting were also excused from property taxes; she emphasized the irony: ". . . the moment the black man died, the name of the widow or daughter was put on the assessors list & the taxes extorted."[102] Suffragists were not always above mixing a case for gender equality with an appeal to class inequality. An 1879 Massachusetts statute, supported by Bowditch, offered the right to vote for members of local school committees to any female citizen over twenty-one who could "read the constitution in the English language," write her name, had lived in the state a year and in her town for six months, and had paid "a state, county, city or town tax assessed on her or her trustee within two years"— the same terms which qualified men to vote in all elections. Two years later the terms were expanded to include property-holding women who voluntarily offered to pay a poll tax of fifty cents.[103]

Women's taxpayer suffrage pitted class against gender, offering the power of propertied women to buttress privileged classes in the political system. Richard P. Hallowell's critical testimony, challenging Bowditch before a Massachusetts legislative committee in 1878, captured these concerns well; published in pamphlet form, it was reprinted again more than twenty years later.[104] Hallowell announced himself to be a supporter of "Impartial Suffrage, without regard to sex." Taxpayer suffrage for women was not a step in the right direction, but a selfish move by women who "for years have regarded the Woman Suffrage movement with hostility or indifference." Taxpayer suffrage for women perpetuated "class rule," and encouraged "the establishment of an aristocracy of wealth." The decent thing would be for propertied women to wait until they were prepared "to demand for others what they now ask for themselves alone."

Women's taxpaying suffrage was not, Hallowell warned, a harmless entering wedge, opening the door to all women. It was more likely to prepare the way "for an assault by male property holders upon the political rights of a vast number of worthy citizens"; he cited efforts in New York to limit suffrage to property holders in elections of people who will be "entrusted with the expenditure of money." As Hallowell warmed to his task, he offered simultaneously a denial that wealth was a reliable proxy for intelligence and a defense of the integrity of the working classes: "Grant this petition . . . and in addition to the many worthy women who will gain the ballot, you will enfranchise all the Flora McFlimseys of the State—women who never earned a dollar, who never could earn a dollar, and who own their property solely through the accident of inheritance. Such women know nothing of political duty or responsibility. . . . You are asked to enfranchise them, while others who, by constant toil with hand and brain, support worthless husbands and rear families of children, are to remain on a political level with the paupers of the State. . . . The theory that the property tax-payer alone has the right to say to what extent the State shall levy taxes and expend money is . . . very dangerous."[105]

Taxpaying women throughout the country also supported a more capacious compromise: legislation to permit all women to vote on matters related to taxes or to school affairs. By 1913 some states—among them Iowa, Michigan, Kansas, Montana, and Louisiana—allowed women to vote on matters relating to bond issues and taxes in school districts and some municipalities on the same terms as men. Women could vote on school issues in some New York towns—but not cities—and several municipalities in Delaware.[106]

The achievement of suffrage on a national scale quieted many discussions of taxation and representation but drove others underground. When Puerto Rican women attempted to register to vote in 1920, the U.S. Bureau of Insular Affairs decided that the Nineteenth

Amendment did not automatically apply to U.S. territories. Suffragist groups mobilized in Puerto Rico, lobbying throughout the next decade both on the island and in Washington, D.C., with support from the National Woman's Party. In 1929 the territorial legislature granted suffrage to women restricted by a literacy requirement; not until Puerto Rico became a commonwealth in 1952 was universal suffrage established.

Most southern states had excluded African-American men from voting by using intimidation, "literacy" tests, and poll taxes; in those states black women could vote no more easily than black men, and suffrage was an empty victory. Poll taxes applied to whites as well as blacks, and represented a class and gender barrier as well as a racial one. In states where the tax was cumulative and interest and penalties were added for each year of nonpayment the tax quickly became a major expense; in states where married men controlled the earnings of their wives, husbands understood themselves to have the burden of paying their wives' poll taxes. Since there were substantial disparities between the median incomes of men and women—in 1959, legal historian Ronnie Podolefsky points out, the median income of women in Virginia was 37 percent of men's—poll taxes weighed far less heavily on men than on women. The state of Georgia effectively discouraged white women from voting by providing that any woman who did not choose to register to vote did not have to pay the poll tax. This law, which encouraged white women—and their husbands —to see voting as an expensive extravagance, was challenged by Nolen Breedlove, a white man who owed $13.50 in cumulative poll taxes, with the support of the ACLU. Despite lucid argument on his behalf by the distinguished attorney Arthur Garfield Hays, the Supreme Court upheld the Georgia law in 1937. In exempting women from the obligation to pay poll taxes, "in view of burdens necessarily borne by them for the preservation of the race," the Court used a racialized motherhood to trump civic obligation.[107] A campaign against poll taxes, in which both black and white women were deeply engaged, continued until the mid-1960s, when the Twenty-fourth Amendment and a Supreme Court decision made such taxes unconstitutional. African-Americans found registrars' offices inhospitable places even when they were willing to pay the tax; reformers found that the claim that white men disapproved of women's voting could be used to screen the shame of not being able to afford the poll tax for their wives.[108]

Considerations of gender have continued to permeate American tax policy, especially in the structure of income and inheritance taxes. The same generation that experienced expanded suffrage for women also experienced the establishment of a permanent national income tax in 1913. Over the years, income tax policy has been reshaped in various ways to recognize that most households are composed of interdependent individuals, and the rules by which taxes were calculated have been substantially reconstructed several times in the twentieth century in efforts to recognize this interdependence. Early income tax policy was based on the assumption that individuals would pay taxes on their own income; husbands and wives who earned income filed their own separate returns.

As taxes became more substantial and also more progressive in the 1930s and 1940s, the tax burden of a household with a single earner whose income was, say, $50,000 a year was greater than a household made up of two earners who each earned $25,000 and so paid lower marginal rates. Families with single earners—almost always husbands—searched for devices that would permit them to split their income (fictive transfers of real estate between husband and wife was a favorite) and found the most successful strategy in the practices of community property states. These states, among them California, Louisiana, New Mexico, descended from French and Spanish colonies and had taken from them civil law traditions in which husbands did not receive as extensive ownership rights to the family property as the practice of coverture gave them in Anglo-American legal regimes. In community property states, wives were understood to own one-half of the family property, whoever was the earner, and to pass it down to their own heirs—which, in the case of childless marriages, could well be different than the heirs of their husbands. In 1930, the U.S. Supreme Court permitted husbands and wives in community property states to split their income for the purposes of federal taxes as well as state taxes.[109]

This decision set off an explosion of efforts to adopt community property regimes—and their tax advantages—throughout the country. Community property systems, however, entailed acknowledging the wife's direct control of one-half of the family property, whether or not she had contributed it to the family account. Tax history is usually arcane, but legal historian Carolyn C. Jones's account of the struggles over tax policy of the 1940s is wickedly funny. Jones quotes the complaint of a Pennsylvania court: "Might he so much, indeed, as buy a cigar or a newspaper with money one-half of which belonged to his wife without at least the technical duty of accounting to her for her portion of the money thus expended?" and newspaper headlines like "Community Property Law Can Aid Wives in Putting Mates over Barrel."[110] To recognize domestic partnerships could potentially undermine elements of the old law of domestic relations which forbade paying wives for the performance of services to the family; work in a family business was considered to be part of "wifely duty" and did not entitle her to make her own claims on the family's wealth. In a context in which state laws rarely asserted the obligation of the married woman to support her family but did establish that obligation for men, a wife's contribution to the family partnership was interpreted as activity which enabled husbands to fulfill their own obligations. Jones quotes *Newsweek*: "In most states, if a husband left his wife or if a wife went home to mother, the best she could hope for was a nominal support allowance. In any community-property state, the woman automatically came out with half the family bankroll."[111] *Newsweek* clearly thought its readers would regard the second sentence as unfair.

The adoption of the joint tax return in 1948 was a conservative compromise, offering tax reduction comparable to what was available in community property states "without any change in the legal rights between spouses."[112] In effect, the joint tax return accomplished a tax advantage without renegotiating the limited authority which women could claim over family income. A tax advantage for the one-earner household was simultaneously counterbalanced by, as Grace Blumberg, the first scholar to offer a gender critique of the Internal Revenue Code, put it, "a serious disincentive for married women who wish to work as well as a disproportionately high tax liability for single people."[113] When the idea of a joint income tax was first raised, in 1942, a coalition of women's organizations had attacked it on the grounds that a joint income tax amounted to a restoration of the concepts of coverture and the old law of domestic relations. "Women have worked for many years to break down the old common-law doctrine that husband and wife are one, and that one the husband," complained the president of the National Federation of Business and Professional Women. "Women are individuals, even when married. . . . It took many years of struggle to secure laws which recognize the separate property of husband and wife, and this proposal is a step backward."[114]

In the tax system that was in effect between 1948 and 1970, the woman who was part of a family in which she was fully supported by her husband was greatly advantaged; the woman who was part of a two-earner family was understood to be the "secondary earner" and was severely disadvantaged. Reform of tax law was on the agenda of many feminist legislators who entered politics during the revitalized feminist movement of the 1970s.[115] Some of the most obvious of these disadvantages were removed in the 1969 revision of the tax code, and many thought that the "marriage penalty" had been eliminated, but complex rules continued to burden two-earner families. Tax analyst Edward J. McCaffery has argued persuasively that lowest income earners still face a pronounced marriage penalty; among middle-class and wealthier two-parent households, "the high marginal tax rates facing a potential earner and the inadequacy of the child-care credit strongly encourage one spouse to stay home."[116] U.S. tax structures continue to combine with social traditions to sustain a system in which wives are understood to be secondary earners and their participation in the waged labor force understood to be a matter of choice. "If a married mother leaves the home to go into the workforce," McCaffery points out, "she must earn at least *double* the costs of child care and other work-related expenses because for every dollar she earns, the government will take one-half. . . . working wives are taxed without being benefited; stay-at-home spouses are benefited without being taxed."[117] Women who work not only gain income but also maintain and improve their professional skills; studies have shown that married women who earn money have a more emphatic role in family decision making than those who do not. Yet the prediction of many feminists in the early 1970s that men's as well as women's career patterns would change as more women entered the workforce did not turn out to be accurate; at this writing less than 5 percent of married fathers work part-time. Traditional beliefs that fathers' work is inflexible and mothers' work is flexible are sustained by what

McCaffery calls "the deep skew of the tax system against working wives."[118]

In the 1940s a few prescient feminists had warned of the special biases of inheritance law. Prompted by the complaints of farm wives, feminist legislators of the 1970s recognized that estate taxes often disadvantaged widows in order to privilege children. Estate taxes on real property, especially farms, failed to give ownership credit to widows who had worked side by side with their husbands to increase the value of the farm. In some states, when a farmer died intestate and childless, the bulk of the farm stayed in his family line, inherited by his parents or siblings and their heirs, not his wife. It took nearly a quarter century of legislative work to change these patterns.[119]

Thus married and widowed women's relationship to tax structures—including Social Security—continued to take into account their relationship to their husbands. By the 1990s, same-sex couples were pointing out that heterosexual couples received not only cultural support for their relationship but measurable benefits in taxation and inheritance practice.[120] Federal estate tax law permitted a wealthy spouse to pass on unlimited property to a surviving spouse; cohabiting couples—heterosexual as well as same-sex—could not; they "face much more severe tax consequences than their married counterparts," observed the authors of one rulebook.[121] Lesbians and gay men began to argue that they should enjoy the same tax advantages as husbands and wives, including joint wealth free of gift and estate taxes. They pointed out that the expansive fringe benefits which employers provide to spouses of employees are often exempted from taxation. The equality they sought could be achieved either by a thorough reconsideration of the joint income tax system or by the recognition of same-sex marriages.[122]

In short, despite many changes made in the interests of gender neutrality, tax law has continued to be structured by designs that imagine heterosexual households, with men working outside the household and women working inside in the service of husbands and children. At the turn of the twenty-first century, the obligation to pay taxes is no longer filtered through husbands' "virtual" representation of women in the political order. But it remains embedded in the political economy of marriage.

4

"WOMAN IS THE CENTER OF HOME
AND FAMILY LIFE"
GWENDOLYN HOYT AND JURY SERVICE
IN THE TWENTIETH CENTURY

"I wanted my husband not to die"

Gwendolyn Rogers Hoyt was thirty-two years old when she killed her husband, Clarence, an Air Force pilot, with a broken baseball bat. Theirs had been a rocky marriage. Children of working people, they grew up in a mill town north of Boston. They dated in high school, and were married in 1942 when Gwendolyn Rogers was seventeen. Clarence Hoyt enlisted in the Air Force and was soon sent to England; while he was overseas Gwendolyn Hoyt began having "convulsive episodes," later diagnosed as epilepsy.[1] Not long after Clarence's return in 1945, Gwendolyn divorced him "because she found him with another woman in their apartment."[2]

Two years later, Gwendolyn Hoyt was charged with stabbing Clarence and a woman with whom he was living, but by the time the case of mutual assault and battery was heard they had remarried. Gwendolyn Hoyt was placed on probation for three years and ordered to make $500 reparations.[3] A year later they had a son.

In the spring of 1950, the Hoyts took their troubled marriage to

Florida, where Clarence was stationed at MacDill Air Force Base in Tampa. They bought a modest one-story home at the end of a quiet dead-end street close to the base, where many military families lived. The street was full of children and the noise of their games. Tampa was a small city in those days; the Florida land boom was still concentrated on the east coast. Tampa was a strenuously segregated city.[4]

In April 1956, Clarence was assigned to the 19th Air Refueling Squadron at Homestead Air Force Base, nearly two hundred fifty miles away. Gwendolyn remained with their son in Tampa, and Clarence returned on weekends and three-day passes. Within a year the visits had become irregular, the marriage had become problematic, and Gwendolyn's epilepsy had increased—with dizziness, faintness, occasional hallucinations of a streak of light, episodes of numbness and slight paralysis, and periods of stuttering. She and Clarence told her doctor that they believed her attacks were "precipitated by emotional disturbances and nervous tension."[5] Meanwhile, as Gwendolyn Hoyt's attorneys would later say, she felt that Clarence Hoyt's conduct toward her and "their child changed completely . . . [he] began to ignore [her] . . . , their child, and their home life . . . he did not come home except on rare occasions and on those occasions he would be very grouchy and critical . . . [of her] and their child; . . . marital and sexual relations deteriorated. . . . [Clarence Hoyt] was receiving telephone calls from strange women."[6] Gwendolyn Hoyt tried to reach him by telephone and "made several trips to Homestead, Florida, to try to get [Clarence] . . . to reform himself and to get a home near the base where he was stationed, all to no avail." In July 1957, she went to Homestead and found him unshaven, looking "as if he had been drinking."[7] He rarely came home to Tampa; on one of those visits he "became extremely angry . . . and beat her unmercifully; . . . [she] could see her marriage crumbling before her."[8]

On September 18, Gwendolyn Hoyt tried a desperate tactic to gain Clarence's attention; she sent a false message that their son was dying in a hospital in Tampa. When Clarence appeared, she "tried every conceivable way to save something out of the marital life of the parties, including sexual attraction and all other means known to females."[9] They spent the evening visiting with friends who knew of their marital troubles; when they returned home "I put on this gown which he liked," she said at her trial. "But when I went to him where

9. On December 19, 1957, while the jury was
considering its verdict, the Tampa *Daily Times* ran
this photograph of Gwendolyn Hoyt.

he was lying on the davenport . . . [h]e says, 'Don't. I won't touch
you.' And we just had to discuss our marriage, our problems. I said,
'You just got to discuss them. We've just got to,' and then, the little
dog, he was barking. And he said, 'Go out and let the dog in,' and
so I went out and I let the dog in and I went out, I was turning
around, I saw the bat and I picked it up. I thought I'd put it into the
trash when I went out to put my little doggie to bed. . . . I went in.
I didn't want to miss anything he was saying. And I, when I went in
there, he turned over and he said, 'Don't bother me. Get away. I'm
going back to Homestead in the morning, and that'll be the end of
it.' That's when I hit him."[10] "I just picked up that horrible bat to
throw it away," she told reporters two days later. "The room was
dark, and I struck out to hurt him. If it hadn't been for [that horri-
ble][11] bat, I would have slapped him—and then he probably would've

10. Clarence Hoyt, 1957.

gotten up and slapped me back and none of this would have been."[12]

Gwendolyn Hoyt called her family doctor, who refused to come. She called MacDill Air Force Base, which did send an ambulance; while she waited she remembered what she had learned about shock in a course she had taken, and she covered Clarence with a blanket, offered him water, tried to stop the bleeding. "I said, 'Please lay still for your own sake,' and I asked him to forgive me. And he smiled at me and he patted my arm. . . . I wanted my husband not to die."

The headline in the Tampa *Morning Tribune* on September 21 read: "Tampa Wife Beats MacDill Hubby to Death with Bat." When Clarence Hoyt died on the morning of September 20, Gwendolyn Hoyt was arrested on a charge of first-degree murder, placed in the county jail without bond,[13] and transferred to Tampa General Hospital's psychiatric ward. By September 25, a bond of $3,500 was set. Newspapers described her as "quiet" and "buxom"; they said she had been "irked" by her husband's behavior. None mentioned—then or after it had come out in the trial—the violence that had characterized the household. A county grand jury, unable to find premeditation, indicted her for second-degree murder on October 1. Her defense attorneys pled "not guilty by reason of temporary insanity" and tried to get the charge reduced to manslaughter; their plea was denied. They also objected to the all-male jury.[14]

"The lamp that shows that freedom lives"

We know very little about what actually happens inside jury rooms, for jurors are normally forbidden to take notes out when they leave, and so must reconstruct their deliberations from flawed memories. Moreover, the people who are most interested in the patterns of jury deliberations—lawyers, political scientists, scholars of criminal justice—are often for that very reason excluded (formally or informally) from jury service. Those who write about juries have rarely heard a real jury deliberate. In the mid-1950s, the Chicago Jury Project tried to change this by taping jury proceedings in order to analyze them. The resulting national scandal included public censure by the Attorney General of the United States and the Internal Security Subcommittee of the Senate Judiciary Committee and a wave of new statutes explicitly forbidding the practice.[15] The place of the jury long seemed magical. Until the closing years of the twentieth century, Americans hesitated to inquire too much.

People who believe the legal system leans against their interests often want to demystify the jury—to ask if it is indeed "the lamp that shows that freedom lives."[16] In twentieth-century America, these critics have often been feminists and civil rights activists—sometimes one and the same person, sometimes not.

Juries have long held a significant and powerful place in American public life. Like voting, jury service is one of the basic rituals by which Americans affirm their participation in society. Unlike voting, it is a civil obligation; the citizen who does not respond to a summons to serve on a jury faces sanctions ranging from fines to contempt of court. The first colonial reprint of an English lawbook, in 1693, was a tract demanding an increased range of activities for juries.[17] At least since the time of the trial of John Peter Zenger in 1735, when a New York editor persuaded a jury to override the established law that truth was not a defense against the charge of seditious libel, American courts have recognized a wide-ranging power of juries to determine law. The power of juries was particularly strong in the prerevolutionary era, when juries had virtually unlimited power to find the law as well as the facts; they spoke for a community view of justice and morality which stood as a countervailing force against provincial and royal authorities.[18] During the revolutionary era, the British attack on juries' independence—by extending the jurisdiction of admiralty cases, which were decided by boards of judges without juries, and by moving cases to Nova Scotia, where the jurors would not be neighbors of the accused—was a major issue in the agenda of patriot complaints and figured in the list of charges against George III in the Declaration of Independence. "[N]o right was made more central in the configuration of rights created by lawyers, legislators and pamphleteers in the decade of the American rebellion," writes historian Kathryn Preyer. "In their view, the right to trial by jury constituted the most effective mode of popular check on arbitrary power."[19] The right of an accused criminal to trial by jury was quickly embedded in each of the new states' Declarations of Rights, in state constitutions, in the Federal Constitution and in the Bill of Rights. It is the only guarantee of an individual right to be so unanimously enumerated.[20]

Members of the founding generation construed jury service to be central to the process of democracy; it was the context in which average citizens exercised reflective judgment. Republics rested on the virtue and intelligence of their citizens; virtue and intelligence were trained and tested in the jury box. Jefferson described the jury as the "school by which [the] people learn the exercise of civic duties as well as rights."[21] For James Wilson, a Philadelphia jurist and signer of the Federal Constitution, jury service challenged ordinary citizens' ability to understand and to make fine distinctions; voters "come to know, to shape, and thus to admire the law . . . through their participation on juries."[22] Although judges instructed juries in the applicable law, members of the founding generation were insistent that—as John Adams asserted in 1771—a juror had not only the right but the "Duty . . . to find the Verdict according to his own best Understanding, Judgment and Conscience, tho in Direct opposition to the Direction of the court."[23] When Alexander Hamilton faced a sedition charge he insisted that conceding to juries a broad range of discretion was an important protection for the citizen against arbitrary judges.[24] By the early nineteenth century, however, judges were asserting greater control over juries, claiming heightened authority to find the law, to supervise the fact-finding process, and to narrow the range of jurors' independence. Although no state now sustains the right of the jury to judge the law—limiting juries rather to judgment of facts alone—the assertion of the claim of "jury nullification" continues to thrive, as juries in the late twentieth century exercise their power to bring in a verdict that challenges both law and facts as the judge has summarized them.[25]

Emphasis on the role of juries continues to be a distinctive mark of the American system of justice. France adopted a form of jury service in the era of the French Revolution, but only echoes of it remain.[26] Western European nations now commonly use mixed panels of lay jurors who sit with professional judges.[27] The Japanese constitution, negotiated by a victorious United States with a defeated state, echoes the American constitution in many respects—and goes it one further by embedding an equivalent of the Equal Rights Amendment directly in the text—but has no provision for jurors; the victors did not trust the judgment of the defeated, nor were juries familiar devices in Japanese traditions of justice. Not all former British colonies have adopted Britain's jury system; it is strong in Canada and Australia, but not in India.

"Covered" by their husbands' civic identity, Anglo-American women traditionally had entered civil courts linked to their husband or to a "prochein ami"—a male "next friend." In England, Scotland, and the colonies, women's jury service had been strictly limited to their role as witnesses in cases in which a woman's pregnancy was in question. Long after the traditional role of the jury as witnesses to the facts had died out, "juries of matrons" were summoned to exercise their skills as midwives in cases in which female felons "pled their belly" and called upon their pregnancies to postpone death sentences, or in which widows were suspected of feigning pregnancy in order to enable a fictive heir to inherit the estate, or as inspectors of women's bodies in cases of infanticide or witchcraft.[28] William Blackstone, the author of the English treatise on which American lawyers relied in the revolutionary era, and who can be counted on to reveal his prejudices, identifies women as one of the many groups ineligible for regular jury service, cheerfully dismissing them as suffering from a "defect of sex" without telling us of what this defect consists.[29]

Judith Sargent Murray was the member of the founding generation who wrote most extensively about women's relationship to the state; she was well known in New England for her short stories and political essays, published from the mid-1770s until the end of the century. "Are not women equally concerned with men in the public weal?" she asked, and she did not mean her question to be rhetorical. Murray formulated her generation's major structural criticism of a system of jury service that excluded women, a criticism that would be echoed late into the twentieth century. In 1797 she wrote to a friend: "I have sometimes thought that we Women are hardly dealt by since strictly speaking, we cannot legally be tried by our Peers, for men are not our Peers, and yet upon their breath our guilt or innocence depends—thus are our privileges in this, as in many other respects, tyrannically abridged. . . . I object to a male decision upon a female question."[30]

In short, the founding generations understood juries as the place where the people continued their participation in lawmaking, a point that Alexis de Tocqueville, a generation later, saw clearly. "[T]he jury," he wrote after his tour of the United States in 1835, "which is the most energetic means of making the people rule, is also the most efficacious means of teaching it how to rule well."[31] But Tocqueville did not ask of whom "the people" consisted; he did not ask Judith Sargent Murray's question. Are women and men peers? In what sense are they peers? In what sense are they not? What are the ingredients of "a male decision"? What characterizes "a female question"? These issues, which by the end of the twentieth century would be spoken of as the dilemma of resolving equality and difference, are issues which emerged with the emergence of the nation.

The Federal Constitution promises "trial by jury" in criminal cases in the state where the crimes were committed (Article III). The Seventh Amendment guarantees jury trial in civil suits "where the value in controversy shall exceed twenty dollars," and also ensures that facts, once tried by a jury, may not be reexamined in any court unless the rules of common law permit. The Sixth Amendment promises that the trial is to be "speedy" and "public" and that the jury shall be "impartial" and drawn from "the district wherein the crime shall

11. "What We May Confidently Look For." This 1870 cartoon conveyed that African-Americans and women were unpleasant and disruptive presences in the courtroom.

have been committed." The Constitution does not specify the size of a jury; the twelve-person tradition eroded in some jurisdictions in the 1940s and 1950s. The conditions of impartiality are not spelled out; the Constitution promises neither "a jury of one's peers" nor one drawn from a "cross section" of the community.[32] Yet a long customary tradition has linked the concept of the jury with "peers," neighbors, and a sample of the community in which the crime is committed and from which the jury is chosen. The judgment of court officials has traditionally entered into the selection process, often through the device of requiring "good character," which in turn is vulnerable to subjective assessment. The qualifications for "peers" have varied greatly over time, and included property qualifications at least since the time of Henry II. Property qualifications dropped out of U.S. practice for petit juries gradually during the nineteenth century, but remained in force for grand juries in some jurisdictions until the mid-twentieth century.[33]

An extended train of cases, dating to Reconstruction, has linked impartiality to the *process* by which the jurors are selected, equating

↑ how peers are selected

"impartial" with a "cross section" of the community and defining "peers" as people chosen randomly. In 1879 *Strauder v. West Virginia* tested a statute that limited jury service to white men. Strauder, an African-American being tried for the murder of his wife, claimed that he had "a right to a trial . . . by a jury selected and impanelled without discrimination against his race or color." In a 7–2 decision upholding his claims, and ruling that the statute denied black men equal protection of the laws under the Fourteenth Amendment, the Supreme Court made it clear that the question was *not* "whether a colored man . . . has a right to a . . . jury *composed* [emphasis mine] in whole or in part of persons of his own race or color, but . . . whether, in the composition or selection of jurors by whom he is to be indicted or tried, all persons of his race or color may be excluded by law." If it would be wrong to exclude other classes of citizens—of Irish descent, whites in a county in which blacks were in the majority—then it was wrong to exclude black men from juries. The Court offered a ringing statement of its conviction: "The right to a trial by jury is guaranteed to every citizen of West Virginia by the Constitution of that State, and the constitution of juries is a very essential part of the protection such a mode of trial is intended to secure."

But from these generalizations the Supreme Court backed off almost immediately, affirming that a state may

> prescribe the qualifications of its jurors, and in so doing make discrimination. It may confine the selection to males, to freeholders, to citizens, to persons within certain ages, or to persons having educational qualifications. We do not believe the Fourteenth Amendment was ever intended to prohibit this. . . . Its aim was against discrimination because of race or color.[34]

Of the groups whose exclusion was permitted by this list, women were the only ones who could not change their condition. People get older, they can change and improve their educational qualifications or economic condition, albeit often only with difficulty. But sex, like race, resists change.

For nearly a century, *Strauder* would be used to confirm the haphazard development of patterns of women's jury service. Courts comfortably quoted *Strauder* to the effect that deep prejudice against blacks required that the state protect their right to be judged by a jury from which other blacks had not been excluded. They used the reasoning in *Strauder* to insist that other ethnic groups not be barred from jury service, and expanded it to include those who received weekly wages rather than monthly salaries (a stand-in for class).[35] "It is part of the established tradition in the use of juries as instruments of public justice," observed the Supreme Court in 1940, "that the jury be a body truly representative of the community."[36] But neither courts nor the liberal community was prepared to concede that the continued exclusion of women from jury service was a mark of deep prejudice against women. The concept of obligation was repeatedly confused with claims of rights. When they had claimed the vote in return for fulfilling their obligation to pay taxes, women had received the response that the right to vote was not connected to the obligation to pay taxes. When women defendants demanded that other women fulfill an obligation to be available for jury service so that a full cross section of the community could be drawn upon, they met the claim that women had the "right" to be excused from jury service. Women were understood to be *favored* by the culture, and exemption from jury service was understood to be one manifestation of that privilege.

A good window onto these issues is a frequently reprinted short story, by Susan Glaspell, published in 1917. "A Jury of Her Peers" is set in an unnamed rural community. The story is based on the 1901 trial of Margaret Hossack, of rural New Virginia, Iowa, who killed her husband with an ax while he lay sleeping in their bed. The trial created a sensation; Mrs. Hossack was arrested "just as the sexton was throwing the last clods on the grave of her murdered husband," and as many as 1,200 people crowded the courthouse when the trial opened. Glaspell covered the trial for the Des Moines *Daily News*.[37]

In "A Jury of Her Peers" two women—Mrs. Peters, the wife of the sheriff, and Martha Hale, the wife of the neighbor who discovered the body—accompany their husbands and the county attorney to the isolated farmhouse where John Wright has been discovered in his bed, strangled by a rope around his neck. Minnie Wright, who admits she was sleeping in the bed with him, denies any knowledge of the crime; " 'I didn't wake up,' " she says, "pleatin' at her apron"; 'I sleep sound.' "

The women who have come to the farmhouse are timid, hesitant, inarticulate. The men are sure of themselves, boisterous, talkative. "Nothing here but kitchen things," sniffs the sheriff. They doubt that the women would "know a clue if they did come upon it."[38]

While the men are in the upstairs bedroom trying to reconstruct the circumstances of the death, the women hang around the kitchen, noticing details: the shabby clothing Minnie Wright wore, a sharp contrast to the pretty clothes on which she had prided herself twenty years before, "when she was Minnie Foster, one of the town girls, singing in the choir." They notice work interrupted, particularly a quilting block sewed so erratically it looked "crazy." They find a birdcage with a broken door, its hinge pulled apart. They remember that a peddler has recently been by, selling canaries. They think that Minnie Wright "was kind of like a bird herself. Real sweet and pretty, but kind of timid and—fluttery. How—she—did—change." And when they find the dead bird carefully wrapped in Minnie Wright's sewing box, its neck broken, they understand that "if there had been years and years of—nothing, then a bird to sing to you, it would be awful—still—after the bird was still."

For the men, it is "all perfectly clear, except the reason for doing it. But you know juries when it comes to women." For a jury to convict a woman, they need "some definite thing . . . that would connect with this clumsy way of doing it." The two women, communicating in silence, hide the dead bird, refuse the evidence. They are indeed Minnie Foster Wright's peers: farm women like her, they have done the endless work that she has done, known isolation as she has known it, suffered intimidation by men. They understand the power relations in the Wright household because they have experienced these power relations themselves, though in a milder form. Thus these two women, truly a jury of her peers, judge Minnie Wright. In effect they lower the charges from murder, which requires premeditation, to manslaughter, and find her innocent due to mitigating circumstances.

Ought the Minnie Wrights of the world have a right to have women on the juries that try them? Ought the Martha Hales have an *obligation* to serve on such panels? Is jury service a right or an obligation? Is it a compliment or an insult to women to offer them easy excuses from jury service? Is it in the interests of defendants to have women on the jury? For what kind of defendant is the presence of women on the jury an advantage? For whom a disadvantage?

In these questions have been embedded much that was otherwise left unexpressed about women's relationship to the political community and about the capacities of women's minds. All the themes that are present in Glaspell's short story reappeared in legislative battles and in test cases throughout the twentieth century. Some argued that women don't "belong" in the courtroom; that they are already advantaged by a cultural tradition that offers women a certain indulgence because of the weakness of their sex; that they are too frivolous to take serious matters seriously—or that they take them *too* seriously. Others argued that there are things women intuit better than men do or that their experience and interests are distinct from men's and that courtroom equity requires their presence. In reconstructing the history of jury service, and exploring what this struggle suggests about the citizenship of women, distinctions have to be made between the *right* of citizens, if they are accused of crime, to an impartial jury and to equal protection of the laws and the *obligation* of citizens to serve on juries.

"Something very like a second suffrage campaign"

Debates over appropriate jury service for women were infused with a variety of understandings of women's minds and the nature of women's civic obligation. The history of women's jury service is complex, because rules that bound trial juries did not always also bind grand juries; rules that bound state juries did not apply to federal juries. This history of women's jury service stretches over the entire course of the twentieth century; the first permanent state statute which permitted women to serve was not passed until 1898 in Utah, and the right of a *defendant* to a jury drawn from a list on which women's names are placed on the same terms as men's names have been placed was not firmly established until 1975. Not until 1994 did the Supreme Court rule that peremptory challenges cannot be used to screen jurors on the basis of gender.[39]

As women achieved the right to vote, one state at a time, jury service sometimes followed on its heels. Men and women were entitled to "equal enjoyment of all civil, political and religious rights and privileges" when Wyoming entered the Union in 1889, but shortly after women began actually to serve on juries, men mobilized to overturn the statute permitting them to do so. Jury service followed suffrage in Utah (1898), Washington (1911), Kansas (1913), California (1917), New Jersey (1917), and Michigan (1918).[40] But this was not a uniform pattern. Although women had been voting in Wyoming since the 1870s and in Colorado since the 1890s, they did not serve on juries there, and would not until the 1940s.

In some states, where statutes defined as competent jurors "all qualified electors" the achievement of jury service followed painlessly on the heels of the Nineteenth Amendment. A 1921 Oregon jury service statute was especially emphatic, providing that "in all cases in which a minor under the age of eighteen years is involved, either as defendant or as complaining witness, at least one half the jury shall be women."[41] But even in those states, the first man who was found guilty by a jury that included a woman often challenged his conviction, and state Supreme Court judges had to rule on that specific point. In Michigan the court held that even though the jury statutes had used the term "man," "the moment a woman became an elector under the constitutional amendment she was entitled to perform jury duty, if she was possessed of the same qualifications that men possessed."[42]

In most states, however, new statutes were required. In California women began to serve as soon as they began to vote in 1911. But the California statutes had been framed in terms of "a body of men," and men convicted of crimes successfully challenged their conviction on the grounds that women had been part of the jury, forcing the legislature to pass a new statute in 1917.[43] In 1925 the Illinois Supreme Court ruled that because only men had been voters in 1874 when the jury statute had been passed, the terms "legal voters" and "electors" referred only to male persons. Not until 1939 did the Illinois state legislature permit women to serve on juries.

Early in the 1920s, the National League of Women Voters drafted a "Women's Bill of Rights": an agenda which sought to remove a long list of legal discriminations against women. The National Wom-

Reject the Susan B. Anthony Amendment

WOMAN SUFFRAGE IN ACTION!

Would Southern Men Approve of This?

≡ VOTES FOR WOMEN MEANS JURY DUTY FOR WOMEN ≡

Suffragist leaders are careful never to mention to their audiences in the East or in the South the subject of jury duty for women. When questioned about it, one of them replied: "Oh, that can be arranged very pleasantly." Let us see how it is arranged in the States where women vote.

For many weeks of the spring of 1917 a big I. W. W. murder trial was in progress in Seattle. Six of the jurors were women. Mrs. Sarah J. Timmer was juror No. 11. She had received word before she entered the box that "her children had contracted the measles." Calling the jury in, Judge Donald said to Mrs. Timmer:

Mrs. Timmer, I have been informed that you are worried about your children. I'm powerless to let you go home, but both sides agree that I may communicate to you any word your family physician desires to convey. Don't let your attention be attracted by anything but the trial. We'll keep you advised and you will have no cause to worry. Remember, no news is good news." (Seattle *Post-Intelligencer*, March 8, 1917.)

It must be a grand and glorious feeling for a woman to be drawn as a juror in a murder case, likely to last two months, when the children of her family have contracted the measles!

A month later the Seattle *Post-Intelligencer* said: "The confinement imposed on juries in murder trials is beginning to tell on most of the members of the Tracy jury, *especially the women jurors, the majority of whom have families*. During the last month numerous stipulations have been arranged between attorneys for both sides, allowing children of the jurors to see their parents for a few minutes in the presence of witnesses. The defense attorneys estimate that it will be nearly two weeks yet before they are through submitting evidence."

WOMEN OF WEALTH MANAGE TO ESCAPE JURY DUTY

One of them told how an eastern friend how she did it. She said: "I was determined I would not serve on that jury, so I got a doctor to give me something which would make me violently sick for a little while; then I called another doctor, who finding me very sick, gave me a certificate that I was not able to serve on the jury." The poor man's wife cannot afford to pay two

doctors' bills to escape the disagreeable duty which suffragists have forced upon her, so she is obliged to serve.

An article from the *Spokesman Review* of Spokane, Washington, a suffrage State tells how the jury law works there:

"While the law is so stern that it refuses a mother permission to go to her baby while she is doing jury duty, there is nothing to prevent a baby going to its mother, at least that is how the law was interpreted in the court of Judge William Huneke, when baby Margaret Hackett went to the courthouse for her dinner.

"Father rushed Margaret, aged three months, in an automobile to the courthouse. Mother gave baby her 6 o'clock meal, and father and infant retired, subject to hurry calls during the night.

"Mrs. R. W. Hackett was serving on a jury which failed to agree." It has also been reported directly by letter that a two-months-old baby has been left at a day nursery while its mother serves on a jury.

WOMEN IN THE SUFFRAGE STATES ARE SERVING ON JURIES IN MURDER CASES, COMMERCIALIZED VICE CASES, AND WHISKEY CASES.

A court official of many years experience states that his observation of criminal trials has shown that at almost every term of court language is used and incidents recited from the witness stand that grate on the sensibilities of all refined men present. Profanity, obscenity and the detailed narration of the immoral acts and doings of the lowest type of humanity are brought out in all their revolting nakedness. A suffragist naively argued that if women were on the juries all this would be "cut out!" This is childish. It is a fact that it is not cut out in the suffrage States. Most judges are refined men and would eliminate all such testimony if they could legally and justly do so.

The National Suffrage Program says: "Laws should provide that women be subject to jury service."

See Proceedings National Suffrage Convention, Chicago, February, 1920. Page 64.

Men of the South, do you like this prospect for your wife, your daughter, or for the woman who may become your wife? If not,

Wake up and fight Suffrage in order to protect Southern
Women from having jury duty forced upon them

12. Jury service and suffrage were linked in this North Carolina attack on the ratification of the Nineteenth Amendment, probably printed in 1920.

an's Party also committed itself to the removal of a wide range of legal discriminations against women.[44] Neither group, however, was committed to fighting discrimination against black women or to asking whether a cross section of the community was complete without African-American citizens; to do that would have required them to take a position defending civil rights for all African-Americans, which few among them were prepared to do. Had they done so, however, they might have paid more attention than they did to fighting poll taxes, which, as we have seen, bore heavily on African-Americans and on white women simultaneously.[45] High on the agendas of both the League and the National Woman's Party were unequal guardianship laws, unequal eligibility to make contracts and to hold civil office, the dependence of the citizenship of married women on their husband's status—as Ethel Mackenzie's had been—and equal obligation to jury service.[46] The League believed that the absence of women from juries was part of the larger problem of the way in which sex bias intruded on the equal administration of justice; they kept mandatory jury service statutes high on their agenda. Repeatedly they asked the Sixth Amendment question: "If a jury ought to represent a cross-section of the community, is a cross-section of the community complete without women?"[47]

By 1923, eighteen states and the territory of Alaska had arranged for women to serve on juries; most provided easy exemptions for women unwilling to serve.[48] But between the mid-term elections of 1922 and the presidential election of 1924 it became clear that women did not vote as a bloc, and legislators found it less urgent to treat them as an interest group. In states that did not yet have statutes, arduous legislative battles followed.[49] In Florida, Massachusetts, and New York—the states from which the actors in the drama that was the Hoyt case would come—no women served on juries long after national suffrage was achieved.

In Florida mandatory jury service was on the legislative agenda of the League of Women Voters throughout the 1920s and 1930s. In 1929 the Florida legislature defeated a bill the League had sponsored.[50] In 1939 the Florida Supreme Court denied a claim by a woman that she had the right to be tried by a jury for which other women were eligible to serve. *Strauder* had established that the access to jury service for African-Americans was intended to protect them against continuing and real potential for oppression because of their race. But the court held that women had been favored by the law. "Women had not been enslaved," claimed Judge Armstead Brown, ignoring all African-American women. "They had long been generally recognized in this country as the equal of man." Indeed, he continued, "the spirit of chivalry, and of deep respect for the rights of the opposite sex, have not yet departed from the heads and hearts of the men of this country."[51]

In 1943, Representative Mary Lou Baker, who had been active in the St. Petersburg chapter of the League, introduced a jury service bill in her first speech to the Florida House of Representatives. Baker's original draft required that 50 percent of any jury list be names of women, but she displayed her moderation by promptly agreeing to strike that provision, as well as to add one that provided that "no female may be made to serve against her will." The bill was thus rapidly transformed from mandatory equal jury service—the 50 percent provision would have made it the strongest in the nation; there is none like it today—to permissive jury service. In its weakened form the bill attracted more support than many had anticipated; one early move to dismiss it was deflected only by a tie vote.

Even though Florida jury commissioners were notorious for their success in keeping blacks off juries, opponents immediately denounced Baker for making white women vulnerable to service with black men, summoning up visions "of women serving on coroner's juries called into negro districts."[52] One representative was certain that women "would be worrying about the children back home" and not keep their minds on the case. Others complained of the cost of added rest rooms in county courthouses and of women bailiffs when juries had to be sequestered. Some House members were sure that they "did not want their wives and sisters exposed to the embarrassment of hearing filthy evidence."

Baker responded that "in cases involving sex offenses a mixed jury is especially desirable"; warned her colleagues against facing women's anger in the next election; assured them that a male juror was more likely "to rush a verdict 'to get to his meal on time' than a woman, and ended by reading five full verses of a Kipling poem with the refrain "The female of the species is more deadly than the male." Her motion lost by a vote of 38–50.[53]

Not until 1949 did the Florida legislature again consider a women's jury service bill. It squeaked to passage in the state Senate by the narrow margin of 20–18, "despite warnings from opponents that it would 'degrade womanhood.' "[54] The House was somewhat more skeptical. Its version obligated a woman to jury duty only after she had "registered with the Clerk of the Circuit Court her desire to be placed on the jury list."[55] When the amended bill finally reached the floor, it was taken as welcome comic relief and passed easily, the St. Petersburg *Times* reported, "after a good deal about the likelihood of 'busybodies and gossips' qualifying for jury service for lack of anything better to do."[56] "It will be interesting," the Tampa *Tribune* observed, "to see what percentage of women citizens will register their willingness to go into the jury box."[57] The Hillsborough County clerk did not place dates next to the signatures of the women who signed up in Tampa, but across the bay in Pinellas County, which included St. Petersburg and its suburb of Clearwater and was roughly equivalent in population to Hillsborough, 200 women registered within six months.

News of the women's jury service bill commanded little public attention in a week in which Governor Fuller Warren ceremonially made himself the first state employee to sign a loyalty oath, and the retired dean of the University of Florida Law School told the House committee investigating Communism in the state universities that there are "fifty to a hundred radicals" on the University of Florida faculty.[58] But two law students at the university, C. J. Hardee and Carl Durrance, whom we shall meet later in this story, took notice.

Mary Lou Baker's experience in Florida differed only in detail from the experiences of her colleagues elsewhere. In New York State, for example, where women's groups were considerably stronger than in Florida, the struggle for a mandatory jury service law absorbed a substantial amount of energy of the League of Women Voters, the Women's City Club, and the National Woman's Party for decades.

The arguments in New York were less racist than those heard in Florida, but their general drift was similar. "Women may be tenderhearted but they are not soft-headed," advocates said.[59] New York Bar Associations resisted, arguing that women should not be compelled to listen to sordid evidence; that lawyers like to talk "man to man" to jurors; that it was inappropriate to sequester women in the

13. "The Little Closed Spaces Where Men Are
Men," Boston *Herald* cartoon by Carl J. Rose,
September 12, 1931.

same room with men. To the last point, Eleanor Roosevelt observed
that "it never occurs to us to be disturbed if we are locked up all
night in an airplane, so why should we get excited about chances of
being locked up in a jury room?"[60]

A 1937 law made New York women eligible to serve on the same
terms as men but offered them the opportunity to claim exemption
by submitting a simple affidavit. Exemptions from jury duty could be
claimed by "a clergyman . . . officiating as such . . . ; a practicing
physician, surgeon or surgeon dentist having patients requiring his
daily professional attention, a licensed pharmacist . . . a person belonging to the army, navy or marine corps . . . A captain, engineer,
or other officer, actually employed upon a vessel making regular trips
. . . a woman."[61] Easy exemption for women jurors would not end in
New York until the mid-1970s. By prearrangement, the first New
York jury with women on it sat in August 1937 in the same federal

courthouse in Canandaigua in which Susan B. Anthony had been convicted for voting in 1873.[62]

Although the voting statutes in Massachusetts were written in terms of electors, a 1921 advisory opinion of the Massachusetts Supreme Judicial Court indicated that a new, specific statute would be required. Failing to make progress in the Massachusetts legislature, the National Woman's Party tried a test case, challenging the $50 fine Genevieve Welosky had received for violating prohibition statutes. Despite prominent coverage in the newspapers, which emphasized the irony of interpreting a statute framed in terms of "persons" to exclude women, the NWP lost in Massachusetts, and the U.S. Supreme Court refused to hear its appeal.[63] Not until after World War II, when more women sat in the legislature and a 1946 state referendum in support of women's jury service won in every county, was a permissive jury service statute enacted. Even after the referendum, three years of lobbying were required before the statute finally passed; by that time, writes its historian, it "was no longer a contested issue."[64] Even then, a woman could not be required to serve in any trial in which the presiding judge had reason to believe she would "likely be embarrassed by hearing the testimony or by discussing [it] in the jury room."[65]

"Getting the word 'male' out of jury statutes is requiring something very like a second suffrage campaign—laborious, costly and exasperating," observed the executive secretary of the League of Women Voters in 1930. The lengthy struggles in Florida, New York, and Massachusetts suggest that what may seem self-evident now was once highly problematic.[66]

Everywhere the case for women jurors seesawed back and forth between an emphasis on women's and men's sameness (implying that excluding women from jury service was a foolish and impractical limitation on the number of those eligible to serve) and an emphasis on women's and men's difference (implying that to exclude women meant excluding people who could bring a usefully distinctive perspective or a different set of skills to the jury process). The case against women jurors also seesawed back and forth between an emphasis on women's and men's sameness (arguing that since men and women were equal, jury pools completely composed of men did no disservice to women) and an emphasis on women's and men's differ-

"NOT GUILTY!"—ON ACCOUNT OF HIS GOOD LOOKS

14. "Not Guilty—On Account of His Good Looks." A 1910 illustration from *Harper's Weekly* predicted the outcome of an all-woman courtroom. Drawing by R. F. Schabelitz.

include

ence (arguing that women were, for a variety of reasons—emotionalism, inability to sustain logical and rational argument, prior commitment to domestic chores—less capable than men). The images alternated, often in the same memo, sometimes in the same paragraph, their internal contradictions and oxymoronic nature reflecting deep cultural ambivalence.

In the 1920s and early 1930s, when equal jury service was high on the list of the League of Women Voters' priorities, the national office conducted a survey, hoping to find prominent jurists who would publicly support equal jury service. The League's Committee on the Legal Status of Women commissioned pamphlets that used these responses.[67] Meanwhile the Illinois League, facing the need for a new statute that explicitly recognized women, took its own particular interest in the issue, and conducted its own surveys. The responses to these inquiries by many dozens of local judges capture much of the complexity and ambivalence characteristic of the time.

Occasionally, but only occasionally, the responses of proponents of women's jury service were grounded straightforwardly on simple issues of equal citizenship and equal obligation. Guy Miller, judge of the Circuit Court for the Third Judicial Circuit of Michigan, which included Detroit, wrote that he saw "no reason why any distinction should be made as between women and men in the matter of jury service." Miller confessed that "through what turned out to be a mistaken sense of chivalry" he had once excused women from juries involving rape or "revolting or gruesome details." But he found, "somewhat to my surprise," that "the women on the jury panel were very indignant over the discrimination." Since that time, he had instructed the prosecutors to warn jurors of potential embarrassment; "there have been only one or two instances where women jurors have declined to serve."[68]

There were respondents who were flatly opposed to women's jury service; a New Orleans judge said that he "frankly . . . would consider the woman, who, voluntarily, took this grievous task upon her shoulders, a _____ [sic] FOOL."[69]

The League of Women Voters, of course, had made its own position clear. It publicized many supportive opinions that stressed women's difference from men in ways that implied that women were better than men: that the woman juror took her responsibilities "more seriously" than male jurors; that women were "more free than men from the influence of business, politics, lodge affiliations, etc., which tend to prevent that fair attitude demanded of jurors."[70] Jennie Loitman Barron, a young Boston lawyer who in later years would be the first and for decades the only woman judge on the Massachusetts Superior Court, argued that women jurors were "specially needed in cases involving women and girls, and in cases affecting public morals; first, because women can appreciate women's condition best; and second, because women are generally more interested than men in the morals of their community. A shabby, poverty-stricken, adolescent girl victim is not as interesting to some male jurors as is a clever, well-dressed, handsome adventuress."[71]

Yet most of these supportive opinions, even the published ones, were in some way ambivalent, warning against women's difference even as they offered support for statutes that would provide for equal service. Like the White Queen in *Through the Looking Glass*, supporters of women's jury service were capable of thinking of two contradictory things before breakfast. Thus the Chief Justice of the Ohio

Supreme Court reported that women jurors had displayed "conscientiousness, courage and good judgment" and were not "predisposed in favor of litigants of their own sex." But he also warned "that the natural trustfulness of women and . . . their admitted lack of knowledge of the ways of the world detracts from their value as jurors. . . . [T]hey do not reason with the same accuracy as men. . . . On the other hand, these defects may be fully compensated by an intuition, which is perhaps a better guide to separate the false and the spurious from that which rings true."[72]

The most intransigent responses were based in some measure on the premise that women would neglect their household duties. Men who were untroubled by fears that jury service would lead men to neglect their familial or professional duties were adamant in their insistence that women could not be relied on to maintain households properly if they were burdened by jury service. At the root of this paradox lies the traditional law of domestic relations which had placed married women's bodies and property firmly under the legal control of their husbands. Michael Grossberg and other historians of legal change have emphasized how vigorously many elements of family law were revised in the early republic.[73] But the relationship of husbands and wives was considerably slower to change; the first fragile married women's property acts only began to emerge in mid-century. Meanwhile the role of the republican mother had linked middle-class women to the new republic; women would perpetuate the republic, it was said, by their refusal to countenance lovers who were not devoted to the service of the state, and by their commitment to raise sons who were educated for civic virtue and for responsible citizenship. They would also raise self-reliant daughters who, in their turn, would raise republican sons. The concept of the "republican mother" had developed in the era of the American Revolution as a way of deflecting male criticism that the woman who "meddled" in political ideas necessarily desexed herself; it also developed, as Elizabeth Blackmar has argued, as a language that permitted the wives of upwardly mobile, entrepreneurial men to account for their household responsibilities as productive, even civic, duties requiring them to supervise working-class women as domestic workers.[74]

In the early republic, to claim the role of the republican mother was to claim a role of expanded scope, to claim powers of mind that most men denied women had, and to claim convictions and resolution of which most men thought women incapable.[75] But as used in the twentieth century, women's domestic duties were understood not as a way by which women might make claims on the state, but as an obligation overriding the claims the state might make upon women's time and energy. George Wickersham, partner in the elite law firm of Wickersham and Taft in New York, and appointed by Herbert Hoover as chairman of the National Commission on Law Observance and Enforcement, observed that "women . . . have other duties that seem to me to rise far beyond the heights of serving on juries, and these I think should not be interfered with by the requirement to do what men can do without serious interference with the most important primary occupations they have in life."[76]

In 1924, Jennie Loitman Barron sought to dismiss the objection based on household obligation. First, she observed, nearly 20 percent of adult women worked for pay, and the ease or difficulty with which they could perform jury service was comparable to that experienced by their male counterparts; indeed, since women's wages were already low, there was less contrast between their wages and "the compensation they receive as jurors." As for looking after babies, those with real child-care responsibilities could be excused for cause, just the way men with professional responsibilities were, but the " 'babies' of many women are school teachers, clerks, doctors, and in our stores and factories. These babies probably would not miss mother's care more than usual." Those women who enjoyed household help could substitute jury service for a bridge party or two; those who lacked household help could use their pay as jurors to hire someone in their absence. But, most important, although women already left their homes frequently for clubs, for volunteer work, and for waged labor, Barron wrote ruefully, "grace and charm have not departed from the American home; family life has not been destroyed . . . children have not gone, in greater numbers than before, breakfastless to school. There is no recorded increase in the burning of soups."[77]

In 1944 and 1945 tragic headlines of war news were interspersed with a titillating series of articles about juries which brought the issue of women jurors to national attention. One series of trials involved fifty-four-year-old Charlie Chaplin, who, on the eve of his marriage to his fourth wife, eighteen-year-old Oona O'Neill, was faced with a paternity suit by Joan Barry, an aspiring actress. The Justice Department added a federal suit charging him with a violation of the Mann Act, which prohibited taking women across state lines for "immoral purposes"—Barry and Chaplin had taken a train from New York to Los Angeles.[78] Chaplin and his attorneys made clear their belief that women jurors would be more sympathetic than male jurors to the uneasy plight of a male movie star, and more resistant to the image of a weeping Joan Barry on the witness stand.[79] A jury of seven women and five men did acquit Chaplin of violation of the Mann Act; but a jury of eleven women and one man—a selection that had made Chaplin's lawyers ecstatic—found him guilty in the paternity case.

While the Chaplin cases filled columns of newsprint, another series of trials that would have a far more significant impact on the law was proceeding in the same jurisdiction—the Federal District Court for the Southern District of California. The "I Am" movement believed that Guy and Edna Ballard and their son Donald were divine messengers for St. Germain, a French bishop who had died in A.D. 448. The Ballards, in the words of the court, claimed that they "had attained a supernatural state of self-immortality, which enabled them to be entirely free from ailments common to man and to conquer disease, death, old age, poverty and misery" and that "they could and would transmit that supernatural state to others willing to pay." Guy Ballard died before the trial, but Edna Ballard, her son, and a number of their colleagues were charged with mail fraud for soliciting substantial amounts of money as "love gifts" to the movement (since the end of the world was coming, individuals would no longer need money), and for selling charts, books, and pictures purporting to show a visitation of St. Germain to Guy Ballard. The group claimed that their movement was religiously inspired and therefore protected under the First Amendment. They also claimed that the women defendants were being denied equal protection of the laws because women had been excluded from the group from which the members of the grand jury and trial jury had been drawn.[80]

As we have seen, the California legislature had admitted women to jury service in the state courts under its jurisdiction shortly after they were granted suffrage. But federal judges controlled the practices in their own courts, and no changes had been made in federal court practice. They readily admitted that the practice was a mere continuation of habit, "not traceable to any lack of proper accommodation for mixed juries" or to any other practical problem. "Back of the policy," observed the district judge inexplicably, "is also the conviction of many that as the federal jury is the common law jury, it must, of necessity, consist of men only." Edna Ballard and her colleagues charged that exclusion of women from jury lists in a federal district located in a state where women had long since served on juries was arbitrary, discriminatory, and a violation of the due process and equal protection clause of the Fifth Amendment. The Federal District Court decided that the only strict constitutional limitation on jury selection was *Strauder*'s prohibition of race discrimination. Although the California law had been changed from "men" to "persons" in order to make it *possible* for women to serve on juries, the use of women as jurors was not mandatory and was part of the discretionary power invested in the jury commissioner and the clerk of the court. The judge cited a 1928 California Supreme Court decision to the effect that "there is nothing in the state or Federal Constitutions, or in any statute, which guarantees one accused of a crime a trial by a jury *composed of men and women, or of only men, or of only women, or of any definite proportion of either sex*" (emphasis in original). As would often occur in these arguments, the judge lost track of whether it was the jury itself or the *pool* from which it had been selected that was at issue. Edna Ballard and her colleagues were addressing the issue of the pool, but the decision focused on the actual jury and insisted that she was claiming a favorable jury rather than an impartial one.[81]

The conviction was upheld by the U.S. Court of Appeals for the Ninth Circuit. The Ballards appealed to the Supreme Court; with some measure of irony, the Justice Department assigned a woman attorney, Beatrice Rosenberg, to argue the case against insisting that women be part of the jury pool.[82]

Justice William O. Douglas wrote a strong opinion for the 8–4 majority, reversing the conviction. It would be the last Supreme Court decision on the subject for fifteen years. Douglas quoted approvingly a dissenting judge in the Circuit Court of Appeals, who had been persuaded that Ballard was involved in a "mean and vile . . . conspiracy," but had nevertheless been willing to reverse because of

the exclusion of women from the jury pool. The judge had observed
that on religious matters, women had experiences so different from
men that they might well come to different conclusions: "the souls
of children in their infant and early adolescent bodies receive the first
and most lasting teaching of religious truths from their mothers. . . .
In the churches of all religions the numbers of women attendants on
divine service vastly exceed men." He thought that a woman juror
who was, perhaps, a Christian Scientist might have reasoned that Mrs.
Ballard's income was comparable to the "trust created by Mrs. Eddy
for the Christian Science Monitor."

Justice Douglas emphasized repeatedly that the Sixth Amendment
demand for an impartial jury, which had been interpreted, over the
years, to mean one drawn from a cross-section of the community, was
an issue of "basic democracy." He reiterated the Supreme Court's
ruling earlier that year that daily wage earners—as contrasted with
those who drew a weekly or monthly salary—could not be excluded
from juries, for wage earning was an obvious metaphor for class.[83]
Douglas' reasoning and his rhetoric caught national attention. His
opinion in *Ballard* would be repeatedly quoted in subsequent arguments and decisions. "If the shoe were on the other foot," Douglas
wrote, "who would claim that a jury was truly representative of the
community if all men were intentionally and systematically excluded
from the panel? The truth is that the two sexes are not fungible; a
community made up exclusively of one is different from a community
composed of both; the subtle interplay of influence of one on the
other is among imponderables. . . . [A] flavor, a distinct quality is lost
if either sex is excluded. The exclusion of one may indeed make the
jury less representative of the community than would be true if an
economic or racial group were excluded."[84]

Douglas' words would be repeated for thirty years. They offered
to reformers a promise of what they wanted to hear: exclusion of
women meant that something dangerous happened to the cross-
sectional quality that everyone agreed was essential to the proper jury.
"A distinct quality is lost," Douglas said; he challenged men to acknowledge that they would resist being judged by a jury fully composed of women. But it was also clear that Douglas' argument
proceeded from an assumption of an essential *difference* between men
and women—"the two sexes are not fungible"—and when feminists

of the 1970s read his decision, they were not at all certain it was one they welcomed. "What did he mean, 'a flavor'?" asked a young law student when she studied the opinion in the late 1960s.[85]

"We still had ten ladies' names left in the box"

Not long after midnight on September 20, 1957, the phone rang in the emergency room at the MacDill Air Force Base hospital. It was, testified Army captain Dr. Farid Karam at the trial, "a lady who said that she had her husband bleeding, and she wanted an . . . ambulance rushed in emergency."[86] John J. Howarth, a driver for the B. Marion Reed [Ambulance] Company was sent to 3003 Meadows Street, where he found Clarence Hoyt slumped "on the couch . . . bleeding from the head, one eye was almost closed, swollen, and he had vomited all over the floor and couch and everything." Howarth asked Gwendolyn Hoyt "if she wanted to go to the hospital with him, and she said, no, somebody had to take care of the children."[87] Clarence Hoyt was unconscious when Dr. Karam encountered him. Hoyt "smelled [of] alcohol and he was severely bleeding from two cuts, one over the forehead and the other was over . . . the left eye. . . . his eye was black and he had been bleeding from his nose, too, and he had a fracture of the nasal bone on the left side. . . . He was resisting even being taken to the X-ray and he . . . mumble[d] a few words uncomprehensibly, I couldn't understand." The chief of surgery, Captain Garth Dettinger, anticipated what the X-rays would show: "by gentle feeling of the area of the skull, you could feel the bone beneath moving, indicating that there was extensive fractures of the skull. . . . it was possible to move the nose about." At the trial, Dettinger would observe, "I had never seen as much damage in a patient who was still alive in my experience which extends back some twenty-one years."[88]

The only word which Clarence Hoyt could say was his last name. "I needed something to go by to treat him medically," Dr. Karam said at the trial, and asked an aide to dial the Hoyts' home. "And she said, 'Are you from the police?' And I told her, no, I was an officer at MacDill Air Force Base and I needed some information concerning the treatment of this patient, and she . . . said that she hit her husband several times with a bat."[89] That conversation triggered a phone call to the police, who quickly appeared with a photographer. Gwendolyn Hoyt let them in. "There was," Detective A. L. Ford said at the trial, "a damp area on the rug in the front of a sofa, and also on the sofa was dampness about the area, as if something had been just washed recently."[90] The police claimed the bat as evidence.

Now Gwendolyn Hoyt was a suspect. Accompanied by Detectives Ford and Raul Riveiro, she left her son at a friend's home, and went with them to the police station.[91]

"We asked her if she wished to give us a handwritten statement, and she stated that she did so," said Detective Ford at the trial.[92] The statement was on a printed form with blanks filled in with her name, the date, and the time—3:55 a.m.—and the standard paragraph: "having been warned of my constitutional rights, I understand that I need make no statement which might tend to incriminate me and that if I do, it may be used in court against me. No force or coercion has been used in obtaining the following statement." Since the attack took place nine years before the Supreme Court decision in *Miranda v. Arizona* that established rights of criminal suspects, no one was required to apprise Gwendolyn Hoyt of her right to remain silent, to call a lawyer or to have one appointed for her. At the trial, Judge Grayson asked Ford, "Did you exhibit any force or make any threats to her before you took this statement?"

"No," said Ford. "None whatever."

"Did you intimidate her in any fashion at all?"

"Not at all."

"Did she give the statement to you voluntarily and of her own free will?" Grayson asked.

"Yes, she did."[93]

After she signed the confession, Gwendolyn Hoyt was released on $100 bond.[94] But news of the event had already reached the press, and Tampa *Morning Tribune* reporter Bob Fellows quickly made his way to 3003 Meadows Street.[95] "Almost drugged by horror at the nightmare which had taken sudden possession of her life," Fellows wrote, striking the tone that would be characteristic of much of the newspaper reporting of the event, Hoyt "appear[ed] almost glad for someone to talk with."[96]

15. Newspapers emphasized the irony of a child's sporting
equipment as a lethal weapon. Two detectives examine the
baseball bat, September 21, 1957.

When Clarence Hoyt died on the evening of September 20, the
police returned; this time they brought Gwendolyn Hoyt to the
county jail.[97] By that time, Fellows' story had run in the *Tribune*, and
a friend who lived in the neighborhood called the jail. He wondered
if there was anything he could do; when he learned Hoyt had no
lawyer, he offered to call one.[98] Gwendolyn Hoyt was very lucky; her
attorney would undertake her defense with emotional commitment
and intellectual intensity.

Charles Jay Hardee, Jr., whom everyone, in the southern manner,
called C.J., was the same age as Gwendolyn Hoyt. His great-uncle
had been a governor of Florida in the early 1920s; his father was a
prominent lawyer who took segregation and class hierarchy for
granted, and expected that his talented son would one day reclaim
the governorship for the family.[99] After serving in the infantry during
the last years of World War II, and rising to the rank of sergeant
major, Hardee entered the University of Florida, an institution reserved for white men and staggered by the return of thousands of
veterans, many of them married.[100]

While Hardee studied law, anxieties about gender separation, international Communism, and racial segregation pervaded daily life

and often disrupted university politics. The state college for white women was more than 150 miles away in Tallahassee. Male students energetically—one sign read: "Life ain't normal. We want women" —and successfully demanded coeducation at both the university and the state college.[101] (The single black college in the state was already coeducational.) Accusations of Communist infiltration flourished in the late 1940s; at one point the association of Communism with attacks on segregation erupted in the demand that black faculty testify to their own support of segregation in order to clear themselves of charges of Communism. In C. J. Hardee's senior year—law was an undergraduate degree in those years in Florida—two black students sought admission to the law school. Their lawyer was simultaneously defending three black men who had almost been lynched in the central Florida town of Groveland, charged by a grand jury from which blacks had been completely excluded.[102]

Hardee's own politics developed along a considerably more liberal pattern than his father's, sustained as he was by the energy of Patricia Felsher, a smart and lively young woman from New Orleans. They married shortly before C.J.'s graduation, and worked hard for the liberal Democrat Claude Pepper in the bitter Senate campaign of 1950, to the dismay of C.J.'s family. "He was a fervid Democrat," Pat recalls. "We used to have records of labor songs. We read Eugene V. Debs. We just wallowed in that stuff." Pat was a Stevenson delegate at the National Democratic Convention in 1956; in 1958 C.J. would be elected president of the Young Democratic Clubs of Florida.[103] Pat, who had a teaching degree, gave birth to four children in five years. She found time to be active in the League of Women Voters, one of the few actively liberal organizations in Tampa in the 1950s, and she registered for jury service.[104]

After five years of practice with his father, C.J. formed a partnership with Truett Ott, who was older and somewhat more conservative. "We handled labor law in a time when it was dangerous to do that," says Dallas Albritton, who joined their firm after studying labor law with the distinguished jurist Louis Pollak at Yale. "You never wanted to be picked up for speeding or anything, because the cops would really have it out for you. Labor lawyers were hard to find in those days," says Albritton; "C.J. was a courageous man." The partnership of opposites was successful; at its height, Albritton says, they "made a lot of money. They had years when they made a quarter of a million *each* when that was *real* money." But they also did a substantial amount of pro bono work. "I used to kid him about taking this free case. Maybe half of what we did was either on a contingency basis or free."[105]

When Hardee agreed to defend Gwendolyn Hoyt, he asked Carl Durrance, who was practicing law in Tampa, to help him.[106] Durrance had been a year or two ahead of Hardee at the university, and he too had absorbed from his years there a skepticism about excluding broad categories of citizens from jury service. "We had that statute which did not permit women to serve," Durrance recalls now. "He and I both felt that was absolutely wrong."[107]

When Gwendolyn Hoyt came to trial in 1957, nearly 46,000 women made up 40 percent of the registered voters of Hillsborough County, but only 218 women had volunteered for jury service.[108] The actual process of compiling the pool of names from which the prospective jurors were pulled was so informal that it verged on the sloppy, and proved hard to reconstruct in later trial testimony. The inability of most of the participants to do simple arithmetic added to the confusion.

The Florida jury service statute, like those in many states, had always permitted, even required, that jury commissioners exercise a wide range of discretion in compiling jury lists. "In the selection of jury lists," the 1949 statute read, "only such persons as the selecting officers know, or have reason to believe, are law-abiding citizens of approved integrity, good character, sound judgment and intelligence, and who are not physically or mentally infirm, shall be selected for jury duty."[109] This discretion was widely used for keeping blacks off juries. Charged with finding black men of "integrity, good character, sound judgment and intelligence" in a segregated state in which whites assumed that none of these qualities were characteristic of blacks, jury commissioners throughout the South regularly placed in jury pools the names of a handful of black ministers, funeral directors, and perhaps a shopkeeper or two, and assumed that the entire African-American community was therefore represented on the jury. "We checked the list," Hillsborough County jury commissioner

James Lockhart explained at the beginning of the Hoyt trial, the vagueness of his criteria making clearer than he perhaps realized the discretion which the commissioners exercised. "They consider the age, the occupation, might be a freeholder, something along that line."[110] No one asked him what occupations the commissioners deemed unsuitable for jury service, or whether people who did not own property were generally taken off the jury lists. Indeed, the situation would become a crisis a few months after the Hoyt trial, when a jury panel of sixty names drawn for a trial included ten people who had been charged with crimes ranging from robbery, prostitution, being AWOL from the Army, and running the illegal gambling game known as bolita.[111]

When jury commissioners were given the opportunity to include women who registered willingness to serve, they also made their own interpretation of the law. The strategies used to place women's names on the jury lists had the effect of limiting women's presence on juries even more severely than the requirement of personal registration. Although the law said nothing about maximum age, Lockhart excluded everyone over sixty-five; he also, without explanation, excluded all women who had signed up before 1952, leaving only thirty-five women in the pool. In his testimony, Lockhart implied that he thought that women who had registered in the immediate aftermath of the passage of the law were politically identified with the campaign for change and were therefore not trustworthy. He also implied that he thought they were too old to serve.[112] "The same women were then called over and over for jury duty," Carl Durrance recalls. "But few ever served. It was a foregone conclusion the state would not permit any woman to serve on this jury, and the state had ten peremptory challenges."[113]

It was the practice of county jury commissioners to establish a list of 3,000 names of male voters from which panels of sixty would be called to appear for each jury trial; from those sixty the actual six-person jury would be selected. In 1955 the Florida legislature required that this basic list be expanded to 10,000 names, and the first long list was developed in 1956. The list that was used to choose the jury for the Hoyt trial began as a list of 10,000 names compiled in 1956. Over the course of 1956, between 2,500 and 3,000 names were drawn for use in trials. In 1957 it was necessary to replenish the list.

"I used the list from my card index file that I'd made in 1956 and added approximately 2,500 names," said Katherine McPhillips, who worked in the office of the clerk of the Circuit Court. ". . . I went back two or three, four years, and noticed how many women they had put on before and I put on approximately the same number . . . Mr. Lockhart told me at one time to go back approximately two or three years to get the names because there were no recent women that had signed up." McPhillips added no new women's names. "We just used the ones we had," said McPhillips. "We had ten women in the 7,000 left that had not served. . . . So we did not take their names out of the box, or out of the file that we use to compile the list. . . . we still had ten ladies' names left in the box from the 1956 list." Asked how she distinguished between men's and women's names, McPhillips said that she looked over the full list of 10,000, and checked the names that looked like female ones against the original list of 218 that were already in the women's special registration book. Judge Lawrence A. Grayson, who presided at the Hoyt trial, agreed that it was not always easy to tell from the name alone whether a person was male or female. "Of course, when they came in the court-room, I readily caught on."[114] When a panel of jurors was drawn from a box of 3,000 men's names and 35 women's names—a box, that is, in which 1.2 percent were the names of women—it came as no surprise that all 60 were men.

When Hardee and Durrance moved to dismiss the jury panel on the ground that the Florida statute on jury service denied Gwendolyn Hoyt her constitutional right to a fair trial, Judge Grayson denied the motion, partly on the grounds that given an eligibility list of 68,000 male jurors and 218 women, the 10,000 names in the jury box represented "about 27 percent of the eligible women and about 15 percent of the eligible men, so I believe, percentagewise, . . . that there certainly isn't any discrimination of the nature of which you complain."[115] Four years later, law clerk Timothy B. Dyk, preparing a memo for Chief Justice Earl Warren, observed acidly, "The trial judge . . . was not a very good mathematician."[116] The correct figure for the women was 4.6 percent. As for whether the Florida jury ser-vice statute was constitutional, Grayson maintained that the claim was so basic that "we ought to have the Appellate Court first to declare the act unconstitutional, if it is unconstitutional."[117]

Lawrence Ayres Grayson had recently been reelected for the third time to the Criminal Court bench by the largest majority ever given a candidate for public office in Hillsborough County.[118] Even now, lawyers in Tampa are cautious about what they say about Grayson, but everyone begins by mentioning that he was born in Virginia; despite more than thirty years among Tampa's elite, Grayson continued to be perceived as something of an outsider.

Grayson was, Durrance observes carefully now, "a man of very strong feelings and opinions." Durrance gives his infectious grin. "One thing that made me what I felt was a good lawyer, [in his courtroom] I felt I had to fight *both* the judge and the prosecutor."[119] Once, trying three teenagers charged with burning a cross, Grayson asserted, "As far as I'm concerned the KKK and the NAACP are just alike—regardless of what some cockeyed newspaper editors may say."[120] The death of Clarence Hoyt shared headlines with Eisenhower's sending troops into Little Rock. Grayson ordered the bailiff to open his court that day by declaiming: "Hear ye, hear ye, hear ye, the Criminal Court of Record of Hillsborough County is in session. God save the United States of America, the great state of *Arkansas*, and this honorable court."[121] When, after months of planning, Tampa merchants carefully and quietly desegregated their stores, Grayson canceled his accounts.[122] Long after the county courthouse had been desegregated, blacks and whites sat separately in Grayson's courtroom. He endorsed public humiliation and whippings for juvenile delinquents, wife beaters and nonsupporting husbands. In his decision on Gwendolyn Hoyt, he gratuitously threw in his own opinions: "Throughout our entire history . . . women have been treated as superior to men, until they sought to get equal rights and got brought down to our level. They are now our equals and no longer our superiors."

No bar association ever censured Grayson; indeed the year after the Hoyt trial he was elected the first president of the Criminal Court of Record Judges Association, a group of judges from nine Florida counties. In 1961, when Grayson died of a heart attack, editorial writers remembered the occasions on which he had stood up for freedom of the press and memorialized him as "honest and courageous," "a firm fighter for those principles and causes in which he believed," and a man who would be known for his "satiric and trenchant commentaries on the politics of our time."[123]

The opening of the Hoyt trial commanded large headlines in Tampa, but went uncovered in the papers of St. Petersburg, twenty-two miles away on the other side of Tampa Bay. The St. Petersburg *Times* had its own sensational trial to cover, one of "a handsome French war hero for the murders of a retired Army general and the general's wife," whom he had served as "chauffeur-companion."[124] "It is obvious to the spectators," observed the St. Petersburg *Times* reporter, "that the sad loneliness which surrounds this man from France would appeal to the mother instinct in women." For this trial, the defense wanted women on the jury and it would—briefly—have its chance; when thirty-nine names were drawn for a jury panel in the Pinellas County courthouse, on the very same day as the all-male Hoyt panel was being drawn, six of the names belonged to women.

As recently as the previous year, the process of women's registration for jury service in St. Petersburg and its suburb of Clearwater had been the same as that across the bay in Tampa. As in Hillsborough County, registrations had dropped off in Pinellas County after the first wave of enthusiasm; by 1956 only 248 women had registered.[125] In 1955 the state legislature required the expansion of jury lists to 10,000 names. In Tampa, Lockhart had taken the position that only ten of those names needed to be those of women. In Clearwater, Circuit Court clerk Avery Gilkerson took a different position: if new names had to be added to his list, Gilkerson was determined that half of them should be women's.

Avery Gilkerson had an expansive definition of his job as clerk of the Circuit Court—officially he was "recorder of deeds, collector of delinquent taxes, accountant to the County Commission, county treasurer, clerk of the Pinellas Water and Navigation Control Authority." Unofficially he "cherished" his role as "public watchdog"; he was known for refusing to pay bills incurred by county commissioners until he was persuaded they had legal authority for incurring them. Gilkerson understood that his most likely recruits were the many newcomers to the state, women who had been accustomed to jury service in their former residence, and who were much more likely than native-born Floridians to vote for Gilkerson's Republican Party.[126] He formed a women's committee for jury service, chaired by the president of the local League of Women Voters, another woman who had long been active in civic clubs, and himself. Over a single weekend, the committee called 230 ministers, asking them to urge church women to volunteer, and 550 women's civic, church, and school groups. The first substantive response to their appeal was from a black minister, the Reverend C. A. Strickland of the Negro Baptist Evangelist Church, who came in with a list of church women who were likely to volunteer.[127] Within a month, Gilkerson's campaign had yielded more than 1,000 women's names, and registrations of women were continuing at an average rate of seventeen a day. Pinellas County soon had more women jurors registered than any other in the state.[128]

It had, in short, been no accident that six women's names were in the jury pool for the French war hero's trial. Six women delighted the defense, but appalled the prosecution, which used its peremptory challenges against them. After the first few had been dismissed, "the women when called were not even bothering to rise and enter the jury box. They awaited the challenge with a smiling expectancy. It came. The calling of the roll of the . . . jurors . . . provided a touch of humor in the otherwise tense proceedings." Judge John U. Bird, "a courteous gentleman of the old school, felt obliged to explain to the women jurors, 'This is no reflection on the ladies. We'll get you on cases later.'" The reporter observed, "To the layman, the strategy of defense attorney Harry Fogle in trying to get women on the jury seemed like a switch on something out of a pocketbook thriller: Where the defense seeks an all-male jury and then puts its beautiful defendant with (always) lovely legs on the stand."[129]

Across the bay in Tampa, Hardee and Durrance were trying to avoid becoming "a pocketbook thriller." Though their defendant fully met the qualifications for sensationalist reporting—she was young and attractive enough that a reporter would subsequently be fired for illicitly selling one of the newspaper's photographs of her to *Front Page Detective*, a pulp magazine—Hardee and Durrance went directly against the grain of what was generally understood to be the common view of the matter.[130] The shared wisdom at the time recommended that if a lawyer were representing an attractive young woman, there should be as many men jurors, old or young, as possible. Younger men were expected to be drawn to her beauty, and older men to feel protective. (Indeed, at the trial the prosecutor would specifically warn the jurors against the sympathy they would normally feel for "a lady in trouble.") Most lawyers agreed that women, whom they expected to be jealous of beauty, were to be strenuously avoided as jurors in cases where sympathy was needed for a female.[131]

Hardee and Durrance wanted women jurors. Gwendolyn Hoyt would claim in her own defense that she had killed her husband "out of passion." Hardee and Durrance argued that she would be discriminated against "if forced to trial by jury with an all-male panel who do not have the same passions and understanding of females and their feelings as other women would have." She was entitled to be tried by a jury drawn from a list with the same proportion of female names as on the voting lists.[132] But there was no Avery Gilkerson in Hillsborough County.

The Hillsborough County courthouse has not been substantially remodeled since Gwendolyn Hoyt was tried there. The large, squat white building spreads across two square city blocks in central Tampa. Its facade is aluminum Art Deco; inside, the wood-paneled courtrooms are large and windowless. In 1957 the courthouse was still segregated and inhospitable to African-Americans; although the courtroom was packed, Jeanette Durrance remembers no blacks in the crowd.[133] Gwendolyn Hoyt's trial opened on December 17; the Tampa *Times* gave it three-column banner headlines: "Mrs. Hoyt Testifies She Was Scorned." Three days of what the *Times* called "bitter and intimate" testimony followed.[134]

The county solicitor who conducted the prosecution was Paul Johnson, a conservative Democrat, one of the established circle of courthouse regulars. As Johnson's seniority in the position grew and he could make choices about which cases he would try, he sought out murder cases. "I tried most of the murder cases," Johnson reflected more than thirty years later, "because I felt murder is the type of crime you can never restore." If C. J. Hardee was driven by moral conviction, so was Johnson. Indeed, Johnson believed that the original

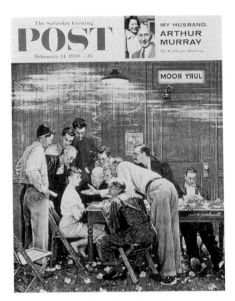

16. "The Holdout," by Norman
Rockwell, implied that young women
could not be counted upon to engage in
reasoned argument in the jury room.

charge of first-degree murder—vulnerable to capital punishment—
was appropriate; "the husband was induced to come over" from
Homestead to Tampa, suggesting the premeditation that distinguishes first-degree murder from the lesser charge that Gwendolyn
Hoyt faced.[135]

After the challenge to the jury failed, the trial turned to the question of whether Hoyt was guilty of second-degree murder. On the
stand, Gwendolyn Hoyt testified to the unpredictability of the onset
of her epileptic episodes. She described domestic violence the previous July, when Clarence had been in "a rage and he started to throw
things around in the kitchen . . . and then he went after me and he
tore my dress off and I tried to run out of the house and he went
and he got me and he twisted my arm . . . and he started to choke
me and said he would kill me." Durrance did not pursue the topic.
Johnson, cross-examining, avoided the topic, observing mildly, "Your
marriage was not working out too successfully. Is that pretty much
the sum and substance of your testimony? . . . In other words, you
all would have problems and then you would reconcile and then you

would have other problems?" There was testimony from competing psychiatrists, unsuccessful efforts of the defense to introduce testimony from Clarence Hoyt's Air Force associates, and successful efforts of the prosecution to introduce hearsay evidence from a babysitter that Gwendolyn Hoyt had spent the night with a man in a hotel the week before the murder.[136] Years later, both Paul Johnson, the county solicitor, and Dallas Albritton, then a young partner with the firm of Hardee & Ott, recalled their belief that the babysitter's testimony had been crucial in undermining Gwendolyn Hoyt's credibility.[137]

It took the six-man jury only twenty-five minutes to convict Gwendolyn Hoyt of second-degree murder; on January 20, 1958, she was sentenced to imprisonment at hard labor for thirty years.[138]

Hardee and Durrance appealed. They claimed that the constraints placed on women's jury service had deprived Hoyt of her rights under the Sixth and Fourteenth amendments to a jury drawn from a pool from which women had not been excluded. While the appeal was pending, and Hoyt was free on bail, she sent her son to stay with relatives in Massachusetts, and C.J. invited her to stay in a small apartment over the detached garage on his home property. She sometimes cared for the Hardee children when C.J. and Pat went out.[139] The Supreme Court of Florida sustained the conviction, primarily because the basic list "did contain some names of women who had registered for jury service." In his opinion, Judge E. Harris Drew situated women's "household duties" as their "primary responsibility" and placed those duties in conflict with their public service. He did not think that excusing women from jury service implied that they were incapable of it. As he put it:

> Whatever changes may have taken place in the political or economic status of women in our society, nothing has yet altered the fact of their primary responsibility, as a class, for the daily welfare of the family unit upon which our civilization depends. . . . [To excuse them from jury service recognizes] that such demands might place an unwarranted strain upon the social and domestic structure, or result in unwilling participation.[140]

Judge T. Frank Hobson, who also served on the Florida Supreme Court, declined at first to question the constitutionality of the Florida statute. But he criticized the practice of permitting a clerk, rather than the jury commissioner himself, to choose the names for the pool. And he severely criticized Grayson's conduct of the trial, particularly the introduction of "purely hearsay testimony" about Gwendolyn Hoyt's date with a man and their use of a baby-sitting agency to care for her son while they went out. Although it was true that she had been depicting her husband as "a flagrant philanderer," Hobson thought it was "recrimination," not "rebuttal," to try in this way to place Gwendolyn Hoyt's own character at issue.[141]

Hardee petitioned for a rehearing; in April 1960 the Florida Supreme Court turned him down, but Hobson had had time to reflect on his partial concurrence. Now he was prepared to say flatly that the Florida law was unconstitutional and that Gwendolyn Hoyt had not been "confronted by a jury of her peers." Hobson wrote a dissenting opinion that caught most of the issues that Hardee wanted to raise: women were a "class . . . discriminated against by the statutory limitation"; with their entry into "business and professional life," the traditional reason for exclusion as a class—their duties as homemakers—no longer existed; finally, if the Florida law on women's jury service was constitutional, "then we must hold that the legislature could validly require all women to serve but limit male service to volunteers and thus, in effect, create an all-female jury system."[142]

But even Hobson, describing the night of September 18 sympathetically, had only stereotypes to deploy to capture the emotions of that evening.

> . . . she became emotionally upset, as would forsooth even a *normally stable* wife under such circumstances. The record clearly shows Mrs. Hoyt was far from "normally stable"; indeed she was, at least, neurotic if not psychotic.
>
> The oft repeated quotation "Heaven has no rage like love to hatred turned, Nor hell a fury like a woman scorned" has been accepted as apodictic throughout the ages.[143]

"The only bulwark between chaos and an organized and well-run family unit is our woman of the day"

Gwendolyn Hoyt returned to her mother's home in Massachusetts. Hardee was determined to appeal to the Supreme Court, but he was not certified to plead before it; moreover, it would be difficult for a lawyer in Florida to conduct the appeal with the defendant a thousand miles away. Hoyt's minister consulted his friends for advice about a new lawyer, and they led him to Herbert Ehrmann, of the prominent Boston firm of Goulston & Storrs.[144]

After graduation from Harvard, Ehrmann was unable to find work in a law firm (possibly because he was Jewish).[145] He began instead as a Legal Aid lawyer, working at first without pay, and throughout his life he would be responsive to people who needed help.[146] Ehrmann's most notable service was as junior counsel in the defense of Sacco and Vanzetti.[147] The experience would mark Ehrmann and his wife, Sara Rosenfeld Ehrmann, for life, setting their identities as supporters of the vulnerable and opponents of state violence. Shortly before he was executed, Vanzetti presented to her a necklace which a fellow prisoner had made in the prison workshop; for the rest of her long life Sara Ehrmann would be a prominent opponent of the death penalty.[148] Each year the Massachusetts Civil Liberties Union now bestows the Sara Ehrmann Award on the person who has done the most to undermine the death penalty.[149] At Goulston & Storrs, a firm founded by Jewish lawyers, Herbert Ehrmann continued to be notable for his interest in pro bono cases; in 1943 he defended several Jewish boys arrested during anti-Semitic disturbances in Dorchester, a Boston neighborhood.[150]

When he agreed to help Gwendolyn Hoyt, Ehrmann had never actually argued a case before the U.S. Supreme Court—his first would come in 1960, and he would lose.[151] Ehrmann undertook Hoyt's defense pro bono; it was understood that her minister would raise money for the expenses. Because he would be busy as president of the American Jewish Committee, Ehrmann hired a young lawyer to work with him.

Raya Spiegel Dreben had graduated from Radcliffe in 1949. Be-

17. Herbert B. Ehrmann, mid-1960s. Inscribed to Raya Dreben.

cause Harvard Law School did not then admit women, she had entered Columbia. The following year Harvard decided to admit women, but when Dreben applied she was told they would not accept transfer students. She was eventually admitted; she graduated high in her class in 1954. After a federal clerkship and a period as a teaching fellow at Chicago Law School—where she met Harry Kalven, but was not involved in the Chicago Jury Project that he led—she returned to Boston. The opportunities for women lawyers in Boston in the late 1950s—even those who had come out first on the state bar examination and held distinguished postgraduate appointments— were dismal, generally limited to staff positions in insurance companies or in real estate law. Neither option intrigued Dreben, whose

18. Raya Dreben, mid-1960s.

law school peers had moved directly into entry positions in major law firms. She had young children. "I offered my part-time services *free*," she says now, still amazed, "to legal aid and voluntary defenders. They turned me down." When Ehrmann asked a friend if he knew a good lawyer who was available on a part-time basis, Dreben welcomed the chance. At Goulston & Storrs, her name would not be on the door. "I had to write letters to clients on stationery that had every name in the firm on it except for mine. It was humiliating." Only a decade before, she recalls, "some Boston law firms had placed typewriters on the desks of women lawyers, so that visiting clients would take them for secretaries. It was less embarrassing to the firm than to admit that they had actually hired women attorneys."[152]

Although Ehrmann met occasionally with Gwendolyn Hoyt, he turned over to Dreben most of the work of preparing the case for the Supreme Court.[153] She had no staff apart from modest secretarial help. For assistance in making the argument that it was anachronistic to excuse women from central obligations of modern society, she turned outside the profession, to Barbara Miller Solomon, a historian who was developing the fledgling Radcliffe Women's Archive, and Esther Peterson, head of the Women's Bureau of the Department of

Labor in Washington.[154] Reflecting now on what goes into the making of a case that could convince the Supreme Court to break a long-standing precedent, Dreben muses, "It's chance. It's chance and money. Now you have women justice projects [like the Women's Rights Project at the ACLU]. If this had happened later, after feminist issues had been articulated more publicly, I would have had more assistance."[155]

She did have C. J. Hardee, who continued to send helpful advice.[156] Their work together was facilitated by the speed of the U.S. mail in the 1950s, which delivered Dreben's letters from Boston to Tampa on the following day. Hardee was determined that others understand the significance of Gwendolyn Hoyt's case. "I have had a notion," he wrote modestly to Ehrmann, "that if the argument were clearly presented to the major public interest organizations which logically ought to be expected to be interested in the affair, namely the American Civil Liberties Union, the League of Women Voters and the American Association of University Women, they might see fit to take our case as a test case."[157]

Raya Dreben framed the requests and conducted the correspondence. To the original three groups she added twelve others, including the National Federation of Business and Professional Women, the American Bar Association and its Boston chapter; the National Association of Women Lawyers.[158] With only one exception, all replied that they wished Raya Dreben well but they could not possibly get involved.[159] "The League worked hard," wrote Virginia Smith, the president of the Florida League of Women Voters, to get the 1949 permissive jury service statute passed. "Since 1949 nothing has been done by the Florida League in this area or in any area that involves the status of women." Pitting the politically conscious Miami women against the less committed Tampa counterparts, Smith sniffed: "In Dade County, where I live, there do not seem to be any administrative difficulties at all . . . League members in this County have been urged to register for jury duty and a great many have. . . . Of course, I do not know what goes on in Hillsborough County, but we have had no complaint from the Tampa League."[160] The president of the Mississippi League of Women Voters reported that her organization had been seeking legislation "permitting women to serve on juries," but for six years it had either not emerged from committee or, if passed by one house, was defeated by the other. "If Florida women are not called for jury service then it must be because the majority do not wish to be called, which is one of the main reasons we have not met with success in Mississippi."[161]

The single exception was the American Civil Liberties Union. Rowland Watts had moved from the Workers Defense League to become the ACLU's general counsel, and he quickly responded that "of course" the ACLU was interested and predicted that the executive committee of the ACLU would quickly "agree that we should appear amicus."[162] The filing of a "friend of the court" brief was a more rare occurrence in 1959 than it has since become. The ACLU had never before filed an amicus brief in a sex discrimination case.[163] In its entire history, the Supreme Court had accepted only a very few cases in which sex discrimination was claimed—two, *Muller v. Oregon* (1908) and *Adkins v. Children's Hospital* (1923), explicitly requested protective treatment, and the Court had upheld only *Muller*. The others—*Bradwell, Goesaert*, and a few more—which asked for equal treatment, had failed to persuade the Court. Indeed, as recently as 1947, the Supreme Court had ruled that New York's practice of offering women the option not to serve on "blue ribbon" juries if they were called was not a denial of equal treatment under the law.[164] By the time Raya Dreben was ready to file her brief for equal treatment, it was accompanied by one written by Dorothy Kenyon for the ACLU.

When she entered the case, Dorothy Kenyon had been an articulate exponent of women's right to serve on juries—and of the need of defendants to have women on their juries—for more than thirty years. Born in 1888 to a wealthy New York family—her father and two brothers were leading patent lawyers—Dorothy Kenyon had graduated from Smith in 1908 and from New York University School of Law in 1919. The first word that comes to mind to describe her career is "feisty." In 1922 she and a woman colleague set up their own independent practice; when in 1937 the New York Bar Association, worrying more about its tax status than about equal opportunity, finally admitted women, Kenyon was among the first fourteen women admitted. Mayor Fiorello La Guardia appointed her to a short term as municipal court judge; for the rest of her life she was often referred to as "Judge Kenyon."[165] She had been a member of the ACLU board of directors since 1931. As early as 1959 Kenyon was leading the ACLU toward supporting the legalization of abortion on the grounds that "women have a right to choose what shall happen to their bodies."[166]

Throughout the 1920s and 1930s Kenyon had been prominent in the efforts of New York women's groups to pass a jury service statute.[167] She had once interrupted an off-Broadway play in which a mock jury was selected from the audience and insisted that women should be included too.[168] As chance would have it, she was among the women included when women's names were drawn in New York for the first time.[169] In her files were texts of at least a dozen speeches she had given defending equal jury service for men and women. It was an easy matter for Kenyon to respond to Raya Dreben's plea.[170]

Kenyon quickly completed her draft; sending it to Watts, she offered not only to trim some of its verbiage but also to expand its argument on women's rights. Watts thought the brief was "both cogent and fun"; he was inclined to "expand and make this a major effort on behalf of women's rights."[171]

Although Goulston & Storrs handled the case pro bono, there were charges for secretarial expenses and for Ehrmann and Dreben's travel to Washington, D.C., for the argument before the Supreme Court, which Hoyt's minister and Bishop Henry Knox Sherrill, the former Episcopal Bishop of Massachusetts and recently retired Presiding Bishop of the Episcopal Church in the United States, worked hard to raise.[172] "I remember I bought a new hat for the occasion," Dreben says now. It was her first Supreme Court case. "And when I got there the sergeant at arms made me remove it; ladies didn't wear hats!" Hardee made the trip from Florida, and Ehrmann formally presented him to the bar of the Supreme Court.[173] Dorothy Kenyon was there, but she slipped out at the end, and Dreben did not meet her. Gwendolyn Hoyt had no money to come.

Ehrmann, Dreben, Hardee, and Kenyon went to Washington to try to persuade at least five Supreme Court justices to agree to an argument which had not been persuasive before. In what they said and what they chose to ignore, in the argumentative choices they made, both lawyers and judges revealed their assumptions about what were appropriate relations between men and women. What lawyers said

19. Dorothy Kenyon, Deputy Commissioner of Licenses, filing
for jury duty, September 1, 1937.

was shaped by the capacity of judges to hear what the attorneys were
trying to say. What counted as acceptable and reasonable argument
in 1961 was grounded in the social setting, in the time and culture
in which they all lived.

The four lawyers were not making an "acceptable" argument, nor
were they personally located in the mainstream of the profession.
Each may have seemed at first glance—and certainly to Gwendolyn
Hoyt—to be solidly part of a national professional community. But
each lived in some sense on its outer boundaries: Hardee as a liberal
labor lawyer in a conservative family and conservative political community, Ehrmann as a Jew who had experienced anti-Semitism and
as a defender of Sacco and Vanzetti, Dreben and Kenyon as women
in a profession that aggressively defined itself as male. Dreben's iden-

tity as a Jew and Kenyon's identity as a single woman marginalized them further. Even Dreben's doubt about whether to wear a hat suggests how far removed a woman lawyer was from the dress codes of her own profession, how uncertain of her place in it. The legal profession embedded its understanding of the proper relations of men and women into its institutional arrangements—bench, bar, and jury. There were only a handful of senior women judges, only two in federal courts.[174] No Supreme Court justice was accustomed to women as colleagues; no justice had yet hired a woman clerk. "My wife would object"; "My secretary would quit"—these reasons expressed the general sense that relationships among men were reliably professional ones, but relationships between men and women could not help but include an erotic component. To those who thought this way, having different rules for women's and men's jury service made sense, echoing as they did the different rules for employing male and female courtroom personnel.

Ehrmann and Dreben brought their argument to a Supreme Court that was one of the most distinguished in the nation's history. Less than seven years before, the Court had handed down its momentous decision in *Brown v. Board of Education*, pronouncing separate educational facilities for blacks and whites "inherently unequal" and a violation of the Fourteenth Amendment guarantees of equal protection. Even though the decision provided that changes should be made with "all deliberate speed," resistance was massive, ranging from passive resistance to mob violence and disrupting American society and politics for at least a decade. Perceiving that much of the credibility of the *Brown* decision would be lost if the Court did not seem to speak with a single voice, Warren and some of his colleagues went to extraordinary lengths to reach a consensus so that the decision would be a unanimous one. This quest for unanimity would characterize the Warren Court, which continued to take forthright stands on equal treatment unanimously or by wide margins.

But if the members of the Warren Court generally were certain that discrimination on the basis of race was not equal treatment under the law—that you could not have difference and equality at the same time—they were not at all certain that discrimination on the basis of sex was equally questionable. They lived in a culture that thought it had resolved the question by offering women the right to vote forty years before and had not subsequently entertained wide discussion of the matter. Separations on the basis of sex pervaded American society—from the way men and women dressed to single-sex schools to single-sex occupations. (In 1960 roughly 70 percent of working women had jobs in which a majority of other workers were female.[175]) Separation on the basis of sex was generally defined as marking women's privilege, not women's inferiority. William O. Douglas had written, as we have seen, an opinion sustaining the obligation of women to serve on juries, but Felix Frankfurter had written the opinion for *Goesaert v. Cleary* in 1948, when the Court ruled that if the state of Michigan wished to exclude all women from tending bar without the presence of a male bartender, even women who owned their own taverns, even in the knowledge that the statute had been initiated by a male bartenders' union, it was not a denial of equal treatment under law. Both men still sat on the Court.

As far as the state of Florida was concerned, the case was an easy one. The facts were not in dispute. Not unlike the fictional John Wright in Susan Glaspell's story, Clarence Hoyt had been lying on a couch, vulnerable to attack. "Her husband did not in any way harm her physically, threaten her with any form of violence, chastisement, upbraiding or punishment," observed Florida Assistant Attorney General George Georgieff. Maybe Clarence Hoyt had been exercising "superhuman control," wanting simply to end the marriage without further argument.[176] What Gwendolyn Hoyt really wanted, Georgieff said, was not justice, but favoritism. "She has no constitutional right to female friends on the jury."[177] " 'Impartiality' is a *state of mind*. Its existence or absence does not depend upon whether the juror is male, female, black, white or what have you."[178]

To the argument that times had changed since the Court's ruling in 1879 that it was reasonable to exclude women from jury service, and that women's suffrage, as well as their entry into a wide range of public activities rendered older assumptions anachronistic, Georgieff responded with a heartfelt entreaty:

Ever since the dawn of time conception has been the same. Though many eons may have passed, the gestation period in the

human female has likewise remained unchanged. Save and except for a number of beneficial precautions presently available,
parturition is as it well may have been in the Garden of Eden.
The rearing of children, even if it be conceded that the socio-
psychologists have made inroads thereon, nevertheless remains
a prime responsibility of the matriarch. The home, though it no
longer be the log cabin in the wilderness, must nevertheless be
maintained. The advent of "T.V." dinners does not remove the
burden of providing palatable food for the members of the family, the husband is still, in the main, the breadwinner, child's
hurts are, almost without exception, bound and treated by the
mother. . . . *The only bulwark between chaos and an organized and
well-run family unit is our woman of the day.* She and she alone
ministers to our wants and needs as the partner in marriage, the
mother in travail, and the healer and comforter during illness
and sadness.[179]

need women around to be women [handwritten margin note]

Hoyt was a spoiler; she was trying to have it both ways:

> If we again accept appellant's argument, we find that women
> have sought for many, many years to achieve the ultimate—the
> status of men. This appears, over the years, to have been based
> on their sincere belief in themselves as the equivalent of men.
> . . . in many respects, truly they are. That being so, must we not
> assume that inasmuch as she was tried by an all-male jury, she
> had attained the ultimate pinnacle to which she (as a member
> of our female body politic) had aspired[?][180]

Gwendolyn Hoyt's attorneys generally let the point of Clarence's
passivity at the moment of the attack ride. They could make no claim
that Gwendolyn Hoyt had struck her husband in immediate self-
defense. They could not connect what they knew of his violence in
the past to the events of the night of the attack lest they inadvertently
support a charge of premeditated murder in the first degree.[181] (The
more wide-ranging understanding of the potential for sex bias in the
law of self-defense, which feminist attorneys would pioneer in defense
of battered women, lay far in the future.[182]) Instead they argued that

the effects of her epilepsy *combined* with the normal response of a
woman to her husband's infidelity had triggered Hoyt's attack.

Since second-degree murder required an act "evincing a depraved
mind regardless of human life," wrote Ehrmann and Dreben, "the
issues before the all-male jury involved the determination of a woman's state of mind."[183] A defense framed this way needed women on
the jury to confirm that Gwendolyn Hoyt's had been a *woman's* response. It therefore seemed to be a denial of due process for Gwendolyn Hoyt to be tried by a jury that made an additional requirement
for women's service. To argue this point effectively, they had to stress
the *difference* between men and women.

Raya Dreben amused herself by taking an informal survey, asking
men of her acquaintance what they would think of a case in which a
man who had killed his wife in anger because she had found out about
his mistress was tried by an all-woman jury; every single one said that
such a trial would be unfair.[184] More formally, the defense used the
findings of a study by the Chicago Jury Project which, like the recent
work of Carol Gilligan, seemed to show that in jury deliberations
women exhibit "more social and emotional specialization," while men
are more "task-oriented"; that women "tend to play the role of me-
diators, and to break tensions more than men."[185] As a woman, Gwendolyn Hoyt had a right to women in the pool from which jurors were
drawn because women's distinctive emotional configuration would
make it more likely that women could understand her plea. In effect,
the defense had to call on stereotypes similar to those that the prosecution used, but deploy the stereotypes differently. It is not surprising that Georgieff reduced their argument to a plea for "female
friends."

But if the defense wanted to stress the difference between men and
women, they simultaneously wanted to stress equality; they needed
both halves of what Martha Minow has called the dilemma of difference.[186] For the heart of the defense case was that Gwendolyn Hoyt
had been denied her rights to equal treatment under law and to due
process. Equality, as the defense saw it, had two sides; equal capacity
and equal obligation. The prosecution—in between its arias about
home and mother—generally conceded equal capacity. But the defense had to establish that if the state, in its wisdom, wished to define
jury service as an obligation for men and a voluntary act for women

it was in violation of equal protection of the laws. If men and women were equal, why could women not permit men to speak for them? If women were a separate and different class, did fairness require that they be treated differently? Was not offering to women the privilege of easy exemption from jury service a recognition of that difference? Framing the question this way drove the discussion unavoidably toward the problem of how the equal right of women to *serve* as jurors was to be construed, and away from Gwendolyn Hoyt's right to be tried by a jury of her peers.[187] But Ehrmann was unable to control the oral argument during the free-for-all of the appearance before the Supreme Court. The questions by members of the Supreme Court—both to him and to Georgieff—largely focused on the issue of jury selection and whether jury service was open or closed to women. Ultimately Ehrmann burst out impatiently, "I am not here urging the right of women to serve on juries. I am arguing the right of my client not to serve thirty years at hard labor!"—but it was no use.[188] The arguments—both written and oral—kept drifting back.

The defense would have to find a way to resolve the difference dilemma. The argument from equality was relatively easy to make *if* it were conceded that registration was a barrier to service and not an advantage. Exclusion of women from jury service, Kenyon wrote, "does great injustice to the female defendant (as in the case at bar) who so badly needs the *diffused impartiality* of a jury drawn from all segments of our society, emphatically including women." But the exemption of women, wrote Kenyon, also "works a real hardship on the male juryman upon whom a greater burden of service is placed than would otherwise be the case."[189] The trouble was that the prosecution would not make that concession, but instead insisted that registration was evidence of chivalric protection of women. If women were so anxious to serve, sneered Georgieff in oral argument, there was nothing to prevent all 46,000 women voters in Hillsborough County from trooping in to register their willingness with the clerk of the court.

The argument from difference was hard to make because the defense had trouble specifying of what the difference consisted. The defense groped for an answer, but were left with imponderables: "Does it not shock our sense of fair play that, because a few young women with small babies at home might find it inconvenient to come to court to hear her case (and of course they would not have to because the Judge would excuse them), this woman should be deprived of even one single woman on her jury!" wrote Kenyon. Dreben could only say that Hoyt's "concern for her child, her despair and frustration at her inability to attract her husband, and her burst of fury when her husband announced his intention to leave are circumstances best or perhaps only understood by a woman." The best they could do was to follow William O. Douglas in *Ballard*, by calling women's emotions into the service of her equality. Douglas had said that a jury made up of women was different from a jury of men and women, but he could not say why it was different, conceding that "the subtle interplay of influence one on the other is among the imponderables."[190] Neither, it would soon appear, could his colleagues on the Supreme Court in 1961.

When the nine justices entered the courtroom, five—Justices Potter Stewart, Charles Whittaker, John Marshall Harlan, Tom Clark, and Felix Frankfurter—were disposed to let the decision of the Florida Supreme Court stand. But a proposal to deny Hoyt's appeal required six votes, not five, and four justices—William Brennan, William O. Douglas, Hugo Black, and Chief Justice Earl Warren—had refused to dismiss.[191] If that division held after the oral argument, Hoyt would still have lost, but by a 5–4 decision.

When he entered the courtroom to hear the case, Chief Justice Earl Warren had already read a memo drafted for him by his clerk Timothy B. Dyk, who excoriated Grayson's calculations, emphasized the arbitrariness of the Florida system, and recommended that Warren vote to overturn the decision in *Hoyt*.[192]

But Dyk felt a duty to articulate every possible argument in favor of the state law; under the standards of review prevailing at the time, the state needed only to demonstrate that the distinctions between men and women that it was making had a rational basis. (Not until the mid-1970s would the Supreme Court require that states that wished to discriminate on the basis of sex had the burden of demonstrating that discrimination is "substantially related" to an important governmental objective.) Dyk, who has made a distinguished career practicing appellate law with a particular interest in First Amendment issues, and who now works collegially with professional women, is still rueful about what he wrote next: although he personally was more comfortable with a system in which all women were called for jury duty but excused upon request, he made the argument that *total* exclusion of women could be "constitutionally permissible." He went on: "Curiously, I think that this statute is the more arbitrary because it permits women to volunteer for jury duty. There are a number of justifications for excluding women altogether: their educational level may not be considered to be as high as that of men; *permitting them to serve on juries may encourage lax performance of their domestic chores*" (emphasis mine). Thus, like Georgieff in his oral argument and, as we shall see, Harlan in his written opinion, even Dyk felt obligated to mention that the state might have an interest in enforcing women's "performance of their domestic chores"; if the obligation of jury service would interfere with that performance, or contribute to its being performed sloppily, or in a "lax" manner, then the state might reasonably refuse to make jury service obligatory. What was the passage doing there? "Well . . . I had only started to work for the Chief Justice in August. Probably I didn't want to seem to be too much of a radical. I'd like to think there was some irony in the way the argument was articulated." He grins. "If I expected the Chief Justice to get it I was optimistic."[193]

In accordance with an old tradition, no one accompanies the justices of the Supreme Court into the private conference in which they vote on the cases they have heard. But often individual justices keep notes of the conferences, and sometimes these notes survive. Douglas' notes of the conference on Gwendolyn Hoyt's case remain among his papers in the Library of Congress. They provide a glimpse of the opening of the conference, conveying to us the positions that the justices, speaking in order of seniority, brought into the room.

As usual, the Chief Justice began. *Hoyt*, said Warren, involves women jurors in criminal cases; he was prepared to reverse the Florida Supreme Court's decision, perhaps on narrow grounds. Florida had "limited women['s] service to ¹⁄₁₀ of one percent—that is tantamount to taking them out." It was not necessary "to get at the section itself and knock it down" because "the subject is dying—only three states keep women off." Hugo Black was also prepared to reverse; he thought it was a "denial of equal protection."

But then it was Felix Frankfurter's turn, and his warm friendship with Ehrmann, which went back to the days of Sacco and Vanzetti, was not enough to convert him to Ehrmann's arguments. Frankfurter had dissented in *Ballard*, and in that case a statute had actually excluded women. He did not think *Hoyt* was analogous to "the Mexican case"—*Hernandez*, in which all hourly workers had been excluded as a way of keeping working-class people off a jury. In Florida women's "exclusion" was more problematic. All the social and demographic data that Dreben had included, all the testimony to changes in women's lives, failed to persuade Frankfurter; when that sort of material had been included in the *Goesaert* briefs, he had observed, "The Constitution does not require legislatures to reflect sociological insight, or shifting social standards."[194] Although six years after *Goesaert*, in 1954, Frankfurter had been part of a unanimous court in declaring that shifting social standards made continued segregation of the public schools unconstitutional, he had had to persuade himself that on this matter he should not defer to legislative discretion. On sex discrimination, he was now prepared to let legislatures follow their own tastes; there had been, he thought, "no systematic exclusion."

Douglas—who had written the majority opinion in *Ballard* and had been among the dissenters in *Goesaert*—was prepared to reverse in *Hoyt*. Three of the four most senior justices were prepared to say that Hardee had been right to challenge Florida law and to agree that Gwendolyn Hoyt's jury had been improperly selected.

But Tom Clark and John Marshall Harlan said they agreed with Frankfurter, and William Brennan "affirm[ed] tentatively." Charles Whittaker observed that if the clerk had "arbitrarily left women out" he would reverse, "but this was not purposeful or systematic"—that is, the foul-up of the clerk in Hillsborough County who added only ten women's names could be separated from the registration requirement; Potter Stewart agreed with Whittaker. Somewhere along the way Brennan removed "tentative" from his vote to affirm, and the alignment stood at 6–3.[195]

"The Chief Justice," Dyk observes now, "put an enormous emphasis on justices getting together and not being divisive. . . . Even in 1961 you were still getting complaints about Brown." And they knew that other major civil rights issues would be facing them; within a single year they faced two decisions nearly as controversial as *Brown* had been. The Court was so divided on *Baker v. Carr*, which required redistricting to reflect the principle of one person, one vote, that it asked for reargument on October 9, 1961, less than two weeks before *Hoyt*. A few weeks after hearing *Hoyt*, it decided to accept *Engel v. Vitale* on the constitutionality of prayer in public schools. When the Court decided such prayer was unconstitutional, "the mail attacking it was the largest in the Court's history," writes Bernard Schwartz.[196]

In that context, the problem that faced Warren was whether the 6–3 lineup was worth spending limited moral capital to announce when he believed "the subject is dying." Although Warren and Douglas and some other justices occasionally took positions skeptical of arbitrary discrimination between men and women, the Court's agenda for the expansion of the principle of equal protection did not extend—as Ruth Bader Ginsburg would observe—to "evening up the rights, responsibilities and opportunities of men and women."[197]

In the end, the Supreme Court's decision was unanimous. "If women are politically aggressive, if they really want not to [be required to] register, William O. Douglas had observed in response to Ehrmann, "the legislature could change the law." The justices seemed undismayed by the minuscule number of women who had volunteered, or even by the reduction of their numbers to ten.[198] It may be that Warren made the best of the situation by asking Harlan to write the opinion, for Harlan had been restrained in conference, unlike Frankfurter, who had forthrightly argued for affirmation. It may even be that Warren was hoping against hope for Harlan to write creatively in a way that opened future opportunities for women; Harlan's grandfather had written the dissent in *Plessy v. Ferguson* in 1897, in which he had referred approvingly to *Strauder* and observed, "In respect of civil rights, all citizens are equal before the law. The humblest is the peer of the most powerful."

Harlan refused to reconsider *Strauder*. Women were not "excluded"; they were "exempted"; the exemption was not arbitrary, but "reasonable." Jury service was positioned against women's obligation to nurture. Harlan wrote:

Despite the enlightened emancipation of women from the restrictions and protections of bygone years, and their entry into
many parts of community life formerly considered to be reserved
to men, woman is still regarded as the center of home and family
life. We cannot say that it is constitutionally impermissible for
a State, acting in pursuit of the general welfare, to conclude that
a woman should be relieved from the civic duty of jury service
unless she herself determines that such service is consistent with
her own special responsibilities."[199]

The phrase "woman is still regarded as the center of home and
family life" would prove to be the most quoted—and, ultimately, the
most problematic—part of the opinion from the moment it was
handed down. Douglas, Warren, and Black—the three who had been
prepared to reverse the Florida court's decision—dissociated themselves from that section of Harlan's opinion, adding instead an ellip-
tical concurring opinion in which they observed that they agreed with
"the reasons set forth in Part II." Part II dealt with technical issues
—particularly whether the jury list had been properly constructed.
But to accept Part II was also to accept a substantial number of sub-
liminal images. For example, Part II accepts Lockhart's argument for
excluding most of those women who had registered before 1952,
quoting for support Lockhart's sweeping generalization—offered
with no substantive evidence—that "a good many of the women folks
now are over sixty-five. In fact, one of them is approximately
eighty."[200] Indeed, the Court accepted his exclusion of all but thirty-
five names.

The three concurring justices also agreed with Harlan in Part II
that "this case in no way resembles those involving race or color.
. . . There is present here neither the unfortunate atmosphere of
ethnic or racial prejudices . . . nor [a] long course of discriminatory
administrative practice." They concluded, with the rest of their colleagues, that there was "no substantial evidence whatever in this record that Florida has arbitrarily undertaken to exclude women from
jury service."

Dreben and Ehrmann had been sure that at the core of their argument had been the claim that Gwendolyn Hoyt had not been tried
by a fair cross section of the community. Only secondarily had they

argued that women were a distinct class and that Hoyt, as a member of that class, had been entitled not to have her own class excluded from the jury pool. It was particularly galling, then, when Harlan also maintained that the defense had been asking for a jury shaped to the particular circumstances of the case; that the defense had wanted a "compassionate" jury. "At the core of appellant's argument is the claim that the nature of the crime of which she was convicted peculiarly demanded the inclusion of persons of her own sex on the jury."

Yet the argument that women were a class that could be used to test whether any given selection from the community was indeed a "fair cross section" was itself a fragile argument in 1961. Douglas' own law clerk, Bernard Jacobs, had advised him to vote not to hear the case at all: "It is undeniable that women constitute a 'class' within the constitutional sense of that word. . . . The question is then . . . whether the limitation of women jurors to the class of volunteers is a reasonable one under the equal protection clause. Reasons might be suggested for the classification; distinctions based on sex do not *seem to meet* with the same disfavor that classifications based on ethnic group or race do [emphasis mine]. Appellant is not entitled to have jury representation of every group she could prove herself to belong to. Yet this case does rouse sympathies: she certainly would have been better off in justifying uxoricide to a jury of women than to a jury of men."

But it was not clear what they got from being a class. Jacobs did not go on to make the connection that would be made in the 1970s: that since women are a class, their class cannot be arbitrarily excluded. Nor did Harlan himself: "the disproportion of women to men on the list independently carries no constitutional significance. In the administration of the jury laws proportional class representation is not a constitutionally required factor."[201] When a revitalized feminist movement came alive in the 1970s, it would seek to break up the assumptions in which Harlan's opinion was embedded: that women and only women were necessarily the center of home and family life, and legally that "women" were not a class entitled to constitutional protection.

Easy exemption from jury service seemed to Harlan and his colleagues a matter of privilege, not of unequal obligation. There was for women no "unfortunate atmosphere of . . . prejudices . . . nor . . .

discriminatory administrative practice." When the New York *Times*, reporting Harlan's opinion on November 21, used his assertion that "woman is still regarded as the center of home and family life" as its "Quotation of the Day," an old friend of Harlan's composed cheerful verses that captured the relationship between Harlan's private relations with his own wife and his vision of women jurors:

> *While never really a misogynist,*
> *You thought that women should not be kissed . . .*
> *Ethel soon changed all of this,*
> *Marriage was right, so too the kiss,*
> *Years of happy matrimony*
> *Have changed ideas which once were phony.*
> *Now as Judge in the highest Court,*
> *Woman's been put right where she ought,*
> *Not with jurors 'midst scenes of strife*
> *But "the center of home and family life."*[202]

"A live lawyer was far more a danger . . . than a dead sharecropper"

When Gwendolyn Hoyt entered the Lowell Women's Correctional Institution at Ocala in 1961, most Americans understood women to be privileged by the law, excused from obligations incumbent on men.[203] As Harlan's opinion made clear, women's obligations to their families substituted for their obligation to public service. When the suffrage movement split in the 1920s, liberals had moved in the direction of emphasizing women's difference from men; those who sought to strengthen protective legislation like minimum wages, maximum hours, and funding for prenatal care generally focused on women's distinctive responsibilities as mothers. Arguments about equal rights for women were increasingly monopolized by the more conservative National Woman's Party, which was prepared to sacrifice protective legislation in the interests of principle. In the 1950s women's rights was territory understood by liberals to be inhabited by the clubwomen depicted in the popular cartoons of Helen Hokinson, who wore frivolous hats, enlarged upon inconsequential matters, and leaned to the right politically.

When Hoyt and her lawyers protested that in order for her to enjoy a right to a fair trial, other women would have to fulfill an obligation to serve on juries, few listened. When they tried to make civil rights claims, they seemed opportunistic. The day that Gwendolyn Hoyt killed her husband, newspapers carried stories of mobs stoning black schoolchildren in Little Rock; it could escape few how many of the stone throwers were women. Ehrmann's claim that women had been excluded longer than any other class sounded at best antiquarian, at worst self-serving.

Yet already many people were groping toward a revised understanding of the social relationships between women and men, and were hesitantly beginning to consider that there might be analogies between the way the law treated women and the way the law treated African-Americans. Analogies between exclusion by race and exclusion by gender were as old as the women's rights and abolitionist movements of the nineteenth century, and new life was breathed into them during World War II. In 1944 the distinguished Swedish economist Gunnar Myrdal devoted a chapter in *An American Dilemma*, his magisterial book about race relations in the United States, to "the important similarities between the Negro Problem and the women's problem." "In the final analysis," Myrdal wrote, "women are still hindered in their competition by the function of procreation; Negroes are laboring under the yoke of the doctrine of unassimilability which has remained although slavery is abolished. The second barrier is actually much stronger than the first in America today. But the first is more eternally inexorable."[204] In 1953 many Americans were reading Simone de Beauvoir's *The Second Sex*, which insisted that the exclusion of women from public life was not simply a matter of sloppy legislation or ignorance but was central to the way men had fabricated public life. Drawing on anthropological studies, Beauvoir argued that women have long been a medium of exchange between men—passed on in arranged marriages, their bridewealth or personal property becoming, as in the laws of coverture, part of the property of the husband. If women have been part of the patrimony of men, of course they could not be put in the position of judging men. Like Negroes, Beauvoir observed, women were only "partially integrated in a civilization that nevertheless regards them as constituting an inferior caste. . . . There is this great difference; the Negroes submit with a feeling of revolt, no privileges compensating for their hard lot, whereas woman is offered inducements to complicity."[205]

Raya Dreben had understood this. She had her own bitter personal experience of how gender difference translated not into privilege but into burden. She had paid particular attention to *Fay v. New York* and had thought it was wrongly decided. The argument in *Brown v. Board of Education* had been heavily based on historical analogy; Dreben had hoped that her *Hoyt* brief might do to *Strauder* something analogous to what *Brown* had done to *Plessy v. Ferguson*.[206] But as a junior lawyer—it did not help that she was female—she would not be the one who directly encountered the justices of the Supreme Court, and when Ehrmann stood before the bench, he did not make the analogy between race and sex part of his oral argument. That analogy, and its connection with the concept of jury service, would have to wait for Pauli Murray, the brilliant feminist, lawyer, and memoirist, who would make it central to her own intellectual career.

In the mid-1960s, the now elderly Dorothy Kenyon and the young lawyer Pauli Murray worked together in the case of *White v. Crook*, which would effectively link the obligation of jury service for women with the same obligation for men, and link exclusion on the basis of sex difference to exclusion on the basis of race difference.

They had first met in 1946, when Pauli Murray was not long out of Howard University Law School and Dorothy Kenyon was fifty-eight, with, Murray recalled, "a barbed wit and a penchant for wearing large floppy hats. . . . She had no job to offer me [but] her identification with my struggle boosted my sagging morale."[207] Determined to escape segregation, Murray had turned down scholarships to black colleges after her graduation from high school in Durham, North Carolina. She had moved to New York City to attend Hunter College, and emerged in 1933 knowing herself to be a writer. After graduation she worked, briefly, for the National Urban League, the Works Progress Administration, and the Workers Defense League, whose director, Rowland Watts, would years later respond so promptly to Raya Dreben's plea for help from the ACLU. Murray found her friendships in the interracial, interfaith civil rights community of the 1930s left.[208] These experiences provided happy examples of the possibility of interracial solidarity but also ever more chilling evidence of the apparent invulnerability of segregation and racism.[209] Traveling home to North Carolina from New York in 1940, she and a West Indian friend refused to sit on broken seats in the back of the bus and were arrested for creating a public disturbance. They were jailed in the city prison in Petersburg, Virginia. But there was no one to play Martin Luther King to their Rosa Parks. Eleanor Roosevelt put in a word with the governor of Virginia but also reiterated that "as long as these laws exist, it does no one much good to violate them." Murray refused to pay the fine; the NAACP, hoping to raise "the issue of the constitutionality of state segregation law in interstate travel," defended her unsuccessfully.[210]

Within five years of her graduation from college, Murray was convinced that she could better defend workers by becoming a lawyer. She applied to the University of North Carolina in the face of its segregation, but also with the ironic knowledge that her own white great-great-grandfather, James S. Smith of Chapel Hill, had been a member of the university's board of trustees in the early nineteenth century. Frank Porter Graham, the liberal president of the University of North Carolina, locked in his own struggles with the board of trustees, felt he had no choice but to deny her admission, but not before Murray had startled the campus—she conducted a sharp debate in print in the student newspaper as well as in the newspapers of the black community—and made national news.[211]

As field secretary for the Workers Defense League, Murray raised money for the defense of Odell Waller, a black sharecropper who had killed his white employer in a bitter fight over the seizure of his crop and was sentenced to death. In 1940 Virginia, jury lists were drawn from voting lists, and voting required the payment of a poll tax. The tax, as intended, put voting far out of the reach of virtually all sharecroppers. "So you had," Murray remembered many years later, "a poll tax jury which, for all practical purposes, was a planters' jury."[212]

The Workers Defense League sent Murray to Richmond, to make an appeal for contributions at a meeting of the Negro Ministers Alliance. To her chagrin she found that she would be preceded on the program by Leon Ransom, acting dean of the Howard University

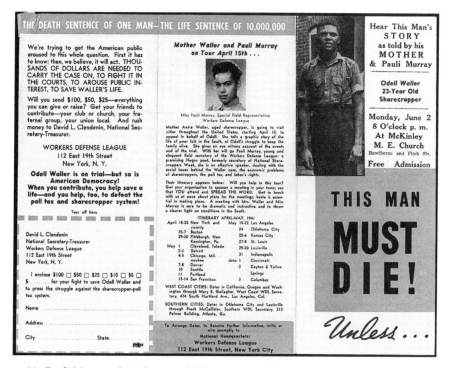

20. Pauli Murray, the "eloquent field secretary of the Workers Defense League," undertook a grueling cross-country tour in 1940 to raise money for the defense of Odell Waller, a young sharecropper condemned by a poll tax jury.

Law School, and Thurgood Marshall, who were asking for money to support the defense of four young black men accused a raping a white woman; no one in the audience could have missed the fear of another Scottsboro case. But Murray made a moving speech; it was one of the rare occasions on which she dissolved in tears in public, and the ministers opened their pockets to her. "[B]ack at the hotel Dr. Ransom . . . and I [were] just kind of, you know, rapping back and forth, [and I] said, 'Well look, if I'm going to be messing around with these cases, I might as well study law.' He said, 'Come on, we'd love to have you.' I said, 'Give me a fellowship and I will.' He says, 'O.K., I'll give you a fellowship' . . . sure enough, he went and sent me the papers." Pauli Murray entered Howard University Law School that fall; Waller was executed in 1942. When Murray graduated in June 1944, at the top of her class, she sent an engraved invitation to her commencement to Virginia governor Colgate Darden with a note "suggesting . . . that a live lawyer was far more a danger to his system than a dead sharecropper."[213]

At Howard she found "the beginning of my conscious feminism." No sooner had classes begun than she spotted a notice on the bulletin board: " 'All male members of the first year class are invited to Dean So-and-so's for a smoker.' There were only two females in the entire school, one of which was myself. I am so stunned." At Howard, where in the 1940s all faculty and students were black, "the sex factor was isolated." Awarded the prestigious Julius Rosenwald Fellowship for graduate work in law, which was normally accomplished at Harvard, she found that Harvard Law School did not admit women; she went to the University of California instead. A year in the district attorney's office in Los Angeles instructed her, she would later remember, in the social construction of racial difference. "Middle-class Negroes, for example, had been able to move into the homes left vacant by the Japanese-Americans who had been interned . . . I began then thinking of minorities rather than just the black-white situation."[214]

For more than a dozen years after finishing her fellowship, Murray struggled to find stable footing as a lawyer and a writer. She found her professional opportunity in 1961, the year that *Hoyt* was argued in the Supreme Court, when Assistant Secretary of Labor Esther Peterson, a veteran of women's rights struggles, persuaded John F. Kennedy to establish the President's Commission on the Status of Women. Pauli Murray found a job on the staff of the Commission's Committee on Civil and Political Rights. In this setting she would do some of the most important work of her life.

Perhaps more than any other single person, Murray linked the civil rights movement with the federal quest for equity for women.[215] The Committee hoped to defuse "troublesome and futile agitation" over an Equal Rights Amendment by exploring the potential of litigation under the Fourteenth Amendment guarantees of equal protection under the law. But even liberals were recognizing that in the climate of New Deal wages and hours legislation, the old protective labor laws were increasingly "protecting" women from better-paying "men's" jobs, just as the label of "privilege" was sustaining many inequalities, among them permissive rather than mandatory jury service. As members of and advisers to American occupation forces in Japan, old New Dealers had made sure that equal rights for women were written into the postwar Japanese constitution. Since Murray had prepared an overview of *States' Laws on Race and Color* for the Women's Division of the Methodist Church, the Commission turned to her to survey the law, making recommendations about the viability of the Fourteenth Amendment for accomplishing what an Equal Rights Amendment might without at the same time putting protective legislation at risk.[216]

Murray welcomed the opportunity. She was aware that all previous efforts to claim rights under the privileges and immunities clause of the Fourteenth Amendment had failed. As early as 1947 she had begun to call discrimination on the basis of sex a system of "Jane Crow." In a biting and deeply personal essay published in *Negro Digest* entitled "Why Negro Girls Stay Single," Murray insisted that the "minority status" of women is suffered "despite their numerical size," and "independently of race, religion or politics." The black woman suffered her own bitter variant, Murray said, at the hands of men of her own race, who turned their resentment against whites "upon himself and the Negro woman."[217]

What was intended to be a brief memo—Murray at first was hopeful that she could have a draft memorandum within a week—became a considerably longer project. She spent her term as a Fellow in Residence at Yale (in the late summer and fall of 1962) writing the lengthy memo. The experience, she would later say, was a consciousness raising one for her; she understood that she herself had experienced, she said, "both 'Jim Crow' and 'Jane Crow' as twin evils."[218]

The memo was intended to be, she said, "a bold imaginative approach" that she thought could "bring about a consensus for a reinterpretation of the Fourteenth Amendment as applied to the rights of women."[219] She would use it to criticize the black community as well as the white; early in its development she wrote explicitly to an editor of the Harlem newspaper the *Amsterdam News*: "Nowhere is there a greater need for appreciation of the rights of women as citizens than in the Negro community itself. Negro women, although they have battled valiantly for 'equal rights,' have not always shared those rights when they were established."[220]

As she prepared to write the memo, Murray gathered materials and advice, and one of the first requests she made was to Melvin Wulf, general counsel of the ACLU, asking him for a copy of the brief "my old friend and your predecessor, Rowland Watts, and Judge Dorothy Kenyon prepared" in *Hoyt v. Florida*. Murray had been struck by Justice Douglas' concurrence, in such apparent contradiction to his position in *Ballard*, and wondered whether *Ballard* "still remains good law . . . Mr. Justice Harlan's opinion in *Hoyt* has tended to narrow the broad principle announced in *Ballard*." She went on:

> What I am after, of course, is to get a clear cut decision from the Supreme Court . . . that the Fourteenth Amendment is applicable to discrimination because of sex, and to get a clarification of the term "reasonable classification" as applied to women against the backdrop of mid-twentieth century notions of democracy.

Wulf sent copies of the records and briefs on *Hoyt* with the request that she take good care of the ACLU's only copies.[221] Kenyon wrote—but belatedly, well after Murray had completed the revised draft—that the *Hoyt* decision really rested on the failure to prove that Florida had *arbitrarily* excluded women from jury service, and that in her opinion, "Mr. Justice Harlan's discussion of the constitutional issue was mere dictum and irrelevant."[222]

But *Hoyt* was relevant to Murray from the beginning. When she needed an example of sex discrimination, jury service was the first contemporary example to which she turned, and she added an eleven-page, single-spaced appendix detailing the history of sex discrimination in jury service. Jury service was, she thought, the issue that most clearly illustrated widespread "confusion" about whether women had been oppressed by the law and required emancipation or favored by the law and permitted chivalrous exemption.[223] Murray sent the first draft of the memo to her old friend Caroline Ware, the distinguished social historian who taught at Howard University and who had, along with her economist husband, Gardiner Means, developed virtually a full second career as a social activist and adviser to labor reformers, black activist students, and New Dealers. Ware agreed that jury service was central to the issues which Murray discussed. Instead of conceding that the *Hoyt* decision had narrowed the broad principle expressed in *Ballard*, Ware urged Murray to "exploit" the potential of *Ballard* "to the fullest." "[O]n the issue of equality of status [and

Fourteenth Amendment rights, *Ballard*] is clear and unequivocal."[224]

Murray reached back to Blanche Crozier's 1935 article on *Strauder* for the argument that "race and sex are in every way comparable classes . . . there are no others like them. They are large, permanent, unchangeable, natural classes. No other kind of class is susceptible to [permanent] implications of inferiority." Murray searched the law reviews; Crozier's analogy had been ignored; indeed hers had been virtually the only substantial study of the constitutional issues of sex discrimination published in major law reviews in more than twenty-five years. Murray was appalled that there had been "no concerted effort to bring to bear upon the courts the body of current knowledge about the capacities, achievements and perspectives of women as individuals nor of the social implications of legal discrimination against them"; there had been for women no equivalent of *Brown v. Board of Education*.[225] Jury service was a particularly strategic locus, Murray suggested, for thinking through issues of the difference dilemma. If women were to deny their difference, would it be possible to continue to claim *any* form of different treatment? That is, could they have equality *and* protective legislation? On what grounds, in what terms, could such claims be made? She had many questions to ask:

When is it "appropriate" to treat women differently from men? To what extent and in what degree does a physiological difference, or the biological function of childbearing, or the social function of child-rearing justify differential treatment? And should such differential treatment apply to *all* women without regard to the performance of the function of motherhood? Is a policy which discriminates in *favor* of women in the same undesirable category as one which discriminates *against* them? When can it be justified on the ground of governmental intervention to protect a traditionally disadvantaged group? And how far is such protection to extend? When does it operate to restrict personal rights in violation of constitutional guarantees?[226]

When, at the end, Murray came to prepare an agenda for the "important issues" crying out for adjudication, jury service, and the reconsideration of *Hoyt*, was first on her list.[227] Appendix I, which described "Selected Court Decisions Determining Validity of Laws

Which Distinguish on the Basis of Sex," began with sections on federal and state jury service; in the latter category *Hoyt* led the list and was given the most extensive discussion. In her summary Murray called for "new legislation . . . to ensure full participation of women as jurors."[228] She proposed that the ACLU or the Justice Department prepare a "Brandeis Brief" which would press "the Supreme Court [to] decide that arbitrary discrimination against women violated the Fourteenth Amendment in the same way racial bias did."[229]

Murray's manuscript was circulated to members of the President's Commission on the Status of Women, lawyers who were part of the project, and old friends. Those who welcomed it did so in part for its simplicity, forthrightness, and clarity. "I feel in my bones that you are making history," Esther Peterson wrote.[230] "I couldn't agree with you more that [the equality clause of the Fourteenth] Amendment is ideally fitted to deal with discriminations against women if only the Judges could be made to see it," Dorothy Kenyon wrote from New York. Relieved that Frankfurter had retired and pleased at the prospect of the two new members, Arthur Goldberg and Byron White, Kenyon looked forward to trying again, "when a better woman juror case comes along than the Hoyt one."[231]

Not everyone was pleased; Erwin Griswold, dean of the Harvard Law School, thought Murray's memo "excellent" but found himself "luke warm" about her conclusions; he was not prepared to untangle the difference dilemma, preferring to leave it in the realm of the inchoate. "Somehow or other," he mused, "it has always seemed to me that there are differences in sex, and that these differences may, in appropriate cases, be the basis of classification for legal purposes. Generally speaking, I dislike carrying any argument to extremes, and your proposal does seem to me at times to carry a good thing perhaps a little bit too far."[232]

Murray's memo became part of the PSCW report, published in 1963 as *American Women: Report of the President's Commission on the Status of Women.*[233] The report was full of surprising information about the range and extent to which sex discrimination was embedded in American law—not only in divorce and child custody but in matters like eligibility for credit, choice of domicile, access to unemployment benefits. Inspired by the President's Committee, many governors appointed state commissions to make similar inquiries, and the state commissions found much the same conditions. The people who were appointed to these commissions were rarely radical; they were likely to be people who had worked in state politics for many years. As a result, hundreds of influential, middle-of-the-road citizens came to be convinced not only of the pervasiveness of sex discrimination in American law, but also that relying on the Fourteenth Amendment and litigating one issue at a time would be exhausting and impractical. An Equal Rights Amendment began to look efficient to many of the same people who had only recently opposed it.

Murray had identified the two most strategic issues as sex discrimination in jury service and in educational opportunity. She gave equal employment opportunity less attention, perhaps because she thought it would follow on the heels of equal access to education. The passage of the Civil Rights Bill of 1964, with its notable Title VII outlawing employment discrimination on the basis of sex as well as race and religion, and the invention of an Equal Employment Opportunities Commission to enforce Title VII, shifted the priorities on the agenda of sex discrimination. There were suddenly possibilities for undermining sex discrimination in the workplace that had not existed when Murray wrote the original memo.[234]

Now she (with a colleague, Mary Eastwood) almost completely recast her argument, publishing "Jane Crow and the Law: Sex Discrimination and Title VII," in the *George Washington Law Review* in 1965. Many of the generalizations of the first draft were the same; the central claim remained that "the rights of women and the rights of Negroes are only different phases of the fundamental and indivisible issue of human rights." The voice was still optimistic and consensual. Although the Supreme Court had never applied the Fourteenth Amendment to sex discrimination, Murray wrote, "[t]he genius of the American Constitution is its capacity, through judicial interpretation, for growth and adaptation to changing conditions and human values." But because Title VII now made substantive change possible, the essay stressed employment issues as "the most serious discrimination against both women and Negroes today." Now *Hoyt v. Florida*'s significance was primarily historical; it was cited as one of the ten major cases in which the Court had upheld sex discrimination by law as reasonable. Jury service still figured, however, along with military service, as a practice that would have to be changed "to be consistent with the principle of equality of rights." In her insistence that "women, though numerically more than one-half of the adult population, occupy a position comparable to that of a racial minority," Murray would provide intellectual grounding for the feminist legal revolution of the 1970s.[235]

Gwendolyn Hoyt's minister and the retired Presiding Bishop of the Episcopal Church, Henry Knox Sherrill, steadily petitioned that she be paroled. C. J. Hardee monitored the situation and kept Ehrmann and Dreben informed.[236] On July 20, 1964, after three and a half years of imprisonment, Gwendolyn Hoyt was paroled. Like many women convicted of murdering their husbands, she did not seem to pose a further threat to the peace of the community.[237]

By the time "Jane Crow and the Law" was in print Pauli Murray had joined the national board of directors of the ACLU. She had no success in her call for a permanent commission on the status of women to continue the work of the PCSW. However, as a member of the ACLU's Equality Committee—joined in alliance with Dorothy Kenyon—Murray could continue to urge a focused and constitutional attack on sex discrimination.[238]

At a series of meetings late in 1967 and early in 1968, maintaining that "classification by sex is almost as pernicious as classification by race," Pauli Murray urged the Equality Committee to "completely revise" ACLU policy on sex discrimination. She sought to keep the focus on women as a "functional rather than a biological class"—that is, to make exceptions for mothers or pregnant women when those conditions were specifically an issue, but otherwise to treat women as individuals just as men are treated. She wanted the ACLU to focus on the guarantees of the Fifth and Fourteenth amendments, for due process and for equal treatment under the law, and to initiate litigation to eliminate discrimination based on sex in "jury service, the criminal law, *domestic relations law*, public education." There was no dearth of cases which could be used to test the usefulness of the Fourteenth Amendment; among the lively ones in the fall of 1967 were cases challenging limits on the number of hours women could work overtime and the use of indeterminate sentences for women, but not men, convicted of crime. The vision developed in the ACLU

Equality Committee in the late 1960s would ground the ACLU's Women's Rights Project, which Ruth Bader Ginsburg would come to New York to head in 1971.[239]

In developing this enterprise, Murray said frankly she hoped to defuse potential tension between white women and Negroes. Her support of the inclusion of sex as well as race as protected categories in Title VII of the Civil Rights Act of 1964 had put her at odds with some old allies. To some black activists, it looked as though white women were riding the coattails of a movement in which black lives had been risked and sacrificed; in this context, Murray's lifelong commitment to ending "Jane Crow" as well as "Jim Crow" was vulnerable to the interpretation that she had cast her lot with white feminists.

The tension broke into dramatic confrontation with a colleague, Floyd McKissick, president of the Congress for Racial Equality (CORE) at the December 1967 meeting of the Equality Committee.[240] Murray had framed an agenda intended to sustain and enlarge a coalition of white and Negro women—indeed, of whites and Negroes, men and women—the coalition of which she had been a part since her days at Hunter College, the coalition that was embodied in the very membership of the ACLU's Equality Committee itself. But that coalition had been destabilized by the rise of Black Power, signaled by Stokely Carmichael's demand in the summer of 1966 that blacks set their own agenda without reference to white concerns, even to the concerns of white allies. For Murray to use the word "Negro" instead of "black" at that moment was to signal the choice of one set of political allies over another. She was being true to what she had learned in her own life as she had lived it, but the position would put at risk her relations with a generation of black activists. In his response, McKissick made clear just how political Murray's wording had been. The Committee's secretary recorded his words: "the circumstances in 1967 are changed. . . . CORE's Board of Directors has decided that black power is the method to be used to bring about equality." McKissick went on to make clear—more explicitly than did almost any of his contemporaries, except perhaps Stokely Carmichael—the gender tensions of the politics of Black Power:

Thus, at the moment CORE is emphasizing black male power, and tomorrow will concentrate on the equality of women. He

21. While serving on the ACLU Equality Committee, Pauli Murray taught at Brandeis University; she would later say that the tensions with militant black students during the winter of 1968–69 felt "like rolling backward down a steep incline in a vehicle out of control." None of the tensions are evident in this 1970 photograph taken in her office at Brandeis.

will defend the ACLU position, but at the same time must maintain his organization's position. He further noted that the black woman in America has traditionally been the spearhead of all movement while the black male leadership has slept. As a result, the real failure to lead the black people is the failure to have the black men as leaders, and the real issue today is to educate black men.[241]

For McKissick, while women might "spearhead," only men could lead; what women had done in the movement was discounted; the "real issue" was to rectify the failure to have enough "black men as leaders." Like so many radical movements before and after, Black

Power told women that "tomorrow" it would "concentrate on the equality of women." "Jane Crow" would have to wait for attention until "Jim Crow" was dead; Murray had long since decided that the two must be destroyed together. Her sensibilities had been shaped by her trust in the interracial relationships which had been central to the reform movements in which she had been involved since her youth. She had found commitment to civil liberties among whites as well as blacks, and she had found scorn for civil liberties among blacks (notably in Ghana, where she had spent 1966) as well as among whites. Her position on these matters increasingly put Murray in a tense relationship with many black activists, especially those younger than she.

Murray's involvement in the ACLU bound her together with Dorothy Kenyon, who was still arguing for equal obligation to jury service. Together they worked on *White v. Crook*, a case that was initiated in Alabama within a few days of the murders of Viola Liuzzo and Jonathan Daniels just after the Selma-to-Montgomery march in the early spring of 1965.[242] The lead attorney in the case was Charles Morgan of the Atlanta chapter of the ACLU. Working closely with ACLU colleagues in Birmingham, he demanded that the trials of the alleged murderers be delayed until blacks and women could serve on juries in Alabama. They failed to delay the trials, which were promptly held in Lowndes County, Alabama—where the population was 81 percent black but no black men had ever appeared on a jury roll and where all women were barred from serving on juries—and the alleged murderers were found innocent. (The three defendants were later found guilty by a federal jury composed of twelve white men after the federal government initiated a suit charging the violation of a Reconstruction-era federal civil rights conspiracy law, making it a crime for two or more persons to "conspire to injure, oppress, threaten or intimidate any citizen in the free exercise or enjoyment of any right or privilege secured to him by the Constitution or laws of the United States.")

White v. Crook brought together arguments against sex discrimination in juries with arguments against race discrimination in juries. Attorneys Charles Morgan in Atlanta and Orzell Billingsley in Birmingham were joined by the national office of the ACLU in New York and the U.S. Department of Justice. Together they had the resources to subpoena and analyze all Lowndes County jury records for the past fifty-three years. They found that a small group of white men—including one of the accused murderers—were regularly recirculated among the juries. Sex and race discrimination were linked; the machinery of equal protection had completely broken down. The plaintiffs argued that since all women and all black men were excluded, only white men, who comprised barely 6 percent of the population of the county, and only 13 percent of adults between the ages of twenty-one and sixty-four, were available to serve, and few of them were actually enlisted in jury service. Anomalies abounded. Women served Alabama within many state agencies and as state Auditor, state Treasurer, and Secretary of State; sitting with others as a Board of Adjustment, they granted damages to citizens who had been injured by the state, a role once performed by grand juries. Annie Lola Price, the presiding judge of the Alabama Court of Appeals, could "reverse the verdict of a jury. She could resign and practice law before a jury. But solely because she is a woman she is not eligible to serve on a jury."[243]

The three-judge panel of the U.S. Court of Appeals for the Fifth Circuit was composed of men who had for more than a decade played a heroic part in ending segregation; Judge Richard T. Rives had written the court's opinion upholding the Montgomery bus boycott; Judge Frank M. Johnson had managed the federal trial that had finally convicted Viola Liuzzo's murderers. The court was already disposed to hear the argument on racial grounds. But the argument on grounds of sex was freshly invoked by Morgan and his colleagues. Kenyon and Murray considered it central; the New York *Times* took it to be "a side issue," reporting:

> Dorothy Kenyon . . . came to Alabama to make an oral argument on that point but was denied this opportunity when the judges called for the submission of written briefs [only]. . . . Judge Richard T. Rives addressed Mrs. Kenyon sharply when she insisted on making her argument despite the ruling.[244]

Despite the unpleasant encounter, the court included a clear acceptance of sex as well as race in its decision. "Jury service is a form of participation in the processes of government, a responsibility and a right that should be shared by all citizens, regardless of sex. . . . [T]he exclusion of women from jury service in Alabama by statutory provision is arbitrary . . . [and] unconstitutional . . ." The court required Alabama to eliminate racial restrictions instantly, but gave the legislature a year to change the system for recruiting women, and left them to choose whether women's service would be mandatory or voluntary. (Alabama made it voluntary.)²⁴⁵

Though the triumph was shared with Charles Morgan and others, Murray recalled that *White v. Crook* was Kenyon's "first victory in a number of attempts to have the equal protection clause of the Fourteenth Amendment judicially applied to cases of sex-based discrimination. . . . The decision was a vindication of her years of effort."²⁴⁶ In 1970, though frail (cancer would kill her within two years), Kenyon joined a women's liberation parade celebrating the fiftieth anniversary of suffrage, organized in New York City "by women young enough to be her great-grandchildren." They offered to have her ride in an automobile, but she insisted on walking with her juniors. "I wanted them to know I was with them," she told reporters.²⁴⁷

"Gender . . . is an unconstitutional proxy for . . . competence"

When thirty-eight-year-old Ruth Bader Ginsburg and ACLU Director Mel Wulf wrote the brief for Sally Reed, the appellant in *Reed v. Reed* in 1971—a case testing the competing claims of separated parents to serve as administrator of their dead son's estate, in which the U.S. Supreme Court would rule for the first time that discrimination on the basis of sex is an unconstitutional denial of equal protection of the laws—they placed the names of Dorothy Kenyon and Pauli Murray on the title page as co-authors alongside their own. Neither Kenyon nor Murray had actually participated in the writing of the brief, but Ginsburg was determined to acknowledge the intellectual debt which contemporary feminist legal argument owed to "those brave women."²⁴⁸ The succession of names on the *Reed* brief was the sign of a torch passed by one generation and aggressively claimed by another.

When Dorothy Kenyon died in 1972, Pauli Murray delivered her eulogy. Disillusioned by her struggles with the Black Power move-

22. Dorothy Kenyon near the end of her life, ca. 1970.

23. Ruth Bader Ginsburg in 1972, during the
strenuous years of litigation.

ment of the late 1960s, which seemed to her to abandon the dream
of interracial, interfaith fellowship, Murray decided that what the
world needed was more ministers like Martin Luther King and fewer
divisive activists. She abandoned her career in the law and the acad-
emy and turned to her religious faith; in a moving ceremony in 1977,
she became one of the first women priests ordained in the Episcopal
Church.

The work to which Kenyon and Murray had been dedicated was
taken on by a younger generation of women lawyers. "It was much
easier for us to do what we did" than it had been for Murray, Ruth
Bader Ginsburg mused many years later; "there were a lot of things
that were very hard for her."[249]

Ruth Bader had been an undergraduate at Cornell in the early
1950s, when only one woman had been admitted to the College of
Arts and Sciences for every four men, and where parietal rules re-

quired women to live in dormitories whether they wished to or not. When she entered Harvard Law School in 1956, one of nine women in a class of some 500 men, she found that the logic of difference could be turned upside down; at Harvard men monopolized the dormitories and women were required to live off campus. Each year Dean Erwin Griswold—who would tell Pauli Murray that some discrimination on the basis of sex had its place—invited the women law students to a dinner at his home; he invited also an equal number of male senior faculty. After dinner, Ginsburg recalls, the dean, not thinking to humiliate and attempting to be gracious, "asked us to explain what we were doing in law school taking a place that could be held by a man." Long afterward, when Ginsburg was a circuit judge on the U.S. Court of Appeals—and then again at her confirmation hearings when she was appointed to the Supreme Court in 1993—Ginsburg talked of the experience. "In those days I smoked," Ginsburg confesses, "and when it came my turn the ashtray I was sharing with distinguished visiting professor Herbert Wechsler slid from my lap onto the floor . . . It was one of life's most memorable embarrassing moments. All I could think of to say was that my husband was in the second year class and it was important for a wife to understand her husband's work. When it came her turn, Miss Flora Schnell had the wit to say 'with so many of them and so few of us, what better place to find a husband!' " The annual ritual was repeated for years.[250]

Ginsburg completed law school at Columbia, graduating in 1959. She joined the faculty of Rutgers Law School, where in 1970 she read Pauli Murray's "Jane Crow and the Law" and used it for what would be one of the first courses in the nation devoted to sex-based discrimination in the law. The following year Ginsburg returned to Columbia with an appointment that permitted her to spend half her time heading the ACLU's new Women's Rights Project, whose basic principle was one Kenyon and Murray had maintained for years—that discrimination on the basis of sex was neither "benign" nor harmless. Ginsburg prepared a short list of four classic cases, ranging over a century, to the overturn of which the WRP was committed; among them was *Hoyt*.[251] When they began, Ginsburg recalled, "the possibility of getting a favorable decision seemed nil. The Supreme Court had held the line so long."[252] Jury service was a particularly strategic issue, Ginsburg thought; "it has both the rights aspect and the obligation."[253]

The Women's Rights Project was heavily dependent on chance for the specific cases testing equal protection of the laws and the order in which they could appeal them to the Supreme Court. There was a thick backlog of complaints. "It wasn't as though we had to go searching for a test case; there were plenty of cases," Ginsburg remembered. In the ACLU files, for example, was the 1966 complaint of a New York City schoolteacher who had been shocked to discover that although the Board of Education compensated male teachers for days lost when they served on juries, she had lost two days' pay for her two days of jury service—on the grounds that since the law permitted her to claim a waiver as a woman she had had "the choice of not accepting the jury service." Maude Matthews protested: "I accepted the summons to serve because the Federal Courts have held that Jury Service is not only a right but an obligation of citizenship."[254]

As it turned out, the first major case in which the Supreme Court ruled that different treatment of the sexes could be a denial of equal protection of the laws involved estate administration, and the second involved dependents' allowances.[255] *Reed v. Reed* tested an Idaho law that provided that when there were several "equally qualified" persons to administer a deceased person's estate, "males must be preferred to females." In the brief she drafted for *Reed*, Ginsburg argued that the state of Idaho should not be able to avoid making choices on the merits of competing claims—here by separated parents to manage a deceased son's estate—by invoking administrative convenience.[256] Two years later Ginsburg argued successfully on behalf of Sharron Frontiero, an Air Force officer who was dismayed to discover that she could not claim dependent's benefits for her husband on the same terms that her male colleagues could for their wives.[257] The *Frontiero* decision was handed down only a few weeks after the Court's decision in *Roe v. Wade*, which held that antiabortion statutes denied women Fourteenth Amendment guarantees of due process.

We can now look back at 1971–75 as years of an extraordinary legal transformation in the situation of women in the United States; the principle that discrimination on the basis of sex was a burden, not a privilege, challenged law and custom in virtually every sector of

American life, from the workplace to schools to intensely private matters of sexuality. As laws were rewritten and freshly interpreted, there was a lot of work for feminist lawyers; the work wove a single fabric, intended to smother Jane Crow as Pauli Murray had intended she be smothered. In the early 1970s, Ginsburg says now, "everything was coming together: the Equal Rights Amendment, the Women's Rights Project, teaching, the casebook, litigation. . . . It was really exhilarating. . . . But we were always tired."[258]

Ginsburg and her colleagues continued to wait for an opportunity to test *Hoyt*. So did the NAACP Legal Defense Fund, which had long been challenging "poll tax juries" and other devices that effectively eliminated blacks from jury pools. As they began to challenge jury pools from which black men had been excluded, they began to make claims on behalf of all women as well.[259] In 1971, a man convicted of rape in Louisiana (a state that discriminated against black men as jurors and, as Florida had done, required women to volunteer for jury service) appealed his conviction on the grounds that he had been indicted by an improperly constituted grand jury. The Supreme Court found the idea that such a defendant would want women involved in the jury selection "novel"—the implication was preposterous; only Justice Douglas was prepared to pursue the issue.[260]

Meanwhile lawsuits that had developed during the antiwar and civil rights movements of the late 1960s were slowly making their way to higher courts of appeal; these cases in their turn raised yet more questions about the composition of juries. (Justice Douglas, perhaps the member of the Supreme Court most sympathetic to arguments for equal jury service, suffered a stroke and had to leave the bench.) The most consequential of these new developments was the invention of new strategies of jury selection, devised almost inadvertently by two New York professors.

In 1971, Jay Shulman, a sociologist at the City University of New York, began to gather together the loose alliance that would later come to be known as the National Jury Project, and put it at the service of Daniel and Philip Berrigan, priests who were being tried in Harrisburg, Pennsylvania, for destroying the files of a draft office. Shulman, who is fondly remembered for his political intensity, had come to know Daniel Berrigan some years before, when Shulman was on the faculty of Cornell University and Berrigan was a minister

there. Now Shulman recruited Richard Christie, a distinguished professor of social psychology at Columbia University; together they began to think through what difference it made when certain sorts of
people were present on a jury.[261] Christie and his colleagues were
looking for unbiased jurors who would listen to their arguments; they
wanted people who resided in a politically conservative district but
who would not necessarily be conservative in their judgments. The
same sort of practice manuals that had told C. J. Hardee and Carl
Durrance to look for men on Gwendolyn Hoyt's jury told Christie
to look for Jews ("Jews have a history of oppression and generally
empathize with the accused," warned a manual used by Dallas, Texas,
prosecutors[262]) or Catholics (who might identify with the priests). But
there were relatively few Jews or Catholics in Harrisburg. Manuals
told them to avoid Lutherans, who were likely to be politically conservative, and to prefer college graduates, who were likely to be liberal, but Christie's polling data reported that neither rule held in
Harrisburg. Unlike many midwestern Lutheran churches, few in the
area were aligned with the conservative Missouri Synod. There were
only two liberal arts colleges in the area; the others were religious
seminaries or teachers colleges. Christie suspected that many young
people went out of the community to go to college; and did not come
back. "Our ideal juror would be a high school graduate who was
Lutheran."[263]

Guided by Christie's profiles, the lawyers used their voir dire challenges counterintuitively; they won their case with a jury heavily pop-
ulated with Lutheran high school graduates. Their published report
of what they had done inadvertently formalized a practice of intentional use of peremptory challenges to shape a jury selection, shifting
the practice from one that in Hardee's day had been intuitive to one
that quickly became commercial. By the 1980s expensive legal counsel
analyzing potential jurors in high-profile civil and criminal lawsuits
had become frequent and by the 1990s it was a well-established specialty of legal practice; it became a matter of widespread public observation during the O. J. Simpson murder trial of 1995. Christie and
others who pioneered the strategy looked on these commercial developments with dismay.

Although the Harrisburg experiment did not raise particular questions of gender, it did encourage further efforts to understand what

difference the composition of juries might make. Lawyers for the defense in civil rights cases increasingly claimed that it mattered that the widest possible range of people were in the jury pool. They had a more than theoretical reason to insist on the principle. The more precisely they were prepared to use their peremptory challenges to shape the outcome they wished, the more they wanted to be sure all shades of opinion were in the pool. And the more they scrutinized jury questionnaires, the less reasonable claims for exemptions turned out to be. When Florida removed the registration requirement for women, it offered exemptions to mothers of children under eighteen; examining jury questionnaires as part of an appeal, Rhonda Copelon and Jay Shulman discovered that nearly half of the women who claimed those exemptions from the obligation of jury service for child care were working full-time. Blanket exemptions did not really address practical hardship in finding substitute child care.[264]

When the Women's Rights Project finally did find a case that tightly linked women's jury service to matters of race they were unable to bring it all the way to the Supreme Court. Ruth Bader Ginsburg still feels wistful about the outcome. Edna Stubblefield was only nineteen when she was indicted for first-degree murder of another woman in a barroom brawl. Stubblefield did not deny having a knife, although she maintained she could not remember what happened in the fight. The club was in the small town of Paris, Tennessee, in a segregated area known locally as "black bottom," and no ambulance would go there. By the time one was found, the other woman had bled to death.[265]

In Tennessee, a woman who was summoned for jury service needed only to notify the court that she did "not desire to serve."[266] Virtually all women, black and white, took advantage of this exemption.[267] The Henry County Jury Commission systematically excluded blacks from both grand and petit juries; in a stunning commitment to maintaining a social order that had not felt the impact of a civil rights movement, the Commission had reappointed the same white man as foreman of the county grand jury since 1937. As one judge pointed out: "A person who consumes no beverage save water deliberately chooses to exclude all other types of drink, and it is not necessary under such circumstances to point out that he has eliminated from his consumption tea or coffee or any other liquid . . . [T]he judge making the appointment . . . had no need of collateral indications of race. He knew to an absolute certainty."[268] The Supreme Court refused to hear *Stubblefield*, but the arguments that Ginsburg developed there would successfully be used elsewhere. Easy exemption "betray[ed] a view of women ultimately harmful to them," and enforced a tradition in which adult women were not understood to be "persons with full civic responsibilities as well as rights. . . . [T]he state types women as persons whose assistance in the administration of justice is not really needed by the community."[269]

As it turned out, the major challenges to *Hoyt* would occur in Louisiana, which had recycled the practice of preregistration for women that Florida had abandoned. The first was consciously structured as a test case, and there was some humor in it. Marsha Healy, a member of the board of the Louisiana Civil Liberties Union, saw an opportunity in a civil suit initiated by a woman who had purchased a defective home permanent that had caused all her hair to break off at the roots. She claimed that a jury with women on it was likely to understand her embarrassment and humiliation and award her higher damages. Healy was a class action suit; it included a number of other women who were actually bringing civil lawsuits, a number of women who claimed that they were disadvantaged because they could not anticipate that a reasonable number of women would ever be on their juries should they be charged with a crime, a number of women who claimed that, as potential jurors, they should not be subject to a sign-up requirement, and a number of men who claimed that they were excessively vulnerable to service on juries because women were excused. Ginsburg sought "a declaration that the exemption provisions violate the rights of the class to Equal Protection and Due Process of the Law, and an injunction against continued enforcement of these laws."[270] The Attorney General of Louisiana echoed *Hoyt*: "Granted, that some women pursue business careers, the great majority constitute the heart of the home, where they are busily engaged in the 24-hour-day task [sic] of protecting and rearing children, providing a home for the entire family, and performing the daily household work . . . the state legislature has permitted the exemption in order not to risk disruption of this basic family unit."[271]

Healy went to a three-judge panel of the U.S. Court of Appeals for the Fifth Circuit, composed of members who were committed to an expansion of civil rights: Alvin Rubin, John Minor Wisdom, and R. Blake West. Among the amicus briefs filed on behalf of Healy was one prepared for the Center for Constitutional Rights by three young women: Nancy Stearns, Rhonda Copelon, and Elizabeth Schneider, a recent law school graduate who had not yet been admitted to the bar. The three were part of a new generation of women lawyers, the first generation for whom the concept of women as a class was unproblematic. Copelon recalled a meeting at the ACLU where older lawyers "were favoring the exemption. And we had a big argument about it. And I remember Ruth calling us back a few days later to say that she was convinced . . . even a neutral exemption was not a practical advance."[272]

Central to the CCR brief was an attack on the core issue in *Hoyt*; "All . . . forms of categorical exemption [reflect] the assumption that women are preoccupied with and continually essential to the maintenance of the home and the rearing of children." In 1973, 50 percent of married women with school-age children (ages six to seventeen) were working; so were nearly 70 percent of widowed, divorced, or separated mothers. Generic child-care exemptions for mothers were unrelated to reality; for most mothers, "jury service would not constitute a disruption of a pattern of continuous child care but rather absence from their employment." Any exemption should, they argued, be based on an individualized showing of difficulty.[273]

In July 1973 Ginsburg flew to New Orleans to argue *Healy v. Edwards*. Knowledge of *Hoyt* was never far from the surface in the oral argument; what Ginsburg had to do was persuade three judges to contradict a well-established Supreme Court precedent, something no panel of senior judges would do lightly.[274] But the Fifth Circuit panel was already disposed to be critical; in the end the three-judge panel was unanimous, and they said explicitly that they were overturning *Hoyt*. "When today's vibrant principle is obviously in conflict with yesterday's sterile precedent, trial courts need not follow the outgrown dogma. Hence we consider that *Hoyt* is no longer binding."[275]

Rubin moved past Justice Douglas in articulating just what it was that women brought to jury service; it was no longer a "flavor," but "qualities of human nature and varieties of human experience." The absence of women "is significant not because all women react alike, but because they contribute a distinctive medley of view influenced by differences in biology, cultural impact and life experience indispensable if the jury is to comprise a cross-section of the community."[276]

In the early 1970s, while ACLU lawyers and appeals courts debated, Pat and C. J. Hardee's son Charles Jay Hardee III was a student at the University of Florida Law School. In his textbooks, *Hoyt* was in the footnotes; his father's name was not mentioned. Charles Hardee had learned in his own family that *Hoyt* had been an important case, and was quietly proud to see it appear in his curriculum.[277]

Louisiana appealed the *Healy* decision to the Supreme Court, and Ginsburg argued it. But another case, also challenging the same Louisiana jury service statute, displaced *Healy*; because it involved a more serious crime it would be the one on which the Court issued an opinion, and *Healy* would be resolved by its outcome. Paradoxically, in *Taylor v. Louisiana*, in order to sustain women's equal access to juror obligation, the Supreme Court would have to support the claims of a man convicted of violent crimes against a woman. Ironically, the Court handed the decision down in response to a man who wanted jurors of the opposite sex, not a woman who, like Gwendolyn Hoyt, wanted jurors of her own sex.

Armed with a butcher knife, Billy J. Taylor abducted a woman, forcing her to drive her car, in which her daughter and grandson were passengers, to a deserted area, where he raped her and robbed them all. Desperate for a technicality, Taylor appealed his conviction on the ground that women had been systematically excluded from the jury pool. His lawyers drew an analogy between his experience and the Court's decision three years before that a white man was entitled to have a jury from which blacks had not been systematically barred. "[W]e think," wrote Judge Byron White, speaking for a majority, "it is no longer tenable to hold that women as a class may be excluded or given automatic exemptions based solely on sex if the consequence is that criminal jury venires are almost totally male. To this extent we cannot follow the contrary implications of the prior cases, including *Hoyt v. Florida*. If it was ever the case that women were unqualified to sit on juries or were so situated that none of them should be required to perform jury service, that time has long since passed. . . . Communities differ at different times and places."

By 1975 feminist lawyers had succeeded in making arguments from equality the common sense of the matter; the "republican mother" no longer figured in the Court's vision of work roles. "What is a fair cross section at one time or place," wrote Justice White in the majority opinion in *Taylor*, "is not necessarily a fair cross section at another time or a different place. Nothing persuasive has been presented to us in this case suggesting that all-male venires in the parishes involved here are fairly representative of the local population otherwise eligible for jury service."[278]

Carl Durrance read the *Taylor* decision in his office; he was a circuit court judge in Plant City, not far from Tampa. "When *Taylor* came down," he says now, "I thought well, at last it's finally done! And I wondered if anyone would know."[279] No one told Gwendolyn Hoyt.

Justice William Rehnquist did not join his colleagues in the *Taylor* decision. Taylor's crime was a major one and he had been fairly convicted; Taylor was not claiming a biased jury, just a flaw in the selection process. Why was this particular jury not to be trusted? The defense—and the Court majority—had not gotten beyond *Ballard*: "the best it can do," complained Rehnquist, "is to posit 'a flavor, a distinct quality' which allegedly is lost if either sex is excluded." This "flavor," Rehnquist went on, "is not of such importance that the Constitution is offended if any given petit jury is not so enriched. This smacks more of mysticism than of law."[280] Long before, in 1917, Susan Glaspell had based her demand for women's jury service not on Douglas' inchoate "imponderables" or even Kenyon's "diffused impartiality" but on the different experiences and *interests* that men and women might have, their different experiences of power.

Elizabeth Schneider had been only twenty-five when work for the CCR on *Healy* challenged her to think seriously about the difference dilemma. "There were tensions around claiming that there are insights that women might bring to juries, that women's minds are of a 'distinctive cast.' " She and her colleagues felt uncomfortable; those were "issues we thought about a lot." Rehnquist's opinion in *Taylor* had also, she would say many years later, forced her to think hard about what difference it did in fact make when women were on juries. Why fight so hard for a "fair cross section"? What difference would a "fair cross section" make? To say, as Douglas had in *Ballard*, that women added a *flavor* was, Schneider thought, "a gross trivialization."[281]

Before the decade was out, Schneider and Nancy Stearns would face this question directly and develop a startling example of the distinctive interests of men and women. As staff attorneys for the Center for Constitutional Rights, they helped develop the appeal of Yvonne Wanrow. Wanrow had a seven-year-old daughter who she had reason to believe had been molested by William Wesler, a man who was nearly a foot taller than the petite Wanrow. Near sunrise, on an August morning in 1972, Wanrow believed that an intoxicated Wesler was breaking into the house where she was staying. She was then using a crutch and had one leg in a cast. Wanrow shot Wesler, and was found guilty of using unreasonable force.

Wanrow fit a pattern in which there were striking disparities of force when a woman killed a man. The fictional Minnie Wright killed her husband when he was asleep; Gwendolyn Hoyt killed her husband when he was lying down. At the time Hoyt came to trial, the only practical defense for such a woman had been to concede that she had been irrational and to try to prove insanity. But in 1979 Schneider and Stearns and other feminist attorneys helped women like Wanrow say that they had been acting in self-defense—that given the lack of state intervention, the different socialization of men and women, and the magnitude of the disparities of force between them and the men they attacked, they had no other choice. Thus the woman who used a pistol to kill an unarmed man who, she believed, was threatening her life or the life of her children could be understood as acting reasonably.[282]

Even if we imagine time folded in on itself, and imagine the "expanded self-defense" argument to have been developed in the 1950s, it is not at all clear that Hardee and Durrance would have found it helpful in their defense of Gwendolyn Hoyt. She did not appear to be a paradigmatic "battered woman" who lives in a household so infected by her husband or lover's violence that she is frightened to leave it; often he controls her by threats to their children. Gwendolyn

Hoyt had herself initiated violence in 1947; Clarence Hoyt was living apart from her most of the time in 1957. Yet we also now know that domestic violence is premised on the assertion of power and control. The arguments that were first made on behalf of Yvonne Wanrow have now been developed in the context of the defense of battered women who have had to defend their lives against their assailants. We know that on at least one occasion he "beat her unmercifully"; and modern analysts of domestic violence emphasize that it is very common for women to deny the level of violence to which they are subjected. In the context of what could be expected at trial in 1957, Hardee and Durrance did not dare explore the extent to which violence permeated the household and intimidated Gwendolyn Hoyt; to do so, they believed, would likely have backfired, providing grounds for charges of first-degree murder, rather than manslaughter.

But if the development of the argument about self-defense does not mean that Gwendolyn Hoyt could have been declared innocent of crime, the defense did emerge in part from reconsideration of the conditions of her trial. Hardee, Durrance, Ehrmann, and Dreben had all, in their various ways, raised questions about the conditions in which Hoyt could receive equal protection of the laws and a trial by an impartial jury. They were certain that Hoyt had been driven by the anxieties of a rejected and tormented wife, and they wanted a jury capable of "hearing" that claim and taking it seriously. They wanted a jury drawn from people who had at least a chance of having experienced power relationships in a household as Hoyt had herself experienced them. Twenty years later, Schneider and her colleagues were also asking, "What will make it possible for a jury truly to 'hear' what Wanrow claimed? What is necessary before the jury will give the woman's story the credibility it deserves?"

The argument about self-defense seemed to move past the stage of "imponderables" to a recognition that men and women may indeed be differently situated as a result of different socialization and social circumstances. Women may also bring to their jury service predictably different experiences and interests than do men. Yet the difference dilemma was not easily resolved, for lawyers working on battered women's defense cases quickly learned that women jurors ranged widely in their opinions, and certainly could not be counted on, as a class, to be sympathetic to battered women. Indeed, says Schneider,

in practice we are more likely to find the "*reverse* of the Glaspell story
. . . many women distance themselves from women caught in violent
households. They deny their own experiences and say, 'If this was
happening to me, I would respond differently.' Male jurors are often
more patriarchially protective of women defendants than are women
jurors."

In the eighteenth century, the argument against women's direct obligation was logically embedded in the law of coverture. To call upon
women to make political decisions freely while their husbands controlled their physical bodies, their earning capacity, and their property
would be to place women in a double bind, which the founding generation refused to do. But eighteenth- and nineteenth-century Americans were not logical when they made the constraints on married
women applicable to *all* women. Unmarried women *did* legally control their own bodies, earning capacity and property, but except for
taxation, they were generally treated by the state *as though* they were
wives, under the control of men. Married women found it hard to
make claims for independent treatment under the law. Much of that
confusion persisted well into the twentieth century. When Justice
Harlan's opinion in *Hoyt* was published, he received a handwritten
letter from a woman he had never met, who had her own bitter personal experience of what could happen when women were classified
as people to whom the state had different civic relations than it had
to men. Elizabeth Snyder's husband had died in an airplane crash;
negligence was proved against the airline company. A man whose wife
had died in the same crash was able to sue the company for damages
for the loss of his wife's "society, services and sexual companionship."
"I told my lawyer my loss and grief was the same, he said he understood but that is not the law. . . . What right have the lawmakers to
say a husband's loss is any greater than a wife's loss[?]" Snyder was
not persuaded of the "enlightened emancipation of women over the
years" that Harlan had emphasized in his opinion; a bill to change
the law was becalmed in the Pennsylvania legislature, waiting its turn
on the agenda behind the choice of the state dog.[283] She linked the
denial of her claim to damages for loss of her husband's companionship to the Supreme Court's decision to uphold different treatment

of men and women prospective jurors; although she did not have the technical language, she did understand that both were parts of a system which privileged husbands' claims over wives'. In the twentieth century, decisions to free women from the obligation of mandatory jury service were generally tangled in similar confusion: because *some women* had domestic obligations as wives and mothers, *all women* were offered easy excuse from jury service.

The decision in *Taylor* destroyed this line of reasoning. In a strongly worded opinion, with only Justice Rehnquist dissenting, the Court explicitly turned away—"we cannot follow"—from its position in *Hoyt*. The issue was the Sixth Amendment right to an "impartial" jury, now defined as a jury *impartially drawn* from the district where the crime was committed; *impartially drawn* was now defined to mean that no *class* of people was intentionally excluded from the pool—not blacks, not wage earners, not people of a specific ethnic descent, not women. Moreover, *intentional* was more broadly understood than it had been. Louisiana law of 1975, like Florida law of 1949, did not fully exclude women from the pool; women could *choose* to register. In 1961 the Supreme Court had ruled that the registration requirement was a reasonable recognition of women's difference from men —whether they had young children at home or not, whether they were even married or not—and if women chose not to register they were not failing their civic obligation. In 1975 the Court accepted Kenyon's argument that placing a requirement in the path of one sex and not in the path of the other poisoned the "impartiality" of the process of jury selection.

In response to *Taylor*, states moved to change their selection procedures. Solutions varied, but broad classes of excused groups were eliminated and broad classes of other groups—like everyone who applied for a driver's license—were added to the pool of registered voters in order to capture a larger set of people. Efforts were made to defuse individuals' unwillingness to serve; some summonses promised only one day of waiting and only a single trial if chosen.

There had been, as we have seen, two roads to *Taylor*, roads that by the late 1970s were running parallel. One road was made up of the cases that tested the exclusion of women from juries; the other of those that challenged exclusion on the basis of race. These roads converged in *White v. Crook*, in *Stubblefield*, and in *Taylor*. The decision in *Taylor* resolved the matter of which names must be made available for random drawing. It did not address the matter of what happened to those names once they entered the pool.

In the American tradition of jury service, as jurors' names are drawn randomly for a trial, the jurors undergo the process of voir dire. Normally in open court, lawyers or judges ask them questions intended to reveal whether they are related to participants in the case, have already heard about the case and made up their minds, or would otherwise have difficulty offering a fair verdict. Lawyers may refuse to seat prospective jurors whose answers to these questions suggest that they are biased toward one or another outcome of the case. Depending on the nature of the case and the jurisdiction in which it is argued, lawyers also have at their disposal a number of "peremptory" challenges: that is, they may exclude prospective jurors from the trial without revealing the grounds or defending these reasons before the judge. (By contrast, in England it is the usual practice to seat the first twelve prospective jurors.)[284]

It did not take a lot of subtlety to notice that once the law was changed to permit classes of people who had previously been excluded from jury service to be called, lawyers often used peremptory challenges to take them off. In using their peremptory challenges, lawyers and judges were guided by what they understood to be the common sense of the matter; assumptions that they thought so obvious that they could barely articulate them. As we have seen, lawyers for the prosecution in the 1957 Chavigny trial in St. Petersburg had effectively excluded the women whom Gilkerson's registration campaign had called up. "This is no reflection on the ladies," the judge said cheerfully.[285] Handbooks of instruction for courtroom practice were full of commonsensical advice, but it was generally common sense as the anthropologist Clifford Geertz has wisely defined the term: "common sense is not what the mind clear of cant spontaneously apprehends; it is what the mind filled with presuppositions . . . concludes."[286] The old guides were filled with presuppositions: "Intellectuals such as teachers, etc., generally are too liberal and contemplative to make good State's jurors. . . . Hunters always make good State's jurors. . . . [Women] make the best jurors in cases involving crimes against children. . . . You are not looking for a fair juror, but rather a strong, biased and sometimes hypocritical individual."[287] After the Harrisburg trials, lawyers were often guided by commercial services and professional specialists who developed complex theories about the characteristics of the juror who would aid their case. They had wide discretion in using their peremptory challenges; the controlling precedent had been established in 1965, in *Swain v. Alabama*, when the Supreme Court sustained a prosecutor in a case involving a nineteen-year-old black man convicted of raping a seventeen-year-old white woman who used his peremptory challenges to exclude the only six blacks eligible to serve in a county where no black had served on any jury since 1950.[288] Even after *Taylor*, peremptory challenges could stand unless the defendant could show that the "state was solely responsible for the absence of a particular group over an extended period of time," that "the state had not used its challenges in a fair and impartial manner," and that there was "a pattern of discrimination."[289]

Civil rights groups, led by the NAACP Legal Defense Fund, launched cases aimed at making it illegal to use peremptory challenges to exclude blacks. By 1986, in the case of *Batson v. Kentucky*, the Supreme Court condemned peremptory challenges *by prosecutors* to exclude blacks from juries in cases involving black *defendants*.[290] It took five years before the Supreme Court extended that position, ruling that the prosecution's use of racial criteria in the selection of a jury is unconstitutional regardless of the races of the defendant or the excluded jurors.[291] It was easy to predict that peremptory challenges on the grounds of gender would soon follow, but the narrow ruling in *Batson* meant that each component of a trial had to be separately tested, and that there would have to be separate test cases for gender. In these cases the issues were often framed as the *right* of a woman who was a prospective juror to be free of implication that she was not equal to a man, rather than on her obligation to serve. Even that was not easy to establish; in 1983 a California woman was held in contempt and sentenced to a day in jail for protesting when a judge asked only the women on the jury panel whether they were married and what were the occupations of their spouses.[292] When the Supreme Court finally did consider the matter, the case could not have been better framed to dramatize stereotypes. A man we know only as J.E.B.

was named in a paternity suit; child support was demanded. Blood tests suggested that there was a 99.2 percent chance that he was the child's father. The panel of prospective jurors was twelve men and twenty-four women; after the court removed three men for cause, the state used nine of its ten peremptory challenges to remove the remaining men. They had achieved the panel that had given editorialists of Charlie Chaplin's time nightmares: the paternity suit judged by twelve women, who did indeed find J.E.B. to be the father of the child and ordered him to pay child support.

By this time Ruth Bader Ginsburg had joined the Supreme Court. On the first day of her confirmation hearings, in response to a request by Senator Edward Kennedy that she speak about the cases that had most meaning for her, Ginsburg had begun by reaching back before the cases that she herself had litigated to tell, in detail, the story of *Hoyt v. Florida*. Now, Justice Harry Blackmun, soon to retire, wrote the opinion in *J.E.B. v. Alabama*, but experienced journalists found Ginsburg's "voice was apparent in the majority opinion, which cited four landmark sex discrimination cases that she successfully argued before the Court in the 1970s, as well as others that she helped bring to the Court."[293] Blackmun's opinion offered a brief history of women's jury service since *Strauder*, reminded readers of *Ballard*, and treated *Hoyt* as hopelessly outdated. He quoted *Taylor* to the effect that a diverse and representative jury was necessary "partly as assurance of a diffused impartiality and partly because sharing in the administration of justice is a phase of civic responsibility." And he concluded that "gender, like race, is an unconstitutional proxy for juror competence and impartiality."

Women's exclusion from juries followed from a vision of the female who owed her primary service to her husband and their family: explaining why it was reasonable to exempt women from obligatory jury service, the Attorney General of Louisiana had announced "the woman is the heart of the home." Metaphors describing how women fulfilled their obligations to their husbands abounded in food imagery: with babies at their breasts or—as Georgieff blurted out in court—"cooking our dinners." That pronoun, "our," which reached across the bench to include the male justices, is key to understanding why the argument in *Hoyt* kept drifting away from Gwendolyn Hoyt's right to a jury drawn from an authentic cross section of her community and toward the "right" of women to be excused from jury service so that they could be free to cook "our" dinners. A few years later, debating revisions in the rules of federal jury service, Congressman Emanuel Celler of New York—who had been supporting women's voluntary service for many years—rose in the House of Representatives to assure Martha Griffiths of Michigan that he was willing to support compulsory service for women if he could be reassured on one issue: "Frankly, I am caught between the urging of the gentlewoman from Michigan and a male constituent, who expects a hot meal on the table when he returns from work. Is it the gentlewoman's desire to come between man and wife?"[294] Georgieff's and Celler's words highlighted the contrast between those whose dinners were cooked and those who had been freed from their civic obligation of jury service so that they could cook those dinners. In this peculiar, bizarre, even tawdry way, the old tradition of republican motherhood, which had understood woman's service to the state to involve nurturing civic virtue in the men of her own and of the next generation—her husband and sons—gasped its last in the Cold War era. No one worried about who cooked Gwendolyn Hoyt's dinner.

Telling the history of women's jury service in the United States relies on understanding the relationship between obligation and rights, compulsion and consent. In the founding era the manikin of the body politic on which the suit of rights and obligations was fitted was explicitly male. Embedded in the argument about whether jury service is a right or an obligation were contradictory understandings of the capacity of women's minds and the propriety of women judging men. When Gwendolyn Hoyt hit her horizontal husband with the baseball bat in 1957, the only way her aggression could be understood was as a result of either a "depraved mind" or temporary insanity sharpened by epilepsy. She was caught in the difference dilemma as it was understood in her generation: if men and women were equal, difference didn't matter and she should have been content to have an all-male jury; if men and women were different, then the request for women on the jury was a request for "female friends" and for favoritism. Only through the critique of marginality developed in the civil rights movement did women's rights activists learn to define women as a class entitled to equal protection of the laws under the Fourteenth Amendment and to deploy that knowledge to link women's claim to equal protection with that of African-Americans; as Pauli Murray said, both links were "phases" of the same movement for equality.

The feminist movement of the 1970s and after also involved a defense of the capacities of women's intellect. Legally this defense took the form of attacks on explicit and implicit exclusions of women from colleges and professional schooling; structurally it was embodied in women's reading groups, feminist bookstores, feminist presses, popular magazines, and academic journals. Intellectually it was embedded in socialist-feminist critiques of Marxism, women's historians' critiques of consensus history, feminist lawyers' criticism of legal theory. In practice, late-twentieth-century feminism has set itself against the traditional assumption that women's minds are unsuited for the abstract reasoning that justice requires.

As a result, thirty years later—that is, within the compass of Gwendolyn Hoyt's sentence—it had become possible to conceive that a woman killing in that situation might actually be acting reasonably. In 1975 and again in 1994, the Supreme Court ruled that gender could not be used as a defining characteristic of jurors' eligibility for service. Both developments would have been enthusiastically welcomed by Hoyt, Hardee, and Durrance in 1961. But over the years, while standards of eligibility increasingly reflected a confident insistence on the equality of citizens—whatever their race, gender, or class—the use of peremptory challenges widened. The purpose of the peremptory challenge, after all, is to do an end run around the randomly drawn panel by finding reasons to exclude on other grounds jurors who might be predicted to be inclined against the attorney's client. The flamboyant use of jury consultants in the O. J. Simpson murder trial of 1994–95 made public what had been known primarily by specialists in the preceding decade. In that trial, both sides used expensive consultants who had made a profession of evaluating prospective jurors and predicting how they might be inclined to decide. The defense in the Simpson trial spent considerably more money than the state on these services. It used consultants not only during the jury selection phase but steadily throughout the trial, relying on the guidance of specialists not only in invoking peremptory challenges but also to study the responses of mock jury panels, and to make choices of which arguments were most likely to persuade that particular group of people.[295]

The obligation of citizens to make themselves available to serve on juries is based on the understanding that a proper jury expresses the moral consensus of the community.[296] Were Gwendolyn Hoyt to be tried today, no part of the community would be exempt from the obligation to serve; in some jurisdictions all adults, even nonvoters, even attorneys and judges, are entered in the jury pool. Hoyt and her lawyers would confidently expect a judgment by representatives of the full community, the judgment of her peers. Ironically, however, the simultaneous growth in the vigorous use of peremptory challenges to shape the jury in ways which attorneys think will serve their purposes testifies to widespread "countervailing doubt, mistrust, and ambivalence" about whether a random cross section of the public is to be trusted.[297] At the turn of the twenty-first century, our concept of the "peer" remains very much in question.

5

"A CONSTITUTIONAL RIGHT
TO BE TREATED LIKE AMERICAN LADIES"
HELEN FEENEY, ROBERT GOLDBERG,
AND MILITARY OBLIGATION
IN CONTEMPORARY AMERICA

"What's a nice girl like you want to go into service?"

World War II brought a large share of sorrow to Dracut, Massachusetts, and to Helen Buyo and her family. Helen's boyfriend was killed in the Philippines. Her brother-in-law also lost his life in the war. "We had a group of five girls that were close friends"; four had boyfriends, one a husband. Only one of the men came back from the war. "I wanted to enlist in the WAACs; I would go down to the recruiting office. The men would say 'What's a nice girl like you want to go into service? No openings now. Come back in two weeks.' " Parental consent was necessary for a woman under twenty-one who wished to enlist; Helen Buyo's mother was skeptical. She had heard troubling stories about WAACs' morals. There were rumors that they slept with soldiers, even that they were prostitutes. She knew that WAACs "got no respect. My mother said the WAACs were not a good life for her daughter. She wouldn't sign the papers."[1]

Frustrated in her desire to serve, Helen continued to live with her family in Dracut, a town north of Boston, and to work as a clerk in the state Division of Child Guardianship. A friend who was not a college graduate enlisted in the Navy and entered officers' training. "There she was humiliated by other officers because she wasn't from Wellesley or Radcliffe." Helen Buyo thought about aiming for law school, "but I had to work to support my mother. I would have had to go to night school for ten years." There was for her no equivalent of the GI Bill, which supported higher education for millions of veterans.

In 1951 Helen married Charles P. Feeney, a veteran who owned a small trucking company. Helen managed the company; they had two daughters in 1952 and 1953. The Feeneys continued to live in Dracut; both were active in local Democratic Party politics. Helen became president of the local Parent-Teachers Association and was approached to run for the nonsalaried town School Committee; no woman had ever served. "My husband encouraged me to do it. It was expected that you would lose once." But it was unusual for a woman to run; she was noticed, and, she observes now, "I was always a very good public speaker." Helen Feeney won her first campaign and quickly established herself as an outspoken official. She remained on the School Committee for three years. She was alert for corruption in building projects and the granting of contracts; she was skeptical of flashy curriculum reform. "I had to fight the superintendent from day one. People were being paid off. But they couldn't hide. I was hung in effigy at a town meeting." But Feeney stayed on; it was the superintendent who left Dracut. The Lowell *Sun*'s reporter called hers "a flamboyant career." Four or five years later, in the early 1960s, Helen Feeney received a phone call from the Town Moderator. "By five o'clock tonight I've got to appoint someone to the Building Committee for the Greater Lowell Vocational and Technical School." She agreed, and for nearly seven years Feeney, the only woman on a seven-person committee, oversaw development of a state-of-the-art regional school that would become one of the nation's largest vocational schools. The Committee visited model schools throughout the country; they developed high curriculum standards and pioneered in self-paced curricula. "I did my homework. Other members would often say, 'If Helen's not voting for it, I'm not voting for it either.'"

In 1963 the Feeneys sold the family business. Helen Feeney was hired as a senior clerk stenographer for the field office of the Massachusetts Civil Defense Agency in Tewksbury, close to home. No veterans passed the exam; she had the highest score. In 1967, on the basis of a promotional exam—a type on which veterans received only a 2-point bonus—she was promoted to the position of Federal Funds and Personnel Coordinator, the only woman among "fifteen or sixteen" service officers at the agency. She would hold the job until 1975. Meanwhile she tried to improve her position and her pay. In 1971 Feeney took the civil service examination for the position of Assistant Secretary for the Massachusetts Board of Dental Examiners. She received the second-highest score, but was ranked sixth on the hiring list, behind five male veterans, four of whom had received lower grades than she. A male veteran with a grade eight points lower than hers was appointed to the job. Before very long, Helen Feeney would find herself in the center of a national argument about what a grateful government ought to owe its veterans.

"I vote for all veteran legislation"

The obligation to serve in the military, which involves substantial physical risk, has never rested evenly on the population as a whole. Women have been recruited by the military in all wars: as volunteers, in support systems of medical care, feeding, spying. Their service has often seemed the more heroic because it was not coerced. In the United States women have always been exempt from the draft; their participation has—to varying degrees—occurred outside the boundaries of civic obligation, and, therefore, outside the boundaries of reciprocity and entitlement.

The language of obligation fits uncomfortably into democratic conversation; talk of obligation is as apt to lead to claims for entitlements as it is to assertions of equal responsibility. Although the reciprocal of the obligation to risk one's life for the state may be the right to bear arms, most veterans speak of the reciprocal of military service as entitlement to veterans' pensions, benefits, and preferences in hiring. We can trace Americans' changing understanding of the meaning of the obligation to serve in the military through the history of conscription; we can also trace that understanding through following arguments over what a grateful nation should owe to those who

**24. Helen Feeney, *Newsweek*,
March 5, 1979.**

have fulfilled their obligation of military service. The association between soldiering and entitlement runs very deep; the first large-scale public welfare system in the United States was invented for veterans of the Civil War, and the assumptions on which that system were grounded continued to shape American thinking about welfare long after the Civil War veterans were dead.[2]

At the end of World War II, Americans assumed that the answer to the question "Does what the state owes to citizens and what citizens owe to the state vary by sex?" was "yes." The state offered white men and women equal opportunity for suffrage; in virtually all other relationships—from Social Security entitlements to jury service to military obligation—sex and race played a defining role. The civil rights movement of mid-century challenged a wide range of distinctions habitually made on the basis of race; the feminist movement that followed and echoed it challenged distinctions made on the basis of sex. Two lawsuits, which reached the U.S. Supreme Court between 1979 and 1981, raised the same questions in different frameworks: Is the obligation to military service fairly distributed? What does the nation—including taxpaying nonveterans—owe to those who have fulfilled their military obligation? Helen Feeney raised the second question; as we shall see, Robert Goldberg would raise the first. The two issues bracketed the experience of military obligation: being drafted occurs before military service has begun; benefiting from veterans' preference policies happens after military service has been completed. One is preservice, the other postservice. When we examine each, we are examining the meaning of military obligation.

Helen Feeney's job competitors had benefited from the practice of veterans' preference, a strategy of indirect rewards for service in the armed forces that dated back to the Revolution, when "special provisions were made for disabled soldiers to serve as customs agents," and to the Civil War era, when the federal government first engaged in the preferential hiring of veterans.[3] The practice of veterans' preference, which represents a reallocation of resources but presumably does not "cost" the government any additional funds, should be distinguished from veterans' benefits, like insurance coverage or tuition payments, whose financial costs are explicit. Preference practices have been understood to be a gesture of gratitude by the community, which offers the jobs in its control and paid for by its taxes to those who have disrupted and risked their lives to protect it. But definitions of who counts as a veteran, and what veterans' preference practices will be, are the result of political negotiation. Often the distinctions between benefits and preferences have been fuzzy, even to those who were most deeply involved in constructing them. Charged with inconsistency in his own voting record during World War II, Representative Beverly M. Vincent of Kentucky snapped, "I am a veteran of the last war and I vote for all veteran legislation."[4]

The most common form is initial hiring preference, but promotional preferences and layoff preferences—treating veterans as first to be promoted and last to be laid off—are sometimes used as well. In its World War II guise, veterans' preference was offered first to disabled veterans, then to wives of disabled ex-servicemen and widows of deceased ex-servicemen, then to any veteran, and then to "natural" *mothers* of men who had died or been completely disabled in service and who were themselves widowed or divorced.[5] Veterans' preference thus privileged not only many men but also some women who were not themselves veterans. Had Helen Feeney married her boyfriend before he left for war, she would have inherited his preference. Widowed mothers of deceased soldiers could claim veterans' preference only if they were the "natural" mothers *and* if the father of the deceased or the husband of her remarriage was disabled. That is, the eligibility of a mother was determined by examining, first, her relationship to a husband and, second, her genetic relationship to her son. What counted as a "natural mother" was contestable. Not until 1960, well after the Korean War, was the provision expanded to include adoptive mothers "and those who served in loco parentis" but explicitly not to include "out of wedlock" mothers, who did not count as "natural." Even these modest changes were vigorously opposed by the Disabled American Veterans, who thought this was one among many efforts to "weaken, if not completely destroy," veterans' preference practices.[6]

Every state and the federal government, and many county and municipal governments, now practice some form of veterans' preference in civil service examinations. A few offer only tie-breaking preferences, but most follow the federal government in granting veterans a point advantage: often ten points are added to an examination score for a disabled veteran and five for one who is not disabled.[7] New Jersey and Massachusetts grant veterans *absolute* preferences—veterans who achieve a passing score are placed in descending order at the top of the civil service list, ahead of civilians who may have achieved higher examination scores than they. (Utah offers absolute preference in certain cases.)

In Massachusetts the veterans' preference legislation has been particularly sweeping. It granted absolute preference for their entire lives to anyone who had served the military in wartime for even a single day, not necessarily in a theater of war. Indeed, wartime was so generously defined in the statute (World War II, Korea, and Vietnam) as to cover the *entire* period from September 1940 to May 1975. Members of the Women's Army Corps and military nurses were specifically included. Those who achieved passing scores for any civil service position were placed on the list in the following order: first, disabled veterans in order of their respective standing on the examination, then veterans, then widows or widowed mothers of veterans killed in action or dead from a service-connected disability (in 1977, this last clause was changed to "surviving spouses and surviving parents"), and then, finally, other applicants.[8]

The practice of veterans' preference seems to have been unproblematic in Massachusetts in the early Cold War era. Virtually all veterans were men. A strict ceiling held the numbers of women in the armed forces to 2 percent between 1948 and 1967 with a brief lifting of the ceiling during the Korean War; before that, custom and practice kept women to only 1 percent of the armed services. Of those veterans, of course, only a small proportion sought civil service jobs when they returned to civilian life, and, when they did, sex segregation in state offices ensured that men rarely applied for jobs held by women—or, rather, ensured that women rarely held jobs that male veterans would find attractive enough to seek. (That is why Helen Feeney had little trouble finding her first job as a stenographer.) Veterans' preference seemed so unproblematic that it was excluded from the purview of the Equal Employment Opportunities Commission established by Title VII of the Civil Rights Act of 1964.

The close of the Vietnam War in 1973 had a sharp impact on this comfortable arrangement. The last years of the war coincided with a revitalized feminist movement. Women in substantial numbers entered nontraditional jobs. As early as 1971, the Equality Committee of the American Civil Liberties Union commissioned a memo on the implications of veterans' preference for equal employment policy which developed the argument that the preferences were excessive as applied to men and discriminatory as applied to women. The author of the memo, Peter Gregware, urged the ACLU to look for an appropriate case that would test the issue. Gregware was skeptical of blanket claims that the military had disrupted the lives of all veterans: indeed, full-time military career people may have retired on generous pensions and "still get a blanket preference in public employment." Even if veterans' preference practices were an appropriate gesture of gratitude, he thought the gratitude not finely tuned, "rewarding equally the soldier who risked his life in combat with the person who operated the stateside officers' club and the person who has received extensive technical training and benefits."[9] Many jobs traditionally monopolized by men for which feminists now demanded an opportunity to compete were in state and civic agencies. Returning Vietnam veterans increased the competition for such jobs; indeed some jobs, like those of police officers and forest rangers, could only be pursued through the public sector.[10] In the past, the Supreme Court had refused to consider claims that veterans' preference denied some groups in the population equal protection of the laws, relying on a 1915 decision that gave states all the range of a private employer in determining whom to hire and fire. But over the years, particularly as a result of the civil rights movement, states' ability to discriminate had been increasingly constrained; Gregware thought it was time to challenge states' options when the result was to discriminate on the basis of sex. Others who studied the problem recognized, as one analyst put it, that it was "almost a statistical impossibility" for women to be appointed to civil service positions.[11] They were pessimistic about the possibility of gathering enough votes in Massachusetts to accomplish legislative change and about the speed with which the recent increase in women's participation in the armed forces was likely to change substantially the proportion of female veterans.

They were right to be pessimistic. In 1973, a federal court in Pennsylvania had refused to question the practice of granting a ten-point bonus to the score of any veteran who received a passing grade on a state civil service examination. The court held that preference was not a denial of equal protection, but added, for the sake of argument, "even if provisions do discriminate against women, they may be justified as a recognition that experience, discipline, and loyalty which veterans gain in military service is conducive to better performance of public duties."[12] And later that year, the U.S. Supreme Court affirmed a lower court's ruling that the Minnesota veterans' preference statute, which, like that in Massachusetts, gave qualifying veterans an *absolute* preference for state jobs, was a rational scheme and within the boundaries of appropriate state action. The discrimination that women experienced was held to be unintentional.[13]

"You are not a veteran, but you could be disabled"

In 1973 Helen Feeney took an exam for the job of head administrative assistant at the Solomon Mental Health Center in Lowell. She received the third-highest grade on the examination; she was ranked fourteenth on the list behind twelve male veterans, eleven of whom had lower scores than she. "After a while, the civil service exams were a cinch for me. I took every one I could get; that let me know the structure of the exams. On one exam I got a 96 and the person who got the job got a 70." In 1974 she took an examination which covered a wide range of administrative assistant positions; her grade would have tied her for 17th place on the list; the veterans' preference formula caused her to be ranked 70th, behind 64 veterans, 63 of whom were men; 50 men had lower examination grades than she.[14] On March 28, 1975, as part of a reorganization of government departments, Helen Feeney was laid off from her position with the Civil Defense Agency.

Meanwhile, Alexander Macmillan, who chaired the state's Labor Relations Commission, was anticipating the demoralization of his own office. Massachusetts offered civil service examinations only intermittently; in interim periods it was possible to hire staff members provisionally. Macmillan had hired a number of young lawyers—including several women who were doing especially good work. Once the new civil service list was published, Macmillan would have to replace them with lawyers who, because they were veterans, would be placed high on the list despite their lower scores and weaker credentials. Macmillan predicted an office thrown into disarray.

Macmillan contacted Ropes & Gray, the distinguished Boston law firm; the task landed on the desk of a young associate, Richard Ward. Meanwhile, John Reinstein, a young lawyer employed by the Massachusetts affiliate of the American Civil Liberties Union, had independently raised the issue of veterans' preference with the committee that reviewed new cases for the Civil Liberties Union. Ward thought the time was right for a constitutional challenge. So did Reinstein; the two groups quickly came together. Because the suit had a major law reform objective beyond the protection of the interests of the individual clients, Ropes & Gray welcomed the institutional sponsorship of the ACLU. For its part, the Civil Liberties Union, with only one full time lawyer on its staff, could not take on the case alone. It needed the resources of a firm like Ropes & Gray.

Less than two years before, in 1973, the Supreme Court had ruled in favor of a female Air Force officer who was appalled to discover that she could not claim dependent's benefits for her husband on the same terms that her male colleagues could for their wives. Ruth Bader

Ginsburg had argued Sharron Frontiero's claim.[15] The decision was a complex one; six justices agreed with Frontiero, but only three drew analogies between discrimination on the basis of race and discrimination on the basis of sex. In their decision, the Supreme Court treated discrimination on the basis of sex with "heightened scrutiny," although they did not treat it with the high level of suspicion reserved for race discrimination. The level of scrutiny established for classifications based on gender in *Frontiero* gave Ward and his colleagues grounds for confidence that the Court would be equally skeptical of absolute veterans preference. "We believe," Ward concluded, "that a challenge of the Massachusetts veterans' preference statute under the Equal Protection Clause, on the grounds that it necessarily and systematically discriminates against women, would have reasonable prospects for success."[16]

The first plaintiffs were women attorneys, some of whom worked for Macmillan. The other women who joined the suit were themselves attorneys who were employed provisionally and faced the loss of their civil service jobs. Among them were Betty Gittes, who had been an activist as a student at Northeastern Law School in the early 1970s and had been seeking a civil service position; Kathryn Noonan, on the Labor Relations Commission; and Carol Anthony, who was Assistant Counsel in the Department of Public Welfare. "If the state had had a point preference I wouldn't have joined it," Anthony says now; it was the absolute preference that dismayed her.[17] Noonan and Anthony had tied with one man for the highest score when they took the Counsel I test in the spring of 1974 but were ranked 57th, behind 56 male veterans, 55 of whom had lower scores than they. They submitted not only accounts of their own experiences, but 50 other eligible lists, dating from 1971 to 1975. On these lists, 38% of the men were veterans in contrast to one half of one percent of the women; in every single list, female eligibles were placed behind male veterans with lower scores.[18]

In April 1975, just before the case was to be argued, the Massachusetts legislature decided to remove all appointments to state and municipal legal positions from the civil service law; that seemed to eliminate Anthony, Noonan, and Gittes. But legislators refused to shift to a point system or to change veterans' preference in any other way. The vote in the lower house was overwhelming: 159–61.[19]

Rick Ward did not believe the case was necessarily moot; absolute preference remained as a principle. But Betty Gittes and the other plaintiffs did want to add a non-lawyer, for whom absolute preference was still a live issue. "We looked at lists and lists," Betty Gittes remembers. "I started looking at the Civil Service lists and looked for women who were at the top but who had been bumped by veterans." She was frustrated. "Lots of people wouldn't talk to us. Still pretty scared. A lot of them were in provisional positions."

Helen Feeney had taken lots of tests. And, most important, "she had solid civil service status; she had been appointed from an examination and was part of the permanent civil service."[20] One summer evening she got a phone call from Betty Gittes.

Helen Feeney found it easy to respond. "I was getting mad. Test after test I would pass at the top." Another explanation is ironic; by then Charles Feeney had died. Many other women in her position, she noticed, were married to men who owed their own civil service employment to the veterans' preference practices. She no longer had "a husband who was a veteran and who would say no way you're getting involved in this case. I received calls from some women who did."

But, most important, as we have seen, Helen Feeney had keen political sensitivities and extensive political experience. "I'm the adventuresome type." She was no stranger to politics; she had already overcome having been burned in effigy at a Town Meeting in Dracut and criticized in editorials in the Lowell *Sun*. To sue the state was to take on the powerful Attorney General, Francis X. Bellotti, who ran the Democratic Party machine and was an effective opponent of the party's liberal wing; but Charles Feeney had been Francis X. Bellotti's campaign manager in Lowell, and Helen Feeney knew Bellotti and was not afraid of him.

When Feeney went to meet the lawyers at Ropes & Gray for the first time, she remembers that they seemed anxious, afraid she'd lose her nerve. As the case dragged on, "they even took me to the Harvard Club for lunch; I had the feeling that I was being reinforced." She grins. They need not have worried; "there was no way I was going to back out." The case lasted four years. Once she was identified in the press as a "52-year-old widow," the adjective stuck; "I remained a 52-year-old widow for four years." Helen Feeney laughs.[21] "Had they billed," Rick Ward says now, "time and charges alone had to have been a half million dollars. We loved every minute of it."[22]

Anthony and her colleagues tried to continue litigating the principle. They believed that if they had not been so poorly listed, they would have been certified and chosen for permanent positions long before the legislature omitted lawyers from veterans' preference. But they asked only for $1 in damages, and a year later the U.S. District Court considered their case moot. That left Helen Feeney. "I felt like the cheese in the nursery rhyme," she says now; "you know, 'the cheese stands alone.' "[23]

From the perspective of Helen Feeney and her lawyers, the national sense of obligation was hopelessly skewed. She was unemployed after repeatedly achieving examination scores that otherwise would have made her a prime candidate for placement in a range of good positions. More than half the men who held civil service appointments in Massachusetts were veterans; fewer than 2 percent of the women were. This was an accurate reflection of rules that had limited the numbers of women in the armed forces to 2 percent until long after World War II, excluded women with children until the 1970s, and required that women have higher entry-level education and aptitude test scores than men.[24] Feeney had once wanted to enlist but had needed parental permission when men her age did not. She argued that she was trapped in a Catch-22; urged by the state to marry and have children, "protected" from Army service for doing so, she was now "being penalized by the state for having exercised her fundamental constitutional right to marry and have children." The allocation of jobs was discriminatory; although women made up 43 percent of the people appointed to the Massachusetts civil service between 1963 and 1973, they were not distributed evenly across the various rankings of jobs. Officially until 1965 and informally until 1971, appointing authorities were free to define virtually any job as "male" or "female"; virtually all advertisements for administrative assistants and for lawyers specified "male."[25] Most women served in lower-grade positions that had actually been reserved for women and for which men traditionally had not applied. "You only got the jobs the veterans didn't want," Feeney remembered.[26]

The practical consequence of the operation of these proscriptions in combination with the veterans' preference formula was, Feeney thought, to make it virtually impossible for her to compete for the most attractive positions in the state civil service. Indeed, it has been estimated that on one of the eligibility lists she entered, "women lost an average of 21.5 places due to veterans' preference, while male veterans gained an average of 28 places." It was, she claimed, an excessive response to the service that men had offered the state. As one analyst put it, the cost of thanking veterans was borne "disproportionately by women seeking equal opportunities."[27] "We tried," John Reinstein observed a decade later, "to make a distinction between veterans' *benefits* like educational subsidies or health care support" and veterans' *preference*. "What was pernicious about veterans' preference was that it took a fixed asset and allocated it" unevenly. "It really closed the door to the sector of the economy that was beginning to evolve." Since most men had entered military service involuntarily, Helen Feeney did not think that she, as a nonvolunteer, was any more to blame for her disadvantaged position than most men were for their advantaged one.

As the Commonwealth of Massachusetts saw it, Helen Feeney had no grounds for complaint. The ratio of men to women in the state's civil service was 57–43; not an overwhelming bias, unless one factored in the point that most of the jobs held by women—file clerks, switchboard operators, stenographers—were jobs for which men did not apply. The veterans' preference statutes had not been intended to disqualify women; indeed, they explicitly included female veterans. Had Helen Feeney served her country, she too could have been bounced to the top of the list. "Two guys get out of high school, one joins the service, the other doesn't. The one that doesn't join has a jump on the other guys, like seniority when the layoffs came," an American Legion member wrote to the Lowell *Sun*. In that vision, permanent preference was a counterweight for the years the military had claimed from veterans' lives, whether or not they had been placed in physical danger.[28] The maintenance of veterans' preference—even absolute veterans' preference—had very strong public support.

To understand the particular intensity of the opposition to revision of preference policies on the part of veterans' groups it is necessary to recapture the particular combination of resentments felt by many veterans in this post-Vietnam War period: resentments constructed out of the knowledge of their own sacrifices and risks, the scorn they

25. John Reinstein,
County Court House, Boston,
1979.

felt they encountered on their return, and the absence of public recognition of their service. "It took a lot of courage to wear the U.S.
uniform during the Vietnam War, even on stateside service," wrote
one disabled veteran.[29] The Vietnam War Memorial would not be
inaugurated until years after the last U.S. soldiers had left Vietnam.
The lasting images of the close of the American involvement in the
war were not the traditional ticker-tape parades (that would not happen until 1985), but the urgent flight of helicopters from the roof of
the American embassy in Saigon in 1975. Long before the fall of
Saigon, the process of reconstructing veterans as victims had already
begun. They were victims, as Susan Jeffords has put it, "of their government, the war, the Vietnamese, American protesters, and the
women's movement—Vietnam veterans are portrayed in contemporary American culture as emblems of an unjustly discriminated masculinity."[30] This sense of being aggrieved, of having been obligated
to risk their lives and not receiving their proper entitlements, would

contribute to the strong support veterans' organizations like the American Legion gave to Ronald Reagan, who was sympathetic to their cause, and their votes contributed to the success of the Reagan-Bush ticket in 1980. Veterans' sense of being aggrieved also fueled their lobbying efforts in the late 1970s and energized their complaint that the traditional reciprocity between obligation and entitlement was not being maintained.

But veterans were themselves a complex category, not a single community. Vietnam engendered the largest opposition movement among its own veterans that any American war had seen. Organized as Vietnam Veterans Against War, they not only offered public testimony in congressional hearings and antiwar parades but also supported rap or consciousness-raising groups in which their developing criticism of the war helped them find, as one historian put it, "a renewed faith in their own moral integrity."[31]

For their part, traditional veterans' groups had a great deal of difficulty recruiting new members from the men who had been in Vietnam. Paul Hunt, a veteran of World War II who played a leading role in persuading the Massachusetts American Legion to contribute substantial funds to develop an amicus brief in the Feeney case and who lobbied vigorously to encourage the legislature not to change the system of absolute preference, was understanding. "The veterans came home, they'd gone through hell, and people spit at them."[32] In that context, Hunt concluded, veterans could be excused if they did not enthusiastically identify themselves. It would have to be the more solidly situated veterans of World War II and Korea who worked on behalf of the younger men. Hunt and his colleagues made no distinctions between the GI Bill and veterans' preference; both were ways of resituating veterans in the community and offering them upward mobility. Activism was the way the older men could help a generation that was getting a raw deal, and pay their own debt of gratitude to a government that had invested in them thirty years before, when they in their turn had been young and vulnerable.[33] Feeney's suit carried far more political and emotional baggage than its technical title—*Helen B. Feeney v. Personnel Administrator of the Commonwealth of Massachusetts*—suggested.[34]

Betty Gittes was sympathetic: "Helen Feeney got harassment. She received hostile mail." One woman wrote, "I hope you are thoroughly ashamed of yourself. If you aren't you should be for objecting to giving veterans first choice of jobs. You seem oblivious of the fact that those men fought and died for you. I wonder if all the members of the 'National Organization for Women' are as mean and small as you are. Such unsympathetic women don't deserve ever to get jobs near the top of the ladder and I hope they never do."[35] There was a postcard signed "Vet," headed "*Women vs. Men*": "Lady, it was the millions of men whose crosses are around the world (I saw them in England, France, Italy, Far East) who were discriminated against *forever*. Also those men whose injuries were and are irreparable—limb or disease. Where were the women in *World War I, World War II, Korea, Vietnam* and others. You and your ilk want the benefits of war but not the *burdens*."[36] One day Feeney came home to find a note in her mailbox: "I am a disabled veteran. You are not a veteran, but you could be disabled."[37]

"May all our Citizens be Soldiers, and all our Soldiers Citizens"

When John Jay, the senior American negotiator in Paris, hosted a ball celebrating the end of the War of the Revolution in the fall of 1783, his wife, Sarah Livingston Jay, made the plans and arrangements. She drafted the expected series of toasts. Most were rhetorically graceful but predictable enough, "The United States of America, may they be perpetual," "Moderation to our Enemies, Concord, Wisdom and Firmness to all American Councils," "Liberty and Happiness to all Mankind." One toast, however, may have struck a discordant note, coming as it did from a woman: "May all our Citizens be Soldiers, and all our Soldiers Citizens." The words testified to Sarah Jay's acceptance of a revitalized relationship between the military and the republican state. But there was a rhetorical imbalance, in which the gender of the listener made a difference. What did Sarah Jay mean by her words? What did her audience hear in them?[38]

Military service has infused the concept of citizenship since its origins. The first Greek polis to develop the practices of citizenship was Sparta, "the dark one," in historian Peter Riesenberg's words, where "citizenship developed against the backdrop of war and fear of re-

bellion," and where public service first meant "the full-time dedica-
tion of most of the citizen's best years to a steady, vigilant, and
dangerous military career." In the earliest, Spartan version of citizenship, "civic virtue is defined in terms of absolute military efficiency."[39]
To the warrior-citizen ideal by which Sparta defined itself Athens
would add political deliberation, service on juries, and voting, round-
ing out the conception of the good citizen who, as Aristotle would
write, "should know and have the capacity both to rule and be ruled,
and this very thing is the virtue of a citizen."[40] When Rome was faced
with invasion from Gaul in 390 B.C., male commoners were offered
citizenship in return for military service; their stake in the commonwealth was measured by the investment in arms that they could afford
to make.

Women cannot be part of this political community for the same
reasons male prostitutes are not part of the political community:
women are thought to put the security of the community at risk because they make their bodies available to please other persons; the
demands of the state come second.[41] The honor of male heads of
households is invested in the purity of their wives and daughters.
Women's vulnerability and sometimes their collusion with an enemy
could put men at risk, but women do nothing to shield the community from risk. In this way of thinking, which would persist for
millennia, women owe their first obligations to their families: unmarried women to their fathers, married women to their husbands.

The classic roles of women in wartime are two: both were named
by the Greeks, and both position women as critics of war. Antigone
and Cassandra are both outsiders, and therefore are less subject than
men to ambivalence about doing their share or abandoning their
comrades. They are free to concentrate on the price rather than the
promise of war. Antigone is the legendary daughter of Oedipus, who,
as an adult woman, confronts her uncle Creon, ruler of Thebes, with
the demand that he give a decent burial to the body of her brother
Polyneices, who had died attacking Creon's city. Creon insists that
Polyneices was a traitor, and the body of the traitor is left to rot,
unburied. Antigone secretly performs the funeral rites and buries her
brother. In Sophocles' *Antigone*, Creon condemns her to death; she
is sealed in a cave, where she chooses a quick suicide rather than slow
starvation. Her death shames the community. In Sophocles' telling

of the legend, Antigone is heroic. She understands that she cannot affect the outcome of battle, but she claims the power to set ethical limits on what men do in war. Cassandra is the daughter of Priam, king of Troy. The god Apollo promises her the gift of prophecy if she will lie with him. She accepts the proposal and the gift; but rejects Apollo. Furious, he declares that her prophecies will never be believed. In Aeschylus' play, Cassandra wanders through the Trojan War, expressing her anxiety and her criticism, foreseeing its tragic end.

To define the woman citizen as Cassandra is to constrain her permanently to the role of outsider as well as critic; at her worst Cassandra merely whines. The role of Antigone, with its claim that women can judge men, is perhaps more appealing, but it is best suited to exhausting moments of dramatic moral confrontation. Moreover, Antigone cannot make her claim effective until she is dead. Both roles maintain the classic dichotomy in which men are the defenders of the state and women are the protected.

The word "citizen" carried military overtones inherited from antiquity. The classical association between civic identity and arms-bearing was muted in the Renaissance, when the key ingredients in a claim to citizenship were ancestry and property ownership; the service a citizen was expected to offer his city took a variety of forms, only one of which was arms-bearing. But the link between arms-bearing and citizenship was central to the work of Machiavelli, who gave a primary role to expansion and violence in maintaining the vitality of political life. The significant members of his imagined republican political community were men with property to protect; men whose willingness and capacity to take up arms in defense of the republic was understood to entitle them to participate in the decision to defend it. There was no room for women in Machiavelli's civic order. The principal section on women and the state in Machiavelli's *Discourses* is entitled "How a State Falls Because of Women."[42]

Arms-bearing was central to this strain of the republican tradition. "The possession of arms," wrote James Burgh, an eighteenth-century English writer of great importance to American revolutionaries, "is the distinction between a freeman and a slave. He, who has nothing, and who himself belongs to another, must be defended by him, whose property he is, and needs no arms. But he, who thinks he is his own master, and has what he can call his own, ought to have arms to defend himself, and what he possesses; else he lives precariously, and at discretion."[43] This way of relating men to the state had no room in it for women except as objects—objects to be protected, burdens to be defended, targets of contempt.[44]

In early modern England, arms-bearing shifted uneasily between right and obligation. In the course of the seventeenth century, years of civil war and political revolutions at home and of colonial expansion abroad, an often onerous and resented duty was turned into a right. Centuries before the invention of civic policing, peace was maintained in the countryside by armed householders who protected their communities against violence by resisting thieves and burglars in their own homes and also by taking turns in the patrols known as "watch and ward." Infirm men and widows who headed their own households were required to pay for substitutes. Free men had the obligation to keep the peace by turning out to pursue bandits and rioters when the sheriff raised a "hue and cry," to join the *posse comitatus* when riots broke out, and to serve in the militia.[45] Similar attitudes prevailed in English colonies. In seventeenth-century Massachusetts, the state put its energies into compelling free adult males to bear arms, even to the point of subsidizing arms for the most impoverished.[46]

Utopian texts written in the sixteenth and seventeenth centuries—Sir Thomas More's *Utopia*, James Harrington's *Oceana*—sustained the point that in a wholesome state armed freeholders protected each other. More's Utopian citizens "despise war . . . they think nothing so inglorious as the glory won in battle." In Utopia, honor lies in winning by shrewdness and intelligence; "wild beasts fight with their bodies." But "both men and women alike carry on vigorous military training, so they will be fit to fight should the need arise." And families accompany mothers and fathers to battle, to help them and to urge them on. "It is a matter of great reproach for either partner to come home without the other."[47]

As royal power expanded, and as it became clear that "militiamen forced to fight for an unpopular cause were unreliable," kings increasingly demanded military forces which they could control. Kings wanted standing armies which they raised, trained, and paid. Unpopular kings distrusted an armed citizenry.[48] James II wanted a standing army which was largely Catholic, or at least sympathetic to Catholics. The more he disarmed Protestants, the more they claimed the right to bear arms. Out of these struggles was born the principle in the 1689 Declaration of Rights—"That the Subjects which are Protestants may have Arms for their Defence suitable to their Conditions and as allowed by Law"—and a century later, in the U.S. Bill of Rights: "A well regulated Militia, being necessary to the security of a free State, the right of the people to keep and bear Arms, shall not be infringed." In the eighteenth-century context, arms-bearing was both a personal right ("the natural right of resistance and self-preservation") and a personal duty (to assist "in the execution of the laws and the preservation of the public peace").[49] The doubled significance of arms-bearing is in some respects analogous to the doubled meaning of jury service. In both, individual vulnerability to an obligatory service simultaneously functions as the empowerment of the citizen and a constraint on governmental power.[50] In twentieth-century England, it is now understood that the obligation to bear arms will be activated only occasionally (such as a draft call) and that the right to bear arms no longer exists.[51]

In the early American republic, patriot men understood themselves to be sons breaking free of the control of their political fathers, but, as we have seen, they did not abandon their own claims to domination over the women of their family and community. The founders brought the law of coverture virtually intact into the republic, maintaining the claims of the married man to his wife's body, her earning power, and her property. It was understood that she had traded these for his protection, both civic and personal; he was the protector, she the protected. Thus a toast offered on the first anniversary of the Declaration of Independence: "May only those Americans enjoy freedom who are ready to die for its defense." In a formulation like this one, to be free required a man to risk death. The connection between the republic and male patriots—who could enlist—was immediate. The connection between the republic and women—however patriotic they might feel themselves to be—was remote.

The connection between the physical defense of the republic and the right to participate in governance periodically surfaced in debates over voting qualifications in the early republic. As we have seen in Chapter 3, virtually all states began by attaching property requirements to the suffrage. But they were challenged by men of little property who had served the republic in the militias and in the Continental Army; these men were shocked when they were not permitted to vote.[52] In the extended struggles over suffrage requirements in the early nineteenth century, property requirements gradually fell under the double assault of the principle of no taxation without representation and the spectacle of Revolutionary War veterans denied the suffrage.[53]

These formulations of citizenship and civic relations in a republic were tightly linked to race and manhood; it was white men who offered military service, white men who sought honor, white men who dueled in its defense. Manliness and honor were sharply and ritually contrasted with effeminacy and dishonor. In *Common Sense*, Tom Paine linked independence from the empire to the natural pride and independence of the grown son. "To know whether it be the interest of the continent to be independent, we need only to ask this easy, simple question: Is it the interest of a man to be a boy all his life?" Addressing his readers as "husband, father, friend or lover," Paine wrote "to awaken us from fatal and unmanly slumbers."[54]

The concept was destabilized in the prerevolutionary years, as those who challenged England's claims of authority struggled to articulate more satisfactory relationships between ruler and ruled, between the individual and state authority. They moved from a medieval language of hierarchical relationships to a system that stressed reciprocity between state and citizen. Building on one aspect of their inheritance from the medieval commune, a language whose "key words are *patria, amor,* and *animus,* which flow into various formulas for the love and service of country," as Peter Reisenberg reminds us, the new definition of citizenship also rested on *allegiance* (as demonstrated by one's physical presence and emotional commitment), which gradually came to be given equal weight with military service. An allegiance defined by race, location, and volition was an allegiance that white women could join. While the old language of republicanism deeply distrusted women's citizenship, a liberal language of independence and individual choice could accommodate white women as full participants in the life of the state. This vision of the republic infused the naturalization policy adopted after the Revolution, which welcomed white immigrants, set low residency requirements, and promised naturalized citizens the same "privileges and immunities" as those born in the United States.[55]

As they emerged from the War of the Revolution, the founding generation transmitted to its successors complex and sometimes contradictory understandings of the meaning of citizenship.[56] Sometimes claims of women's citizenship were aggressively developed independently of arms-bearing, by stressing, as did Judith Sargent Murray in America and Mary Wollstonecraft in England, women's native "capability" and competence as preconditions of citizenship. (Indeed, Wollstonecraft sneered at standing armies, likening uniformed soldiers who were admired for their status and attire to frivolous women, brought up to be deferential and to please their superiors by their manners and their dress.) Sometimes claims for women's citizenship were linked to other ways of risking one's life, such as childbirth.

What historian J. G. A. Pocock has called "the [American] language of myth and metahistory" connects citizenship to military service, and sets the context in which the reciprocity of rights and obligations has been understood.[57] Nine of the original thirteen state constitutions articulated the "duty of the citizen to render military service and the power to compel him against his consent to do so." The generic terms "people" and "citizens" fudged the issue of gender.[58] In the early nineteenth century, even Judge Joseph Story, usually very careful about whom he means when he says "citizen," left it vague when he discussed arms-bearing in his magisterial *Commentaries on the Constitution*: "The right of the citizens to keep and bear arms, has justly been considered as the palladium of the liberties of a republic."[59] Probably he meant only men. When George Mason refused to sign the Constitution because of the absence of a Bill of Rights, he asked rhetorically, "Who are the Militia? They consist now of the whole people"; probably he meant only white men.[60] However, other usages of "people" and "citizens" in the Constitution and in statutes were early understood to denote both men and women—most obviously in the right of petition and freedom of religion. All new citizens—male and female—were required to swear to uphold the Constitution.

During the War of 1812, to which they bitterly objected, Federalists tried unsuccessfully to detach citizenship from arms-bearing.

They argued that granting Congress the power to *raise* armies did not necessarily mean that Congress could *conscript* unwilling soldiers.[61] When in 1856 Chief Justice Roger Taney was writing the decision that denied the reenslaved Dred Scott the protection of the Constitution, Taney founded his assertion that Africans were "a separate class of persons . . . not regarded as a portion of the people or citizens of the Government" in part on the exclusion of African-Americans from arms-bearing and militia service in many free states.[62] Justice Benjamin Curtis drew opposite conclusions from the same basic factual situation: since disabled white men were not required to provide militia service but no one denied that they could be citizens, he thought it logical that other characteristics might also be considered inappropriate for militia service but compatible with citizenship. But Curtis was on the losing side.[63]

During and after the Civil War, the link between the obligation to bear arms and the rights of citizenship was strengthened.[64] The Emancipation Proclamation itself merged emancipation and arms-bearing, welcoming into the armed service of the United States the people whom Lincoln declared free. For enslaved blacks, arms-bearing for the Union was an experience that came before citizenship and helped to set the terms for it. Black men risked their lives for the Union long before the Thirteenth Amendment, and the claim that they had bought their rights with their blood suffused constitutional debate and also the discourse of Reconstruction.

But the more rhetoric linked black men to the republic because they had enthusiastically assumed the obligations of arms-bearing, the more invidious the implicit distinction between those who bore arms and those who did not. Memories of the violence and suffering of battle fed veterans' claims to their own entitlement and also their sense that those who had not been vulnerable to cannon fire were not politically equal. The editors of the New York *World* put it bluntly: "Woman, being exempted by her sex from military duties and responsibilities, holds all her rights by sufferance. . . . The capacity of men for political life does not depend upon their ability to drink tea . . . or spout speeches, but on the hardihood and strength of character which nerves them for military service at the call of the state. . . . It is female soldiering, not public tea-drinking, that must efface this distinction."[65]

For sixty-five years after the Civil War, women suffragists responded with combinations of four different arguments. One was the traditional claim, as old as the Greeks, that the obligation was not arms-bearing per se but risking one's life for the republic, and that childbearing women repeatedly satisfied that obligation. "Whose life is perilled when the soldier is born?" Lucy Stone asked.[66] Lillie Devereux Blake, who as extensively as any woman of her generation analyzed the relationship between civic rights and obligation, made the point firmly at the end of the century: "As women perpetually risk their lives and devote their time to the bearing of children, thus performing the highest duty of citizenship, they should justly be exempt from military duty."[67]

A second argument was that women do indeed provide military service. John Stuart Mill used the Spartan example: "though no less subordinate by law than in other Greek states," he wrote in 1869, Spartan women "were more free in fact, and being trained to bodily exercises in the same manner with men, gave ample proof that they were not naturally disqualified for them."[68] The Civil War experience provided ample documentation of service; at the 1876 convention of the National Woman Suffrage Association, Lillie Devereux Blake asserted what was already common knowledge: "women had actually enlisted and fought in our late war, until their sex was discovered, when they were summarily dismissed without being paid for their services."[69]

A third argument was that suffrage was not actually linked to arms-bearing. When Senator Justin Smith Morrill of Maine argued that the man who exercises the ballot must be prepared to defend it with the bayonet, Senator Aaron Augustus Sargent snapped back, "What do you do with men who are past the age of military service? Do you deprive them of the ballot?"[70] William Ingersoll Bowditch included the argument as part of his massive attack on women's exclusion from suffrage in 1875: "It is not . . . true that the right of suffrage for men is based in the slightest degree on their supposed ability to fight."[71] Some 40,000 men in Massachusetts were over eighteen but under twenty-one; "the very men who are best able to fight are not allowed to vote." One-sixth of all voting men were too old to fight. "But even if it were true," Bowditch went on, that some sort of military service ought to be considered as due from voters generally, why cannot women buy substitutes . . . or pay an equivalent, or be exempted like Quakers or ministers, or act as nurses? . . . [W]hy, if (as the last census proves), in time of peace, nearly as many women as men can be employed in the manufacture of ammunition cartridges . . . if in time of peace, women may be blacksmiths or engage in the manufacture of cutlery, edge-tools, and axes, or in the manufacture of gunpowder, fire-arms, percussion caps, &c.,—why, in the name of common-sense, cannot their labor be utilized in the same or some similar way in time of war? . . . [I]f woman can work out a highway tax, with horse and cart or spade and pickaxe, why cannot she work for the government in time of war?[72]

Yet another strategy—one which was used with increasing frequency in the period between the late 1890s and World War II—was to reject arms-bearing entirely and to juxtapose women's nurture against men's destruction. Instead of military service, women could sustain the republic by bearing witness for peace. Catherine Stebbins of Michigan told the Senate Judiciary Committee in 1880 that armies enacted "a solemn . . . farce . . . [T]he saintly Clara Barton" with her "cordials, medicines . . . lint and bandages" had been part of the same wagon train used by General McClellan to move men to the front lines. "[M]en . . . on both sides fall by the death-dealing missiles. Miss Barton and her aids bear off the sufferers, staunch their bleeding wounds, soothe the reeling brain, bandage the crippled limbs."[73] The assertion that women were a force for peace developed in the years leading up to World War I, embodied in the risks undertaken by the passengers on Henry Ford's Peace Ship and by many progressive feminists after the war was over and suffrage was accomplished.[74] Explaining her opposition to an Equal Rights Amendment in 1921, just after she had returned from an extended trip to postwar Europe, historian Mary Beard denied that she was one of the "equal opportunists to the bitter end." She had seen "so much industrial equality that women sweep the streets and till the land while men drink in the cafés. I believe that women will be conscripted for war in the future. . . . I am not interested one bit if that is all democracy has to offer."[75]

In the twentieth century, the relationship between citizenship and military obligation has generally been most intensely debated in the context of challenges to a wartime draft. Defending the draft during World War I, the Supreme Court expressed a capacious civic obligation to military service: "[T]he highest duty of the citizen is to bear arms at the call of the nation," observed Chief Justice Edward Douglas White, speaking for a unanimous Court. "[T]he very conception of a just government and its duty to the citizen includes the reciprocal obligation of the citizen to render military service in case of need and the right to compel it."[76] When a draft was reconfigured in 1940, the principle by which the legislation was justified was the obligation of every citizen; that only men were made immediately *liable* did not obliterate the principle of equal obligation of all.[77]

The debate over the relationship between citizenship and military obligation has rarely invoked gender. In 1928, however, the Supreme Court forcefully addressed women citizens' obligation to bear arms. When Rosika Schwimmer applied for naturalization, responding to the standard questionnaire, she answered "no" to the question "If necessary, are you willing to take up arms in defense of this country?" No one had ever calculated the number of women who offered the same answer or left the question blank. Indeed, pacifist citizens who applied for passports had to answer similar questions, and had been permitted to add the phrase "so far as my conscience as a Christian will allow." Supporting and defending the Constitution did not necessarily involve physical defense; "especially," observed the Chief of the Passport Division, since the oath "is administered to women and children."[78]

But Schwimmer had an international reputation for pacifism and war resistance; she was also a target of anti-Semites. Journalist Dorothy Bromley believed that the Chicago office of the Naturalization Bureau examined Schwimmer's file critically because they had been alerted by the Women's Auxiliary of the American Legion. Schwimmer's application was treated as a political gesture from the outset.[79]

Her negative reply to question #22 became the basis for denial of citizenship, even though, as Oliver Wendell Holmes would observe in his classic dissent when her case reached the Supreme Court, as a fifty-year-old woman she "would not be allowed to bear arms if she wanted to."[80] But the majority of the Court upheld the denial, asserting, "That it is the duty of citizens by force of arms to defend our government against all enemies whenever necessity arises is a fundamental principle of the Constitution."[81] Reflecting on the experience, Schwimmer thought ruefully of the many essays on citizenship and naturalization she was required to write in the process of her repeated appeals: "The United States had a perfect right to deny citizenship to me; but they owe me a Ph.D."[82]

The *Schwimmer* decision was made the more ironic by U.S. participation in the Kellogg-Briand Pact, which renounced war as an instrument of national policy.[83] In its aftermath, and with the support of the ACLU, Representative Anthony Griffin of New York introduced in 1929 a bill to amend the Naturalization Law of 1906, so that no person would be barred from taking the citizenship oath "by reason of his or her religious beliefs or personal convictions with respect to bearing arms, or the lawfulness of war as a means of settling international differences." A similar bill was introduced in the Senate in 1932 by Bronson Cutting of New Mexico; both were sustained by informal support committees of lawyers and others who had been associated with the Schwimmer case, including Katherine Devereux Blake, Alice Stone Blackwell, and Harriot Stanton Blatch, daughters of leading suffragists, who, with their mothers, had long raised questions about equal obligation of taxation, jury duty, and military service.[84] Neither bill was successful.

Meanwhile, what Griffin called "the heckling question" was taken literally and attention was selectively paid to the answers. The New York Office had asked the arms-bearing question erratically; after the Schwimmer case they took it very seriously. Dorothea Zukierelli, who had been a stenographer at the German embassy, and who became a Quaker in 1937, explained how she had moved from thinking the question inconsequential to regarding it as crucial:

In my petition of 1933 I had answered the question whether I would take the full oath of allegiance with "Yes." . . . I remember distinctly that . . . I was much disturbed about the question. . . . But I thought that women would never be called upon to take up arms, anyway. . . . When it was read to me again [in 1938, after she had become a Quaker], I felt it my duty to tell him what was on my mind and I asked him if the arms-bearing part could not be eliminated in my case.[85]

Shortly after the *Schwimmer* decision the citizenship applications of two conscientious objectors from Canada—Douglas MacIntosh, a minister, and Marie Bland, a nurse—who had served in noncombat roles in World War I, and who rejected arms-bearing on religious grounds, a more conservative position than Schwimmer's—were denied.[86] Their appeals took place in the context of congressional hearings on the Griffin bill, hearings in which women representing patriotic societies—the DAR, the Daughters of Union Veterans, Ladies of the Grand Army of the Republic, the United Daughters of the Confederacy, the American War Mothers—defended the *Schwimmer* decision and attacked proposals for change. "[T]he mothers of the men who have fought for this country beseech you not to give the great privilege of American citizenship to men and women who are not willing to bear arms and to pay the debt of devotion they owe to this country."[87] The congressional hearings helped publicize a trend, and lower and local courts and naturalization bureaus increasingly denied citizenship to women who would not check off an agreement to bear arms. Marie Bland's attorney, Emily Marx of New York City, accused the courts of "reading into the naturalization act a Congressional direction that women must promise to bear arms in order to become citizens."[88]

Not until 1946 were the *Schwimmer*, *MacIntosh*, and *Bland* decisions reversed. "The bearing of arms, important as it is," wrote Justice William O. Douglas, "is not the only way in which our institutions may be supported and defended, even in times of great peril. . . . Refusal to bear arms is not necessarily a sign of disloyalty." In 1950 the McCarran Internal Security Act required that the naturalization oath include a clause in which the new citizen agreed "to bear arms or perform non-combatant service, or take an alternate oath."[89]

The idea of the citizen-soldier was vigorously deployed during World War II. Selective Service was itself based on a concept of universal obligation; the preamble to the 1940 Selective Training and Service Act provided that "in a free society the obligations and privileges of military training and service should be shared generally."[90] Americans remained, however, deeply skeptical of women's service. This skepticism distinguished the U.S. public from its British counterpart, and probably is a measure of geographical distance from the actual fighting. Explicit policy, writes historian D'Ann Campbell, "kept Waves off ships and restricted Wacs from drills with real weapons."[91] In 1942 and again toward the very end of the war there was some thought of drafting white nurses, but enough were recruited as volunteers to make the effort unnecessary. (African-American nurses were segregated in the military.)[92]

Somewhat more attention was paid to the idea of following the British example and drafting women for noncombatant and war industry work. In early 1943, Warren Austin and James Wadsworth, two Republicans who were bitter opponents of New Deal legislation but strong supporters of Roosevelt's international initiatives, proposed universal registration for national service of all men between eighteen and sixty-five, and of all women between eighteen and fifty who did not have children younger than eighteen living with them.[93] "[T]he democratic way," observed Robert P. Patterson, Undersecretary of War, "is to recognize the equality in obligation of all to serve . . . in the way that will best serve the Nation."[94] African-American organizations supported the move but cautioned that there was a need for guarantees against nondiscrimination.

Yet the bill was vigorously attacked, in part by a coalition of women's peace organizations in uneasy alliance with right-wing organizations who defined women's services in the home as a noncombatant service that substituted for the draft. Mildred Scott Olmsted, who had organized the Women's Committee to Oppose Conscription (WCOC), declared in a radio broadcast: "Women are naturally and rightly the homemakers . . . They play their part during the war by 'keeping the home fires burning' . . . and by carrying on the services that hold the community together."[95] Among these services was supervision of adolescents, particularly adolescent girls who were vulnerable to sexual exploitation by servicemen.[96] They warned of an increase in venereal disease if mothers were not home to supervise their children.[97] The far-right group Mothers of Sons did not disagree; they warned that "this bill would nationalize our women and complete the sovietization of our country."[98] Colonel Lewis Sanders of the War Manpower Commission shrewdly pointed out that the women's groups arrayed against the legislation were located on the fringes. He criticized them for "thinking entirely in terms of the privileges and freedoms which a democracy is created to protect, but they ignore completely the fundamental obligations on which the success of any democracy rests."[99]

In fact, the popular understanding of the meaning of the war itself came to be linked to a commitment to define women as fulfilling their civic obligation within their homes. One major distinguishing difference between dictatorships and democracy, as Americans saw it, was that democracies might regiment men but would not regiment women.[100] Americans emerged from the war strongly committed to the concept of a sex-based combat exclusion and the sense that it was a crucial boundary to maintain.

There was a flurry of talk about the relationship between citizenship and military obligation in 1948, in the context of the Soviet Union's explosion of an atomic bomb, a national debate on universal military service, and the restructuring of the Selective Service System. Although General (soon to be President) Dwight D. Eisenhower testified that he expected it would be necessary to draft women in the next large war, the point was not pursued, and what discussion there was was so soaked in misogyny that it is difficult to evaluate for precedent.[101]

During the Vietnam era, opponents of the war and draft resisters often stressed their loyalty to conceptions of citizenship that permitted rejection of some state policies to exist simultaneously with allegiance; loyal citizens could, without putting their own loyalty in question, refuse to participate in ill-considered, ill-founded national policies. Draft resisters pressed to expand the possibilities of a critical allegiance that was grounded in secular conscientious objection. Debate about the link between military service and civic obligation was dampened by the ability of many opponents of the war to avoid service by claiming student deferments or enlisting in the National Guard. It was also dampened by the federal courts' expansion of the terms under which conscientious objection could be claimed.[102] Not long after the draft lottery was instituted the war itself wound down. The initiation of an all-volunteer military force after Vietnam ended the draft and with it discussions of military obligation for men. But as the war wound down, the fight over the Equal Rights Amendment heated up. By the mid-1970s, argument over the ERA was rich in implications about whether equality for women necessarily meant equal military service and equal military risk.[103]

If male citizens were obliged to risk their lives on the battlefield, it was an easy step to the principle that the state was obliged to reciprocate by the provision of at least modest financial support for wounds sustained when the state itself had put the individual at risk. Thucydides' account of Pericles' Funeral Oration after the Battle of Marathon offers an answer to the question "What does the community owe to those who have died for it?" Pericles' answer is both aesthetic and practical; the city will honor its heroes, and it will also support the heroes' children until they came of age.[104] In the 1790s, some modest support was offered to disabled veterans, but Congress did not pass general pension legislation until 1832, or cover surviving widows until 1834, by which time many veterans—and their widows—were dead.[105] Congress committed itself to disability pensions shortly after the Civil War broke out, however, promising immediate pension benefits to disabled soldiers and to their dependent mothers and sisters—statutes that were gradually expanded by amendment and by interpretation after the war until, as Theda Skocpol has argued, the Civil War veterans pension system became a veritable social insurance system for an entire generation of the "righteously privileged," largely middle-class Northern white men. Justified as entitlement by "the deserving core of a special generation," the reciprocal obligation of a grateful nation, the pension system offered the experience of social insurance to a single sector of the population several generations before the New Deal.[106] In the same era, states began to offer preference in civil service jobs to veterans; the first civil service statute in Massachusetts, passed in 1884, offered preference to veterans, "other qualifications being equal," in appointments and promotion.[107] As World War II ended, a capacious system of entitlement—the GI Bill of Rights—was put into place, privileging veterans' entry into postsecondary education and home ownership. Simultaneously, as we have seen, a capacious system of veterans' preference was established, offering veterans privileged entry into the workforce.[108]

But the system was not the same for male and female veterans; for example, the Senate deleted a provision of the Veterans Preference

Act of 1944, initiated in the House by Charles La Follette of Indiana, which "would have given the same preferences to husbands of disabled women veterans and unmarried widowers of deceased ex-servicewomen as the Act allowed" to their female counterparts. Had that provision remained, establishing a system of entitlement which was truly reciprocal as between spouses, it might well have set a model for the equal treatment of dependents of male and female military personnel, and Sharron Frontiero might not have had to turn to the courts to demand a dependent's allowance for her husband in 1973.

"If two things are inextricably tied together, and you can think of one without thinking of the other, why then, you have a legal mind"

Helen Feeney could feel triumphant in March 1976. The Federal District Court held that the permanent and absolute veterans' preference was unconstitutional. As Judge Joseph L. Tauro put it, writing for the majority: "While there is no constitutional right to public employment, once a state decides to provide public service jobs, the Fourteenth Amendment demands that it must do so in a fair and equitable manner." Because the Massachusetts veterans' preference formula was "triggered by decades of restrictive federal enlistment regulations" the selection policy that emerged from it was neither impartial nor neutral; its impact on women "neither fair nor equitable."[109] But the margin of victory was thin; one of the two judges in the majority emphasized "the limited reach of our holding"; the other judge dissented.

"It took a woman to do what no other person or group has been able to establish," said the Boston *Herald-American* the following day.[110] Even Edward Powers, who had been director of the Civil Service Commission and the person in whose name Feeney had brought her suit, agreed that the outcome was a good one: he thought it was "ludicrous in this day and age for a woman professional not to get the job she deserves in public employment."[111] The Civil Service Commission itself was relieved to have lost; the Personnel Administrator wrote immediately to Attorney General Francis X. Bellotti urging him not to appeal the decision. Michael Dukakis, the liberal

Democratic governor, moved immediately to suspend absolute preference and to urge legislation establishing a point system which would give veterans only limited preference.[112] Early one morning Helen Feeney answered her front door, wearing a chenille bathrobe, and found Fred Graham and a CBS camera crew on her doorstep. It is hard to say who was more surprised—she at their appearance or they at her refusal of the publicity.

But the telephone in Helen Feeney's home began to ring with hate calls at 6 a.m. the day after the news was announced. "I didn't think people would be that mean. But they will adjust."[113] "All of us guys who are veterans are very upset today," wrote a local columnist. "I'll tell you what's unconstitutional: it's unconstitutional to give those juicy Civil Service jobs away to the panty-waists and shirkers who never marched proudly in the uniform of their country."[114] The former state commander of the American Legion said the decision hurt the "Vietnam vet, the guy who really needs help now."[115] Judge Levin H. Campbell was attacked as antiveteran for having once participated in a decision "that an antigovernment protester was not desecrating the flag when he wore it sewed to the seat of his pants."[116] Judge Tauro was attacked as a supporter of the women's liberation movement.[117] The legislature quickly passed resolutions demanding an appeal.

Buoyed by the knowledge that the legislature had been unambivalent when the question had been put to it, and by the strenuous urging of veterans' groups, Attorney General Bellotti moved quickly to appeal the decision to the U.S. Supreme Court.[118] For the next four years, Bellotti was joined by Thomas R. Kiley, an Assistant Attorney General, who had been seriously wounded in Vietnam.[119]

Dukakis had no interest in appealing the decision; he urged Bellotti to abandon his effort. Bellotti, who was elected and had his own constituency in which veterans were a substantial segment, set off an unprecedented and high-profile struggle between a governor and Attorney General of the same political party, exposing a fault line between Massachusetts Democrats that would widen over the course of the next decade.[120] A President faced with a similar situation could simply fire his Attorney General, but Dukakis had to beg the Supreme Judicial Court to constrain Bellotti. Could an Attorney General compel the governor to "go forward with litigation against his will"?[121]

Could "the willing attorney . . . make his unwilling client go forward"? Could the Attorney General, a member of the executive branch, be directly instructed by the legislature? It was a humiliation for Dukakis when the Supreme Judicial Court ruled that Attorney General Bellotti had his own responsibility to exercise his judgment about what would further the interests of the Commonwealth and the public he represented.[122]

Litigation wobbled back and forth between the U.S. Supreme Court and the U.S. District Court in Massachusetts for the next two years. Before it would accept the case, the Supreme Court required that the District Court reconsider its decision in light of a new Supreme Court ruling that had recognized that "well-intentioned programs may have uneven side effects: society is too complicated for every discriminatory consequence to disqualify legitimate policies." Was the Massachusetts practice merely "a neutral classification with unintended effects"? Tauro and Campbell stuck to their position that absolute preference—as Campbell put it—"forces women to pay a disproportionate share of the cost of benefiting veterans by sacrificing their own chance to be selected for state employment."[123]

As Helen Feeney's case was restored to the Supreme Court docket, veterans' preference policies once again became the focus of national attention. In Massachusetts the issue was absolute preference, but as the ACLU memorandum of 1971 had signaled, even the federal scheme, which awarded points to every competitive examination score taken by veterans over the course of their lives, came under attack from women's groups and their allies. President Jimmy Carter had long been skeptical of the way in which even limited permanent preferences of this sort marginalized most women; he believed it was an excessive assumption of social obligations toward veterans. In 1978, Carter tried to establish a ten-year limit on the length of time veterans could claim an additional ten points on civil service examinations. He was unprepared for the strength of the resistance from veterans' groups; even after congressional committees extended the time limit to fifteen years, the bill was defeated. It was a straw that showed, perhaps, which way the wind was blowing.[124]

Meanwhile, Helen Feeney was getting more unpleasant experience in being a public figure. "Every time there was news coverage, I got obscene or threatening calls, like 'Have somebody else start your car

26. "You've Come a Long Way, Baby." Cartoon by Bill Clark,
October 13, 1977.

tomorrow.' "[125] The Lowell *Sun*, which could be counted on to be skeptical, linked her case to claims for gay rights and funding for abortion; all were predictors of what an Equal Rights Amendment would accomplish. Feeney, who prided herself on her conservative and respectable dress and demeanor, appeared in a *Sun* editorial cartoon as a flower child: bare midriff, low-slung jeans, cleavage.[126] "Helen Feeney of Dracut is well-known," wrote the editorialist, constructing a figure who had enriched herself by the state jobs and had excused herself from military obligation. "Long interested in government affairs, she followed the traditional route that public office holders frequently take by going from an elective position to state employment. . . . when the male vets she now resents so much were called to the colors, they had no alternative but to go."[127]

The questions brought to the Supreme Court remained the questions with which the case had begun. What are the reasonable bounds of the obligations that a state may assume to those who had risked their lives in its behalf? Was it reasonable to treat all who had offered military service—whether voluntary or involuntary, with or without combat risk—as having been equally obliged, and therefore equal recipients of the state's largesse? "When a man enters the service," observed a disabled veteran, "he's given a serial number and he never knows whether he'll wind up stateside or overseas. He's ready to go wherever he's transferred, whether it's with a combat unit overseas, or with back-up or supporting units."[128] What was reasonable for the state, in turn, to require that its citizens—who paid obligatory taxes to sustain benefits and preferences—return to those who had performed military service? As Judge Campbell put it: "The law was sexually skewed from the outset, since the exclusionary effect upon women was not merely predictable but absolutely inescapable . . . Where a law's consequences are . . . inevitable, can they meaningfully be described as unintended?"[129]

When the case reached the U.S. Supreme Court, each side was supported by a brief from a nongovernmental group. The American Legion emphasized the reasonableness of rewarding service, especially since no one even hinted that preferences had been specifically intended to discriminate against women. Indeed, as more women entered the All-Volunteer Force, the proportion of women eligible for preference was bound to increase over time. A brief signed by the National Organization for Women, the American Jewish Committee, and a half dozen other well-known progressive women's groups—the League of Women Voters, the Women's Equity Action League, the National Federation of Business and Professional Women—argued that permanent preference constituted "invidious discrimination" which ensured perpetuation of past discrimination. The Legion expected things to change slowly as more women entered the armed forces and, in the course of time, became veterans themselves. But NOW and its allies argued that long before that could happen several generations of Massachusetts women—Helen Feeney and her daughters and their daughters—would not be able to make careers in the civil service. "Divorcing impact and intent given the gross quality of the Massachusetts preference," Ruth Bader Ginsburg wrote encouragingly to John Reinstein as he prepared for the Supreme Court, "reminds me of the comment attributed to a famous law professor: If two things are inextricably tied together, and you can think of one without thinking of the other, why then, you have a legal mind."[130]

Bellotti and Kiley carried on their challenge despite the wishes of their governor. They had their odd counterparts in Solicitor General Wade McCree, Jr., and Deputy Solicitor General Frank Easterbrook, who filed an amicus brief on behalf of the United States and in support of Massachusetts even though President Carter personally disagreed with them.[131] Although federal preferences were not as sweeping as those in the state, McCree and Easterbrook thought it was in the national interest to protect flexibility and "to defend the prerogatives of Congress and the Executive Branch."[132] It was widely reported that the President was furious; it was certain that women's groups were.[133] Four women attorneys on the staffs of federal agencies prepared a quite different amicus brief supporting Feeney—"a victory for women's groups and a tacit admission of error by the Carter administration," observed the *Globe*.[134]

Thomas Kiley conducted the argument before the Supreme Court on February 26, 1979; Bellotti joined him at the counsel's table. The argument was organized as an equal protection case under the Fourteenth Amendment; no one in the oral argument used the word "obligation." Kiley insisted that Feeney overstated her complaint; she had, after all, "held a significant civil service position." When Kiley made the point that females held over 42 percent of all civil service jobs, Justice John Paul Stevens pressed him; twice Kiley responded that "traditionally men and women do not always compete for the same jobs," and "common awareness tell[s] us . . . that women and men don't always compete."[135]

"It might also be a truism," said Stevens, "that a lot of women don't even bother taking the test because they are not veterans and they know they can't overcome the great big handicap."[136]

Rick Ward needed to show that 42 percent was not a meaningful figure; those women were mostly secretaries and clerks. When he raised the matter of the expansive categories of women—married, with children, and so forth—who had been barred from service, he was interrupted: "Is it also discriminatory to bar women from combat and then make combat service the basis of the preference?" One justice pursued Ward, urging him to concede that the reasoning he used against veterans' preference would "condemn all the federal veterans' preference legislation." Ward did not flinch; point systems have a "much less significant impact on women."

27. These pastel sketches of Richard Ward and Thurgood Marshall were drawn during the Supreme Court argument of *Personnel Administrator of Massachusetts v. Feeney*, 1979. Justice John Paul Stevens is in the background.

"There has to be some limit when you say that your goal is simply to reward veterans," Ward summed up. "For example, the state couldn't really say that only veterans could practice law in the Commonwealth of Massachusetts or only the children of veterans."[137]

Outside the courtroom, Bellotti hugged Helen Feeney. Betty Gittes, who had initiated the case, was shocked. Feeney was not surprised; Bellotti had confessed to her some "doubt about the fairness of absolute preference, but also said the law was on his side and he would win. He felt that he had won; he was consoling me."

In the decision, which the Court announced in June, Justices Thurgood Marshall and William Brennan agreed with the District Court:

"the absolute-preference formula has rendered desirable state civil service employment an almost exclusively male prerogative. . . . this consequence follows foreseeably, indeed inexorably, from the long history of policies severely limiting women's participation in the military."[138] But they were in the minority; the rest of the Court were unconvinced that the discrimination had been intentional. Moreover, Stevens and White added, *male* nonveterans were also disadvantaged by the practice, and therefore the adverse effects were not the result of invidious *gender*-based discrimination.

The American Legion was delighted: it was "a great day for the commonwealth," said the *Massachusetts Legionnaire*.[139] The Boston *Globe* considered it an "unnaturally static" decision; "past errors are rigidly to be preserved."[140] Ruth Bader Ginsburg was even more skeptical; the Court's rulings on women, she thought, had moved "from no rights to half-rights to confusing rights."[141]

Helen Feeney found a non-civil service job, as executive director of the Dracut Council on Aging. After she finally retired, she started school full-time; in 1989 she earned an M.A. in gerontology at the University of Massachusetts, Boston. She lives in North Andover now, a member of the Democratic Town Committee. Years after the case, she was approached by "the very veterans who opposed me. . . . when the next generation grew up, they would call me and ask to make a contribution to my legal expenses. Because then they had sons who wanted to go on the police force and they couldn't. There hadn't been a war to make veterans."[142]

The Supreme Court decision, observed the National Commander of the American Legion, represented a "restatement of allegiance to the veteran population by a grateful nation."[143] What was at play here was a chimera: the belief that although not every man enrolled in the armed forces had served in combat, or had much chance of serving in combat, every man *might* have served in combat, and so was entitled to be treated as though, having risked his life for his country, he had earned the gratitude of the community and was entitled to civil advantages for the rest of his life. Ignoring the majority of veterans, to whom his words did not apply, Kiley had ended his oral argument before the Supreme Court: "We are talking," he concluded, "about a group of individuals who themselves have sacrificed in time of war and are deserving of the nation's approval."[144] That gratitude, and sense of entitlement, can be activated in a wide range of civilian contexts; as of the year 2000, ten of our forty-one Presidents have been generals.[145] Historian Sheila Tobias, who studied the postwar careers of veterans, found that "service in war gives veterans a stock of political capital"; they can use this capital as evidence of experience, patriotism, and of their claims to "competence in matters of foreign and military policy."[146]

The obligation of military service can be traced indirectly, by measuring the benefits and preferences with which the nation responds to those who have fulfilled it. The Massachusetts veterans' preference legislation was constructed for a community divided between veterans and nonveterans. It was influenced more than its authors realized by the deep-rooted assumptions that were central to the old law of domestic relations: that women are covered by husbands' civic identity; that they experience state power through their fathers' and husbands' service. These assumptions had shaped the language of veterans' preference entitlements throughout its history, including the moments central to Feeney's life: the higher age requirement for her enlistment in World War II; the requirement that her parent approve her enlistment, but not that of a brother of the same age; the entitlement of widows to their husbands' preferences; Feeney's own exclusion, as a mother, from armed service. As Helen Feeney learned, in argument over how extensive benefits and preferences should appropriately be, Americans also found themselves struggling to define the boundaries of military obligation. What is a reasonable response to those who have fulfilled that obligation? Lifetime support from a grateful nation? Limited support to get them on their feet? Ten points advantage in civil service tests? Fifteen points? For ten years after the completion of their service? For the rest of their lives?

Conscription is a more direct way of measuring military obligation, and to argument over the draft we now turn.

"Women of the army"

Though Americans have never embraced policies creating obligations for women to go into combat in the national defense, women have long been part of American military forces to a far greater extent than is usually appreciated.[147] As historian Barton Hacker succinctly explained some years ago, early modern armies—including those in British America—lived off the countryside and traveled with hundreds of civilians who made their livings cooking, selling small items, and laundering for the troops. Many of these civilians were women, and only a small proportion of these camp followers were prostitutes.[148] In British practice, with which the colonists had become familiar during the Seven Years' War, each company had its own allocation of women, usually but not always soldiers' wives and occasionally mothers; when British men sailed, British women sailed with them. In the original complement of eight regiments that the British sent to put down the American rebellion, each regiment had 677 men and 60 women.[149]

In the newly independent states, patriots were skeptical about giving women official status in the army; Washington objected to a fixed quota of women. But the women followed nevertheless. By the end of the war, Washington's General Orders allowed no more than one woman to draw food rations for every fifteen men in a regiment. Some, no doubt, came for a taste of adventure. Generals' wives, like Martha Washington and Catherine Greene, took their right to follow as a matter of course, and spent the winters of Valley Forge and Morristown with their husbands. However, the vast majority of the women who followed the armies were impoverished. Wives and children who had no means of support when their husbands and fathers were drawn into service followed after and cared for their own men, earning their subsistence by cooking and washing for the troops in an era when the offices of quartermaster and commissary were inadequately run and when cleanliness was virtually the only guard against disease. Although these women—certainly many thousands, although estimates vary—were sometimes referred to as "women of the army," they had no official position, and they were never eligible for veterans' pensions or benefits.

The only "woman of the army" who has left us a narrative of her experiences is Sarah Osborn, who was eighty-one years old when Congress made it possible for dependent survivors of Revolutionary War veterans to claim their pensions. She testified to her own service as well as to her husband's in a deposition sworn before the Court of Common Pleas in Wayne County, New Jersey, in 1837. Osborn's husband was a commisary guard; Sarah Osborn traveled with him. Her account tells of working when the army was at West Point in the winter of 1780–81; of the long expedition south, marching proudly on horseback into Philadelphia, and then continuing to Yorktown. At Yorktown she brought food to soldiers under fire. When, standing on the battlefield, she told George Washington that she did not fear the bullets because they "would not cheat the gallows," she was conveying her understanding that her challenge to royal authority was comparable to his; if the soldiers risked being hanged for treason, so would she.[150]

We know that there were women who truly were "of the army," but except for one who claimed a government pension for her service, we know details about very few. In 1782, Deborah Sampson, who was already notable in her community of Middleborough, Massachusetts, because of her height and strength, adopted men's clothing and the name of Robert Shurtleff. She enlisted for service with the 4th Massachusetts Regiment and served with her regiment in New York and possibly in Pennsylvania until she was wounded at a battle near Tarrytown, New York. After her return to Massachusetts she married and bore three children, but the fame of her exploits persisted. When a fictionalized biography was published in 1797 by Herman Mann, she went on a wide-ranging speaking tour, perhaps the first American woman to undertake such an enterprise, and applied for the pensions to which her wartime service entitled her. These were awarded slowly and grudgingly, and she died impoverished in 1827.[151]

George Washington's recruits were part of a radical transformation of European and American armies into modern, bureaucratized institutions. In the years between 1750 and 1860, uniforms increasingly denoted status; camp followers and hangers-on were energetically, though not always successfully, excluded. By mid-century, in the Crimean War and at the outset of the American Civil War, armies had officially excluded all women but nurses and laundresses; the exclusion of women was the mark of a "modern" army.

Nevertheless, there were at least several hundred women at the front in the Civil War; historians continue to find more. The enlistment of many "beardless boys" made it easier for women to cut their hair short and pass. Many were only discovered after they were wounded; others were absorbed into the forces even though their colleagues knew their secret.[152] Jane Schultz has found thousands more women on the margins between civilian and camp life, crossdressing as spies and soldiers, cooking and laundering. Based on federal card files of women who nursed, cooked, and laundered in Union hospitals, Schultz estimates that at least 20,000 black and white women worked at some time during the war in the military hospitals of the Union and the Confederacy.[153]

During World War I, over 20,000 women were recruited as nurses. Thousands more made their way to Europe under the auspices of the Quartermaster Corps and voluntary organizations, serving as physicians, telephone operators and Red Cross workers.[154] None had rank or military status, although many were led to believe they did, since they were welcomed as "women members of the American Expeditionary Force" and were subject to court-martial. When they made claims on the basis of their wartime service—even service abroad, as telephone operators who had been part of the Signal Corps in the AEF in France discovered—their claims were denied.[155] Long after the war was over, American nurses, led by the redoubtable Julia Stimson, embarked on a long campaign to achieve military rank. Ultimately they were granted rank, but it was only "relative"—that is, a male officer would always outrank a woman of similar status.[156]

Not until World War II did women achieve, as Susan Hartmann has put it, "permanent, regular status in the military establishment." Gender and race intersected in the construction of military status. No women served on draft boards until 1967; the decision of which men could be spared from civilian service was consigned to men. Only white female nurses received equal pay and allowances and full military rank. (White male nurses were not commissioned as second lieutenants in the Army or ensigns in the Navy; they were ranked as corpsmen or medics even when they had nursing degrees.) African-

Americans were limited to the lowest grades in the Women's Army Corps and completely excluded from the Navy, the Coast Guard, and the Women's Air Service Pilots. African-American nurses were employed only to care for black wounded and for prisoners of war. By the end of the war, some 350,000 women—4,000 of them African-American—had been involved in military service.[157]

Women were recruited into the Army in two separate stages. First, as members of the Women's Army Auxiliary Corps, in May 1942, on terms that made it clear that they were temporary workers, who would receive no benefits or reemployment rights after discharge. Then, in September 1943, after extended debate, the WAAC was dissolved into the Women's Army Corps, which initially provided full military status and benefits only for the duration of the war and six months thereafter. At her first press conference, the politically astute first director of the WAC, Oveta Culp Hobby, had to field the following questions:

Q: How about girdles?
A: If you mean will they be issued, I can't tell yet. If they are required, they will be supplied. . . .
Q: Will they march and carry arms?
A: They will learn to march well enough to parade, but they will carry no guns.[158]

As the concept of "relative rank" suggests, the juxtaposition of women and military service profoundly disturbed the sexual order. The recruitment of women raised major questions about the relationship of gender to military obligation and service.[159] In developing a rationale for women's units during World War II, military personnel and elected male officials stressed women's docility and usefulness to men. Regulations excluded women from combat duty, limited the numbers who could be accepted and the rank to which they could rise (until 1967 no woman could serve in a command position), and offered fewer fringe benefits than were received by servicemen of the same rank. Women Air Service Pilots (WASPs) were forbidden to carry male passengers and to share a cockpit with a male co-pilot.[160] Women would never supervise male personnel. "In 1944," Susan Hartmann writes, "the Marine Corps got around the ticklish problem of female authority by ruling that it was proper for a woman officer to direct men when her orders were construed to be *emanating* from her male superior."[161] At the war's end, the Veterans of Foreign Wars banned women from membership.[162]

To receive dependents' assistance, women veterans had to prove that they provided the major support; male veterans did not have to offer this proof.[163] WASPs were ineligible for veterans' benefits.[164] For their part, advocates of women's service generally stressed the willingness of women to share the responsibilities of citizenship. They were cautious about how much equality they asked for and hesitated to criticize asymmetry of status with men.

Demobilization at the end of World War II seemed to restore traditional gender relations to the military. In 1945, the Army included 153,600 enlisted women, which represented more than 2 percent of the force. This number was quickly reduced to some 10,000. Although General Dwight D. Eisenhower spoke of women's wartime service with admiration at hearings on the reorganization of the Selective Service system in 1948, and observed that he was "convinced that in another war [women] have got to be drafted just like men," there was little discussion of the point, and between 1945 and 1968 the number of women in the Army ranged from 10,000 to 15,000, which accounted for only 1 percent of the force.[165] However, by the early 1960s, manpower specialists in the Pentagon were beginning to worry about the quality of male recruits; the pressures of the Vietnam War further eroded some of the traditional restrictions. As a result, the percentage of women was allowed to rise to 2 percent, women were found giving orders to men, and by 1967 women began to serve on draft boards.[166] Beginning in 1967, women could serve in command positions, but until 1970 the Air Force abruptly terminated any woman who "became a parent."[167] Self-consciousness remained. All-female services had strict rules about makeup and hairstyle; the Women Marines distributed photographs of a model barracks, with stuffed animals on every bed.

The shift to the All-Volunteer Force at the end of the Vietnam War took place, as Morris Janowitz has pointed out, not only in an international context of a trend toward "a great reliance on volunteer armed forces" but also in the context of "the most extensive anti-military sentiment" in American history. The delegitimization of the

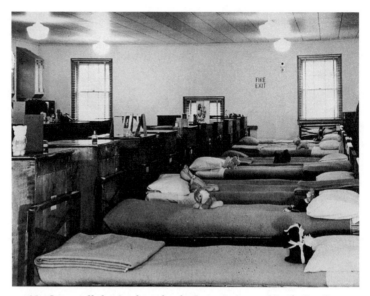

28. One stuffed animal per bunk, Camp Lejeune, North Carolina.

military made recruitment—especially of men—harder. Although women's liberation had been associated with the antiwar left, the military also represented a fortress to be stormed. Women who entered the military, even during its post-Vietnam demoralization, could still make the claim—to themselves, to others—that they were engaged in a progressive effort. The hostility they met in the ranks paradoxically confirmed that view.[168] But those officials who planned the All-Volunteer Force faced severe shortages of male recruits; they were desperate for women.[169] The passage of the Equal Rights Amendment would make different age, marital status, and educational standards for male and female recruits illegal. Recognizing that women generally brought to their military service higher levels of education than their male counterparts, they urged the extension to women of benefits equal to those offered men and the aggressive recruiting of women.[170]

The development of the All-Volunteer Force led to extended analyses of whether women were capable of what were called "nontraditional" assignments, including jobs traditionally performed by men. Military women were less likely to be viewed primarily as people who freed men to do "men's" jobs.[171] The service academies—West Point,

Annapolis, Colorado Springs—opened their enrollment to women in 1976; the Women's Army Corps and other separate women's units were absorbed by the male services.

Statutes continued to foreclose the assignment of women to combat or combat-related duties in the Navy, Air Force, and Coast Guard, but the Army remained governed only by its own policies. What counted as a combat position had always been fluid. During World War II, the British had successfully trained women to serve as spotters in an antiaircraft team, figuring coordinates for the trajectory of the gun which a male teammate would fire. Because the flash of the antiaircraft gun itself made the team a visible target, these were risky roles, even though they were not located in an official theater of war. D'Ann Campbell has shown that Secretary of War Stimson secretly and successfully trained a group of American WAACs as spotters during World War II, but then backed away from developing the practice lest it raise more general opposition to the enlargement of the service into the WACs.[172] In the 1970s, the combat/noncombat distinction was increasingly accused of functioning as a social marker rather than a substantive boundary.[173] "If all the women were discharged tomorrow," Major General Jeanne Holm observed in 1982, "most of the distinctions would be abandoned the day after."[174]

"It does not suffice . . . to treat women kindly because we love them"

The Vietnam War burst into America's high schools by way of the draft. In Philadelphia, anxiety about taking a position—registering for the draft, refusing to register, registering and simultaneously claiming conscientious objector status—may well have been heightened by the strong Quaker presence; Philadelphians knew of a tradition of draft refusal that stretched back before the Revolution. In the spring of 1971, the antiwar group Philadelphia Resistance enlisted three students at Central High School, a selective public school for boys—Andrew Rowland, his younger brother David, and David Sitman. David Freudberg from Cheltenham High School, just outside the city limits, joined them.[175] Andrew Rowland was already eighteen and had registered for the draft; the others had not quite reached their eighteenth birthdays.[176]

Rowland and his colleagues were challenging the Military Selective Service Act of 1967 on an expanded idea of moral and ethical objection. Facing the Vietnam War after My Lai, they connected entry into the Army with being "forced . . . to participate in . . . the Commission of War Crimes," and they believed they would be participating in "an illegal and unconstitutional war."

The firm to which they turned—Kohn, Savett—had been handling many draft classification claims pro bono. Stuart Savett, who had a national reputation as an expert on draft classification issues, initially became interested in the field after having counseled a close friend who was successful in challenging his classification as eligible by a draft board's arbitrary decision despite serious medical problems.[177] Rowland's case was turned over to the firm's youngest associate, Donald Weinberg, who had joined the firm in part because of the appeal of doing pro bono work.[178] Donald Weinberg had mounted his own quiet resistance to the Selective Service system, keeping questions about his eligibility for the draft alive until he safely reached his twenty-sixth birthday.[179]

The Rowland case was one of the very first of Weinberg's career, and he would stay with it all the way to argument in the Supreme Court, a decade later.[180] Within six months of the decision, Donald Weinberg would be diagnosed with lung cancer; he died in 1983, at the age of thirty-seven.[181]

The early briefs used something of a "kitchen sink" approach, Joanna Weinberg recalls now. Donald Weinberg had met his wife in law school. After working in public interest law she was now teaching in the law and social policy program at Bryn Mawr, and she followed the case closely. The original brief claimed the Selective Service Act was "arbitrary" and "capricious"; that it violated the Fifth Amendment by "taking, against their will and accomplished only by coercion and threat of criminal sanction . . . their bodies, their earning capacity as civilians and their labor and services while in the armed forces, all without just compensation"; that it violated the Thirteenth Amendment by forcing them "into involuntary servitude"; and that it violated the Fourteenth Amendment's promise of equal protection of the law by conscripting only males. Years later Joanna Weinberg remembered, "Everything went in: the war was unconstitutional; the draft was unconstitutional; the draft was gender-specific for men." She thought "no one initially took the sex discrimination claim very seriously; it's one of the ironies of the case."[182]

The first American citizens to deny the obligation of military service were Quakers and members of pietist Protestant sects, often of German origin. Only governments with systems of Anglo-American law had even limited patience with their claims; in Western Europe and elsewhere, male war resisters were likely to be imprisoned—or worse. In the era of the American Revolution, Quakers and other pacifists were understood to be weakening the patriot effort by their refusal to participate in rebellion; they were generally suspected of being Tories or Tory sympathizers, and leading Philadelphia Quakers were removed from the city and placed under house arrest in back-country Virginia. Throughout most of the twentieth century, the burden of proof rested on objectors to show that they were part of a religious community with a solid history of absolute pacifism, or at least that their objection was based firmly on religious training and belief in a Supreme Being. During World War I, hundreds of conscientious objectors who refused alternative service were imprisoned; during World War II, thousands of conscientious objectors were permitted to perform alternative service under civilian authorities, but those who refused any service at all still faced prison.[183] Through the years of the Korean War, most of those who claimed conscientious objection were white men connected with relatively small churches; even when virtually all claims from these groups were granted their absence did not make much difference to military mobilization.

However, in the years before World War II, inspired in part by Gandhi's successes in India, a different kind of conscientious objection began to be voiced by African-Americans. They were dismayed by the hypocrisy of having their own patriotism measured by their willingness to join a segregated Army that claimed to be fighting racism. Refusing the draft, Bayard Rustin contended that American segregation, in the Army and outside of it, sustained "the moral error that racism (American) can overcome racism (Fascist)."[184] Whether or not they persuaded their draft boards, their secular arguments

29. Donald, Paul, and Joanna Weinberg at Joanna's
graduation from Harvard Law School, June 1972.

helped widen the scope of available argument. Many black men did alternative service or, like Rustin himself, were imprisoned during the war; some among them emerged to be key initiators of the civil rights struggle in the 1940s and 1950s.

As the United States became more deeply involved in an undeclared war in Vietnam, the question of what was to count as moral objection to conscription was raised again. The Selective Service Act had required that objectors believe in a "Supreme Being"; it had excluded "political, sociological or philosophical views or merely a personal code." In 1965, the same year that Congress declared the burning of one's draft card a federal crime, the Supreme Court ruled that those seeking an exemption need not necessarily believe in God or in a Supreme Being; what was required was "a sincere and meaningful belief which occupies in the life of its possessor a place parallel to that filled by the God of those admittedly qualifying for the exemption."[185] In 1970 the Supreme Court recognized "ethical and moral beliefs."[186] This meant that Jewish men like Sitman, who were not members of traditionally pacifist churches and who were not opposed to all wars—indeed, some years later Sitman served in the Israeli Army—could make the claim that they should not be conscripted.

The four teenagers were among thousands of men who simultaneously tested the boundaries of this expanded definition of moral and ethical objection. In the years between 1965 and 1975, some 22,500 men were indicted and nearly 9,000 convicted for draft law violations. Only 7 percent came from historic peace faiths.[187] The press tracked those who lost their appeals and went to Vietnam, or prison, or fled abroad, but Rowland and his colleagues could only hope when they filed their complaint that the risk they took was—measured statistically—shrewd. By 1972, Charles Moskos and John Whiteclay Chambers II write, "for every hundred young Americans inducted into the armed forces, 131 [others] were exempted as conscientious objectors."[188]

The suit was initiated on June 16, 1971. The Justice Department responded almost scornfully. It was simply "not a controversy." Three of the plaintiffs hadn't yet registered for the draft; the fourth had not yet been ordered to report for induction.[189]

Conscription laws had long stood against a wide range of constitutional challenges, including all those listed by Rowland and his colleagues. These challenges had been based on the First Amendment (it was not unreasonable, courts had repeatedly ruled, that conscripts lose much of their right of free speech and petition, and are subject to the narrow constraints of the Military Code of Justice); on the Thirteenth Amendment (courts had repeatedly ruled that military service is not involuntary servitude); and on sex discrimination and a denial of equal protection of the laws under the Fifth or Fourteenth Amendment (federal courts had held that excluding women from the draft, like excluding clergy, "has rational basis which is reasonably related to Congressional power to raise and support an army").[190] Indeed, only two years before, a nineteen-year-old Fordham University student had failed to persuade the U.S. District Court in New York that a male-only draft constituted a denial of equal protection of the laws and sex discrimination. "[T]he teachings of history," observed Judge Dudley Bonsal at that time, show "that if a nation is to survive, men must provide the first line of defense while women keep the home fires burning." He mused, "The theory was that women would stay home and have children so there'd be some soldiers for the next war, wasn't it?"[191]

If there were inequities, the Justice Department now told the Philadelphia judges, it was for Congress to change them, not the courts.

> It is obvious that not everyone who is registered under the Selective Service Act is inducted. Not everyone who is ordered to report for induction . . . is sent to Vietnam. Not everyone who is in Vietnam commits war crimes. The Selective Service Act does not force an individual to commit war crimes.[192]

Ruefully, Weinberg responded that his clients were not questioning "the power of the Executive Branch to *wage* an illegal and unconstitutional war. Plaintiffs merely seek to *restrain the use of unwilling conscripts in that war*."[193]

It was on sex discrimination that the government, arguing that their burden was merely to show a "reasonable relation" between the goals of the Army and the denial of equality, had made its weakest case, and it was on sex discrimination that Weinberg focused; in the end, it was the only argument that survived. The government leaned on federal court rulings to the effect that so long as Congress offered a rational basis for a male-only draft, courts would not interfere.[194] Only the year before, a federal court had used language reminiscent of Gwendolyn Hoyt's criminal trial in 1957:

> [Even] . . . if modern thinking is to equalize the status of men and women in every respect possible . . . this would not itself remove the physical characteristics which differentiate the sexes. As they are born so they are created and no amount of legislation or "modernization" will change their distinguishing and distinctive physical characteristics. . . . for the most part physical strength is a male characteristic, and so long as this is so, the United States will be compelled to establish and maintain armed forces of males which may at least physically be equal to the armed forces of other nations, likewise composed of males, with which it must compete.[195]

Weinberg must have enjoyed pointing out the hollowness of the argument "in light of the front-line and combat use made of women by our adversaries, actual or potential. North Vietnam, the People's Republic of China and the Soviet Union have both a tradition and a present practice of utilizing women in large numbers for hazardous duty."[196]

On April 27, 1972, Judge James H. Gorbey dismissed the complaint. He refused to be drawn into an argument about the constitutionality of any reasonable aspect of the Selective Service system.[197] It looked like it was all over; Freudberg and Andrew Rowland registered with their draft boards. But Donald Weinberg found a way to appeal, and after a year, during which the U.S. involvement in the Vietnam War slowly and ungracefully ended, the Court of Appeals for the Third Circuit held that all but one element of the appeal were unconvincing or moot. That one element was the claim of sex discrimination.[198] A three-judge panel was named to consider the case —Gorbey, Joseph S. Lord III, and Max Rosenn.

The three judges on the panel all had their own memories of military service. Lord, who served on the U.S. District Court from 1961 to 1991, had attained the rank of lieutenant commander during World War II, serving in the Navy as an air intelligence officer on the staff of Admiral Halsey in the Pacific. Rosenn, who had been appointed to the Court of Appeals for the Third Circuit in 1970, had enlisted in April 1944; he eventually served on the staff of General Douglas MacArthur in the Philippines. And Gorbey had enlisted in the Marines as a private in 1942; he was severely wounded in the battle of Iwo Jima.

Once again the Justice Department tried to convince the panel that the case was moot; the war was over, some of the plaintiffs had long since registered, the All-Volunteer Force was in place, no one was being drafted. Donald Weinberg responded that the Justice Department was trying to have it both ways. First the plaintiffs had been too young to complain; now they were too old.

Was the case moot? There was an aspect of the draft that few except specialists understood. Even after the authority of Selective Service to induct had expired, those who already held deferments remained technically draftable: members of the ROTC, noncitizens deferred by the President, elected and judicial officials—Weinberg was stretching here—and "medical and allied field students" were all "subject to a sudden and rude awakening."[199] Weinberg's argument worked. Taking "judicial notice of the frequency of Selective Service prosecutions which have come before us in recent years," the panel —by a 2-1 decision—denied the Justice Department's motion to dismiss the case.[200]

The reconstruction of the case sent shock waves through the original group of plaintiffs. The case had begun, after all, as an antiwar, antidraft enterprise; gender discrimination was thrown in almost inadvertently. To argue primarily, or, as was now required, *only* on the grounds of gender discrimination meant to concede the rest: to concede that the government might justifiably declare war, to concede that the draft was *not* equivalent to servitude, to concede, in short, the substance of all that had driven them. To argue primarily on the grounds of gender discrimination was to concede that if women were drafted, a draft would be acceptable. This was not at all what the four Philadelphians had signed on for. All but Sitman dropped out, and he was ambivalent.[201] If Weinberg couldn't find another plaintiff, one who was fully comfortable with relying completely on gender discrimination, he would have no case to argue. Weinberg and his new colleague, Cecily Waterman, who had graduated from law school at Boalt Hall the year before, hoped that plaintiff would turn up.[202]

Robert Goldberg turned out to be the person they dreamed of. Cecily Waterman was acquainted with him; he lived in her apartment building and was a medical school classmate of one of her friends. Goldberg was young to be in medical school. Politicized by the events of 1968–71, he had graduated from Haverford High School in 1971, just after the institution of the draft lottery. "It was the first year when you couldn't avoid thinking about Vietnam because of student deferments; you had to confront what the war meant to you." Goldberg turned down a scholarship to Yale so he could enter an accelerated B.S.-M.D. program at Penn State, in the hopes of hastening his progress toward a medical deferment. He began college that summer, and immediately became interested in conscientious objection. Penn State had counseling services focused on the ethical and legal dimensions of objection, and Robert Goldberg sought their help. He would turn eighteen in August.[203]

"When I was eighteen or nineteen," and thinking through the possibility of being a conscientious objector, Goldberg says now, "my issues were what they had been for the original plaintiffs. I had always opposed supporting the killing. . . . I had seen the Army medical manual—which conveyed that doctors were an integral part of the fighting force so they could repair people to go and kill. It said nothing about relieving pain and suffering. It was a perversion of medicine."[204]

Goldberg's lottery number was 329.[205] He filled out his classification questionnaire, claiming "to be a conscientious objector by reason of my religious training and moral & ethical belief."[206] He never completed the process. Draft needs were cut back in 1972—Selective Service only called numbers up to 125—and Goldberg finished his liberal arts requirements and moved on to medical school in Philadelphia. But even when the general draft ended and an All-Volunteer Force was substituted, physicians remained subject to the draft. Goldberg's draft status was 1-H, the category for medical students who were deferred "pending further processing at a time within the discretion of the Selective Service authorities"—that is, Selective Service retained its claim on his service.[207]

By the time that Goldberg met Cecily Waterman, the Rowland lawsuit had refocused on sex discrimination. As neighbors and acquaintances they conversed about the case; Goldberg felt it suited his thinking precisely. "I grew up in the great era of women's liberation. If one assumes the tenets of that movement are correct, why say in this area, where life and death issues exist, why say women are valued more?" Goldberg was being trained side by side with women in medical school; if he were challenged to support the war he thought it reasonable that all his fellow students receive a similar challenge. "So I said to the lawyers, sure, why not? They didn't have to talk me into it. They didn't have to make arguments. I had no idea how big this thing would get, but it was what I was feeling. So I became part of it."[208]

There followed years of procedural maneuvering. The courts have always granted Congress wide latitude in defining what is necessary for the common defense, and Selective Service had many precedents at its disposal, ranging from Justice Arthur Goldberg's sharp opinion in 1963: "The powers of Congress to require military service for the common defense are broad and far-reaching, for while the Constitution protects against invasions of individual rights, it is not a suicide pact,"[209] to a new decision, handed down in January 1975, which reasserted the principle that it was not necessarily arbitrary to omit women from military categories.[210] For his part, Weinberg accused the Justice Department of seeking to dispose of the case on procedural grounds, willfully refusing to engage the issue at the best time to resolve it intelligently. The year 1975 was "a time of zero draft calls, when the transition to a male and female system of conscription could be undertaken without fear of disruption to the flow of inductees to the military." It was a year of dramatic and rapidly moving social change. Weinberg laid before the court a sheaf of newspaper clippings, showing the first waves of female coal miners, truck drivers, and merchant marines, and the Marine Corps's first woman tank mechanic. In 1975 the Supreme Court handed down its decision in *Taylor v. Louisiana* that women and men were equally obligated to jury service, pounding the last nail into the coffin of the *Hoyt* decision and making it impossible to claim, as Judge Bonsal had claimed only seven years before, that women's civic duty was "to keep the home fires burning."

Even as Bonsal spoke in 1968 his words were becoming archaic; his own footnotes cited not only Harlan's words in 1961 that "woman is the center of home and family life" and therefore reasonably exempt from jury service should a state choose to exempt her, but also a 1966 federal court opinion undermining that rule and requiring women's names to be placed in federal jury pools.[211] In 1970, when Ruth Bader Ginsberg took over the newly established Women's Rights Project at the American Civil Liberties Union, two of the major cases on which Bonsal rested his reasoning—*Hoyt v. Florida* and *Goesaert v. Cleary*—were among her central targets;[212] they would both be overturned within five years. Indeed, the years 1973 to 1975 can now be seen as a time of extraordinary expansion of the meaning of equal treatment under the Constitution. In 1973, upholding Sharron Frontiero's demand for dependent's allowance for her husband, the Supreme Court treated gender discrimination as something less serious than race discrimination but close to a "suspect classification," requiring the discriminator to show not merely that discrimination was "reasonable" but that it was *necessary* in order to achieve a constitutional objective. The more time passed, the more decisions to which Weinberg would be able to point. In preparing their reply, the Justice Department had ignored a decision handed down only a week before in the federal court in the District of Montana, in which Senior U.S. District Judge W. D. Murray had articulated words that Weinberg wanted to put in the mouths of his own three-judge panel. Ruling in favor of a draft resister who had refused induction on the grounds that it was unequal treatment on the basis of gender, Murray wrote: "[T]he requirements of serving in the armed forces will undoubtedly be an unpleasant experience for many women; but it is an equally unattractive experience for many men. . . . the sexual distinctions in the legislation which make him subject to induction are suspect classifications." And he concluded: "Women, just as men, are persons and citizens, and in the scheme of government under the Constitution they must be treated as equals of men both as to their rights and obligations. It does not suffice under the Constitution to treat women kindly because we love them. We must treat them rightly. The burdens of citizenship must be borne by all citizens."[213] (Murray's decision would be overturned the following year, but Weinberg could not know that.)

Weinberg lost patience with the Justice Department's delaying strategies: "The Government of the United States is, we hope, effectively eternal. Plaintiff, of course, is not." Complaints did no good, nor did a change of administration. After Jimmy Carter became President, the only apparent change was that a new Assistant Attorney General, Barbara Allen Babcock, signed requests for extensions.[214]

When draft resisters made the claim in 1968 that the male-only draft represented unequal treatment of men and women under the law, they did so in a social context in which unequal treatment of women and of men was increasingly questioned but in a legal context in which unequal treatment was pervasive. When Rowland and Sitman and their colleagues raised the same question a few years later, the social and legal context was changing. By May 1975, when Robert Goldberg joined the case, every one of the old precedents—*Mueller v. Oregon* (which had upheld protective legislation for women), *Goesaert*, *Hoyt*—had been undermined or actually overturned. In the process, the traditional language of protection had eroded, at least so far as civil affairs were involved. If it could no longer be said with a straight face that women's civic obligation was "to keep the home fires burning," then of what *did* women's civic obligation consist? The remaining participants in the Goldberg suit were prepared to say that it consisted of going to war, along with everyone—read: men—else.

"A constitutional right to be treated like American ladies"

When President Jimmy Carter proposed universal mandatory draft registration in his State of the Union address in 1980, the obligatory dimensions of military service once again became the subject of widespread popular debate. Robert Goldberg's challenge to a male-only draft was suddenly infused with political vitality, transformed from a low-profile case on the calendar of a busy federal court into a suit of national significance. President Carter was seeking a measured response to the Soviet Union's invasion of Afghanistan, one that would safely send an assertive, military signal that the United States took this invasion seriously. With the administration under daily attack for cowardice as Iran continued to hold American hostages, the gesture suited the government's agenda. Universal mandatory draft registration was to be a sign of public readiness; conscientious objectors could register and appeal later.[215]

Carter's proposal that women as well as men register was consistent with his characteristic skepticism regarding the gendered traditions of the military services. His administration had attempted to change what it took to be excessive veterans' preference policies in civil service hiring.[216] But his recommendation was also a sharp departure from his previous skepticism about draft registration. Representative Patricia Schroeder, who had led a successful Democratic challenge to draft registration only the previous fall, filed a Freedom of Information Act request for a copy of the first draft of Carter's State of the Union address; she was furious at the administration's "180-degree turn."[217]

For Robert Pirie, Richard Danzig, and their colleagues who staffed the manpower section of the Pentagon, Carter's proposal was full of ironies. They did not disagree with the President on the point that if registration should become necessary women should be registered. But for them, the main problem was the survival of an All-Volunteer

Force against conservative efforts to reinstitute Selective Service and the draft.

Women did indeed enlist in the armed services, and the All-Volunteer Force depended on their presence. The costs the military had to pay for their enlistment—particularly those related to their discomfiting capacity to become pregnant—were counterbalanced by their substantially lower rates of AWOL and of violent off-duty behavior.[218] Richard Danzig, who served as Principal Deputy Assistant Secretary of Defense for Manpower in the Carter years, observed that by the late 1970s "it was evident that recruiting women was a good thing. You were [drawing in] more [recruits] from the higher [qualifications]; you were taking 9 percent of the total force, and you didn't have to reach in to the [less qualified men] in the pool. . . . Every woman was a substitute for a man at the bottom of the pool . . . The women cost less to recruit; they stayed in longer. . . . Women were performing impressively. Statistical indicators [showed] that women were doing well. We [in the Office of Manpower] kept asking the services to add to the number of women they took; to raise their targets higher than 10 percent."[219] The Defense Department also asked Congress to repeal the laws excluding women from combat duty; congressional committees refused.[220] In 1981 nearly 74,000 women were in the Army alone; there were more female Army officers than there had been female enlisted personnel twenty years before.[221]

Only the previous fall, Richard Danzig had encouraged thirty-five-year-old Bernard Rostker, an economist and personnel specialist who had been Principal Deputy Assistant Secretary of the Navy for Manpower and Reserve Affairs, to leave the Pentagon and take on the job of director of Selective Service. Rostker's first task was to develop a practical and efficient registration system that would not start operating until mobilization actually occurred. They believed having such a plan could insulate the All-Volunteer Force until it actually required supplementation by a draft. Estimating that current practices, which relied on freestanding Selective Service boards and election boards, were slow and expensive—registration in California alone had a price tag of some $25 million—Rostker turned to post offices as the sites of registration, Social Security numbers for identification and enforcement, and postcards as the medium. Since the post offices and the Social Security numbers already existed, the new process was speedy and cheap, although the use of Social Security numbers raised problems of privacy, and the plan would be attacked by the American Civil Liberties Union on those grounds. Since the program could be initiated when it was needed, it would have a high degree of accuracy—young people of draft age are among the most mobile elements of the population, and getting the address of a nineteen-year-old one year is little guarantee that it will be the same the next. Since the system would not be activated until it was needed, debate on its theoretical aspects could be postponed. Within two weeks of Carter's State of the Union speech, Rostker and his colleagues were scheduled to deliver a report that said registration on reaching age eighteen would be "redundant and unnecessary."[222] Their plan would cost only $21 million for the entire nation, could be instituted *after* the call to mobilize, and would have recruits ready when training bases were ready to receive them. The scheme was something of a tour de force; they were very proud of it.

Years later, Rostker was still rueful. "And right in the eleventh hour," he recalled, "the President says not only are we going to have a standby registration but we're going to register. And we all had a lot of warning of that—maybe two or three hours." Robert B. Pirie, Jr., Assistant Secretary of Defense for Manpower, Reserve Affairs, and Logistics, had a bit more. Pirie, who had joined the Pentagon after a distinguished naval career, had gone in to his office on Saturday afternoon and "as I was in there the hot line rang. One of the two times I think that [Secretary of Defense] Harold [Brown] rang me on the hot line. Harold said, 'Come down, I want to talk to you.' I came down, and he said, 'Write up a paragraph for the President's State of the Union address that says that we are reinstituting registration. I said [that's a really crummy idea] and he said, 'Thanks for your interest in national security. Go write the paragraph.' " The paragraph was worked over by several people, including Brown, before it went to the White House.[223]

Women in the military was a second-order issue for the President—who believed in equal obligation but was primarily concerned with responding to the Soviet Union—and for the analysts Danzig, Rostker, and Pirie, who had already concluded that women were in the All-Volunteer Force to stay. But once they discussed their subjects—whether it was standby registration or the All-Volunteer Force—they could not avoid gender. The All-Volunteer Force regularly met the criticism that its logical consequence was women in combat. "One of the ways to shore up the All-Volunteer Force was to broaden the labor market base by bringing in more women," observed Pirie. "More women meant that there was substantial chance that women would be involved in combat. We in fact went forward and asked for a change to the exclusion that gave the other faction the opportunity to say, 'Look at these guys. Their agenda is to have women in the trenches, fighting with bayonets.' " Once the argument moved out of the executive branch into Congress and the public, women in the military became central to the discussion.

The planners thought there was no necessity, from a manpower perspective, to establish immediate registration; a standby system was adequate. They understood that the President wanted to send a signal of resolve to the Soviet Union; in that context, they supported registration. They agreed that when the time came, there should be, as Rostker put it, "a gender-specific parallel draft . . . to fill noncombat vacancies." That in fact was the way Selective Service had always worked: "Whatever you needed people for, you drafted people to fill those occupations," observed Danzig. Whether or not women were actually to be placed in combat, he thought they could be drafted.

Carter's formal statement of his proposal to register women unwittingly embodied the ambivalence that even proponents of the measure felt. He began by describing universal registration as a recognition of changing times ("Women are now providing all types of skills in every profession"); then he called it an obligation ("There is no distinction possible, on the basis of ability or performance, that would allow me to exclude women from an obligation to register"). He promised to retain women's combat exemption but almost immediately added that women were already very close to combat exposure. He raised the political stakes by linking registration to women's expanded willingness to meet "the responsibilities of citizenship" and to the proposed Equal Rights Amendment: "Just as we are asking women to assume additional responsibilities, it is more urgent than ever that the women in America have full and equal rights under the Constitution. Equal obligations deserve equal rights."

Then he backed away by emphasizing that registration would not necessarily mean equal vulnerability to combat duty. "Equity" does not require, Carter said, "that men and women be inducted in equal numbers. . . . Equity is achieved when both men and women are asked to serve in proportion to the ability of the Armed Forces to use them effectively."[224]

The House and Senate Armed Services Committees held extended hearings on the President's proposal; now Rostker, Pirie, and Danzig had to testify in support of the President's initiative although it was a program of which they were at best skeptical and in some moods scornful. Rostker could understand that if "the President felt that in this day and age with the Russians it was important to an extra level of security to have the registration, I can support that. I can support submitting a plan and having the President rationally say that he wants more than the plan gave him, but I was not going to be dragged through the mud of Washington about how I had produced a lousy plan." If the original plan was vilified, he was prepared to "resign and defend it."[225]

The analysts were somewhat surprised by the intensity of congressional resistance and by the extent to which the argument came to focus on the registration of women.[226] The President and his supporters sought to separate the issue of universal registration from the issues of the actual draft and the use of women in combat. They thought that decisions on whether women would actually be drafted (and, if so, whether mothers would be exempted) and whether women would be placed in combat positions could be left for future debate. They also claimed that registration did not necessarily mean that one would be drafted; men who planned to request medical or conscientious exemptions were still required to register. Opponents insisted that the issues were linked. They argued that since the primary goal of Selective Service was to identify combat-ready men, there was no need to register women if they were not going to be used in combat.[227]

Ultimately Congress authorized a male-only draft registration; once they did, Robert Goldberg's challenge to the constitutionality of Selective Service for men only leapt to center stage. These debates—in Congress and in the courts—forced many people on both sides of the issue to put in words what they thought about the appropriate military roles and obligations of men and women. They revealed ambivalence and anxiety, both on the left and on the right, which filtered also into the simultaneous debate on the Equal Rights Amendment; the two issues intersected with each other. Indeed, the political scientist Jane Mansbridge has virtually blamed the defeat of the ERA on the failure of proponents to defuse the military issue, and has argued that feminists unconsciously and occasionally consciously restricted debate about women in combat. But as historians Jane De Hart and Donald Mathews have shown, even when discussion of the implications of the ERA for military obligation was encouraged, as it was in North Carolina, opponents were not convinced.[228]

One of the major rocks on which the ERA debates foundered was the claim that proponents were flinging innocent young girls into the military machine—there to be treated as no better than men and to be brutalized. " 'Today,' a mother wrote Senator Sam Ervin after the ERA had passed the Senate, 'I am ashamed and terrified at what the future holds for my three little girls. Will my shy, sweet Tommy be drafted in six years? So modest I can't even see her undress. Oh God! . . . I can't stand it. I just can't bear it.' . . . To this mother, 'Sex' meant the intimate privacy of shy little girls and equality meant ravaging them, stripping away the protection of innocence and thrusting them into battle." It is impossible to understand the opposition to the ERA without appreciating this dimension of military obligation: for opponents, the ERA stood for defilement; to resist the ERA was a rite of purification.[229]

In the anxious debates on military service, the ancient connection, still not well understood, between arms-bearing and citizenship, and between citizenship and manhood, remained a subtext. Occasionally the subtext was clearly revealed. Richard White, chair of the Military Personnel Subcommittee, observed that choices about registration were contingent on whether one believed all young people "owe a certain number of years to the U.S. government."[230] The subtext had its own novel dimensions; since the administration was not challenging the combat exemption, increasing the numbers of women available to fill noncombat assignments would actually *increase* the proportion of drafted men who would be exposed to combat or combat-related positions.[231] And, although supporters of registration tried to keep their distance from its implications for the exercise of violence by women, many regarded it as a slippery slope—from registration to the voluntary exercise of violence by women, to a future in which women would be required to train for and exercise violence.[232]

"[We] have known since 1972," asserted *The Phyllis Schlafly Report,* "that one of the major objectives of the pro-ERA, women's liberation, feminist movement was to force the drafting of women *and* the assignment of drafted women to *all* military combat jobs." The sequence of events that Danzig, Rostker, and Pirie understood to be simply the flow of normal political life was understood by the Eagle Forum to be "a three-step scheme." The first two steps had already taken place: the unsuccessful Pentagon effort in 1979 to repeal the combat exemption and the President's 1980 proposal to reinstate draft registration for men and add women. The third, the Forum predicted, would occur "after the November 1980 election"; they were sure that if Carter was reelected, the military would be required to assign drafted women to all tasks, including combat. The Forum organized the Coalition Against Drafting Women; its leadership included Senator Jesse Helms, the Reverend Jerry Falwell, and a number of conservative organizations, including the National Council of Catholic Women, the Moral Majority, and Young Americans for Freedom. "We were prepared for the Congressional battle because we always knew that the feminists would eventually try to force women into the army."[233]

Feminists and liberals who testified on the issue rarely supported either registration or the draft. Most opposed the entire package.[234] For pacifists there was no problem at all; their thorough objection to militarism covered the present situation easily. "We are against the draft for women and men," observed the March 1980 newsletter of the Women's International League for Peace and Freedom. "Although we believe that women are capable of doing the job, we believe that it's not a job worth doing."[235] Congresswoman Pat Schroeder of Colorado, who had led a successful campaign against registration the previous fall, now sneered at draft registration as an idle gesture and a waste of money that could be better spent buying spare parts so that we really *could* frighten the Russians.[236] African-American men's groups, aware that the critics of the All-Volunteer

Force had focused on the high proportion of blacks in it, suspected that a Selective Service system was a thinly disguised effort to whiten the Army.[237] When pushed into a corner, however, liberal feminists generally conceded the legitimacy of a draft, merged the right of arms-bearing with the obligation to military service, and demanded that if there *had* to be draft registration, it should include women as well as men. No one played Rosika Schwimmer. No one played Antigone, no one played Cassandra.

Testifying for NOW before the House Armed Services Committee, Judy Goldsmith asserted that if there were to be registration and a draft, "they must include women. As a matter of fairness and equity . . . Any registration or draft that excluded females would be challenged as an unconstitutional denial of rights under the Fifth Amendment."[238] Former congresswoman Bella Abzug was similarly stuck: "Feeding our daughters and our sons into the draft registration machinery can only have detrimental and divisive effects on our country . . . [but] if we have registration, I think clearly both men and women should be included and I believe that if they are not and it goes to the courts, the courts would probably so decide, with or without the ERA."[239]

African-American feminists were in a particularly awkward situation. The Conference on a Black Agenda, organized by the Black Leadership Forum and several organizations of black elected officials, meeting in Richmond, Virginia, in March 1980, passed a strong resolution against the reinstatement of registration and of the draft. Congressman Ronald Dellums of California condemned the military budget and called on blacks to "challenge the insanity of war." But Dorothy Height, president of the three-million-member National Council of Negro Women, urged women to register for the draft, "because if we're to be equal in one area, we have to be equal in another." To which one delegate responded, "My daughter won't go until Amy [Carter] goes."[240]

Judy Goldsmith focused on what acceptance of a military obligation would do for women in a nonmilitary context; it would enable them to claim the veterans' preferences that permeated the social order. These preferences were implicit: "Those who oppose the registration and draft for females say they seek to protect women. But omission from the registration and draft ultimately robs women of the right to first-class citizenship and paves the way to underpaying women all the days of their lives. Moreover, because men exclude women here, they justify excluding women from the decisionmaking of our nation."[241]

These preferences, Goldsmith said, were also explicit, embedded in federal and state civil service laws which barred well-paying jobs in precisely those fields, like police work, which women were just beginning to enter, and in the jobs and training which the military itself offered:

> The military provides thousands of jobs, training programs, and educational opportunities which are, for the most part, presently closed to women. Military pay, which is on the average some 40 percent higher than female civilian pay, could be the only way out of poverty for countless young women. Restrictions on women in the military, far from protecting them, serve to continue their second-class citizenship, pay and opportunity. And this discrimination exercised by the military affects women's lives, and employment opportunities and wages throughout their entire work lives, because of veterans' benefits.[242]

She concluded by returning to the combat exemption: "Being told that they are unfit for combat training, that they need protection, women are more readily victims of violence of every kind. Without training and the confidence that they can defend themselves, most women live in daily fear of physical assault. One must ask . . . whether a would-be rapist would be less likely to attack a woman if he thought she had been trained as a Marine."[243]

To which Kathleen Teague, representing the Eagle Forum in the absence of Phyllis Schlafly, replied, "The purpose of the military, of course, is the defense of our country. It is not to provide upward mobility or career opportunities for women."[244]

Teague was an effective voice for the opposition, catching all its ambivalence as well. The thirty-year-old president of the Virginia STOP ERA headed her own public relations firm. She was also the executive director of the American Legislative Exchange Council, ALEC, an association of conservative legislators. On the one hand, the "right" to be excused from the draft was a right "which every

American woman has enjoyed since our country was born." Teague wanted to know what they would get for giving up their "constitutional right to be treated like American ladies."[245] In seeking equitable treatment of men and women, Goldsmith and her colleagues had emphasized the equality of men and women; the implications of equality, as Assistant Secretary of Defense Robert Pirie observed during the hearings, led straight to a military obligation: "Since women have proven that they can serve successfully as volunteers in the Armed Forces, equity suggests that they be liable to serve as draftees if conscription is reinstated."[246] Teague and her colleagues emphasized difference, a difference embedded in traditional patterns of "respect, chivalry," and religious culture. "Servicewomen are not fungible with servicemen," said Teague; "on the average women have only 60 percent of the physical strength of men. . . . Motherhood is not fungible with fatherhood. . . . Our daughters are not fungible with our sons. The drafting of wives is not fungible with the drafting of husbands."[247] Registration was preparation for real conflict. Teague refused to treat it as a symbolic gesture or an emblem of equal status under law. "We expect our servicemen to be tough enough to defend us against any enemy—and we want our women to be feminine and human enough to transform our servicemen into good husbands, fathers and citizens upon their return from battle." Like Tommy's mother, she harbored no illusions about military life; the Tailhook scandal a decade later would not surprise her. "We don't want our daughters subjected to the Army environment where there is little or no privacy, where the rape rate is considerably higher than in civilian life, where there is open toleration of immoral sex . . . where illegitimate births receive equal honor and financial rewards with legitimate births."[248] For Teague, the maintenance of gender difference was a matter of civil rights: "Our young women have the right to be feminine, to get married, to build families and to have homes. Our daughters should not be deprived of rights which every American woman has enjoyed since our country was born."[249] Most importantly, in making this proposal, the supporters of the ERA had finally shown their hand: Teague and her colleagues were not going to give up this right to be free of a military obligation "just because a handful of women, unhappy with their gender, want to be treated like men."[250]

"Draft's 4-F—Greetings: All-Male Sign Up Blocked"

In June 1979, a few months before the Soviet invasion of Afghanistan, Donald Weinberg received a notice from the clerk of the court for the Third Circuit. Since no action had been taken for a year, the Goldberg case would be dismissed unless Weinberg did something to activate it within thirty days.[251] The Justice Department had renewed its request that the entire case be declared moot because of the shift to an All-Volunteer Force; the three-judge panel again denied their request. There was a "flurry of activity," Joanna Weinberg remembers, as Weinberg and his colleagues prepared, finally, for their court appearance.[252]

As they made their preparations, President Carter proposed universal Selective Service registration and Congress began to debate it. "It hit the press; there was immense publicity," Joanna Weinberg recalls. "[D]eluged by people who want to join the suit," Donald Weinberg began to work with Isabelle Pinzler of the ACLU Women's Rights Project in New York and feminist attorney Barbara Brown, choosing additional plaintiffs and laying the grounds to make the case into a class-action suit.[253] While they worked, Congress held hearings, debated the issue, and established a male-only draft registration. Iran had seized the American embassy and held American hostages; the longer they were imprisoned, the more inadequate American power seemed to be. On June 27, 1980, President Carter signed the House Joint Resolution which authorized funding for a revitalized Selective Service system. Goldberg's trial was scheduled for July 1, 1980, just before the Republican nominating convention. The administration had called for universal draft registration but Carter had not vetoed the congressional bill establishing a male-only draft; now the Carter administration was placed in the odd position of having to defend the statute it had originally opposed.

Courtroom 3B is a modest-sized room off a characterless corridor in an anonymous hallway; as in many other courthouses built in the 1950s and 1960s, nothing in the bland corridors, lit by fluorescent lights, suggests with any precision the significance and meaning of the building. It could be a high school or a hospital. The furnishings were designed for trials requiring only a single judge; Lord, Rosenn,

30. Donald Weinberg argues before Judges Joseph S. Lord, Max Rosenn, and
Edward N. Cahn, June 1980.

and Edward N. Cahn (who had entered the case after Gorbey's death
in 1977) squeezed themselves behind the raised bench. Judge Max
Rosenn presided.[254] Even after years of preparation, much happened
at the last minute. The final volume of documentary evidence that
Pinzler of the ACLU and Weinberg had prepared—mostly newspaper clippings showing new roles for women—was not given to the
judges until the afternoon before the trial. Still unsettled was whether
this was to be a class-action suit, covering not only Goldberg and
Sitman but all other men who were required to register. The trial
opened with the question of whether the decision should apply only
to the plaintiffs.[255]

"If this act were to be declared unconstitutional," observed Judge
Lord, thinking of what would happen if it were not a class-action suit,
"it would spawn a million lawsuits, wouldn't it?"

"Yes, your honor," carefully replied Andrew Wolfe for the Justice
Department, which wanted the case handled on the narrowest

grounds, "it might well spawn a considerable number of lawsuits."

". . . And you are suggesting that the law ought to countenance such chaos as that?"

Wolfe: "We do not view it as chaos."

Lord: "You are not sitting up here."

Wolfe pleaded that the court consult their own sense of propriety. Did they really mean that "three young men from the Eastern District of Pennsylvania . . . would have within their power the ability to paralyze the entire Selective Service system and potentially prevent the conscription of any person anywhere across the country"?

"Only if they win," observed Lord, dryly.[256]

It took the court less than five minutes to decide to authorize a class-action suit; they settled down to hear the arguments. Weinberg spent much of his time on technical issues and introducing historical material intended to show that what was at issue was less a matter of reasonable congressional prerogative than it was flat out sex discrimination. If he was calm enough to register the point, he may have realized he was in sympathetic hands when Rosenn interrupted him to observe, "While Eisenhower's statement does have a certain amount of nostalgic interest, don't you really have something very substantial to offer from the testimony of Deputy Secretary of Defense Danzig?"[257] It took Weinberg a while to get back on track, and when he did, he emphasized that women were used "manning the batteries of the anti-aircraft missiles . . . servicing the tank in the front lines." He thought it was contradictory for Congress to send the ERA to the states and simultaneously insist on male-only draft registration; that it was unequal treatment under the law when "men have to prove ineligibility for the draft, whereas women get it presumed . . . like the Social Security case where women's dependency is presumed but men had to prove dependency in order to get benefits." He was thinking of *Weisenfeld v. Weisenfeld*, a case which Ginsburg had argued, in which a young widower with a baby sought "widow's" benefits; Weinberg could as easily have been thinking of *Hoyt*, when women had been presumed ineligible for jury service.[258]

"Even in the age of nuclear weapons," said William Elliott, when it came to be the Justice Department's turn, "war connotes combat between armed adversaries. . . . Women cannot engage in combat. That is the policy . . . of every nation in the world." Elliott summoned up the legend of the Battle of the Bulge: when "the combat support troops were called in from France, and . . . they cleaned the kitchens out, gave them 24 hours training with a gun and sent them to the front." To that, Weinberg replied, "The Battle of the Bulge argument presupposes that the women can't fight. The record is, of course, to the contrary."[259]

"My experience in Domestic Relations Court," Judge Rosenn put in, "is they can fight."[260]

The day after the trial, President Carter announced that all men born in 1960 and 1961 were required to register in the two weeks beginning July 21. Millions of dollars had already been spent on what Bernard Rostker described as "complex arrangements for computer support from the Internal Revenue Service." Radio and television public service announcements spread the word; 34,500 post offices received posters to display and forms to distribute; thousands of postal workers had been trained in new duties.[261]

But three days before the system went into effect, the court handed down its decision. As Andrew Wolfe had feared, the handful of young men had indeed made good on their threat to "paralyze the entire Selective Service system."[262] Writing for a unanimous panel, Judge Edward N. Cahn quoted the Supreme Court's decision in *Feeney* to make the point that "classifications based upon gender, not unlike those based upon race, have traditionally been the touchstone for pervasive and often subtle discrimination."[263] The court regarded gender discrimination as a "badge of inferiority"; it would not accept "outdated stereotypical notions" or "administrative convenience." Even if "protection" were intended for women's benefit, the court would look at it skeptically. Cahn concluded: "It is incongruous that Congress believes on the one hand that it substantially enhances our national defense to constantly expand the utilization of women in the military, and on the other hand endorses legislation excluding women from the pool of registrants available for induction," and found the Military Selective Service Act of 1980 in violation of the Fifth Amendment.[264] It was late in the afternoon of July 18. Compulsory registration was less than three days away.

William Elliott immediately requested a stay; unsurprised, Judge

Joseph S. Lord III heard the request "in open court" at 5 p.m. Elliott had signaled in the trial that the government would immediately appeal any decision that went against it. "We sort of expected that the Court would allow the registration," Bernard Rostker recalled fifteen years later. Elliott was already armed with a memorandum and five affidavits, all of which stressed that "the United States will be irreparably harmed if registration is not allowed to proceed as scheduled . . . next Monday."[265] The District Court's decision, said Elliott, "flatly denies the United States the ability to conscript military forces in response to a national emergency or military attack."

"No, it doesn't," said Lord, who was beginning to enjoy this. "It only says you can't discriminate. We have not said you can't go ahead and do it some other way."

"Not without congressional amendment to the Military Selective Service Act," responded Elliott.

"Of course," said Lord flatly. "That is what Congress is for."

"However, your honor, the Congress conceivably could not act within a short period of time."

"We did," responded Lord.

"[B]ut you were in session; the Congress is not."

"They can be."

Elliott tried again. "Congress, as it must, must study the question at length."

"Why?" asked Lord. "It is a very simple answer. They just can register women. . . . [Y]ou are telling me that . . . Congress has to study it."

"That is correct."

"Why do they have to study it? Don't they regard the separation of powers as between the Executive, the Legislative, and the Judicial? . . . The Judicial has declared this as unconstitutional. What more study is there to be?"

When it came his turn, Donald Weinberg began by expressing skepticism of the government's complaint that it could not recover from a delay in registration. "I begin to believe," he mused, "that the Government can do anything it wants to in a very, very fast time, because ten minutes after I got a copy of the court's opinion I received this marvel of a stay application with five affidavits." Even if there were registration, a national emergency would still require Congress to be called back into session and to decide whether to authorize conscription. How "sudden" was a response that stretched from the invasion of Afghanistan in December 1979 to a registration that began in late July? This was not exactly, Weinberg observed dryly, "springing into action like Pearl Harbor."

In the affidavits, the government complained that it had spent $400,000 for promotional material specific to July 21, which would be wasted if the date were changed. Weinberg responded that whatever training post office personnel had would keep until a later date; so would the cards already printed; the taped radio and TV advertisements could be run later. Lord was losing his patience: "What is the $400,000? What is the complaint about that?"

"That is the amount that the Selective Service has spent in gearing up for this draft registration," said Weinberg.

Lord, breathing relief: "That is only about one-half of the deficit of the Senate lunchroom."

Elliott, one more time: "Clearly the harm to the plaintiffs if a stay is granted in this case is minimal. It only requires them to go forward and to register in the next two weeks."

"Only," repeated Lord. "But that is what we held was unconstitutional."

It did not take Lord very long to come to a conclusion. "I perceive only mischief in the granting of a stay. I can perceive confusion, I can perceive wastage of money, and I see no sound prospect of success on the part of the Government ultimately. . . . I will deny the Motion." The hearing had lasted twenty-five minutes.

Suddenly it appeared that no one would have to register. Three judges had stopped draft registration in its tracks. The headline of the Philadelphia *Journal* read: "Draft's 4-F—Greetings: All-Male Sign Up Blocked."[266] Donald Weinberg went to New York for an appearance on *Good Morning America*; when he entered Isabelle Pinzler's apartment building, the young doorman hugged him. "Oh, Mr. Weinberg, thank you, thank you!"[267] That was not the only hug he got. That weekend there was a picnic at the home of a senior judge for all the judges in the Philadelphia Federal Courthouse and their families; the talk was of nothing else. "Well," says Judge Louis Pollak now with a grin, "I thought it was a very aggressive thing to do!"[268]

Even as Donald Weinberg savored what he had accomplished, a federal marshal was making his way to Nantucket, where Supreme Court Justice William J. Brennan, Jr., who had responsibility for appeals from federal courts in the mid-Atlantic region, spent his summers.[269] Brennan responded quickly. "[T]he case," he observed, "is a difficult and perplexing one." In the end Brennan would agree with the Philadelphia judges that a male-only draft was unconstitutional, and join Thurgood Marshall in dissent. But in deciding whether to issue a stay of execution during the appeals process, Brennan was bound by explicit rules. "My task . . . is not to determine my own view on the merits, but rather to determine the prospect of reversal by this Court as a whole." Brennan had no trouble certifying that there was a "reasonable probability" that four justices would agree to consider the case; and he had to grant "that there is a fair prospect" that the Supreme Court would indeed overturn the lower court's judgment. He disagreed with Lord on what would happen in the interim; he thought that if the registration were ultimately ruled unconstitutional, those who had registered unnecessarily would merely have been subjected to "inconvenience," whereas the government would have to spend the money a second time. Brennan stopped the enforcement of the District Court's decision.[270] Lord's decision had lasted barely a day.

Brennan may not have halted the registration, but he certainly introduced a note of uncertainty into the process, and by signaling that in his judgment the Supreme Court would want to hear the case, he had given it national visibility. On both sides, supporters offered their help. Amicus briefs poured in, including one from the Washington Legal Foundation, which included Congressman Newt Gingrich of Georgia and both senators from Utah, Jake Garn and Orrin Hatch. They argued that the judiciary moved out of its realm when it reviewed "legislative branch determinations as to what military strength is necessary for the safety of our nation or how such strength is to be raised or composed."[271] There was a brief against registering women from the Orthodox Jewish Coalition, who feared that it would "create conflict and disharmony between the majority of our society and substantial minority groups who could not conscientiously cooperate with it." Registration of Orthodox women could not be handled within the normal categories of conscientious objection, since Orthodox Jews did not, for the most part, conscientiously object to all forms of war. Mennonite and Quaker women could have claimed CO status on the same terms as their male co-religionists; Orthodox Jewish women could not.[272]

The Eagle Forum organized a group of sixteen draft-age women, who emphasized "societal reasons" and claimed that exempting women from military service was analogous to exempting clergy—it had long been a way of sustaining family solidarity in time of war. Among the signers was Stacey Acker of Alabama, who "would like to marry and have children" and believed that "women should not be conscripted during their best childbearing years . . . mothers have a greater responsibility to care for their small children than to engage in military service." Kathryn Barr of Wisconsin "has engaged in competitive sports and knows that she cannot compete successfully against males in any contest which requires upper body strength . . . this important physical characteristic . . . may be a matter of life or death in military combat." Almeda Cannon of Tennessee "does not want to serve in the Armed Forces because she fears sexual abuse." Monica Dewitt of New Jersey "fears that if she were ever captured by the enemy, she could not survive as a prisoner of war . . . if women were . . . captured in actual conflict, they would be subject to much worse treatment than men." Others in the diverse list claimed religious scruples, both Christian and Orthodox Jewish, relating to modesty and their "nature as a woman."[273]

There were briefs in support of Goldberg. Most stressed the same issues that supporters of universal registration had stressed in congressional hearings and that Weinberg had emphasized in his arguments. NOW filed a brief; so did a large group of women's rights organizations—the Women's Equity Action League, the American Association of University Women, the League of Women Voters, the National Federation of Business and Professional Women, Federally Employed Women—coordinated by the Women's Legal Defense Fund.[274] Another brief, emphasizing the legislative history, came from liberal members of Congress.[275]

As the lawyers prepared their appeal, wrote their briefs, and sought supporting briefs from amici, the rest of the nation proceeded with a presidential election. Danzig and Pirie knew that they would not be welcome in Ronald Reagan's administration, and they made plans to leave. But the question of how the new administration would stand on registration and the draft was unsettled, and the White House kept Rostker on long after the transition.[276] The Coalition Against Drafting Women saw more than irony in the spectacle of the Carter administration defending a position it did not embrace wholeheartedly: "The case did not present sincere adversaries. The Justice Department . . . used only the weakest of the dozens of good reasons for exempting women from the military draft."[277]

Robert Goldberg had graduated from medical school in 1976 and moved to California for residency training in family medicine, a new specialty. In 1978 he opened a private practice in family medicine in the town of Oakdale, just outside Modesto; he married the following year. He continued to call himself a humanist—"I didn't want to cut up people for a living"—and involved himself deeply in community affairs. When he was asked to join the board of one of the first battered women's shelters to be founded in the state, "I didn't know what it was." Within a few years he had become president of the Stanislaus Women's Refuge, attracting support from the community, moving the enterprise from "an emotional basis that gets these things off the ground" to a practical one with reliable funding, and in the process "doing battle with the heads of the local United Way," whom he accused of "turning their backs on the battered women of the community."

The Supreme Court set the arguments for early Tuesday afternoon, March 24, 1981. Goldberg, describing himself as "just this little family doc from Oakdale," flew to Washington a few days before. He spent some time lobbying local congressmen for funding for the Stanislaus Women's Refuge. Donald Weinberg took him around—to have lunch with Lawrence Tribe, the Harvard Law professor who had helped with writing the Supreme Court brief, and to meet Eleanor Smeal at NOW and the attorneys at the ACLU, among them Goldberg's high school classmate David Landau.

Landau was startled. "*You're* the Goldberg?"

"He couldn't believe it," observes Goldberg. "*I* couldn't believe it." He was moved by the thought that so many attorneys had worked so hard on the amicus briefs; that he had been in some measure the catalyst that had brought them together. Later, inside the Supreme

Court building for the first time, sitting in the front row, "I felt—this is unbelievable. These attorneys are representing *me*."[278]

Solicitor General Wade McCree was making one of his final appearances before he was replaced by a Reagan appointee; Donald Weinberg was young to be arguing before the Supreme Court for the first time. Weinberg was there because his own senior colleagues, recognizing all the work he had done, had not claimed the role; it had been a temptation, Stuart Savett would confess years later, "but I was not going to pull rank."[279] The Weinberg children came, and Donald's parents and Joanna's father; Joanna sat at the counsel table. Phyllis Schlafly came, wearing a bright pink suit. Bernard Rostker was there; so was Senator Sam Nunn. David Sitman remained in Israel. Lawrence Tribe sent a telegram: "I'm with you in spirit, which is the best way to get the benefits of solidarity without the burdens."[280] People had lined up to wait; the courtroom was packed.

The eighty minutes of argument were, the *National Law Journal* would report, "an unusually animated and probing interrogation punctuated by joking remarks and asides."[281] The ironies of the case continued to imbue the argument; the focus was more on the relationship of Congress and the military than on women's equal obligation. Women's issues were not placed directly before the Court. The issue was framed as "invidious discrimination against males"; men brought the suit, men argued it, an all-male bench asked questions. Isabelle Pinzler would observe that it was "the most important yet least understood case in years." The dialogue was framed in terms of whether Congress was being reasonable; Weinberg's goal was to persuade them that "substantial" was not a sufficient standard for gender-based discrimination. Over the argument hovered the spirit of *Craig v. Boren*, a case the Court had decided in 1976, concluding that "classification by gender must serve important governmental objectives and must be substantially related to achievement of those objectives."[282] Weinberg's goal was to persuade the Court to move past *Craig v. Boren* and to say that when sex discrimination is claimed, just as when race discrimination is claimed, the highest level of scrutiny must be used. Even if the justices had then gone on to uphold a male-only registration because combat-eligibility lurked in the wings, Weinberg would have achieved an extraordinary victory.[283]

McCree repeated the Battle of the Bulge argument, but met the response that there were many roles in the modern Army that were never exchanged for combat. Weinberg assured the Court that if he won it would not mean "that every past registration and conscription act of this country is unconstitutional," not even the decision in *Feeney*. Indeed, since the disproportion of men drawing veterans' preferences in *Feeney* was a direct "result of the inequality of conscription," the future might well be different.[284]

Afterward, on the steps of the courthouse, network newspeople swarmed. Goldberg was amazed to hear Senator Nunn tell an interviewer that a Goldberg victory would "destroy the U.S. military."

William Brennan kept notes when the justices met to discuss the case; his notes enable us to enter the normally secret conference. Most justices took different routes to the same opinion—that the choice of registering women, like the choice of drafting women (whether or not for combat), was in the hands of Congress.[285]

Justice William Rehnquist wrote the opinion, which began with the proposition—a proposition that Danzig, Rostker, Pirie, and Goldberg had, in their various ways, denied—that the "purpose of registration was to prepare for a draft of combat troops." Since women were not used in combat, he thought it was reasonable for Congress to conclude "that they would not be needed in the event of a draft." He denied that the draft was a differential burden on two similarly situated groups. An all-male draft was not like an "all-black . . . or an . . . all-Lutheran" Army. "The Constitution requires that Congress treat similarly situated persons similarly, not that it engage in gestures of superficial equality."[286]

Justice Byron White did not think that excluding women would "offend the Constitution," but he dissented on the grounds that Congress had not "concluded that every position in the military, no matter how far removed from combat, must be filled with combat-ready men." Since women were useful to the military, he thought they should be registered.

Justice Brennan joined in the ringing dissent Thurgood Marshall wrote. Justice Marshall objected on the principled grounds of equal civic obligation. He thought that in accommodating Congress, the Court was itself avoiding its own "constitutional obligation" to judge congressional enactments by "the standards of the Constitution," which involve equal protection of the laws. "The Court today places its imprimatur on one of the most potent remaining public expressions of 'ancient canards about the proper role of women,' " he asserted. Upholding differential registration "categorically excludes women from a fundamental civic obligation."

Abandoning Antigone

It took more than a century, from the Revolutionary era to the first decades of the twentieth century, before it was firmly established that women not only had a negative obligation to refrain from treason but a positive obligation to offer allegiance and loyalty. It took nearly a century to develop a precise understanding of the behaviors required of jury service and to arrive at a general consensus that jury service is an obligation that rests equally on citizens regardless of gender. But on bearing arms there is still nothing resembling a consensus.

In the Progressive era, criticism of war was a major part of a feminist critique of the public order, as the career of Jane Addams attests. Given institutional form in the Women's International League for Peace and Freedom and in Women Strike for Peace, pacifism remained a strong part of the feminist social critique through the Vietnam era. In our own time the meaning of conscientious objection has expanded as it has been claimed not only by members of traditionally pacifist churches but also by members of mainline religions and also explicitly on secular moral grounds. But although many feminists maintained a pacifist skepticism deep into the 1970s, increasing numbers found that skepticism difficult to maintain in the presence of an All-Volunteer Force and the campaign for the Equal Rights Amendment. The first removed the threat of a draft; the latter drew them into a rhetoric of equal opportunity and equal obligation. By the late 1980s virtually all liberal women's advocacy organizations were linking military participation to first-class citizenship.

There is no doubt that women form an increasing proportion of military strength and that they have been placed in positions which erode simple distinctions between "combat" and "noncombat." With increasing frequency in recent years, scholars and activists have suggested that construing the Second Amendment to mean the right of *men* to be part of militias, the National Guard, and the Army, Navy, Air Force, and Coast Guard has allowed men to monopolize the agencies of state violence. It seems increasingly clear that among the social implications of this monopoly has been the valorization of male violence outside formal military institutions.[287] In the last quarter century, male monopolization of state violence has been effectively contested: first in urban police forces, where now women daily demonstrate their competence as agents of state power, and then in the All-Volunteer Force, where women are increasingly trained to use force. Even before the Gulf War of 1991 women were placed in positions on patrol ships and stationed on the fringes of the defense perimeter; they were in "combat support" units in Panama and in Saudi Arabia. In the Panama invasion of 1989 Army captain Linda Bray led a military police unit in an exchange of fire while conducting what had been expected to be a police mission; in the Gulf War women were killed and at least one taken prisoner. The "lesson" of Vietnam, that units must be kept together, means that women members of companies will not be pulled out when the entire company is placed in increasingly vulnerable positions. At the end of the Gulf War, women pilots were demanding an end to the combat restrictions—although, notably, enlisted women were not. Embarrassment about the Tailhook scandal of 1992 and the Aberdeen sexual harassment scandals of 1996 and what they revealed about the culture of heterosexuality in the military, and subsequent debates on the military status of gay men and lesbians, have deflected arguments about women in the military and eroded clarity about the difference between "combat" and "noncombat" assignments.[288]

The erosion of the "noncombat" category means that it is harder to draw a distinction between military roles that both men and women may play and those reserved to men. That helps explain why attention has turned to those who occupy ambiguous gender space— gay men, lesbians, transsexuals—and to strengthening distinctions between heterosexuals (men and women) and others. Whether the military will be able simultaneously to welcome women, to respect the privacy of sexual expression, and to maintain its capacity for the controlled exercise of violence remains to be seen. No major military force in history has yet attempted that.

The erosion of the "noncombat" category also means—and, for all I know, may already have meant—that once a woman citizen has voluntarily entered the Army and sworn an oath of obligation, she may not refuse an order from her commanding officer that she enter a combat situation. Sooner or later we will find a court-martial testing this point. But the erosion of the combat exemption does not necessarily or directly tell us about Americans' understanding of whether *all* women, like all men, have an obligation to bear arms, to put their lives at risk when the Commander in Chief decides it is appropriate. The use of women in the Gulf War may increase the likelihood, but does not ensure, that women will also be drafted—that is, that all women will be understood to have a military obligation.

The relationship of women to state violence challenges us to know considerably more than we do now about the relationship between gender and aggression and to consider more precisely the way this relationship has been, and ought to be, deployed by the state.[289] We live at a time when traditional markings of systems of gender difference are changing. What we are learning—in the enrollment of women into other units of state force and violence, notably police departments and corrections forces, as well as the gradual absorption of women into military roles accompanied by scandals like Tailhook and the vulnerability of gay servicepeople to loss of jobs and to violent physical attack—is that it is possible to revise even this most traditional system of gender difference while at the same time keeping systems of male domination intact.

Testifying before the House Armed Services Committee, Judy Goldsmith of NOW had suggested that women and men had different expectations of state protection against violence. Men could expect to be trained to use it in their own defense; women could not. "Without . . . the confidence that they can defend themselves, most women live in daily fear of physical assault." Robert J. Cottrol and Raymond T. Diamond have observed, "Throughout American history, black and white Americans have had radically different experiences with respect to violence and state protection. . . . for many of those who shape or critique constitutional policy, the state's power and inclination to protect them is a given. But for all too many black Americans, that protection historically has not been available."[290] What we are learning now about the prevalence of domestic violence is making it increasingly clear that men and women have also had radically different experiences with respect to violence and state protection. Women as a class have not been able to count on the availability of state protection.[291] As Wendy Brown has recently put it, "when the most routine victims of this 'right' are . . . urban Black men between the ages of sixteen and thirty-four, for whom homicide is the leading cause of death, and women, one of whom is raped every six minutes, one out of three times at gunpoint or knifepoint . . . is there anything more than quaintness to a republican justification of our right to bear arms?"[292] In the context of widespread domestic violence, the tradition that women can confidently rely on men for protection is sadly misleading.

We have slid into a situation in which the protective exclusion of women from the obligation to carry out state-directed violence is eroded. Judy Goldsmith was prescient in linking women's ability to use physical force with resistance to sexual violence. As our estimates of the vulnerability of women to domestic violence grows and the case for improving women's capacity for physical resistance strengthens, the promise that women can rely on men for physical protection looks increasingly like an empty one. The process will be—as in the development of other civic obligations—an extended one. It is likely to be accompanied by hostility against feminists for their complicity in developing an ideology in which it appears that traditional immunity against military obligation has been traded off for inchoate opportunities that many traditional women do not understand to be an advantage, an ideology that also abandons Antigone's ancient claim to stand as skeptic and to voice the claims of higher obligations than those that the state would place upon them.

EPILOGUE

We spend our lives submerged in civic obligations. Most of us, most of the time, are only dimly aware of what we owe. Even taxes, which one way or another we pay daily and are high-profile political issues, are so embedded in the transactions of daily life that they often elude our consciousness. Withholding softens the blow of annual income tax returns; unless the salesclerk says "and 3 percent for the governor" as the bill is rung up, point-of-sale taxes are generally imperceptible.

Other obligations are claimed so erratically as to be virtually invisible. Although many people will receive a summons to serve on a jury at some time in their lives, the appearance of the summons is unpredictable. Most individuals who are summoned will be excused. Relatively few individuals will actually be charged with vagrancy. Only a handful of individuals over the entire course of American history have ever been accused of treason. Even in time of war and a full-scale draft, only a small proportion of Americans are obligated to perform military service.

Consciousness of civic obligation is minimized even more because obligations are often linked to and confused with rights. Gwendolyn

Hoyt could not experience *her own right* to trial by a jury drawn from a cross section of the community unless *other* women were *obligated* to serve. During World War II, while the federal government was invoking Caucasian men's *obligation* to bear arms, the obligation was not demanded of Japanese-American men in relocation camps, some of whom, in turn, demanded their *right* to bear arms.

Women's civic obligations have also been vulnerable to a confusion between privilege and exclusion. It is not difficult to see why permissive rather than obligatory jury service would be regarded as a privilege, and even easier to understand that voluntary rather than obligatory military service is a great privilege. Indeed, to rephrase W. E. B. Du Bois's pithy analysis of the "wages of whiteness," many women have thought themselves to be collecting the "wages of gender." To use Katherine Teague's language, every woman, whatever her class position, could upgrade herself to a "lady."

But the wages of gender are not privilege. They are the residue of the old system of domestic relations, the system of coverture that excused married women from civic obligation *because* married women owed their primary obligation to their husbands. Women never collected the "wages of gender." They paid the wages of gender directly to their husbands rather than directly to the state. Unless we look at the entire system of rights and obligations, we will not understand that.

Rights and obligations are reciprocal elements of citizenship. Rights are pleasing to contemplate: it is invigorating to be assured, as historian Hendrik Hartog has phrased it, that Americans share "an intense persuasion that . . . when we are wronged there must be remedies, that patterns of illegitimate authority can be challenged, that public power must contain institutional mechanisms capable of undoing injustice."[1]

Obligations are less pleasing to contemplate. In the best of all possible worlds, citizens would embrace them voluntarily as welcome civic responsibilities. Indeed most citizens do indeed embrace socially responsible activities: grass-roots politics, voluntary societies, and philanthropic organizations. Democracy requires for its social glue, as Jean Bethke Elshtain correctly insists, "a mode of participation with one's fellow citizens that is animated by a sense of responsibility for one's society."[2] But if citizens could be counted on to carry out all their duties freely, as expressions of what Georgie Anne Geyer has recently called the "patriotic civic conscience," there would have been no need to make them obligatory.[3] In this book I have tried to emphasize the distinction between social duties voluntarily undertaken and obligations imposed by the state.

As long as married women were understood to owe virtually all their obligation to their husbands they could make no claims of rights against the political community. The *feme covert*, the Massachusetts Supreme Judicial Court had been told in 1805, had "no *political* relation to the *state* any more than an alien." The system of coverture filtered the claims of married women through their husbands. American political theorists recoiled from making voting—the most explicit gesture of consent—a federally protected right or an obligation of citizenship. This hesitancy helped in large measure to sustain the gendered construction of the American citizen.

The family law of the early republic retained the traditional elements that made husbands the recipients of the civic obligations of free women except the obligation to refrain from treason. The gradual deterioration of coverture was accompanied by the substitution of obligation to the state for obligations to husbands and family—understood as privilege if one approved, disability if one did not—and engendered its own debates on a timetable independent of the timing of debates about the obligations of male citizens. As women's independent rights to property, suffrage, and bodily integrity were slowly established, the complementary practices of substituting family duties for civic obligation slowly crumbled. The role of the Republican Mother, who fulfilled her civic obligations through her service to her family, substituting private choices for public obligation, had been marked as problematic as early as the 1840s by Elizabeth Cady Stanton and her colleagues. But well into the twentieth century, American law and practice continued to breathe oxygen into the customs of coverture, for all the world as though the Republican Mother were the Resusci-Annie manikin now widely used in cardiopulmonary resuscitation training.

The confusion between privileges and rights has had important consequences for the feminist movement of our own time. The agenda of Second Wave feminism, the women's movement of the late twentieth century, included many items that attacked elements of the old law of domestic relations still vibrant after more than two hundred years. Thus a flyer for the Equal Rights March in New York City on August 26, 1970, the fiftieth anniversary of the passage of the suffrage amendment, included in its list of grievances: "Women cannot buy property without their husband's signature (they don't need yours); Women cannot be sterilized without their husband's signature (again they don't need yours)."[4] Married women had an obligation to permit their husbands sexual access to their bodies in every state until New York's marital rape statute of 1975; even now the laws defining what counts as rape within marriage are complex and erratic.

Criticism of housework was central to the rhetorical attack of the revitalized feminism of the 1970s. Many skeptics have taken that to be a criticism of domesticity itself, and conservative critics have derided feminists on these grounds. But criticism of housework was also criticism of a domesticity that was understood to substitute for other competencies. Feminists warned that the woman who had devoted herself to family obligations at the expense of all other claims would discover herself to be at great *legal* disadvantages should her marriage fail and she needed to face the world as an individual. The 1963 report of the President's Commission on the Status of Women clearly revealed that women—whether single, married, or formerly married —were severely disadvantaged in seeking credit, on the job market, or when they turned to alimony for support. Second Wave feminism was soaked with suspicion of republican motherhood and maternalist credits, permeated by skepticism that civic credits banked as wives and mothers could be reliably reclaimed, filled with anxious warnings to young women to distrust the promises of coverture.

Central to the agendas of feminism, from Elizabeth Cady Stanton's time to our own, has been a program of legal change that sought to eliminate the legacies of coverture. The ending of coverture has been an extended process, accompanied by an almost willful insistence by many scholars that coverture and the problems it raised never really existed, or existed so long ago as to be antique.[5] The political history of women in the United States is generally told as three separate stories. The first is the long struggle for suffrage, successful in 1920; the second, sometimes omitted entirely, is the period 1920–70 that some historians have called "the doldrums," during which little progressive change was made; the third is the account of Second Wave feminism, energized by the Supreme Court's decision in 1971 that discrimination on the basis of sex could indeed be recognized as unequal treatment in violation of the Fourteenth Amendment.

But the political history of women in the United States is better understood as a single narrative. Different generations brought to their tasks different energies and faced different opponents, some more formidable than others. Even after suffrage, the agenda that Elizabeth Cady Stanton and her colleagues had articulated at the Seneca Falls convention in 1848 largely remained to be accomplished. Rather than describing the years after 1920 as "the doldrums," we can now see them as a period when the resistance to progressive change for women was powerful and successful. The American Medical Association had not seriously resisted suffrage, but it did fight vigorously the Sheppard-Towner legislation of the 1920s, which sought to expand prenatal care for pregnant women; the National Association of Manufacturers had not resisted suffrage, but it did fight effectively against the Child Labor Amendment; the opening of vast educational opportunities to male World War II veterans was accompanied by attacks on women for taking up classroom seats that could be held by a man. Reformers who learned their politics in the years of "the doldrums" would be indispensable to the successes of the 1970s and thereafter; they are part of the same narrative. That is why Ruth Bader Ginsburg put Dorothy Kenyon and Pauli Murray's names on her brief in *Reed v. Reed*.

Over the years, one by one, the legacies of the old law of domestic relations were attacked by the argument that difference was not privilege; that different treatment left women vulnerable, not protected. When the Supreme Court ruled in 1971 that discrimination on the grounds of sex was unequal treatment under the law it was confirming claims that Susan B. Anthony and Virginia Minor had made a century before. Subsequently one after another of old legal distinctions between the rights and obligations of men and women fell. But many remained, hiding in the fine print of state legal codes. Not until 1992 did the Supreme Court specifically announce that it would no longer recognize the power of husbands over the bodies of their wives. That is the moment when coverture, as a living legal principle, died.[6]

When I began to write this book, I expected that I would find that succeeding generations brought successive issues to closure; that the fragility of women's independent citizenship in the early republic would be resolved by the married women's property acts of the mid-nineteenth century; that the taxation of women without representation would be resolved by the achievement of suffrage; and that only the matter of whether women would be obligated to military service remained sharply contested. But as we turn into the twenty-first century, virtually every issue remains alive, though in a somewhat different form than when Americans first encountered it.

Whether accessibility of civic opportunities is to be filtered through spousal relationships continues to be a concern for immigration lawyers; whether and how to acknowledge the relationship of spouses continues to bedevil reformers of tax codes; whether Congress should invoke the long-established Supreme Court ruling that women may be required to place their bodies in harm's way during time of war could become a lively policy question during a national emergency. The story I have told is not what historians once called "Whig history": a single narrative of progress from the era of the Revolution to the present. Instead it is a set of complex accounts, often circling on themselves, in which we are challenged to be attentive to the relationship between obligation and rights, and through which we can understand that women, like men, have always been part of the national political culture. We cannot embrace the rights without acknowledging the obligations. Nor do we have the option of limiting ourselves to the voluntarily embraced duties; there waits a steel hand in a velvet glove to enforce obligation.

In these contests, often bitter ones, over what counts as obligation, feminists are often blamed for undermining female privilege; shortsightedly trading security for insecurity in the name of abstractions. "There was a time . . . when feminism had real tasks to accomplish, real inequities to overcome," writes one critic. "Though they take the credit, feminists, radical or otherwise, actually had little to do with the progress of women in the latter half of this century."[7] Feminists today are attacked as responsible for the corruption of domestic roles, for undermining wholesome family relationships, for jeopardizing efforts to protect women in the workplace, for putting in question the traditional exclusion of women from military service.

What, opponents ask, will women get for giving up their "constitutional right to be ladies"?

I do not think that is the right question. I hope that this book has persuaded its readers that the basic obligations of citizenship have always been demanded of women; it is the *forms* and *objects* of that demand that have varied over time. Impoverished women, whether black or white, have never been able to claim the fictional "constitutional" right to be "ladies." Women with property have at least the responsibility to be realists: to ask at whose expense they have claimed that fictive right. And even if, having considered the situation, a majority of women should conclude that they do indeed want to be "ladies" and to collect the "wages of gender," as a historian I can only reply that those wages are not there to collect.

Feminists were as much the *namers* of change as they were the *makers* of change. By the time Second Wave feminists named the practices, they were naming hypocrisy. Dorothy Kenyon and Pauli Murray and Raya Dreben knew that. So did all the lawyers and legislators who examined their own states' laws for gender disparities and found husbands' privilege embedded in places like inheritance law and probate law that only experts could excavate. The quest was often archaeological, but the relics sparkled amid the debris and they had consequences in real life.[8] Gwendolyn Hoyt learned that the hard way.

Whether one is male or female, racially marked in a system that treats Caucasians as "normal," married or single, heterosexual or homosexual, continues to have implications for how we experience the equal obligations of citizenship. How one is taxed, whether or not one's loyalty to the state is filtered through one's marital partner, whether one owes the state physically risky military service—all vary by gender. What we in our generation understand to be the fair and equal obligations of men and women is in part an abstraction enduring over time, developed out of philosophical traditions and logical argument. But it is also an understanding, still developing, that has evolved historically out of the troubles and tragedies of many men and women, some long dead, some our contemporaries.

"All men are created equal," reads the Declaration of Independence. As Abraham Lincoln said in the Gettysburg Address, those words "dedicated" the nation to a principle.[9] That principle was expanded during the Civil War to "all persons, born or naturalized in the United States," entitled by the Fourteenth Amendment to "the equal protection of the laws." There is no constitutional right to be a lady or a gentleman, excused from obligations borne by ordinary women and men. Equality is the great principle, and in Anglo-American legal tradition equality has always meant simultaneously common law and equity, sameness and difference shaped to authentic equality in the world which living people inhabit. What is experienced as equal obligation has shifted over time as social relations between men and women have shifted. The principles remain steady and inviolate, but the work of maintaining them in our lives will have no end.

NOTES

1. "NO POLITICAL RELATION TO THE STATE"

1. James Martin (Plaintiff in Error) *versus* The Commonwealth and William Bosson and Others, Ter-tenants, *Reports of Cases Argued & Determined in the Supreme Judicial Court* (Sept. 1804–June 1805), vol. 1, pp. 347 ff. Hereafter *Martin v. Commonwealth*. The manuscript file papers related to this case, including the writs submitted to the court and detailed descriptions of the property involved, are in the records of the Supreme Judicial Court, Suffolk County, March 1805, Archives of the Commonwealth of Massachusetts, Columbia Point, Boston.

2. William Martin is described in E. Alfred Jones, *The Loyalists of Massachusetts: Their Memorials, Petitions, and Claims* (London, 1930), p. 211, and Peter Wilson Coldham, *American Loyalist Claims* (Washington, D.C.: National Genealogical Society, 1980), p. 335. Details about his life can be gleaned from documents that are part of *Martin v. Commonwealth*, which includes some materials reprinted from the lost records of the Court of Common Pleas at Cambridge, Dec. 24, 1782. Other clues to Martin's life are found in *Martin v. Gordon*, 1773, Court Files No. 148.113, Superior Court of Judicature Records, Suffolk County, Archives of the Commonwealth of Massachusetts, Columbia Point, Boston; *Martin v. Gordon*, June 14, 1773, Record Book, Superior Court of Judicature, Suffolk County, 1773–74, pp. 20–21, Archives of the Commonwealth of Massachusetts, Columbia Point, Boston; Massachusetts Archives, manuscript vol. 154, p. 253, in Archives of the Commonwealth of Massachusetts, Columbia Point, Boston; *A List of the General and Field Officers, as They Rank in the Army* (London, 1763–84); "Memorial of Colonel William Martin of the Royal Regiment of Artillery, Massachusetts & N. Hampshire," London, 15, 1784, Great

Britain, Public Record Office, Records of the American Loyalist Claims Commission, Film 263, Audit Office Transcripts microfilm (hereafter AO) 13/47/622–25; "Examination of Colonel William Martin of the Royal Artillery . . . February 5–7, 1789," AO 12/71/102–8. See also AO 13/6/370.

3. William Martin to James Gordon, May 22, 1752, "Letters communicated by Mr. Noble," in Massachusetts Historical Society *Proceedings*, 2nd ser., vol. 13 (1900), p. 382.

4. James Gordon to William Martin, Oct. 18, 1753, Suffolk Court Files 148,112, p. 66. The letter appears without underlining in MHS *Proceedings*, p. 385.

5. James Gordon to William Martin, Sept. 10, 1765, Suffolk Court Files, reprinted with some silent corrections of language in MHS *Proceedings*, pp. 393, 396.

6. Massachusetts Archives (manuscript), vol. 154, p. 253, Archives of the Commonwealth of Massachusetts, Columbia Point, Boston. See also p. 391, where Mrs. Anna Martin is listed as someone to whom the Estate of Thomas Hutchinson owed £14.8.6 For the printed statute, dated Oct. 16, 1778, see *The Acts and Resolves, Public and Private, of the Province of Massachusetts Bay . . .* , vol. 5 (1769–80) (Boston: Wright & Potter, 1886), ch. 24, pp. 912–18.

7. Brigadier General James Pattison to [William Martin], Philadelphia, March 31, 1778, Pattison Letterbooks, Royal Artillery Institution Library, Woolwich, England, microfilm copy at the David Library of the American Revolution, Washington's Crossing, Pennsylvania. I am deeply grateful to Wayne Bodle for identifying this letter. See also Public Record Office Microfilm AO 13/6/376 and the "Minutes of a Commission (1783) to investigate the causes of the Fire in New York City," Manuscript Division, New-York Historical Society.

Like most regular officers, Martin held a confusing series of titles, since he received temporary wartime promotions in the "army" at a faster rate than his permanent promotions in the regiment. When colleagues testified for him before the Loyalist Claims Commission after the war, his status gyrated wildly. Colleagues may be pardoned their confusion. The published Army Lists establish that he was commissioned a captain in 1757. In 1772 he was still a captain in his regiment, but was promoted to major in the army. In 1779 he was promoted to a major in his regiment, but he was already a lieutenant colonel in the army.

8. Court Files, Case 148.112, pp. 58–62, Superior Court of Judicature, Suffolk County, includes record of *Gordon v. Martin*, Court of Common Pleas, Middlesex County, Sept. 8, 1772. The total debt claimed was £2239.9.5. Gordon's lawyer was the well-known, soon to be loyalist attorney Jonathan Sewall. When Martin won the suit, Gordon appealed to the Supreme Judicial Court, which upheld the county court's decision. See *Martin v. Gordon*, June 14, 1773, Record Book 1773–74, pp. 20–21, Superior Court of Judicature, Suffolk County (Judicial Archives, Archives of the Commonwealth, Boston).

9. AO 12/71/105. See also listing in MHS *Proceedings*, 2nd ser. vol. 10 (1895), pp. 180–81. The Braintree property is described in AO 14/47/637–38. The New Hampshire property is described in AO 13/47/622–38. The properties and their disposition can be traced in Suffolk County, Probate Docket, vol. 72, pp. 281–84, 524; vol. 76, p. 22; vol. 102, pp. 302, 377, 415; vol. 106, p. 507, and file papers 14734, Office of Register of Probate, Suffolk County Courthouse, Boston.

10. The destruction of the house can be followed in PRO microfilm AO 13/6/376; Sept. 27, 1778. After the British evacuation of Boston, the property was sold to John Bosson, Benjamin Cargyll, Winslow Parker, and Levi and Paul Thayer. Account of sale of estates of "Conspirators and Absentees," Massachusetts Archives (manuscript), vol. 154, p. 338: Oct. 3, 1781, Archives of the Commonwealth of Massachusetts, Columbia Point, Boston. The only closely parallel situation I have been able to find is a suit apparently brought in the U.S. Circuit Court by Ward Nicholas Boylston to recover his family estate in Roxbury. It had been confiscated from his father, Benjamin Hallowell, who was named as a "notorious conspirator" in the statute of April 13, 1779; Boylston (who had taken his mother's maiden name) claimed that the property had actually been owned by his mother, and that consequently the confiscation could operate "upon the life estate of Mr. Hallowell, in right of his wife, but did not convey the fee." The estate had been sold to a French immigrant, Lewis Leprilete in 1791. Boylston's suit was successful in 1803. *Ward Nicholas Boylston et al. v. Lewis Leprilete*, Circuit Court, District of Massachusetts, Oct. 26, 1801; *Leprelite v. Rand*, Suffolk County Court of Common Pleas, Jan. 1802; *Rand v. Leprilete*, Supreme Judicial Court, Jan. 1802; all in Department of Archives, Supreme Judicial Court, Boston. See "Confiscated Estates," *New England Genealogical and Historical Register*, vol. 12 (1858), pp. 71–72; Jones, pp. 281–84; I am deeply grateful to David Maas for this reference, and to Elizabeth Bouvier, Archivist of the Supreme Judicial Court, for research assistance.

11. Pattison to Martin, March 31, 1778, Pattison Letterbooks, New-York Historical Society.

12. [Sarah Cooke] "Supreme Court Extracts: re: naturalization of James Martin, of the City of New York, counsellor." Item A. Copy of the statement of the Attorney General to the Supreme Court, Sept. 1791, Miscellaneous Papers—Box 34, Francis Dana Papers, MHS.

13. See the lucid discussion on this point in Maeva Marcus et al., eds., *Documentary History of the Supreme Court of the United States, 1789–1800*, vol. 6 (New York: Columbia University Press, 1997), pp. 199–205, and the documents that follow.

14. *Supreme Court Extracts*, Items D, E, and F, Dana Papers, MHS. Item D is the court's refusal to admit James Martin as an attorney without taking the oath, Feb. 21, 1792; Item E reports exchanges among James Martin, the clerk of the Supreme Judicial Court, and Francis Dana; Item F, dated March 24, 1792, is a note from Martin asking for a reconsideration of the denial: "in a temper very different from resentment Sir . . . I am still ready to receive from the Clerks of the Court the copies of the papers I want." This is endorsed in Dana's hand: "Tell your Master I shall give him no answer to his Letter." These documents are reprinted in Marcus et al., vol. 6, pp. 205–11.

15. Thomas Hobbes, *Leviathan; or, the Matter, Forme, and Power of a Commonwealth, Ecclesiasticall and Civill* (1651; New York: Oxford University Press, 1996), Part II, ch. 21.

16. *Inventing the People* (New York: W. W. Norton, 1988), p. 153. The term "imagined community" is Benedict Anderson's: *Imagined Communities: Reflections on the Origin and Spread of Nationalism* (London: Verso, 1983).

17. John Winthrop's Journal, "History of New England," 1630–49, ed. James Kendall Hosmer (New York: Scribner's, 1908), vol. 2, p. 239.

18. Gerda Lerner, *The Creation of Patriarchy* (New York: Oxford University Press, 1986), pp. 190–93.

19. James Otis, *The Rights of the British Colonies Asserted and Proved* (Boston 1764), reprinted in Bernard Bailyn, ed., *Pamphlets of the American Revolution, 1750–1776* (Cambridge, MA,: Harvard University Press, 1965), 419–22.

20. Emphasis mine. Sally Tickle, New York *Journal and General Advertiser*, Jan. 21, 1773. I am grateful to T. H. Breen for this reference.

21. Abigail Adams to John Adams, June 17, 1782, in L. H. Butterfield et al., eds., *Adams Family Correspondence* (Cambridge, MA: Harvard University Press, 1963–   ), vol. 4, p. 328.

22. See, for one among many examples, George Washington to James Warren, Oct. 7, 1785, in John C. Fitzpatrick, ed., *The Writings of Washington, From the Original Manuscript Sources, 1745–1799* (Washington, DC: Government Printing Office, 1931–44), vol. 28, p. 290.

23. Edwin Burrows and Michael Wallace, "The American Revolution: The Ideology and Psychology of National Liberation," *Perspectives in American History*, vol. 6 (1972), pp. 167–306. See also Winthrop D. Jordan, "Familial Politics: Thomas Paine and the Killing of the King, 1776," *Journal of American History*, vol. 60 (1973), pp. 294–308.

24. Now on display in the Museum of Decorative Arts there. Michael Grossberg, *Governing the Hearth: Law and the Family in Nineteenth Century America* (Chapel Hill: University of North Carolina Press, 1985), also stresses the persistence of patriarchal thought.

25. Tracing changes in voting law in New Jersey, Joan R. Gundersen shrewdly argues that in the early republic "dependency" was redefined as a "sex-specific trait, [transforming] dependent males into independent voters, while subsuming single women, who were in every practical sense independent, into a category of dependence." "Independence, Citizenship and the American Revolution," *Signs: Journal of Women in Culture and Society*, vol. 13 (1987), p. 66. See also Ruth Bloch, "The Gendered Meaning of Virtue in Revolutionary America," *Signs*, vol. 13 (1987), pp. 37–58, and Carroll Smith-Rosenberg, "Dis-covering the Subject of the 'Great Constitutional Discussion,' 1786–1789," *Journal of American History*, vol. 79 (Dec. 1992), pp. 841–73.

26. Carole Pateman's searching examination of the theory of social contract reveals that it treated men as entering the social contract as free agents, but virtually all women as entering already bound by marriage and by antecedent obligations to their husbands. Carole Pateman, *The Sexual Contract* (Stanford: Stanford University Press, 1988), pp. 48–49 et passim.

27. Alfred F. Young, "George Robert Twelves Hewes (1742–1840): A Boston Shoemaker and the Memory of the American Revolution," *William and Mary Quarterly*, 3rd ser., vol. 38 (Oct. 1981), pp. 561–623.

28. Gerda Lerner was early to warn that women's status should be evaluated in relationship to changes in men's status in the early republic; see "The Lady and the Mill Girl: Changes in the Status of Women in the Age of Jackson," *Midcontinent American Studies Journal*, vol. 10 (1969), pp. 5–15.

29. Abigail Adams to John Adams, March 31, 1776, in Butterfield et al., vol. 1, pp. 369–70.

30. See, for example, "An Act for annulling the Distinction between the crimes of Murder and Petit Treason," March 16, 1785, in Asahel Stearns et al., eds., *The General Laws of Massachusetts* . . . , vol. 1 (Boston: Wells & Lilly, 1823), p. 188. On the persistence of petit treason in the slave South, see Kathryn Preyer, "Crime, the Criminal Law and Reform in Post-Revolutionary Virginia," *Law and History Review*, vol. 1 (1983), pp. 56–58.

31. Tapping Reeve, *The Law of Baron and Femme, Parent and Child, Guardian and Ward, Master and Servant, and of the Powers of the Courts of Chancery* (1816; Burlington: Chauncey Goodrich, 1846), p. 73.

32. Reeve, pp. 78–79.

33. Reeve, pp. 98–99.

34. *The Laws Respecting Women* . . . (London: J. Johnson, 1777), p. 183; Nathan Dane, *General Abridgment and Digest of American Law* (Boston, 1823), pp. 341–42; Reeve, p. 162.

35. Well into the twentieth century, courts sustained the understanding that husbands retained property rights in their wives' bodies and fathers retained property rights in the services of their daughters. See Rogers M. Smith's shrewd comments here: " 'One United People': Second-Class Female Citizenship and the American Quest for Community," *Yale Journal of Law and the Humanities*, vol. 1 (1989), p. 269, citing *Tinker v. Colwell*, 193 U.S. 473 (1904) and *In re Freche* 109 F. 620 (D. N.J. 1901).

36. The North Carolina statute provided, for example, that those judged guilty of high treason "shall suffer Death without Benefit of Clergy, and his or her Estate shall be forfeited to the State." April 1777, in *First Laws of the State of North Carolina* (1984; Edenton: Hodge & Wills, 1791), vol. 1, p. 284; "Act for Constituting a Council of Safety," Sept. 1777, in *Acts of General Assembly of New Jersey*, p. 87.

    A New York statute against spying provided that "he or she" might be put to death after court-martial. See *Laws of New York*, vol. 2, June 30, 1780, p. 282, and March 30, 1781, p. 370. See also discussion in Bradley Chapin, *The American Law of Treason: Revolutionary and Early National Origins* (Seattle, 1964), pp. 37–45.

37. "An Act Against Treason and Misprision of Treason," passed by the General Court February 1, 1777, when sitting in exile from Boston at Watertown. *Acts and Resolves, Public and Private, of the Province of Massachusetts Bay*, vol. 5 (1886), ch. 32, p. 615, modeled on the treason statute of the Continental Congress, June 24, 1776. For an insightful examination of the gradual transformation of the concept of the king's "subject" to the republic's "citizen," see James H. Kettner, *The Development of American Citizenship, 1608–1870* (Chapel Hill: University of North Carolina Press, 1978), ch. 7.

38. Chapin, p. 46. There were no executions in Virginia either. There were dozens of arrests for treason in New York, New Jersey, and Pennsylvania, however, and some executions. Chapin, pp. 48–62.

39. Harold M. Hyman, *To Try Men's Souls: Loyalty Tests in American History* (Berkeley: University of California Press, 1960), pp. 63–64.

40. The fullest account of confiscation in revolutionary Massachusetts is found in David E. Maas, *The Return of the Massachusetts Loyalists* (unpublished Ph.D.

dissertation, University of Wisconsin, 1972), esp. ch. 6. Maas concludes that in Massachusetts confiscation "failed as a method of financing the revolution" (p. 313). This failure would make it practical for Tories to return and reclaim their land after the war. See also Harry B. Yoshpe, *The Disposition of Loyalist Estates in the Southern District of the State of New York* (New York: Columbia University Press, 1939).

41. How restrained American revolutionaries were on revising the law of inheritance is a recently reopened question: Carole Shammas, Marylynn Salmon, and Michel Dahlin, *Inheritance in America from Colonial Times to the Present* (New Brunswick: Rutgers University Press, 1987), stress the limits of the changes made in inheritance law in the revolutionary era; note esp. pp. 63–79; Holly Brewer, "Entailing Aristocracy in Colonial Virginia: 'Ancient Feudal Restraints' and Revolutionary Reform," *William and Mary Quarterly*, 3rd ser., vol. 54 (1997), pp. 307–46, stresses the radical impact of the end to primogeniture and entail. The history of dower awaits its historian.

42. Connecticut made no mention of dower right at all: "An Act directing certain confiscated Estates to be sold," *Acts and Laws of the State of Connecticut in America* (New London: Timothy Green, 1794), pp. 56–57. "An Act, for the forteiture and sale of the estates of persons who have adhered to the enemies of this State . . . 22 October 1779," *Laws of the State of New York* . . . (Albany: Weed, Parsons, 1886) vol. 1, pp. 173–84. See also "An Act for the speedy sale of the confiscated and forfeited estates . . . 12 May 1784," ibid., pp. 736–59. Rhode Island and South Carolina claimed all property of loyalist absentees, whether held "in possession, reversion or remainder."

Other states—among them New Jersey, Delaware, and New York—seem to have included dower right by implication in the "just debts" which were to be liquidated before confiscated property was transferred or sold. "An Act for taking Charge of and leasing the Real Estates, and for forfeiting the Personal estates of certain Fugitives and Offenders . . . April 18, 1778, *Acts of the General Assembly of the State of New-Jersey, From the Establishment of the Present Government . . . to . . . 24th Day of December, 1783* . . . (Trenton: Isaac Collins, 1784), pp. 43–52; "An Act for forfeiting to, and vesting in, the State of New Jersey, the Real Estates of certain Fugitives . . . ," Dec. 11, 1778, ibid., pp. 67–68; "An Act to direct the Agents of forfeited Estates . . . to proceed to the Sale . . . ," Dec. 16, 1783, ibid., pp. 354–56. "An Act of free pardon and oblivion . . . ," June 26, 1778, *Laws of the State of Delaware* (New Castle: Samuel and John Adams, 1797), vol. 2, pp. 636–43; "A Supplement to an act, intitled, An act of free pardon . . . ," June 5, 1779, ibid., pp. 658–65; "An Act, for the forfeiture and sale of the estates of persons who have adhered to the enemies of this State . . . ," Oct. 22, 1779, *Laws of the State of New York* (1777–84) (Albany: Weed, Parsons, 1886), vol. 1, pp. 173–84; "An Act for the speedy sale of the confiscated and forfeited estates . . . ," May 12, 1784, ibid., pp. 736–59. But after the Revolution, the New York legislature passed a number of private bills which restored dower claims. See, for example, "An Act for the relief of Clara Service and others," vol. 3, pp. 717 ff.

43. In Pennsylvania, the justices of the Supreme Court could set aside parts of forfeited estates to support wives and children of absentees and traitors; dower may have been treated as an encumbrance on the estate. See "An act for the

attainder of divers traitors . . . ," March 6, 1778, *Laws of the Commonwealth of Pennsylvania* (Philadelphia: Mathew Carey and J. Bioren, 1803), vol. 2, pp. 165 ff., esp. pp. 173–76.

New Hampshire provided that Committees of Confiscation (in 1778) and probate judges (in 1779) might "make such allowance for the wives and children of such absentees out of their estates as they shall judge proper." No specific mention was made of dower or of the necessity to reside in the United States. "An Act in Addition to an Act intituled 'An Act to Confiscate the Estates of Sundry Persons . . . 26 June 1779,' " in Henry Harrison Metcalf, ed., *Laws of New Hampshire* . . . (Bristol: Musgrove Printing House, 1916), vol. 4, pp. 216–18.

44. "An Act for attainting such persons as are therein mentioned of high treason, and for confiscating their estates . . . 1778," in Robert and George Watkins, eds., *A Digest of the Laws of the State of Georgia* . . . (Philadelphia: R. Aitken, 1800), pp. 208 ff., esp. sect. 22, p. 218. See also "An Act for inflicting penalties on, and confiscating the estates of such persons as are therein declared guilty of treason . . . ," 1782, ibid., pp. 242 ff., sect. 12.

45. In Virginia, widows or wives without children could claim dower. The property of British subjects with children, whether the wife was alive or not, was exempt from confiscation if they resided in the state. William Waller Hening, ed., *The Statutes at Large: Being a Collection of All the Laws of Virginia* . . . (Richmond, 1823), vol. 10, p. 71: ch. 14, May 1779. For a discussion of loyalist wives who remained, see Adele Hast, *Loyalism in Revolutionary Virginia: The Norfolk Area and the Eastern Shore* (Ann Arbor: UMI Research Press, 1982), pp. 127–31.

North Carolina also reserved dower claims for wives of absentees who remained "in or under the protection of the . . . United States." North Carolina added the provision that in small estates, wives of absentees could receive "so much of the personal property, including all the household goods . . . as will be sufficient for the reasonable support of the wives, widows and children," and if the lands were small and impoverished, the county court might set aside as much as 100 percent of it for the support of wife and children. "An act to Carry into effect . . . An Act for Confiscating the Property . . . 1778," in Walter Clark, ed., *The State Records of North Carolina* . . . (Goldsboro, NC: Nash Brothers, 1905), vol. 24 (Laws 1777–88), pp. 209–14; note esp. sects. 6, 15. North Carolina went further than other states by specifying that confiscated properties could also be reserved for the support of aged parents of the absentee who were otherwise unable to maintain themselves. See also "An Act to carry into effect . . . Act for confiscating the property of all such persons as are inimical [of Nov. 1777]," Clark, vol. 24, p. 268, sect. 17; and "An Act directing the sale of Confiscated Property," Clark, pp. 424–29 (1782), ch. 6, sect. 26.

46. Richard D. Brown, "The Confiscation and Disposition of Loyalists' Estates in Suffolk County, Massachusetts," *William and Mary Quarterly*, 3rd ser., vol. 21 (1964), pp. 537, 540.

47. "An Act for Confiscating the Estates of Certain Persons Commonly Called Absentees," May 1, 1779, ch. 49, *Acts and Resolves*, vol. 5, pp. 968–61. Details of the legislative history of this statute appear on pp. 1053 ff. On the law of dower, see Marylynn Salmon, *Women and the Law of Property in Early America* (Chapel Hill: University of North Carolina Press, 1986), ch. 7. The efforts of

one absentee's wife to have set off to her one-third of her husband's real estate, "for her dower therein during her life & continuance within the United States of America," may be traced in detail in the John Chandler Transcripts, Octavo Volume C and Folio Volume C, American Antiquarian Society, Worcester, MA, and in Andrew McFarland Davis, *The Confiscation of John Chandler's Estate* (Boston: Houghton Mifflin, 1903).

48. Acts 1778, ch. 48, Massachusetts Archives, manuscript draft, Oct. 8, 1778. Archives of the Commonwealth of Massachusetts, Columbia Point, Boston. This packet includes three other versions drafted between Oct. 1778 and April 1779.

49. "Supreme Court Extracts," Box 34, Dana Papers, MHS.

50. Maeva Marcus and James R. Perry, eds., *Documentary History of the Supreme Court of the United States, 1789–1800*, vol. 1 (1985), pp. 206–7, 210–13. For rough drafts of the original minutes, see pp. 362, 366, 368, 373. See also *Documentary History of the Supreme Court*, vol. 6, pp. 202–4, 212–14; for his admission to practice in New York, see particularly p. 203, n. 22.

51. The other judges were Theodore Sedgwick, Simeon Strong, and George Thatcher. Strong had been briefly arrested as a loyalist during the Revolution. He was appointed to the bench by Federalist governor Caleb Strong in 1801. See William T. Davis, *Bench and Bar of the Commonwealth of Massachusetts* (New York: Da Capo, 1974), p. 246; Gerard W. Gawalt, *The Promise of Power: The Emergence of the Legal Profession in Massachusetts 1760–1840* (Westport, CT: Greenwood Press, 1979), pp. 48, 69; Clifford K. Shipton, in *Sibley's Harvard Graduates: Biographical Sketches of Those who attended Harvard College . . .* (Boston: Massachusetts Historical Society, 1968), pp. 93–95.

52. For long-standing tension among Dana, Sullivan, and Sedgwick, see Thomas Dwight to Theodore Sedgwick, March 20, and April 21, 1798, Vol. C, Theodore Sedgwick Papers, MHS; for tension among Parsons, Dana, and Sullivan, see Theophilus Parsons II, *Memoir of Theophilus Parsons* (Boston: Ticknor and Fields, 1859), p. 79; for tension between Parsons and Sedgwick, see Richard E. Welch, Jr., "The Parsons-Sedgwick Feud and the Reform of the Massachusetts Judiciary," *Essex Institute Historical Collections*, vol. 92 (1956), pp. 171–87. For Sullivan's role in shaping the postwar judiciary system in Massachusetts, see "Bills Drawn by James Sullivan, 1782," in Robert Treat Paine Papers, MHS. Sullivan dedicated *The History of Land Titles in Massachusetts* (Boston: I. Thomas and E. T. Andrews, 1801) to "Francis Dana, Esq. Chief Justice, and the Associate Judges of the Supreme Judicial Court of the Commonwealth of Massachusetts." On the culture of courts and lawyers in this period, see Gawalt, chs. 2 and 3, and Van Beck Hall, *Politics Without Parties: Massachusetts 1780–1791* (Pittsburgh: University of Pittsburgh Press, 1972), pp. 46–48.

53. Thomas C. Amory, *Life of James Sullivan: With Selections from His Writings* (Boston, 1859), vol. 2, p. 88. George Blake (1769–1841) graduated from Harvard in 1789 and studied with James Sullivan; he was admitted to the bar in 1792, and served as U.S. attorney 1801–9. Alfred S. Knofsky and Andrew King, eds., *The Papers of Daniel Webster: Legal Papers—The New Hampshire Practice* (Hanover, NH: University Press of New England, 1982), vol. 1, p. 137.

54. Some years later he would lead the opposition to full disestablishment of religion in Massachusetts. In the 1820s and 1830s, when moderate Jeffersonians had moved into the ranks of Jacksonian Democrats, Blake would be a leader of the

Whigs, along with conservative Jeffersonians and many former Federalists. Blake's positions on disestablishment can be traced in William G. McLoughlin, *New England Dissent 1630–1883: The Baptists and the Separation of Church and State* (Cambridge, MA: Harvard University Press, 1971), vol. 2, pp. 1074, 1158, 1173, 1177–78, 1218–19. His later legal career and his friendship with Daniel Webster can be followed in Charles M. Wiltse, ed., *The Papers of Daniel Webster: Correspondence* (Hanover, NH: University Press of New England, 1974, 1976), vols. 1 and 2.

55. For Parsons' politics, see Parsons, *Memoir*, pp. 27 ff., and David Hackett Fischer, *The Revolution of American Conservatism* (New York: Harper & Row, 1965), p. 254. For Parsons' conservative views of marriage, see Grossberg, pp. 72–73. James Sullivan's biographer stresses the collegial relations the two men maintained on circuit; see Amory, vol. 2, pp. 39–42. Daniel Webster was then a young man reading law in Boston; his admiring comments on Parsons and his critical comments on Sullivan appear in his note "Some characters at the Boston Bar, 1804," in *Papers of Daniel Webster: Legal Papers*, vol. 1, pp. 41–42.

56. William Willis, *A History of the Law, the Courts and the Lawyers of Maine from its First Colonization to the Early Part of the Present Century* (Portland: Bailey & Noyes, 1863), pp. 114–15. Willis says that the office of Solicitor General had been "created especially" for Davis, and when he retired from it, the office was eliminated. I am grateful to Alan Taylor for this reference.

57. See *Columbian Centinel* (Boston), March 6, 13, April 20, 1805.

58. John Adams to Abigail Adams, June 29, 1774, in Butterfield, vol. 1, p. 113; Amory, vol. 1, p. 28. The best biographical essay on Sullivan is Shipton's; see *Sibley's Harvard Graduates*, vol. 15, pp. 299–322. From the prerevolutionary war years and throughout their lives, Sullivan supported Sam Adams and John Hancock. This often meant that he was to be found in alliances which John Adams opposed; in 1788 Sullivan tried to gather support for Hancock instead of Adams as Vice President. For Sullivan's defense of Stamp Act rioters and Adams' defense of their target, see Butterfield, vol. 1, 132–33.

59. Biddeford, Maine, elected Sullivan to its Committee of Safety and sent him as its delegate to three prerevolutionary congresses in 1774 and 1775; in 1776 he became its delegate to the new state legislature. In 1778 Sullivan moved to the central Massachusetts town of Groton, and soon afterward was appointed to the Superior Court of Judicature, the predecessor of the Supreme Judicial Court. He continued to serve concurrently in the legislature.

60. Amory, vol. 1, pp. 138 ff. Sullivan undertook the defense of returning Tory Sylvester Gardiner in return for title to one of Gardiner's estates, an arrangement which was revealed only by David Maas in 1972. Another Tory he assisted was William Vassall. Maas, pp. 526, 533.

61. In 1798 Judge Francis Dana nearly threw Sullivan out of the courtroom for his expressed sympathy for squatters. Thomas Dwight to Theodore Sedgwick, April 21, 1798, Sedgwick Papers, MHS. But Sullivan also took positions which the speculators endorsed; "The Federalist Great Proprietors," Alan Taylor writes bitterly, "should have known that they had little to fear from the new politicians, because so many of the leading Jeffersonians used to work for them." Sullivan had among his clients the Plymouth Company and Henry Knox. Alan

Taylor, *Liberty Men and Great Proprietors: The Revolutionary Settlement on the Maine Frontier* (Chapel Hill: University of North Carolina Press for the Institute of Early American History and Culture, 1990), p. 216. See also pp. 23–24. Sullivan's fullest statement of his understanding of the marketplace appears in a pamphlet in which he bitterly denounced Alexander Hamilton's Bank of the United States for favoring speculators in stocks and bonds and strongly urged making bank stock available to small investors. [James Sullivan] *The Path to Riches. An Inquiry Into the Origin and Use of Money: and Into the Principles of Stocks and Banks, to which are Subjoined Some Thoughts Respecting a Bank for the Commonwealth* (Boston: P. Edes for I. Thomas and E. T. Andrews, 1792).

62. Amory, vol. 1, p. 221. See also [James Sullivan] *A Dissertation Upon the Constitutional Freedom of the Press . . .* (Boston, 1801).

63. In this pamphlet, Sullivan powerfully defined the United States as a postrevolutionary society; if Americans were unrepentant—as he thought they should be—for tar and feathers, for the humiliation and jailing of traitors, for confiscated estates—then they had ought not castigate the French for similar vigor; indeed they ought to acknowledge their similarities and their debt. Novion [James Sullivan], *The Altar of Baal Thrown Down: Or, the French Nation Defended, Against the Pulpit Slander of David Osgood, A.M. Pastor of the Church in Medford* (Boston, 1795). *An Impartial Review of the Causes and Principles of the French Revolution. By an American* (Boston: Benjamin Edes, 1798) is also attributed to Sullivan; in this too he makes comparisons between the French and American experience. See esp. pp. 33, 65, 84, 98. See also *Columbian Centinel*, March 23, 1805. Sullivan denied that he had written the group's constitution but insisted there was nothing wrong with the Massachusetts Constitutional Society. *Independent Chronicle* (Boston), March 11, 1805.

64. On Quock Walker, see Amory, vol. 1, pp. 115, 120, and John D. Cushing, "The Cushing Court and the Abolition of Slavery in Massachusetts: More Notes on the 'Quock Walker Case,'" *American Journal of Legal History*, vol. 5 (1961), pp. 121 n. 6, 137. Sullivan's most extended comments on slavery appear in James Sullivan to Jeremy Belknap, April 9, July 30, 1795, in MHS *Collections*, 5th ser., vol. 3 (1877), pp. 402–3, 412–16.

65. See essay signed "Marcus" in *Independent Chronicle*, Feb. 7, 1793, and essay signed "Plain Truth," *Independent Chronicle*, Aug. 2, 1793.

66. *An Appeal to the Impartial Public by the Society of Christian Independents Congregating in Gloucester* (Boston: Benajmin Edes, 1795). See also James Sullivan to [?], June 25, 1785, Sullivan Papers, MHS. In 1785 Sullivan served as lawyer for the Universalist minister John Murray—future husband of the brilliant writer Judith Sargent Murray, who was already a member of his congregation—when members of his independent church in Gloucester sought to be excused from paying taxes to support the established Congregational church. In this case, Theophilus Parsons was one of the lawyers for the Congregational parish. Although the judges at first sided with Parsons, the jury overrode their opinion, and in a subsequent case, the judges, who included Francis Dana, made "a remarkable reversal," admitting Sullivan's arguments and upholding Murray's claims to church taxes. For an extensive discussion of Sullivan's role in this and related cases, see William G. McLoughlin, *New England Dissent 1630–1833: The Baptists and the Separation of Church and State* (Cambridge, MA: Harvard

University Press, 1971), vol. 1, pp. 654–59. Sullivan was a member of the liberal Brattle Street Church, a church which drifted toward Unitarianism. McLoughlin finds that Sullivan was not a thoroughgoing supporter of disestablishment; he wanted exceptions to the system of tax support for churches, not the entire dismantling of the system.

67. James Sullivan to Elbridge Gerry, May 6, 1776, in Robert J. Taylor et al., eds., *Papers of John Adams* (Cambridge, MA: Harvard University Press, 1979), vol. 4, pp. 212–13. Sullivan had read his Paine: "Government is founded on the Authority of the people, and by them only is Supported and is as the writer of Common Sense observes, not founded so much in human Nature, as in the depravity of it." He suggested a two-tier voting system which took relative wealth into account.

68. John Adams to James Sullivan, May 26, 1776, in Taylor et al., vol. 4, pp. 208–13.

69. Kathryn Kish Sklar, "Popular Sources of Change in the Schooling of Girls in Massachusetts, 1750–1820," unpublished paper, c. 1990. Cited with permission of the author.

70. Sullivan to Thomas Jefferson, June 20, 1806: "I am now before a Supreme Judicial Court, artful, malignant, and cruel, fully determined to ruin me if possible. . . . I can not endure the idea that these malignant men should review me as in a situation chased away by the federalists, and neglected by my own party . . ." See also Sullivan to Jefferson, June 20, 1805, April 21, 1806, Sullivan Papers, MHS. On the election rivalry, see Moses Sampson, *Who Shall be Governor, Strong or Sullivan? Or, the Sham-Patriot Unmasked* (Hudson, NY, 1806).

71. *Martin v. Commonwealth*, p. 361.

72. *Martin v. Commonwealth*, p. 363.

73. *Martin v. Commonwealth*, p. 364.

74. J. G. A. Pocock comments on this relationship in *The Machiavellian Moment* (Princeton: Princeton University Press, 1975), p. 89.

75. *Martin v. Commonwealth*, p. 361.

76. *Martin v. Commonwealth*, p. 376.

77. Sullivan's position was, indeed, congruent with the traditional understanding that the husband who abjured the realm was civilly dead, leaving his wife as *feme sole* and thus vulnerable to the direct claims of the state. See, for example, *The Laws Respecting Women*, p. 171; Dane, p. 335; Reeve, pp. 98–105. I am grateful to Hendrik Hartog for this observation. In these cases, however, it was assumed that in leaving the realm the husband had surrendered his claim to the body of his wife.

78. *Martin v. Commonwealth*, p. 373.

79. *Martin v. Commonwealth*, p. 374.

80. He might here have cited the Treason Act of 1777, which had specified "All persons . . . owe allegiance and are members of the State."

81. To this effect, Davis had cited Burlamaqui on *The Principles of Natural Law*: "Reason being the first rule of man, it is also the first principle of morality, and the immediate cause of all primitive obligation."

82. David Maas reports that as a member of the General Court in the early 1780s, Sedgwick had voted against harsh treatment for returning Tories and had enthusiastically arranged for the return of Peter and Henry Van Schaack, even to

the point of bribing the justices of the peace. See Maas, pp. 402, 422, 444 ff.

83. *Martin v. Commonwealth*, p. 391. A fifth judge, Samuel Sewall, was not present but noted that he agreed with the decision; p. 399.

84. Jan Lewis, "The Republican Wife: Virtue and Seduction in the Early Republic," *William and Mary Quarterly*, 3rd ser., vol. 45 (1987), pp. 689–721.

85. The Martin case is unusual for the clarity with which the matter of women's status was discussed. There are some similarities between it and *Lessee of Pemberton v. Hicks*, 1799, in Horace Binney, *Reports of Cases Adjudged in the Supreme Court of Pennsylvania* (Philadelphia: William Farrand and Co., 1809), vol. 1, pp. 1–24, in that the property of the wife of a loyalist was also at issue. But the facts of the case were significantly different: Joseph Galloway had not only been a loyalist but an attainted traitor, who had fled to England. He had held property "in right of his wife," Grace Galloway, who, like Anna Martin, had inherited land from her father which Joseph held as tenant by curtesy. But Grace Galloway had met the requirement that she stay in the United States in order to maintain her claim on the property. As a traitor, Joseph Galloway was regarded as "civilly dead." All rights reverted to Grace Galloway and for civil purposes she was treated as a widow. When she willed the property to her son-in-law the Supreme Court of Pennsylvania upheld her claim.

86. David Maas finds that with a few brief exceptions in the immediate postwar period, Tory claimants won more cases than they lost. *Divided Hearts: Massachusetts Loyalists 1765–1790: A Biographical Directory* (Society of Colonial Wars . . . & New England Historic Genealogical Society, 1980), p. xxiii. Also Maas, *Return of the Loyalists*, pp. 524–25 et passim.

87. See Catharine Maria Sedgwick, *Hope Leslie: Or, Early Times in the Massachusetts*, ed., Mary Kelley (New Brunswick: Rutgers University Press, 1987), pp. ix–xxi. I owe this paragraph to conversations with Alan Taylor.

88. Grossberg, pp. 296 ff.

89. Not until 1806 did a Boston newspaper mention the Martin case or Sullivan's connection with it. Then, William Bosson, who had purchased the confiscated property and lost it in the lawsuit, charged that Sullivan, although acting on behalf of the state as Attorney General, had also and inappropriately charged him (Bosson) a twenty-dollar fee for legal services. Sullivan defended himself in print; see Boston *Chronicle*, March 24 [?], 1806, reprinted in Amory, vol. 2, pp. 413–14.

James Martin subsequently brought five different and successful ejectment actions against holders of property he claimed he inherited from his mother. These cases can be traced in Docket Book vol. 2, 1804–9, Record Book vol. 2 1806–11, and accompanying file papers for *James Martin v. John Bosson; Martin v. Benjamin Cargyll; Martin v. Winslow Parker; Martin v. Levi Thayer; Martin v. Paul Thayer.* U.S. Circuit Court, Massachusetts, Federal Records Center, Waltham. Blake served as Martin's attorney in all the suits; Sullivan, in his private capacity, was counsel for Bosson and for Cargyll.

90. *Esther Sewall v. Benjamin Lee*, Oct. 1809, in Dudley Atkins Tyng, ed., *Reports of Cases Argued and Determined in the Supreme Judicial Court of the Commonwealth of Massachusetts*, vol. 9 (Boston, 1853), pp. 363–70. Esther Sewall had fled with her husband, Jonathan, to New Brunswick.

The *Martin* decision was reaffirmed by Theophilus Parsons, now in his role as Chief Justice of the Supreme Judicial Court, in *Esther Sewall v. Benjamin Lee*, 9 *Mass. Reports* (1812) 363–70. See also Lewis Bigelow, *A Digest of the Cases Argued and Determined in the Supreme Judicial Court of the Commonwealth of Massachusetts from Sept. 1804 to Nov. 1815* . . . (Cambridge, 1818), p. 238.

91. *Kempe's Lessee v. Kennedy*, 9 *U.S. Reports* (5 Cranch) 173, 174–79. See also Irwin S. Rhodes, ed., *The Papers of John Marshall* (Chapel Hill: University of North Carolina Press, 1974–   ), vol. 2, p. 11. In a delicious irony, in 1812 the Supreme Judicial Court of Massachusetts decided that children born in the colonies could claim birthright citizenship even if they had spent the war years and after in British territory, and therefore were entitled to claim ancestors' estates that had been confiscated during the Revolution. In that case the plaintiff was a grandson of the Gordon family, and, as the historian who discovered this relationship points out, "the defendant, who had insisted that the plaintiff was an alien incapable of inheriting, was the plaintiff's uncle—James Martin." The decision was written by Theophilus Parsons. Marcus et al., vol. 6, p. 205.

92. *Ann Shanks et al. v. Abraham Dupont et al.*, 28 U.S. (3 Peters) 242–68 (1830). As a member of the state legislature Story had served on a committee that examined the contested election returns in 1806; although a Republican, he had refused to vote along party lines and had awarded the disputed election to Caleb Strong rather than to James Sullivan. R. Kent Newmyer, *Supreme Court Justice Joseph Story: Statesman of the Old Republic* (Chapel Hill: University of North Carolina Press, 1985), pp. 56–57 and p. 401 n. 88.

93. William Wetmore Story, ed., *Life and Letters of Joseph Story* (Boston: Little, Brown, 1851), vol. 1, p. 24.

94. *Shanks v. Dupont*, 28 U.S. (3 Peters) 242, 246–48, 253 (1830). It was left to the dissenting judge to complain that "the very innocent act of marrying a British officer" had been "tortured into 'taking a part in the present war.' "

95. Rogers Brubaker, *Citizenship and Nationhood in France and Germany* (Cambridge, MA: Harvard University Press, 1992), pp. 80, 87. The one exception to equal citizenship is that only those who acquire citizenship at birth may stand for election to the presidency. The idea of *jus soli* has been treated much more capaciously in the United States than elsewhere; for example, in France children born on French soil to aliens may be citizens *if* they reach the age of eighteen, have lived in France for five years, and have committed no crime. In some other countries, citizenship is ascribed *only* on the basis of descent. Birth on German soil and prolonged residence have no bearing on citizenship. German opposition parties have recently proposed that children born in Germany be citizens. Children born on United States soil to aliens become citizens at birth.

96. It is ironic that Dred Scott could bring a suit as a citizen in a federal court, but the court ruled that he and other blacks could not enjoy the privileges and immunities of citizenship. Kettner, *Development of American Citizenship*, p. 325.

97. Kettner, pp. 235–36.

98. *Amy v. Smith*, 11 Ky. (1 Litt.) 326, at 333, 339–42 (1822); quoted in Kettner, pp. 321–22.

99. "Act to Secure the Right of Citizenship to Children of Citizens . . ." ch. 71, 10 *Stat.* 604 (1855).

100. *Kelly v. Owen*, 74 U.S. (7 Wall.) 496 (1868).

101. Grossberg, pp. 83; see also p. 52, 67 et passim.

102. "Page Law," 18 Stat. 477. (1875).
103. James Schouler, *A Treatise on the Law of the Domestic Relations; Embracing Husband and Wife, Parent and Child, Guardian and Ward, Infancy, and Master and Servant* (Boston: Little, Brown, 1870), p. 51.
104. Schouler, pp. 10–11.
105. Schouler, pp. 11–12, 18–19.
106. The fullest discussion of these issues is found in Candice Lewis Bredbenner, *A Nationality of Her Own: Woman, Marriage, and the Law of Citizenship* (Berkeley: University of California Press, 1998).
107. House Joint Resolution No. 238, 55th Cong., 2nd sess. (May 18, 1898), 30 Stat. 1496. John L. Cable, *Decisive Decisions of United States Citizenship* (Charlottesville, VA: Michie Co. 1967), pp. 41–42.
108. Emphasis mine. *MacKenzie v. Hare*, 239 U.S. 299, 306–8, 311–12 (1915). The fullest discussion of this case and its context is found in Bredbenner.
109. New York *Times*, May 4, 1918; see also Bredbenner, ch. 2.
110. This section is indebted to Cable and Bredbenner and to Virginia Sapiro, "Women, Citizenship, and Nationality: Immigration and Naturalization Policies in the United States," *Politics and Society*, vol. 13 (1984), pp. 1–26. For the effort to deny the election to Congress of William Jennings Bryan's daughter because she had married a foreigner, see Cable, pp. 48–49; for an example of passport denial in the 1950s, I am indebted to a conversation with Lawrence Gelfand, Sept. 24, 1991.
111. *Villanueva-Jurado v. Immigration and Naturalization Service* 482 F. 2nd 886 (5th Cir. 1973) 887.
112. *Elias v. United States Department of State* 721 F. Supp. 243 (N.D. Cal. 1989). See Gary Endelman, "Mother Knows Best: A New Look at an Old Law," *Immigration Journal*, April–June 1990, pp. 29–31, 36.
113. 8 U.S. C§1401(g) (1994).
114. *Lorelyn Penero Miller v. Madeleine K. Albright*, No. 96-1060, U.S. Supreme Court, decided April 22, 1998. Ginsburg's dissent took the form of a meticulous history of the laws on the transmission of citizenship from parent to child. Justices Stephen Breyer and David Souter joined her in dissent; Breyer wrote a second dissent in which Ginsburg and Souter joined.
115. *The World's Women—1995: Trends and Statistics, Social Statistics and Indicators*, Series K, No. 12 (New York: United Nations, 1995).
116. New York *Times*, Oct. 12, 1996, p. 1; *In re Fauziya Kasinga*, File A73-476-695, U.S. Department of Justice: Executive Office for Immigration Review, Board of Immigration Appeals, Interim Decision 3278, June 13, 1996; see account in New York *Times*, September 11, 1996.
117. See Janet Calvo, "Spouse-Based Immigration Laws: The Legacies of Coverture," *San Diego Law Review*, vol. 28 (1993), 593-644, and Felicia E. Franco, "Unconditional Safety for Conditional Immigrant Women," *Berkeley Women's Law Journal*, vol. 11 (1996), 99-141.
118. *Adams v. Howerton*, 673 F. 2nd 1036, 1037 (9th Cir. 1982). At the time the Adams case was decided, gays and lesbians were subject to exclusion—even if they could fit within a visa category, they still could not immigrate, under sect. 212(a) of the INA. That was repealed in 1990, but the bar on spousal visas remains. For an insightful and wide-ranging analysis of practices that treat sex-

uality as "a fundamental index" of legitimacy, see Lauren Berlant, *The Queen of America Goes to Washington City: Essays on Sex and Citizenship* (Durham: Duke University Press, 1997).

119. On the continuing understanding of obligation as central to Americans' conceptualization of citizenship, see Linda K. Kerber, "The Meanings of Citizenship," *Journal of American History*, vol. 84 (1997) 833-54, and Gerald L. Neuman, *Strangers to the Constitution: Immigrants, Borders, and Fundamental Law* (Princeton: Princeton University Press, 1996), esp. pp. 4–9 and 52–71.

2. "I AM JUST AS FREE AND JUST AS GOOD AS YOU ARE"

1. James M. Smallwood, *Time of Hope, Time of Despair: Black Texans During Reconstruction* (Port Washington, NY: Kennikat Press, 1981), p. 8; Patsy Moses, in George P. Rawick, ed., *The American Slave: A Composite Autobiography—Texas Narratives, Parts 3 and 4*, vol. 5 (1941; Westport, CT: Greenwood Press, 1972), p. 142.

2. William Mathews, quoted in Rawick, p. 70; see also Barry A. Crouch, *The Freedmen's Bureau and Black Texans* (Austin: University of Texas Press, 1992), p. 15.

3. Quoted in Dan T. Carter, *When the War Was Over: The Failure of Self-Reconstruction in the South, 1865–1867* (Baton Rouge: Louisiana State University Press, 1985), p. 23, citing Minetta Altgelt Goyne, ed., *Lone Star and Double Eagle: Civil War Letters of a German-Texas Family* (Lubbock, TX, 1982), pp. 172–73.

4. William L. Richter, *Overreached on All Sides: The Freedmen's Bureau Administrators in Texas, 1865–1868* (College Station: Texas A&M University Press, 1991), p. 28.

5. Bvt. Lt. Col. J. C. De Gress to Maj. Gen. Mower, Nov. 13, 1865, filed as D-5 1866, Registered Letters Received, ser. 3620, Texas Assistant Commissioner, Records of the Bureau of Refugees, Freedmen, and Abandoned Lands, Record Group 105, National Archives [FSSP A-3208]. The bracketed number at the end of a citation is the number under which a photocopy of that document is filed in the collection of the Freedmen and Southern Society Project (FSSP) at the University of Maryland. Subsequent notes will use the abbreviation BRFAL-RG 105, NA, followed by the bracketed number.

6. Richter, p. 28.

7. Houston *Telegraph*, no identification but presumably Nov. 20, 1866; clipping enclosed in J. C. De Gress to Bvt. Lt. Col. H. A. Ellis, Nov. 20, 1866, D-94 1866, Registered Letters Received, ser. 3620, TX Asst. Comm., BRFAL-RG 105, NA [FSSP A-3220].

8. Robert J. Steinfeld, *The Invention of Free Labor: The Employment Relation in English and American Law and Culture, 1350–1870* (Chapel Hill: University of North Carolina Press, 1991), p. 60; 5 Eliz. c. 4, quoted in Steinfeld, p. 23.

9. The ordinance is available in the *Houston City Directory for 1866* (Houston, 1866), p. 71.

10. Arthur H. Sherry, "Vagrants, Rogues and Vagabonds—Old Concepts in Need of Revision," *California Law Review*, vol. 48 (1960), pp. 559–60.

11. Joanna Innes, "Prisons for the Poor: English Bridewells, 1555–1800," in Francis Snyder and Douglas Hay, eds., *Labour, Law and Crime: An Historical Perspective* (London: Tavistock, 1987), p, 102.

12. Tapping Reeve, *The Law of Baron and Femme, of Parent and Child, Guardian and Ward, Master and Servant, and of the Powers of Courts of Chancery; With an Essay on the terms Heir, Heirs, and Heirs of the Body* (1816; 2nd ed.; Burlington: Chauncey Goodrich, 1846), pp. 339–77, esp. p. 343. Christopher Tomlins reflects on these connections in "Subordination, Authority, Law: Subjects in Labor History," *International Labor and Working Class History*, no. 47 (Spring 1995), pp. 56–90. Provisions for binding out the children of poor persons as apprentices may be found in the statute books of many of the states. Rev. Stat. Vt. 1839, p. 345; Rev. Stat. N.Y., vol. 2, p. 154; Stat. Conn. 1838; North Carolina Act 1792. See also Richard B. Morris, *Government and Labor in Early America* (New York: Columbia University Press, 1946), and Robert Steinfeld's unpublished paper "The Mythic Rise of Free Labor: A Critique of Historical Stage Theory," copyright 1995. The Articles of Confederation denied the privileges and immunities of citizenship to vagrants and vagabonds, but the Federal Constitution of 1787 did not repeat the provision. Gerald L. Neuman, *Strangers to the Constitution: Immigrants, Borders, and Fundamental Law* (Princeton: Princeton University Press, 1996), p. 24.

13. Reva Siegel, "Home as Work: The First Women's Rights Claims Concerning Wives' Household Labor, 1850–1880," *Yale Law Journal*, vol. 103 (March 1994), pp. 1073–1217.

14. Zephaniah Swift, *A System of the Laws of the State of Connecticut* (Windham: John Byrne, 1795), vol. 1, pp. 169–70.

15. A thoughtful overview of the problem is Anthony G. Amsterdam, "Federal Constitutional Restrictions on the Punishment of Crimes of Status, Crimes of General Obnoxiousness, Crimes of Displeasing Police Officers, and the Like," *Criminal Law Bulletin*, vol. 3 (1967), pp. 205–42; see esp. pp. 230–31.

16. *People v. Wilson*, 145 Cal. App. 2nd 1, 6, 301 P. 2nd 974, 977–78 (1956). Quoted in Sherry, p. 565.

17. For the construction of household labor as work-free, see Jeanne Boydston, *Home and Work: Housework, Wages, and the Ideology of Labor in the Early Republic* (New York: Oxford University Press, 1990).

18. Personal communication, Jan. 29, 1996.

19. Michael B. Katz, *The Undeserving Poor: From the War on Poverty to the War on Welfare* (New York: Pantheon, 1989), p. 14.

20. For example, the Texas "Act Regulating Contracts for Labor" had a special section for domestic servants, who "shall, at all hours of the day or night, and on all days of the week, promptly answer all calls, and obey and execute all lawful orders and commands of the family in whose service they are employed. . . . And it is the duty of this class of laborers to be especially civil and polite to their employer, his family and guests. "An Act Regulating Contracts for Labor" (Nov. 1, 1866), *The General Laws of the Regular Session of the Eleventh Legislature of the State of Texas* (Austin, 1866), ch. 80, p. 79.

21. Eric Foner, *Reconstruction: America's Unfinished Revolution 1863–1877* (New York: Harper & Row, 1988), p. 56.

22. Foner, pp. 199–200; Donald Nieman, *To Set the Law in Motion: The Freedmen's*

Bureau and the Legal Rights of Blacks, 1865–1868 (Millwood, NY: KTO Press, 1979), pp. 73–97. *Laws . . . of the State of Texas*, ch. 80, pp. 76–77.

23. Gerald David Jaynes, *Branches Without Roots: Genesis of the Black Working Class in the American South, 1862–1882* (New York: Oxford University Press, 1986), pp. 12–13.

24. Harold D. Woodman, *New South—New Law: The Legal Foundations of Credit and Labor Relations in the Postbellum Agricultural South* (Baton Rouge, Louisiana State University Press, 1995), p. 109.

25. The most elegant statement of this development is the essay "The Wartime Genesis of Free Labor, 1861–1865," published as ch. 2 in Ira Berlin et al., *Slaves No More: Three Essays on Emancipation and the Civil War* (Cambridge: Cambridge University Press, 1992), pp. 77–187, and as the introduction to ser. 1, vols. 2 and 3, of *Freedom: A Documentary History of Emancipation 1861–1867* (Cambridge: Cambridge University Press, 1990).

26. Sherry makes a distinction between U.S. vagrancy law, which generally is framed in terms of status as well as behavior, and the English Vagrancy Act of 1824, which "placed almost exclusive emphasis on *conduct*. . . . [Being a] common prostitute . . . was not made punishable unless she wandered in the public streets behaving in a riotous or indecent manner" (p. 564).

27. Julie Saville, *The Work of Reconstruction: From Slave to Wage Laborer in South Carolina 1860–1870* (Cambridge: Cambridge University Press, 1994), pp. 23–27, 46–47, 86; Leslie A. Schwalm, *A Hard Fight for We: Women's Transition from Slavery to Freedom in South Carolina* (Urbana: University of Illinois Press, 1997), esp. pp. 223–31.

28. Houston *Tri-Weekly Telegraph*, Jan. 28, 1866; Richter, pp. 21–24.

29. Saville, p. 104.

30. John Eaton, Jr., to Col. Smith, May 22, 1863, vol. 74, p. 54, Letters Sent by John Eaton, General Superintendent of Contrabands, ser. 2027, MS Asst. Comm. Pre-Bureau Records, Records of the BRFAL-BG 105, NA [FSSP A-4001]: "The dealers in this Sort of horse-flesh are not particular about colour. The promiscuous arrivals of quadroons or mulatto women in town without direction has furnished an opportunity for these vile traders to insure the objects of their traffic. Genl Veatch & Genl Hurlbut have been very anxious that all blacks around loose should be got out of town. But this class when taken out have been constantly returning." He suggested that the solution would be a contraband camp on the outskirts of town.

31. From the Waco *Register*, reprinted in the Houston *Tri-Weekly Telegraph*, Jan. 19, 1866.

32. Houston *Tri-Weekly Telegraph*, Jan. 28, 1866.

33. Richter, p. 9.

34. "An Act establishing a General Apprentice Law . . . ," Oct. 27, 1866, *Laws . . . of the State of Texas*, pp. 61–63.

35. Saville, p. 104 n. 9. See the classic article, Rebecca Scott, "The Battle over the Child: Child Apprenticeship and the Freedmen's Bureau in North Carolina," *Prologue*, vol. 10 (1978), pp. 101–13.

36. William Cohen, *At Freedom's Edge: Black Mobility and the Southern White Quest for Racial Control 1861–1915* (Baton Rouge: Louisiana State University Press, 1991), p. 33.

37. Nieman, pp. 73–75, 84–85, 90–97, 165. In South Carolina, freedpeople who did not have a fixed home and contracted employment were vagrants who could be forced to work without pay for private individuals for up to a year.

38. Smallwood, p. 40.

39. *Laws . . . of the State of Texas*, ch. 80, p. 78.

40. Bvt. Lt. Col. H. A. Ellis to J. C. De Gress, Oct. 26, 1866, vol. 4, p. 363, Letters Sent, ser. 3616, TX Asst. Comm., BRFAL-RG 105, NA [FSSP A-3225].

41. "Biographical Sketches," [T.B. Hadley, Piety Hadley] *Texas Historical and Biographical Magazine* II (April, 1892), 247–48.

42. The ordinance is available in the *Houston City Directory for 1866*, p. 71.

43. See Houston *Telegraph* for 1866, passim; Crouch, p. 78.

44. *Houston City Directory*, p. 71.

45. Houston *Telegraph*, Dec. 21, 1866.

46. Houston *Telegraph*, March 28, 1866. Mary Brittain, a Negro woman arrested for "blackguarding" (that is, abusing or reviling "in scurrilous terms") Elizabeth Wheeler, was sentenced in the Recorder's Court to pay a fine of $11.50. "She was sent to the streets in default." Houston *Sunday Telegraph*, Dec. 16, 1866.

47. Houston *Daily Telegraph*, June 1, 1866.

48. Houston *Daily Telegraph*, Dec. 8, 1866.

49. Houston *Daily Telegraph*, June 2, 1866.

50. "A Wife and Mother" to the Houston *Telegraph*, July 7, 1866, urging the importation of white domestics from Europe.

51. Special Orders no. 63, Sept. 29, 1863, filed as E-2 1865, Letters Received, ser. 15, Washington HQ, Records of the BRFAL-RG 105, NA [FSSP A-4023].

52. Capt. Lewis Kooker to Col. M. T. Donohoe, May 4, 1865, vol. 19/58 24AC, p. 159, Letters Sent, ser. 7000, 1st Brigade, 3rd Division, 24th Army Corps, Records of U.S. Army Continental Commands, pt. 2, no. 478, Record Group 393, National Archives [FSSP C-3185].

53. Special Orders no. 15, Office Assistant Commissioner, Bureau of Refugees, Freedmen, and Abandoned Lands, Jan. 31, 1866, enclosed in Col. T. W. Osborne to Maj. Gen. O. O. Howard, Feb. 19, 1866, F-59 1866, Letters Received, ser. 15, Washington HQ, BRFAL-RG 105, NA [FSSP A-1444].

54. *Laws . . . of the State of Texas*, ch. 80, p. 77.

55. Mary H. Blewett, *Men, Women, and Work: Class, Gender and Protest in the New England Shoe Industry, 1780–1910* (Urbana: University of Illinois Press, 1988), p. 45. Blewett distinguishes between "the family labor system . . . joint family effort coordinated by the male head" and the "family wage system," in which women were paid directly for outwork.

56. J. L. Tharp to Lt. John Tyler, April 30, 1867, Narrative Reports of Operations from Subordinate Officers, ser. 242, AR Asst. Comm., BRFAL-RG 105, NA [FSSP A-2486].

57. Houston *Telegraph*, reprinted Jan. 17, 1866.

58. Susan E. O'Donovan, "Free Labor and African American Households: Reconstruction in Southwestern Georgia, 1865–1868," unpublished paper, 1994. Cited by permission of the author.

59. Order, Bureau of Refugees, Freedmen, and Abandoned Lands, Office Act. Subasst. Comm., District of Thomasville, Nov. 27, 1865, vol. 379, p. 20, Letters

Sent, ser. 1036, Thomasville, GA, Subasst. Comm., BRFAL-RG 105, NA [FSSP A-5216].

60. Jno. A. Hart to Col. O. D. Kinsman, Nov. 26, 1867, Unregistered Letters Received, ser. 9, AL Asst. Comm., BRFAL-RG 105, NA [FSSP A-1865].

61. J. L. Tharp to Lt. John Tyler, April 30, 1867, Narrative Reports of Operations from Subordinate Officers, ser. 242, AR Asst. Comm., BRFAL-RG 105, NA [FSSP A-2486].

62. J. D. Harris to Gen. Tillson, July 23, 1866, Unregistered Letters Received, ser. 632, GA Asst. Comm., BRFAL-RG 105, NA [FSSP A-5402].

63. M. Wells to Maj. William, July 3, 1866, Unregistered Letters Received, ser. 1431, Alexandria, LA, Asst. Supt., BRFAL-RG 105, NA [FSSP A-8697]. Wells tried to force the issue: "I have stopped the rations of the women, but that has no effect, they steal stock, poultry, & other articles."

64. Alice Kessler-Harris, *Out to Work: A History of Wage-Earning Women in the United States* (New York: Oxford University Press, 1982), p. 123. See also U.S. Department of Commerce, Bureau of the Census, *Historical Statistics of the United States, Colonial Times to 1970*, pt. 1 (Washington, DC, 1975), pp. 131–32.

65. Crouch, p. 25.

66. *Minutes of the Meetings of the Board of Mayor and Aldermen*, Book 11, Memphis and Shelby County Archives, May 4, 1866, p. 888. I am grateful to Hannah Rosen for this reference.

67. Capt. Chas. H. Millar to Capt. Geo. S. Darling, Dec. 15, 1864, vol. 299 DG, p. 756, Press Copies of Letters Sent, ser. 1839, Provost Marshal, Dept. of the Gulf, Records of U.S. Army Continental Commands (pt. 1), Record Group 393, National Archives [FSSP C-1071].

68. W. [L.] Strickland to Lt. Van Ornum, July 13, 1865, Letters Received by the Provost Marshal General, ser. 1515, St. Charles Parish, LA, Provost Marshal Field Organizations, Records of U.S. Army Continental Commands (pt. 4), Record Group 393, National Archives [FSSP C-1012].

69. Jno. A. Hart to Col. O. D. Kinsman, Nov. 26, 1867, Unregistered Letters Received, ser. 9, AL Asst. Comm., BFRAL-RG 105, NA [FSSP A-1865].

70. J. C. De Gress to Bvt. Lt. Col. H. A. Ellis, Oct. 27, 1866, D-56 1866, Registered Letters Received, ser. 3620, TX Asst. Comm., BRFAL-RG 105, NA [FSSP A-3225].

71. Foner, p. 170.

72. Barbara Fields, "Ideology and Race in American History," in J. Morgan Kousser and James M. McPherson, eds., *Region, Race and Reconstruction* (New York: Oxford University Press, 1982), p. 165.

73. William Cohen, "Negro Involuntary Servitude in the South 1865–1940: A Preliminary Analysis," *Journal of Southern History*, vol. 42 (Feb. 1976), pp. 33–34.

74. Joanne L. Goodwin, " 'Employable Mothers' and 'Suitable Work': A Reevaluation of Welfare and Wage-Earning for Women in the Twentieth-Century United States," *Journal of Social History*, vol. 29 (1995), p. 256.

75. W. E. B. Du Bois, *Black Reconstruction in America: An Essay Toward a History of the Part Which Black Folk Played in the Attempt to Reconstruct Democracy in America, 1860–1880* (1935; New York: Atheneum, 1973), pp. 700–1.

76. "More Slavery at the South. By a Negro Nurse," *Independent*, vol. 72 (Jan. 25, 1912), pp. 196–200; quoted in David M. Katzman, *Seven Days a Week: Women and Domestic Service in Industrializing America* (Urbana: University of Illinois Press, 1978), pp. 24–25.

77. David R. Roediger, *The Wages of Whiteness: Race and the Making of the American Working Class* (London and New York: Verso, 1991), p. 19, citing David Halle, *America's Working Men: Work, Home and Politics among Blue-Collar Property Owners* (Chicago, 1984), pp. 202–30.

78. Sophonisba Breckenridge, "The Home Responsibilities of Women Workers and the 'Equal Wage,'" *Journal of Political Economy*, vol. 31 (1923), p. 543.

79. Katzman, p. 199.

80. Tera Hunter, *To 'Joy My Freedom: Southern Black Women's Lives and Labors After the Civil War* (Cambridge, MA: Harvard University Press, 1997), pp. 227–32. West Virginia's statute requiring that every able-bodied male resident between the ages of sixteen and sixty should regularly and steadily engage for at least thirty-six hours per week in some employment was overturned by its state court, but a similar Delaware statute was upheld. Rollin M. Perkins, "The Vagrancy Concept," *Hastings Law Journal*, vol. 9 (1958), p. 239.

81. Goodwin, p. 257. See also Edith Abbott and Sophonisba Breckinridge, *The Administration of the Aid to Mothers' Law in Illinois* (Washington, DC: Children's Bureau, U.S. Department of Labor, 1921), Pub. No. 82, pp. 109–10.

82. Mark Leff, "Consensus for Reform," *Social Service Review*, vol. 47 (1973), p. 414.

83. Jill Quadagno, *The Color of Welfare: How Racism Undermined the War on Poverty* (New York: Oxford University Press, 1994), p. 157.

84. Alice Kessler-Harris, "Designing Women and Old Fools: The Construction of the Social Security Amendments of 1939," in Linda K. Kerber, Alice Kessler-Harris, and Kathryn Kish Sklar, eds., *U.S. History as Women's History* (Chapel Hill: University of North Carolina Press, 1995), pp. 91–92.

85. Ibid., p. 94.

86. Quadagno, pp. 157–58.

87. Goodwin, p. 260.

88. Donald Howard, *The WPA and Federal Relief Policy* (New York: Russell Sage Foundation, 1943), p. 279, quoted in Nancy E. Rose, "Gender, Race and the Welfare State: Government Work Programs from the 1930s to the Present," *Feminist Studies*, vol. 19 (1993), p. 324.

89. Eileen Boris, "The Racialized Gendered State: Constructions of Citizenship in the United States," *Social Politics*, vol. 2 (1995), p. 170; the letter to FDR is quoted in Jacqueline Jones, *Labor of Love, Labor of Sorrow: Black Women, Work and the Family from Slavery to the Present* (New York: Basic Books, 1985), p. 219.

90. Goodwin, pp. 261–62. See also Grace Chang, "Undocumented Latinas: The New 'Employable' Mothers," in Evelyn Nakano Glenn et al., eds., *Mothering: Ideology, Experience and Agency* (New York: Routledge, 1994), pp. 259–85.

91. *Anderson v. Burson*, 300 F. Supp. 401, 404 (1968); New York *Times*, Oct. 8, 1967, p. 38. See also *New York State Department of Social Services v. Dolores Dublino et al.*, 93 S.Ct. 2507 (1973).

92. Frances Fox Piven and Richard Cloward, *Regulating the Poor: The Functions of Public Welfare* (New York: Pantheon, 1971), pp. 128, 136, 141.
93. Quadagno, p. 120. The best history of NWRO is Martha F. Davis, *Brutal Need: Lawyers and the Welfare Rights Movement 1960–1973* (New Haven: Yale University Press, 1993). Mary Jo Bane argues that the strategies of reformers were counterproductive; see "Politics and Policies of the Feminization of Poverty," in Margaret Weir et al., *The Politics of Social Policy in the United States* (Princeton, NJ: Princeton University Press, 1988), p. 389. In 1996 Bane resigned as Assistant Secretary of Labor to protest the Personal Responsibility and Work Opportunity Act.
94. Quadagno, pp. 124–27.
95. Bane, p. 389.
96. Goodwin, p. 264; see also Sylvia Law, "Women, Work, Welfare and the Preservation of Patriarchy," *University of Pennsylvania Law Review*, vol. 131 (May 1983), pp. 1249–1339.
97. See Jeffrey Adler, "Vagging the Demons and Scoundrels: Vagrancy and the Growth of St. Louis, 1830–1861," *Journal of Urban History*, vol. 13 (1986), p. 12.
98. *State v. Julia Custer*, 65 North Carolina 339–40 (1871). I am grateful to Laura Edwards for this reference.
99. Cohen, p. 52.
100. *Commonweal*, Dec. 11, 1936, p. 188. I am grateful to Robert Steinfeld for this reference.
101. *Workers Defense Bulletin*, Spring 1949. I am grateful to Robert Steinfeld for this reference.
102. Amsterdam, p. 226.
103. Quoted in opinion in *Papachristou et al. v. City of Jacksonville*, 405 U.S. 156, 163 (1971).
104. *Papachristou et al. v. City of Jacksonville*, at p. 171.

3. "WHEREVER YOU FIND TAXEY THERE VOTEY WILL BE ALSO"

1. Julia E. Smith, *Abby Smith and her Cows, With a Report of the Law Case Decided Contrary to Law* (Hartford, 1877), reprinted Arno Press, 1972, pp. 9–10. This volume is a compilation of letters sent to the sisters and articles from newspapers about their campaign. Hereafter cited as Smith. For another treatment of the Smith sisters' protest, see Carolyn Jones, "Dollars and Selves: Women's Tax Criticism and Resistance in the 1870s," *University of Illinois Law Review*, vol. 1994, pp. 265–309.
2. For biographical information in this chapter, I have relied on Kathleen L. Housley, *The Letter Kills But the Spirit Gives Life: The Smiths—Abolitionists, Suffragists, Bible Translators* (Glastonbury: Historical Society of Glastonbury, Connecticut, 1993). Marjorie Grant McNulty, *Glastonbury for Two Hundred Years* (Historical Society of Glastonbury, 1983) is also useful. For a memoir by someone who had met them when she was a child, see Lilliam E. Prudden, "A Paper Written and Read by Lilliam E. Prudden at the Fortnightly Club in New Haven," Connecticut State Library, Hartford.

3. For Brace's political career as a moderate Federalist, see Richard J. Purcell, *Connecticut in Transition: 1775–1818* (Washington, DC: American Historical Association, 1918), pp. 200–1.

4. Hannah Hickok Smith's account books, diary, and letters are in the collections of the Connecticut Historical Society, Hartford; Nancy Cott analyses the diary in *The Bonds of Womanhood: "Woman's Sphere" in New England, 1780–1835* (New Haven: Yale University Press, 1977), pp. 40–44. See also Housley, pp. 41, 43, 60–61.

5. Housley, pp. 55–59: Laurilla taught French there in 1823, two years after it opened. Julia joined her for ten months in 1823–24.

6. "Retrospect: The Smith Sisters," typescript, Historical Society of Glastonbury.

7. Smith, p. 24.

8. Boston *Post*, Jan. 21, 1874, in Smith, p. 24; Hannah Hickok Smith to Abby Kelley Foster, July 25, 1839, in Housley, p. 136.

9. Boston *Post*, Jan. 21 and 22, 1874, in Smith, pp. 22, 26, 30.

10. Smith, Introduction, p. 7: rearranged on the page.

11. Smith, Introduction, p. 7; Hartford *Daily Courant*, Oct. 29, 30, 1869. On the tensions between the New England suffragists and those organized by Stanton and Anthony, see Ellen Du Bois, *Feminism and Suffrage: The Emergence of an Independent Women's Movement in America, 1848–1869* (Ithaca: Cornell University Press, 1978) pp. 167–70; 186–87.

12. They did not throw themselves into politics until they had lived through "sickness and death in the family"; their eldest sister, Hancy Zephina, died in 1871.

13. Abby Smith's speech of Nov. 5, 1873, in Smith, p. 11; on their resentments about the use of the road taxes, see clipping from Boston *Daily Advertiser*, Jan 13, 1874, in Smith, p. 15.

14. On Rosella Buckingham, see Housley, p. 214; she died in 1875, aged forty-two.

15. *U.S. v. Anthony*, 24 F. Cas. 829, 832 (C.C.N.D. N.Y. 1873), *Minor v. Happersett*, 88 U.S. (21 Wall.) 162 (1875). On Anthony's effort to vote, see Elizabeth Cady Stanton, Susan B. Anthony, and Matilda Joslyn Gage, eds., *History of Woman Suffrage* (Rochester, NY: Susan B. Anthony, 1886), vol. 2, pp. 627–98; on Minor, see vol. 2, pp. 715–55.

16. Housley, p. 144; see also *History of Woman Suffrage*, vol. 2, pp. 831–33; attendance reported to be 1,200.

17. Smith, Introduction, p. 8.

18. Smith, pp. 9–10.

19. Smith, p. 11.

20. Smith, pp. 12, 24.

21. Smith, pp. 38–39, 25, 13.

22. Abby Smith to Springfield *Republican*, Jan. 3, 1874, in Smith, p. 13.

23. Abby Smith to Springfield *Republican*, Jan. 3, 1874, in Smith, p. 13; Boston *Daily Advertiser* quoted in Smith, p. 15.

24. Boston *Daily Advertiser*, Jan. 13, 1874. The Springfield *Republican* quickly understood that the Smith sisters were doing the work of the woman suffrage movement, and that in turn they deserved its help. The newspaper called upon sympathizers to contribute money and legal aid; this fund was the *Republican*'s idea. See Smith, pp. 14, 16, 27.

25. Smith, pp. 14, 25.
26. Smith, p. 14.
27. Smith, pp. 14–15; Housley, p. 151.
28. Theodore Brantner Wilson, *The Black Codes of the South* (Tuscaloosa: University of Alabama Press, 1965); Ira Berlin et al., *Slaves No More: Three Essays on Emancipation and the Civil War* (Cambridge: Cambridge University Press, 1992), and Eric Foner, *Reconstruction: America's Unfinished Revolution 1863–1877* (New York: Harper & Row, 1988), are the best introductions to this problem.
29. Quoted in Edmund S. Morgan, ed., *Prologue to Revolution: Sources and Documents on the Stamp Act Crisis 1764–1766* (Chapel Hill: University of North Carolina Press, 1959), p. 136.
30. Quoted in John Philip Reid, *Constitutional History of the American Revolution: The Authority to Tax* (Madison: University of Wisconsin Press, 1987), pp. 109, 88. See ch. 10 for extended analysis of this point.
31. "Thoughts on Government," quoted in Michael Kammen, *Deputyes & Libertyes: The Origins of Representative Government in Colonial America* (New York: Alfred A. Knopf, 1969), p. 200.
32. Robert A. Becker, *Revolution, Reform, and the Politics of American Taxation, 1763–1783* (Baton Rouge: Louisiana State University Press, 1980), p. 14.
33. Chilton Williamson: *American Suffrage: From Property to Democracy 1760–1860* (Princeton, NJ: Princeton University Press, 1960), pp. 79, 98.
34. South Carolina began in 1775 by permitting "all [male] persons who contributed to the general tax . . . to vote for the membership of the local committees to enforce the Non-Importation agreement." New Hampshire established a taxpaying qualification in its constitution of 1775; North Carolina established a taxpaying qualification for the lower house. The revolutionary era constitution of Pennsylvania enfranchised 90 percent of the adult male population by adding to the voting lists all those who held property and "all Military Associators who had paid a tax." Williamson, pp. 95–110.
35. Williamson, p. 103.
36. Williamson, pp. 80–81.
37. Richard J. Purcell, *Connecticut in Transition: 1775–1818* (Washington, DC: American Historical Association, 1918), pp. 220–23, 250.
38. Purcell, pp. 364, 372, 399; Jarvis Means Morse, *A Neglected Period of Connecticut's History 1818–1850* (New Haven: Yale University Press, 1933), p. 323. Williamson offers more examples; Boston extended municipal suffrage to all male taxpayers in 1820, p. 194. See also pp. 201–5, 240.
39. Remonstrance of South Carolina Democrats, quoted in Michael Les Benedict, "The Problem of Constitutionalism and Constitutional Liberty in the Reconstruction South," in Kermit L. Hall and James W. Ely, Jr., eds., *An Uncertain Tradition: Constitutionalism and the History of the South* (Athens: University of Georgia Press, 1989), p. 237. These Democrats of course *could* have exercised a voice, had they not chosen to boycott the elections. That they might well have been outvoted in a fair election is another matter.
40. Emphasis Sumner's; see text in *History of Woman Suffrage*, vol. 2, pp. 168–69.
41. Gerda Lerner, "The Lady and the Mill Girl: Changes in the Status of Women in the Age of Jackson," *Midcontinent American Studies Journal*, vol. 10 (1969),

pp. 5–15; Judith Wellman, "Women's Rights, Republicanism and Revolutionary Rhetoric in Antebellum New York State," *New York History*, vol. 69 (1988), pp. 353–84.

42. *Constitution of the State of New York, Adopted in 1846* (Albany: Weed, Parsons, 1867), pp. 30–31.

43. For Harrington, see her letter to the *Woman's Journal*, Jan. 17, 1874, describing her protest in 1857–59 in *History of Woman Suffrage*, vol. 2, pp. 373–74. Described also in Du Bois, pp. 49–50. For Stone, see Andrea Moore Kerr, *Lucy Stone: Speaking Out for Equality* (New Brunswick: Rutgers University Press, 1992), p. 103. The Boston physician Harriot Hunt refused to pay taxes on the grounds that young immigrant men who could barely read could vote while she was classed with aliens and minors, and while the state collaborated in denying higher and professional education to women. Her protest of 1852 was widely reprinted and widely circulated for years and can be found in Harriet H. Robinson, *Massachusetts in the Woman Suffrage Movement* (2nd ed.; Boston: Roberts Brothers, 1883), pp. 214–16.

44. See the petitions quoted in Wellman, pp. 379–80, and "1846 Petition for Woman's Suffrage, New York State Constitutional Convention," ed. Jacob Katz Cogan and Lori D. Ginsberg, *Signs*, vol. 22 (1997), pp. 427–39.

45. *History of Woman Suffrage*, vol. 2, pp. 168–69.

46. Leonard N. Beck, "The Library of Susan B. Anthony," *Quarterly Journal of the Library of Congress*, Jan. 1975, p. 333; Anthony reprinted *Subjection* in her newspaper *The Revolution*. John Stuart Mill, *Representative Government* (1861) in *On Liberty and Other Essays* (Oxford: Oxford University Press, 1991), pp. 328–29.

47. Douglass is quoted in Du Bois, pp. 56–57.

48. Mill, p. 329.

49. The fullest evaluation of the meaning of these protests is Jones. She urges us to notice that the 1870s tax protesters never mention Henry D. Thoreau. Thoreau's tax protest was rediscovered in the twentieth century by Tolstoy, Gandhi, and others. The contributors to the *Woman's Journal*, which was based in Boston, may well have known him.

50. "Excise taxes, on liquor and tobacco, produced nearly ninety per cent of the government's internal revenue from 1868 to 1913." Lawrence M. Friedman, *A History of American Law* (New York: Simon & Schuster, 1973), pp. 495–98. At the end of the century, in *Pollock v. Farmers' Loan and Trust Co.* (1895), a modest income tax was declared unconstitutional.

51. *Julia E. Smith v. George C. Andrews et al.*, Superior Court, March Term, 1875, No. 793, Connecticut State Library, Hartford.

52. Woodhull's memorial and testimony appear in *History of Woman Suffrage*, vol. 2, pp. 443–48; Congressman A. G. Riddle's comment in *History of Woman Suffrage*, vol. 2, p. 456.

53. See Barbara A. Babcock, "Clara Shortridge Foltz: 'First Woman,' " *Arizona Law Review*, vol. 30 (1988), pp. 673–717.

54. Denver, Jan. 1870: "Rev. Mrs. Wilkes": *History of Woman Suffrage*, vol. 3, p. 716.

55. *Senate Journal* (Des Moines, 1880), pp. 171, 256; see speech by Nancy R. Allen to the U.S. Senate Judiciary Committee, Jan. 23, 1880, in *History of Woman Suffrage*, vol. 2, p. 160: Allen emphasized that women could have different

politics than men: "I have a list showing that in my city three women pay more taxes than all the city officials together. They are good temperance women. Our city council is composed almost entirely of saloon-keepers, brewers and men who patronize them. . . . All these officials are paid, and we have to help support them."

56. Monica Cook Morris, "The History of Woman Suffrage in Missouri, 1867–1901," *Missouri Historical Review*, vol. 25 (1930–31), p. 69.

57. *Missouri Democrat*, Feb. 6, 1869; *Missouri Republican*, Jan. 3, 1869. See Paula Coalier, "Beyond Sympathy: The St. Louis Ladies' Union Aid Society and the Civil War," *Gateway Heritage*, Summer 1990, pp. 38–51. *Missouri Republican*, Jan. 3, Feb. 26, 1869. Francis Minor, born in 1820, was a graduate of Princeton and the University of Virginia School of Law; in 1870–72 he was clerk of the Missouri Supreme Court. *St. Louis Bar Journal*, Winter 1992, St. Louis Mercantile Library Association.

58. *Missouri Democrat*, Feb. 4 and 5, 1869.

59. Jan. 22, 1868. He included a copy of a petition to the state legislature: "The undersigned women of Missouri, believing that all citizens who are taxed for the support of the government and subject to its laws, should have a voice in the making of those laws." *History of Woman Suffrage*, vol. 3, pp. 599–600.

60. *Missouri Republican*, Feb. 6, 1869; *Missouri Democrat*, Feb. 14, 1869.

61. *History of Woman Suffrage*, vol. 3, p. 601.

62. *Missouri Democrat*, Oct. 7, 1869.

63. *Minor v. Happersett*, 88 U.S. 162 (1875); on refusal to support the Centennial, see *History of Woman Suffrage*, vol. 2, p. 842.

64. For voting requirements, see Mass. Statutes 1874, ch. 376, paragraphs 1–15, 56. The strategy of comparing the taxes paid by nonvoting women with the taxes paid by voting men, pioneered by women in St. Louis and enacted in Massachusetts, would become a popular strategy; see *History of Woman Suffrage*: Iowa, vol. 2, p. 160; New York, vol. 4, p. 313.

65. Lois Bannister Merk, *Massachusetts and the Woman Suffrage Movement* (unpublished Ph.D. dissertation, Harvard University, 1961), p. 18; *Woman's Journal*, Feb. 5, 1870.

66. William I. Bowditch, *Taxation of Women in Massachusetts* (rev. ed.; Cambridge, MA: John Wilson & Son, 1875), pp. 3–6.

67. Bowditch, pp. 12, 19–20.

68. Bowditch, pp. 29–32.

69. Bowditch, pp. 26–27. Bowditch warmed to his task: "In Dedham, the men of property save more than one-eighth; in Brookline, more than one-seventh. . . . The men of property in Westfield saved in one year $6,000; in Pittsfield, $7,000; in Northampton, $10,000."

70. Bowditch, pp. 22–26.

71. Bowditch, p. 29. For another eloquent oration linking the issues of taxation without representation in 1773 with those of 1873, see the accounts of Lucy Stone's speech in Faneuil Hall in *Woman's Journal*, Dec. 20, 1873, and Kerr, pp. 181–82.

72. C. C. Dills to Hartford *Daily Times*, Jan. 22, 1874, in Smith, pp. 19–21.

73. Springfield *Republican*, Jan. 6, 1874, in Smith, p. 14.

74. Jan. 1874, in Smith, p. 27.

75. Rosella Buckingham in Providence *Press*, Jan. 19, 1874, in Smith, pp. 18–19.
76. *Harper's Weekly*, Feb. 7, 1874, p. 123.
77. Springfield *Republican*, Jan. 15, 1874, in Smith, pp. 16–17.
78. Smith, p. 28.
79. Smith, p. 44.
80. Ellen Du Bois, "Outgrowing the Compact of the Fathers: Equal Rights, Woman Suffrage, and the United States Constitution, 1820–1878," *Journal of American History*, vol. 74 (1987), pp. 836–62. See also Joan Hoff, *Law, Gender and Injustice: A Legal History of U.S. Women* (New York: New York University Press, 1991), pp. 152–61, 170–74.
81. Thomas Wentworth Higginson, "Let Us Not Predict Too Much," *Woman's Journal*, vol. 7 (1876), p. 105. Quoted in Jones, p. 303.
82. Smith, p. 30.
83. Smith, p. 42; I have reordered the last two sentences and silently corrected "makes" to "make."
84. Smith, April 6, 1874; account is from the Springfield *Republican*, pp. 31–34.
85. Smith, pp. 41–42; petition included in McNulty, p. 77.
86. Springfield *Republican*, Sept. 5, 1874, in Smith, pp. 45–46. I have made a silent change of "powered," which I think is a typographical error, to "powdered."
87. A detailed account, apparently stenographic, of the Feb. 1875 trial in the Court of Common Pleas was published in *Woman's Journal*, Nov. 18, 1876, and reprinted in Smith, pp. 77 ff. Original papers for *Julia Smith et al. v. George C. Andrews* may be found in Records, Court of Common Pleas, February Term, 1875, No. 484, Connecticut State Library, Hartford. The petitions for an equity hearing in the Superior Court are found in *Julia E. Smith v. George C. Andrews et al.*, Superior Court, March Term, 1875, No. 793, Connecticut State Library, Hartford.
88. Hounsley, p. 177; Jones, p. 277.
89. *History of Woman Suffrage*, vol. 3, p. 98. This article says Julia was eighty-three in 1878.
90. See, for example, James Madison, *Federalist* #54.
91. Joseph Story, *Commentaries on the Constitution of the United States* (1833; Boston: Little, Brown, 1858), Book III, ch. 14.
92. When James G. Blaine complained that election fraud had deprived "the people of Maine" of the right to express their opinion at the polls, Lillie Devereaux Blake was furious. "What Mr. Blaine said . . . was nonsense"; no woman had voted. LDB to House Judiciary Committee, Jan. 24, 1880, *History of Woman Suffrage*, vol. 3, p. 164.
93. Bowditch, p. 60 (Opinion of the Judges, Feb. 15, 1811, 7 Mass. 523).
94. Quoted in Herbert Hovenkamp, *Enterprise and American Law, 1836–1937* (Cambridge, MA: Harvard University Press, 1991), p. 29.
95. Thomas M. Cooley, *A Treatise on the Law of Taxation, including the Law of Local Assessments* (Chicago: Callaghan and Company, 1876). A fourth edition, expanded to keep up with legal change, appeared fifty years later.
96. Cooley, pp. 1–2.
97. Cooley, pp. 3–4.
98. John F. Dillon, *Treatise on the Law of Municipal Corporations* (Chicago: James Cockcroft & Co., 1872), pp. 556–57.

99. Dorothy Ross, *The Origins of American Social Science* (Cambridge: Cambridge University Press, 1991), pp. 188–89, 91.

100. Edwin R. A. Seligman, *Essays in Taxation* (New York: Macmillan, 1895), pp. 4–5.

101. Seligman, pp. 36, 54.

102. Patricia G. Holland et al., eds., *The Papers of Elizabeth Cady Stanton and Susan B. Anthony* (Wilmington, DE: Scholarly Resources, 1991), Series 3, Elizabeth Cady Stanton, "Taxation" (Lecture, 1877), reel 19, frames 726–27.

103. Samuel E. Sewall, *Legal Condition of Women in Massachusetts in 1886* (Boston: Addison C. Getchell, 1886), pp. 11–12; *General Statutes of Massachusetts*, 1881, Title 2, ch. 6, paragraph 3; Title 2, ch. 11, paragraph 1.

104. Richard P. Hallowell, *Address . . . Before a Committee of the Massachusetts Legislature, February 6, 1878, in opposition to a Petition to Grant Suffrage in Municipal Affairs to Women Taxpayers* (n.p., 1900).

105. Hallowell, pp. 16, 7–8, 10–12.

106. Shailer Mathews, ed., *The Woman Citizen's Library: A Systematic Course of Reading in Preparation for the Larger Citizenship* (Chicago: The Civics Society, 1913), vol. 7, p. 1796–1802. "[F]ifteen tax-paying women of Davenport" petitioned for the vote in Iowa in 1880 (Iowa *Senate Journal*, 1880, p. 171), and several state senators proposed that the property of all women be exempt from taxation until "given representation by the ballot" (*Senate Journal*, 1880, p. 256). Iowa women received the right to vote on municipal and school tax and bond issues in 1894. See Ruth Gallaher, *Legal and Political Status of Women in Iowa* (Iowa City: State Historical Society of Iowa, 1918), pp. 202–3.

107. *Breedlove v. Suttles*, 302 U.S. 277, 282 (1937). See the important discussion of this case in Rogers M. Smith, " 'One United People': Second-Class Female Citizenship and the American Quest for Community," *Yale Journal of Law and the Humanities*, vol. 1 (1989), pp. 229–93, esp. pp. 280–81.

108. Ronnie L. Podolefsky, "The Illusion of Suffrage: Female Voting Rights and the Women's Poll Tax Repeal Movement After the Nineteenth Amendment," *Columbia Journal of Gender and Law*, vol. 7 (1998) pp. 185–24.

109. *Poe v. Seaborn*, 282 U.S. 101 (1930). See Grace Blumberg, "Sexism in the Code: A Comparative Study of Income Taxation of Working Wives and Mothers," *Buffalo Law Review*, vol. 21 (1971–72), pp. 49–98.

110. Carolyn C. Jones, "Split Income and Separate Spheres: Tax Law and Gender Roles in the 1940s," *Law and History Review*, vol. 6 (1988), pp. 273–74. Jones's essay is a rich resource on this point; see also pp. 270–72 and 301 nn. 66, 67.

111. Jones, "Split Income," pp. 290–91; *Newsweek*, Oct. 13, 1947, pp. 64–65, quoted in Jones, p. 270.

112. Jones, "Split Income," p. 295.

113. Blumberg, p. 52.

114. New York *Times*, March [n.d.], & June 4, 1942, clippings in Dorothy Kenyon Papers, Smith College Archives. Kenyon called a group together that represented a formidable array of women's organizations: Rose Schneiderman for the National Women's Trade Union League, Ruth Whaley of the National Negro Business and Professional Women's Clubs, the Woman's Bar Association of New York, the National Woman's Party, the Daughters of the American

Revolution (rarely linked with the WTUL), the National Federation of Business and Professional Women.

115. See, for example, the section on taxation of income in Kenneth M. Davison, Ruth Bader Ginsburg, and Herma Hill Kay, eds., *Texts, Cases and Materials on Sex-Based Discrimination* (St. Paul: West Publishing Co., 1974), pp. 528 ff.

116. Edward J. McCaffery, *Taxing Women* (Chicago: University of Chicago Press, 1997), pp. 144–46. That marriage brings an advantage to couples in which only one spouse earns taxable income is widely recognized by tax analysts; see, for example, Harvey S. Rosen, "The Marriage Tax Is Down But Not Out," *National Tax Journal*, vol. 40 (1987), pp. 571 ff.

117. McCaffery, pp. 104–5.

118. McCaffery, p. 234. For an example of the continued perception that it is radical for men to commit themselves to flexible work, see "It's His Half-Year to Wash the Dishes," New York *Times*, sect. 3, p. 1; Nov. 16, 1997.

119. These changes have largely been unstudied; they can be traced in Iowa by following the legislative journals for 1979, 1981, and 1986.

120. Patricia A. Cain, "Same-Sex Couples and the Federal Tax Laws," *Law and Sexuality*, vol. 1 (1991), pp. 98–99.

121. Roberta Achtenberg, ed., *Sexual Orientation and the Law* (Deerfield, IL, 1995), pp. 3-49, 3-50.

122. Cain, pp. 98–99, 131.

4. "WOMAN IS THE CENTER OF HOME AND FAMILY LIFE"

1. Brief for Appellant, *Hoyt v. State*, 119 So. 2nd 691 (Fla. 1959). Appeal from the Criminal Court of Record in and for Hillsborough County, Florida Supreme Court, Florida State Archives, Series 49, carton 29,966, p. 23. (Hereafter Appellant Brief, FSC.)

   Other information comes from Transcript of Record of Proceedings (650 pp.), *Hoyt v. State* Appeal from the Criminal Court of Record in and for Hillsborough County, Florida Supreme Court, Florida State Archives, Series 49, carton 29,966. (Hereafter CCHC Transcript)

2. Tampa *Tribune*, Sept. 21, 1957.

3. The event occurred on Sept. 23, 1947; reported in the Tampa *Daily Times*, Oct. 4, 1957.

4. Meadows Street has changed little since the days the Hoyts lived there.

5. Appellant Brief, FSC, p. 24.

6. In the criminal trial, the prosecution objected to this line of questioning.

7. Gwendolyn Hoyt's testimony in Criminal Court, Tampa *Daily Times*, Dec. 18, 1957.

8. Appellant Brief, FSC, pp. 3–4; see also claims made on p. 24.

9. Appellant Brief, FSC, p. 4.

10. Tampa *Daily Times*, Dec. 18, 1957, and from the trial transcript, quoted in Appellant Brief, FSC, pp. 26–27. Note also CCHC Transcript, p. 203: GH's handwritten statement, made 3:55 a.m., Sept. 20, 1957: "I raised the bat to strike his shoulders but instead hit him two, three blows in the head. Then I immediately called an ambulance and my doctor."

11. "Horrible" from account in Tampa *Daily Times*, Sept. 22, 1957.

12. Tampa *Morning Tribune*, Sept. 21, 1957.
13. Before he died, she was simply charged with assault to murder and released under $100 bond.
14. Tampa *Morning Tribune*, Nov. 15, 1957.
15. Harry Kalven and Hans Zeisel, *The American Jury* (Boston: Little, Brown, 1966), p. xv.
16. Justice Devlin, quoted in Kalven and Zeisel, pp. 6–7.
17. Sir John Hawles's *The Englishman's Right* (1693). See Shannon Stimson, *The American Revolution in the Law: Anglo-American Jurisprudence before John Marshall* (Princeton, NJ: Princeton University Press, 1990), p. 169 n. 46. The very first statute in New England—recorded by Plymouth Colony, December 1623—provided that "all Criminall facts, and also all [matters] of trespasses and debts betweene man & man should [be tried] by the verdict of twelve Honest men to be Impanelled by Authority in forme of a Jury upon their oaths." John M. Murrin, "Magistrates, Sinners, and a Precarious Liberty: Trial by Jury in Seventeenth-Century New England," in John M. Murrin et al., eds., *Saints and Revolutionaries: Essays on Early American History* (New York: W. W. Norton, 1984), p. 157; Murrin stresses the ambiguity of colonial understanding of jury service.
18. For the expansive power of juries during the prerevolutionary era, when judges rarely gave instructions on the law to juries, see William E. Nelson, *Americanization of the Common Law: The Impact of Legal Change on Massachusetts Society, 1760–1830* (Cambridge, MA: Harvard University Press, 1975), esp. pp. 3–5, 20–35, and Stimson, pp. 55 ff.
19. Kathryn Preyer, "*United States v. Callender*: Judge and Jury in a Republican Society," in Maeva Marcus, ed. *Origins of the Federal Judiciary: Essays on the Judiciary Act of 1789* (New York: Oxford University Press, 1992), p. 3; and J. P. Reid, *Constitutional History of the American Revolution*, vol. 1: *The Authority of Rights* (Madison: University of Wisconsin Press, 1986). Milton M. Klein argues that the English threat to the integrity of the jury process exacerbated tensions in New York and prepared the way for the Stamp Act crisis; see "Prelude to Revolution in New York: Jury Trials and Judicial Tenure," *William and Mary Quarterly*, 3rd ser., vol. 17 (1960), pp. 439–62.
20. Albert W. Alschuler and Andrew G. Deiss, "A Brief History of the Criminal Jury in the United States," *University of Chicago Law Review*, vol. 61 (1994), pp. 870–71.
21. Quoted in Stimson, p. 88. The American Revolution, historian Shannon Stimson writes, "was not only about widening participation in the making of law—sovereignty—but also about widening the space for reflective judgment about laws once made" (p. 59).
22. Perhaps more than any other signer of the Constitution, Wilson linked the educational function of the jury with the claim of the people to judge for themselves; see Robert Green McCloskey, ed., *The Works of James Wilson* (Cambridge, MA: Harvard University Press, 1967), vol. II, p. 84, and Stimson, p. 132.
23. L. Kinvin Wroth and Hiller B. Zobel, eds., *The Legal Papers of John Adams* (Cambridge, MA: Harvard University Press, 1965), vol. 1, p. 230.
24. See *People v. Croswell*, 3 Johnson, *Cases* (1st ed. 1812) 337 (1804). See also Julius

Goebel, *The Law Practice of Alexander Hamilton* (New York: Columbia University Press, 1964), vol. 1, pp. 810–11, and *Federalist* #83.

25. Morton J. Horwitz, *The Transformation of American Law 1780–1860* (Cambridge, MA: Harvard University Press, 1977), ch. 1 and pp. 141–43; Nelson, ch. 9; Alschuler and Deiss, pp. 903–21. On recent jury nullification, see Jeffrey Rosen, "Annals of Justice: One Angry Woman," *New Yorker*, Feb. 24, 1997, pp. 54–64.

26. See Bernard Schnapper, "Le Jury français aux XIX et XXème siècles," in Antonio Padoa Schioppa, ed., *The Trial Jury in England, France, Germany 1700–1900* (Berlin: Duncker & Humbolt, 1987), pp. 165–240.

27. Albert W. Alschuler, "Implementing the Criminal Defendant's Right to Trial: Alternatives to the Plea Bargaining System," *University of Chicago Law Review*, vol. 50 (1983), pp. 931–1011, esp. pp. 970–95, and John H. Langbein, *Comparative Criminal Procedure: Germany* (St. Paul: West Publishing Co., 1977).

28. The most thorough account of the history of the English jury of matrons, which was occasionally used as late as the 1870s, is James C. Oldham, "On Pleading the Belly: A History of the Jury of Matrons," *Criminal Justice History*, vol. 6 (1985), pp. 1–64. At the height of their use, in the late seventeenth and early eighteenth centuries, "62 percent of all women sentenced to death pleaded pregnancy, and of these 61 percent were successful before juries of matrons. For one five-year period, 1714–1719, during which . . . [Daniel] Defoe was writing *Moll Flanders*, ninety-two of the 112 females sentenced to death—an astonishing 82 percent—pleaded their bellies" (p. 23).

29. St. George Tucker, ed., *Blackstone's Commentaries* (Philadelphia: William Young Birch and Abraham Small, 1803), vol. 1, p. 362.

30. JSM to Mrs. H____, of York, Nov. 25, 1800, letterbook 10, p. 228, and JSM to [Esther Ellery], April 22, 1797, letterbook 10, p. 101, reel 3, Judith Sargent Murray Papers, University of Mississippi. I am grateful to Professor Sheila Skemp of the University of Mississippi for these references. Most of Murray's published work is collected in *The Gleaner* (1798).

31. Alexis de Tocqueville, *Democracy in America* (New York: Alfred A. Knopf, 1945), p. 287.

32. In early English practice, nobility were entitled to a jury made up of noblemen; thus the term "jury of one's peers." On the history of the exclusion from jury trial of a wide range of criminal offenses despite statements of general and absolute entitlement to trial by jury, see Felix Frankfurter and Thomas G. Corcoran, "Petty Criminal Offenses and the Constitutional Guaranty of Trial by Jury," *Harvard Law Review*, vol. 39 (June 1926), pp. 917–1019, esp. pp. 922–28 and 950–69.

33. "The grand jury inquires into complaints and accusations brought before it and, based on evidence presented by the state, issues bills of indictment. It is called a 'grand' jury because it involves a greater number of jurors (in common law no less than twelve and no more than twenty-three) than an ordinary trial or 'petit' jury." Kermit Hall, *The Magic Mirror: Law in American History* (New York: Oxford University Press, 1989), p. 172.

34. *Strauder v. West Virginia*, 100 U.S. 303, 305, 306, 308, 310 (1880).

35. Notably in *Hernandez v. Texas*, 347 U.S. 475 (1954), on the exclusion of Hispanics; for daily wage earners, see *Thiel v. Southern Pacific*, 328 U.S. 217 (1946).

36. *Smith v. Texas*, 311 U.S. 128 (1940).
37. Des Moines *Daily News*, Jan. 14, 1901. The case can be traced in the *Daily News* from the initial report on Dec. 3, 1900, and continuing through the trial, in Indianola, in April 1901. A long feature story, "Her Dreary Easter Day," probably by Glaspell, appeared on April 9, 1901. Reference to the "sympathetic wife of Sheriff Hudson," who sat with Margaret Hossack throughout the trial, appears on April 3, 1901. At end of the trial it was alleged that they had not married for love, but had been married a year after the birth of their first child; some hint that the child was actually the out-of-wedlock child of her sister. The marriage was "stormy"; there were hints of domestic violence. The guilty verdict was appealed to the state Supreme Court on the grounds that the judge's instructions had been faulty; the Supreme Court reversed the decision and sent the case back to the Warren District Court for retrial. 116 *Iowa Supreme Court Reports*, 195. In 1903 Hossack was released on a $15,000 bond. When she was retried in a different county, the jury was unable to reach a verdict, and the case was ultimately dismissed. Margaret Hossack died thirteen years later. I am very grateful to Sharon Wood for assistance with this research. The best account is Patricia L. Bryan, "Stories in Fiction and in Fact: Susan Glaspell's *A Jury of Her Peers* and the 1901 Murder Trial of Margaret Hossack," *Stanford Law Review* vol. 49 (1997), pp. 1293–1364.
38. Susan Glaspell, "A Jury of Her Peers," in Edward J. O'Brien, ed., *The Best Short Stories of 1917* (Boston: Small, Maynard & Company, 1917), pp. 256–82.
39. Women briefly served on juries in Wyoming Territory in 1870 and 1871. When the territorial legislature passed a woman suffrage bill, women's names were placed on jury lists, although there was no specific statute authorizing their inclusion. Many expected that women would excuse themselves if called, but the women who were summoned appeared promptly in court. The spectacle of the first women to serve on a common-law jury anywhere was widely covered in the press; the king of Prussia sent President Grant a congratulatory telegram. Grace Raymond Hebard, "The First Woman Jury," *Journal of American History*, vol. 7 (1920–21), pp. 1293–1341.
40. The Washington Territorial Supreme Court had sustained women's jury service in 1884 (*Rosencrantz v. Territory*, 2 Wash. T. 267, 5 P. 305 [1884]), but when, a few years later, it overturned women's suffrage, it also overturned jury service. *Harland v. Territory*, 3 Wash. T. 131, 13 P. 453 (1887). A new statute was required.
41. R. Justin Miller, "The Woman Juror," *Oregon Law Review*, vol. 2 (1922), pp. 38–39, citing O.L. 1520 as amended, Gen. Laws 121, ch. 273, p. 515.
42. *People v. Barltz*, 180 N.W. 423, 425 (Mich. 1920). See also *State v. Walker*, Supreme Court of Iowa, Dec. 13, 1921, 135 N.W. 619 (Iowa, 1921), a lengthy decision which went into considerable detail to establish the right of women electors to serve on juries.
43. In *People v. Lensen*, 34 Cal. App. 336 (1917), a man convicted of illegal sale of liquor protested successfully that the grand jury which indicted him had included women. The following year, in a case plainly designed to test the law, the court declared women's jury service constitutional; *In re Eban Mana*, 178 Cal. 213 (1918).
44. Their Legal Research Department, writes its chronicler, "drafted over 600

pieces of legislation aimed at equal rights for women. More than 300 of these bills were passed by state legislatures." Thomas C. Pardo, ed., *The National Woman's Party Papers 1913–1974: A Guide to the Microfilm Edition* (Sanford, NC: Microfilming Corporation of America, 1979), p. 2. In 1927 the NWP took credit for successful lobbying for a bill granting the right of women to serve as jurors in the Washington, DC, courts (p. 30).

45. In 1922 Alice Paul assured southern members that the National Council of the NWP would not actively recruit black members. Pardo, p. 13. The League of Women Voters took the position that there could only be one chapter in a region, and refused to charter two chapters, one black and one white, in the same city. Southern chapters generally recruited only white members but some arranged for black members to serve on separate committees.

46. The agenda was devised after Congress had sent the Nineteenth Amendment to the states but before it was ratified. See League of Women Voters, *A Woman's Platform Presented to the Political Parties* (Washington, DC [1920]). See also Louise H. Young, *In the Public Interest: The League of Women Voters 1920–1970* (Westport, CT: Greenwood Press, 1989), p. 46. No woman could run for legislative office in Iowa until 1928, after the revision of the state constitution.

47. "Women's Liability for Jury Service . . . For Use with 'Women Jurors,' " *Papers of the League of Women Voters*, Part III, Series A, reel 18, pp. 491 ff.

48. To the first six (Utah, 1898; Washington, 1911; Kansas, 1913; California, 1917; New Jersey, 1917; Michigan, 1918) Indiana, Iowa, Kentucky, and Nevada were added in 1920; Arkansas, Maine, Minnesota, North Dakota, Oregon, Pennsylvania, and Wisconsin in 1921; Ohio and Alaska Territory in 1923.

49. See Nancy Cott, *The Grounding of American Feminism* (New Haven: Yale University Press, 1987), pp. 100–14.

50. Report of the Committee on the Legislative Status of Women, 1929, *Papers of the League of Women Voters*, microfilm edition, Part III, Series A, reel 18, p. 641. See also p. 610.

51. *Hall v. State*, 187 So. 392, 400–1 (Fla. 1939).

52. Lewis of Port St. Joe. He was reassured—and we are given evidence of how Jim Crow courtrooms were maintained—by a colleague who told him that "court rulings were satisfied if negroes' names were placed in the venire and then not called."

53. Account from St. Petersburg *Times*, April 22[?], 1943; Rudyard Kipling, "The Female of the Species" (1911), *Rudyard Kipling's Verse* (New York: Doubleday, Doran, 1940), pp. 364–66. Baker succeeded when she sponsored a married women's rights law, which gave married women the right to contract, to sue and be sued, and to manage their separate property. Such bills had been passed in many states in the nineteenth century; Florida was late. I am grateful to Gary R. Mormino for this reference.

54. It permitted women to serve on juries except in cases of eminent domain proceedings; the state constitution specified that condemnation trial juries in cases of eminent domain be made up of men. St. Petersburg *Times*, April 9, 15, 1949.

55. *Florida Statutes*, Section 40.01 (1949).

56. A statute regulating the placing of racetrack bets by phone passed amid serious charges that supporters had accepted bribes. No sooner had the House disposed of "the bookie bill," reported the St. Petersburg *Times*, "than it plunged into

a hilarious discussion of the measure to permit women to serve on juries." April 27, 1949, p. 3. See also May 10, 1949, p. 1. Governor Fuller Warren allowed the jury service bill to become law without his signature.

57. Editorial, May 28, 1949.

58. St. Petersburg *Times*, May 25, 1949, p. 3; Tampa *Morning Tribune*, May 25, 1949, p. 1; the *Tribune* immediately ran an editorial, "No Witchhunt Needed" (p. 14).

59. New York *Times*, Feb. 24, 1926, p. 2; comment in a hearing before New York House Judiciary Committee, proposing that women sit on juries. On Feb. 25 an editorial predicted that women would lose their enthusiasm once they actually were eligible to serve. The bill never emerged from committee.

60. Roosevelt quoted in "Clubwomen Plan Jury Duty Schools," New York *Times*, Aug. 13, 1937. Jennie Loitman Barron observed, "Since our country has survived the test of men and women travelling together in sleeping cars, in the care of a male porter, we ought to have nothing to fear from the very rare necessity of men and women jurors spending a night in hotels, in separate quarters . . ." Barron, *Jury Service for Women* (Washington, DC: League of Women Voters, 1924), p. 11.

61. *Laws of the State of New York* (Albany, 1937), ch. 513, pp. 1171–72.

62. New York *Times*, Aug. 28, 1937.

63. *Malloy v. Carroll*, 287 *Mass.* 376 (1934).

64. Diane Joyce Siegel, "Justitia Mounts the Jury Bench: The Campaign for Women's Jury Service in Massachusetts" (unpublished B.A. Honors thesis, Harvard College, 1981), pp. 32–35, 52–56 ff., Schlesinger Library, Radcliffe College.

65. "An Act Regulating Jury Lists . . . ," *Mass. Acts and Resolves* 306, ch. 347, §2 (1949). In addition to a number of crimes against the person (rape, assault, and abuse of child) the Massachusetts code provided at least twenty-six varieties of "crimes against chastity, morality, decency and good order."

66. Gladys Harrison, "Re-Fighting an Old Battle," New York *Herald Tribune Magazine*, Feb. 9, 1930, in League of Women Voters Papers, Part III, Series A, reel 18, pp. 494–98.66.

67. Julia Margaret Hicks, comp., *Women Jurors* (Washington, DC: Committee on the Legal Status of Women, National League of Women Voters, 1928), an extensive compilation of state statutes, remains the best single guide to the status of women jurors at the time.

68. Guy Miller to Illinois Committee for Women on Juries, Aug. 7, 1926, Box 601, League of Women Voters Papers, Manuscript Division, Library of Congress.

69. H. C. Cage, judge of the Civil District Court for the Parish of Orleans in New Orleans, Louisiana, to Esther A. Dunshee, Aug. 11, 1926, Box 601, League of Women Voters Papers, Manuscript Division, Library of Congress.

70. *Ohio's Experience with Women on Juries* (Washington, DC: League of Women Voters, 1929), pp. 2–5. Ohio had required jury service of women on the same terms as men by a revised statute in 1923.

71. Barron, *Jury Service for Women*, pp. 5–6.

72. League of Women Voters, *Ohio's Experience with Women on Juries*. See also the comments of John A. Roeser, St. Cloud, MN, District Court, Seventh Judicial District, Stearns County, to Esther Dunshee, Chicago, Aug. 9, 1926, Box 601, League of Women Voters Papers, Manuscript Division, Library of Congress.

73. Michael Grossberg, *Governing the Hearth: Law and the Family in Nineteenth Century America* (Chapel Hill: University of North Carolina Press, 1985), esp. chs. 1, 8.

74. Elizabeth Blackmar, *Manhattan for Rent: 1785–1850* (Ithaca, NY: Cornell University Press, 1989), p. 117.

75. I have discussed this concept extensively elsewhere; see chs. 1–5 in *Toward an Intellectual History of Women* (Chapel Hill: University of North Carolina Press, 1997).

76. George Wickersham to Belle Sherwin, President, National League of Women Voters, Feb. 18, 1930, *Papers of the League of Women Voters*, microfilm edition, Part III, Series A, reel 18, p. 374.

77. Barron, *Jury Service for Women*, pp. 4–5, 8.

78. Los Angeles *Times*, March 22, 1944.

79. *U.S. v. Chaplin*, 54 F. Supp. 682 (S.D. Cal., Feb. 26, 1944).

80. *U.S. v. Ballard*, 35 F. Supp. 105–7 (S.D. Cal. 1940); for the characterization of the movement, see *Ballard v. U.S.*, 138 F. 2nd 540, 542–43 (9th Cir. 1943).

81. *U.S. v. Ballard*, 35 F. Supp. 105 (S.D. Cal. 1940).

82. The trials can be followed in *Ballard v. U.S.*, 138 F. 2nd 540 (9th Cir. 1943); *U.S. v. Ballard*, 322 U.S. 78 (1944); *Ballard v. U.S.*, 152 F. 2nd 941 (9th Cir. 1946), *Ballard v. U.S.*, 329 U.S. 187 (1946).

83. *Thiel v. Southern Pacific*, 328 U.S. 217 (1946). The jury commissioner and the clerk of the court had removed from jury lists all those who worked for a daily wage, on the grounds that judges regularly excused people who said they could not afford to serve.

84. *Ballard v. U.S.*, 329 U.S. 187, 193–94 (1946).

85. Rhonda Copelon, who would help write an amicus brief for *Healy v. Edwards*, 363 F. Supp. 1110 (E.D. La. Aug. 31, 1973), graduated from Yale Law School in 1970. "Fungible" is a term usually used to describe the interchangeability of forms of money; it was, she thought, an unfortunate metaphor. Interview with Rhonda Copelon, March 1991.

86. CCHC Transcript, p. 214.

87. CCHC Transcript, pp. 188–89.

88. CCHC Transcript, pp. 215, 219, 224–25, 235.

89. CCHC Transcript, p. 216; see also pp. 224–25.

90. CCHC Transcript, p. 196.

91. CCHC Transcript, pp. 196–97.

92. CCHC Transcript, p. 199.

93. CCHC Transcript, pp. 199–200; Hoyt's statement appears in full on p. 203.

94. Tampa *Daily Times*, Sept. 21, 1957.

95. Tampa *Morning Tribune*, Sept. 21, 1957.

96. The story ends: "She moved around her neat kitchen, automatically going through the motions of making coffee for her guests. Then she leaned against the refrigerator and sobbed.

   "A friend supported her to the living room.

   " 'If you become angry,' she said, 'think a long, long time before you let it come to the surface.'

   "Turning her eyes to a rainstorm outside, she whispered:

   " 'What have I done to us?' "

97. Tampa *Morning Tribune*, Sept. 21, 1957.
98. Interview with Pat Hardee, New Smyrna Beach, Florida, March 1990.
99. Interview with Pat Hardee, March, 1990.
100. Tallahassee *Democrat*, July 25, Aug. 16, 28, 1946. Thanks to the tuition benefits paid by the GI Bill, enrollment soared from the depressed level of the war years—only 700 in 1944—to more than 6,000 in 1946–47; there was no room for more than 2,000 eligible male applicants.
101. Tallahassee *Democrat*, April 28, 1946. Married male veterans without children demanded housing at the University of Florida; within the year they had returned to the legislature to announce that one-third of their wives were pregnant and now they needed housing that could accommodate children. Tallahassee *Democrat*, April 30, 1946. What the students were asking for was expensive, and gave housing a higher priority than libraries, classroom buildings, and teachers' salaries, which were among the lowest in the nation. In contrast, the governor's cabinet had provisionally approved only $45,000 for erecting housing units for married veterans at Florida A&M College for Negroes, $15,000 for moving eleven old barracks to the Negro college campus for single war veterans.
102. Even though the U.S. Supreme Court had ruled in 1950 that the exclusion of a black student from the University of Texas Law School was a denial of equal protection of the laws (*Sweatt v. Painter*, 339 U.S. 629 [1950]), Virgil D. Hawkins, who was forty-three, had to fight the battle anew in Florida. See St. Petersburg *Times*, May 14, 26, 1949. Many others, writes Jack Greenberg, "gave up in despair." *Crusaders in the Courts: How a Dedicated Band of Lawyers Fought for the Civil Rights Revolution* (New York: Basic Books, 1994), ch. 7 and pp. 93–99.
103. Interview with Pat Hardee, March 1990.
104. Pat Hardee is mentioned in scattered issues of the *Tampa Voter*, the League of Women Voters Newsletter, League of Women Voters Papers, Library of Congress. "I would be accurate in stating," the chairman of the Florida Civil Liberties Union observed, "that there exist in Tampa the Bnai Brith, a League of Women Voters, the American Jewish Committee, an association of Jewish congregations (but I am not sure of the name) and that is all that I can think of that would be involved in any kind of activity that could be construed as liberal." Howard Dixon to Alan Reitman, Feb. 24, 1961, Box 462, folder 4, ACLU Archives, Seeley G. Mudd Manuscript Library, Department of Rare Books and Special Collections, Princeton University Library. Published with permission of the Princeton University Library.
105. Interview with Dallas Albritton, Tampa, Feb. 12, 1991.
106. Interview with Pat Hardee, March 1990.
107. Carl Durrance thinks that watching his own wife's experiences as she developed a law practice sensitized him to the awkward relationship between women and the legal system. Interview, Clearwater, Florida, Feb. 1991.
108. The precise number is 45,698. CCHC Transcript, p. 9. At the trial, jury commissioner James Lockhart testified that "from 1952 on, I don't believe there has been more than thirty-five names been put on the list." CCHC Transcript, pp. 27–28. The Record Book in the archives of the Hillsborough County courthouse marked "Female Jurors" has columns for marital status, name, precinct,

age, address, occupation, whether the person was a registered voter, number of years in Florida, and number of children. It does not indicate the date on which the prospective juror actually signed until 1952. Fourteen women aged sixty-five or over signed up between 1952 and 1957; Lockhart excluded them although the law had set only a minimum, not a maximum age. It is not clear why Lockhart moved to exclude all women, of whatever age, who signed up prior to 1952.

109. *Florida Statutes*, Section 40.01 (3), 1949. Many other states had similarly subjective standards.

110. CCHC Transcript, p. 22.

111. Tampa *Tribune*, Feb. 6, 1958.

112. CCHC Transcript, pp. 27–29.

113. Durrance interview, Feb. 1991.

114. CCHC Transcript, pp. 34, 39, 42.

115. Appellant Brief, *Hoyt v. State*, Florida Supreme Court, p. 6. See also CCHC Transcript, p. 45.

116. [Timothy B. Dyk] "Bench Memo," *Hoyt v. Florida*, Earl Warren Papers, #219, Manuscript Division, Library of Congress.

117. CCHC Transcript, p. 46. Reprinted in Appeal to FSC, p. 6.

118. Grayson had been born in Virginia in 1895; he came to Tampa in 1925 and practiced law there until 1944, when he was appointed judge of the Hillsborough County Criminal Court, a position to which he was elected in 1948 and repeatedly thereafter. Tampa *Daily Times*, May 29, 1944. For biographical information, see Karl H. Grismer, *Tampa: A History of the City of Tampa and the Tampa Bay Region of Florida* (St. Petersburg: St. Petersburg Printing Company, 1950), pp. 409–10.

119. Interview with Durrance. Durrance argued many cases before Grayson, and, shortly before Grayson's death in 1961, joined him on the Circuit Court bench. The appointment was made only after Grayson had for many years resisted accepting a colleague on the bench despite the heavy workload because he didn't want the liberal governor LeRoy Collins to have a chance to appoint another judge. Editorial, Tampa *Tribune*, June 7, 1961.

120. Tampa *Tribune*, Jan. 15, 1944; May 29, 1961. For other caustic remarks, see Mar. 26, June 20, 1957; July 2, Aug. 8, 1958.

121. Tampa *Tribune*, May 29, 1961. While Gwendolyn Hoyt was awaiting trial, Grayson spoke to the local Junior Chamber of Commerce, blaming "the entire segregation problem today" on Franklin Roosevelt, who had drawn large numbers of blacks into the Democratic Party. "Today," said Grayson, "these same Negroes and their offspring are being coddled and coaxed to come back into the Republican Party." Tampa *Tribune*, Oct. 9, 1957.

122. Steven F. Lawson, "From Sit-In to Race Riot: Businessmen, Blacks, and the Pursuit of Moderation in Tampa, 1960–1967," in Elizabeth Jacoway and David R. Colburn, eds., *Southern Businessmen and Desegregation* (Baton Rouge: Louisiana State University Press, 1982), p. 267 n. 20.

123. Tampa *Tribune*, Sept. 4, 1958; May 30, 1961; St. Petersburg *Times*, May 30, 1961; Tampa *Times*, May 29, 1961.

124. St. Petersburg *Times*, Dec. 17, 1957. Maurice Chavigny was reputed to have fought in the French Foreign Legion and to have been wounded in World War

II. He appeared for trial in a "bemedaled uniform" which he said he wore while fighting for the United Nations forces in Korea, but was required to change into civilian clothing. Chavigny was convicted and sentenced to a long prison term.

125. St. Petersburg *Times*, Jan. 17, 1956.

126. The population of Pinellas County grew from 159,000 to 375,000 between 1950 and 1960—98 percent of the increase due to in-migration. The presence of substantial numbers of northern Republicans had begun to destabilize the Democratic Party's monopoly of political power in the area. See Gilkerson's obituary and the editorial in the St. Petersburg *Times*, June 16, 1963. I am grateful to Ellen Babb of the University of South Florida for this point.

127. St. Petersburg *Times*, Jan. 17, 1956. Within a week Gilkerson and his allies had organized a mass meeting at the county courthouse for prospective women jurors and had registered nearly 500 women. When women said they wished that bus service between Clearwater and St. Petersburg were better scheduled, so that they could arrive at the Pinellas County courthouse at 8:30 a.m. and leave at 5 p.m., Gilkerson made a public demand for more adequate bus service. St. Petersburg *Times*, Jan. 28, 1956.

128. St. Petersburg *Times*, Feb. 17, 1956.

129. St. Petersburg *Times*, Dec. 17, 1957.

130. W. W. Ward, "I Loved Him So," *Front Page Detective*, Jan. 1958, pp. 46–47, 69–71.

131. CCHC Transcript, p. 98; see also his summation, p. 559. The idea that women jurors judge women defendants differently than do men retains its vigor, sometimes as social science, sometimes as "common sense." Nancy S. Marder, "Gender Dynamics and Jury Deliberations," *Yale Law Journal*, vol. 96 (1987) p. 594, reports that one study found that "male jurors judged attractive female defendants guilty less often, assigned them lighter punishments, and rated them better-liked than their unattractive counterparts." For "common sense" views which still resonate, see the delicious versions quoted in Albert W. Alschuler, "The Supreme Court and the Jury: Voir Dire, Peremptory Challenges and the Review of Jury Verdicts," *University of Chicago Law Review*, vol. 56 (1989), pp. 209–11.

132. "Challenge to the Jury Panel," Nov. 8, 1957, CCHC Transcript, pp. 6–10. They wanted them because they believed that women had been "unlawfully, arbitrarily, systematically and intentionally" excluded from the jury list; that Gwendolyn Hoyt would be denied her constitutional rights to an impartial jury and to equal treatment under the Fifth, Sixth, and Fourteenth amendments and Sections 11 and 12 of the Florida Constitution Declaration of Rights.

133. Telephone interview with Jeannette Durrance, April 1991.

134. Tampa *Times*, Dec. 18, 20, 1957.

135. Telephone interview with Paul Johnson, Jan. 28, 1991.

136. CCHC Transcript, pp. 103–105 ff., 276–303, 367 ff.

137. *Hoyt v. State*, 119 So. 2nd at 697–98. For the burden on women defendants when they fail "to appear conventionally female" or to break down and cry, and the observation that prosecutors "score points with juries by suggesting that women have had sexual relations with men who were not their husbands," see Carolyn Heilbrun and Judith Resnik, "Convergences: Law, Literature, and

Feminism," *Yale Law Journal*, vol. 99 (1990), pp. 1913–56, esp. pp. 1915, 1947, and 1951. That Hoyt had cleaned up the blood and vomit so as not to shock her son was also regarded skeptically.

138. On the day she was judged guilty, Gwendolyn Hoyt was released on $2,500 bond and taken to the psychiatric ward at Tampa General Hospital "on the verge of shock." Tampa *Tribune*, Dec. 20, 1957. On the day of her sentencing she was judged insolvent.

139. Interview with Pat Hardee.

140. *Hoyt v. State*, 119 So. 2nd at 694.

141. *Hoyt v. State*, 697–99.

142. *Hoyt v. State*, 700–2.

143. *Hoyt v. State*, 691, 697. Hoyt's epilepsy was organic; there was no medical justification for Hobson's ascription to her of psychosis.

144. Interview with Raya Dreben, Boston, September 1990.

145. Biographical information on Ehrmann may be found in his manuscript autobiography, "The Education of a Liberal," (1964), Herbert B. Ehrmann Papers, Box 22, Folder 7, Harvard Law School Library. See also HBE to Llewellyn Howland, May [n.d.] 1964, in Herbert B. Ehrmann Papers, Harvard Law School. For Herbert Ehrmann's resistance to aggressive anticommunism within the American Jewish Committee, see Stuart Svonkin, *Jews Against Prejudice: American Jews and the Fight for Civil Liberties* (New York: Columbia University Press, 1997), pp. 161–64.

146. Manuscript, ch. 2. Ehrmann was hired, at first without pay, by Reginald Heber Smith, who would soon write the distinguished Carnegie Corporation study *Justice and the Poor* (1919), which insisted that court costs and legal fees weighed so heavily that "the administration of justice is not impartial." Cited in John T. Noonan, Jr., *Persons and Masks of the Law: Cardozo, Holmes, Jefferson and Wythe as Makers of the Masks* (New York: Farrar, Straus and Giroux, 1976), p. 145.

147. A position for which he had been recommended by Felix Frankfurter, who had joined the Harvard Law School faculty just as Ehrmann was graduating. For Ehrmann's recollections of their encounter and subsequent friendship, see his chapter in Wallace Mendelson, ed., *Felix Frankfurter: A Tribute* (New York: Reynal/Morrow, 1964), and Ehrmann's manuscript autobiography, Box 22, Folder 7, in Herbert Ehrmann Papers, Harvard Law School. Ehrmann's interpretation of the Sacco-Vanzetti case appears in his book *The Untried Case: The Sacco-Vanzetti Case and the Morelli Gang* (New York: Vanguard Press, 1933), reissued in 1960 in response to a new claim that Sacco and Vanzetti were guilty published by Robert Montgomery.

148. The necklace is now in the collections of the Harvard Law School Library.

149. "[T]he American League to Abolish Capital Punishment [and] . . . the Massachusetts Council for Abolition of the Death Penalty," observed the *Boston Bar Journal* in 1967, are "both high sounding names but pretty largely no more nor less than Sara R. Ehrmann." See *Boston Bar Journal*, Feb. 1967, p. 3; in that year she was about to testify for the thirty-eighth time. See also Sara R. Ehrmann, "For Whom the Chair Waits," *Federal Probation*, n.p., March 1962.

150. Folder 9, Box 22, Herbert B. Ehrmann Papers, Harvard Law School.

151. *Gallagher v. Crown Kosher Super Market*, 366 U.S. 617 (1961); Raya Dreben was

also on the brief. They argued that the Massachusetts Sunday-closing law is an establishment of religion; they won in the U.S. District Court but lost in the U.S. Supreme Court.

152. Interview with Raya Dreben, Feb. 1, 1998.

153. HBE to Charles J. Hardee, Jr., Aug. 22, 1961: "Enclosed you will find two copies of our brief. This brief was almost entirely the work of Mrs. Dreben. I hope you will agree with me that it is an excellent presentation." Goulston & Storrs Files, Boston.

154. Esther Peterson to Raya Dreben, July 24, 1961, Goulston & Storrs Files.

155. Interview with Raya Dreben, Dec. 8, 1990, Boston.

156. CJH to HBE, Aug. 24, 1961; Ehrmann to Hardee, Aug. 29, 1961—Goulston & Storrs Files.

157. CJH to HBE, May 17, 1960; HBE to CJH, May 20, 1960—Goulston & Storrs Files.

158. RSD to National Woman's Party, the National Federation of Business and Professional Women, the American Women's Voluntary Services, the General Federation of Women's Clubs; and to Frank Grinnell, Boston Bar Association, Feb. 27, 1961; RSD to the Massachusetts Association of Women Lawyers, the National Association of Women Lawyers, the American Bar Association, Feb. 28, 1961, Goulston & Storrs Files. Dreben also wrote to the state offices of the League of Women Voters in Florida, Mississippi, South Carolina, and Texas, where women's jury service was severely constrained or denied. She sent a copy of the brief to Jennie Loitman Barron. RSD to JLB, Aug. 22, 1961; JLB to RD, Aug. 25, 1961, Goulston & Storrs Files.

159. Mrs. Cyril B. Smith (Florida) to RSD, June 28, 1960; Mrs. George Boller (Texas) to RSD, July 1, 1960; Dena Bank (South Carolina) to RSD, July 23, 1960; RSD to Christine Urban, National Office, League of Women Voters, July 22, 1960, Goulston & Storrs Files. Often these organizations, while refusing to get involved, requested copies of Dreben's Jurisdictional Statement and her brief—an expensive burden in the pre-Xerox era when only three carbon copies could be made.

160. Mrs. Cyril B. Smith/Virginia Smith to RSD, June 28, 1960, Goulston & Storrs Files.

161. Patricia Eicholz to RSD, July 27, 1960, Goulston & Storrs Files. The League of Women Voters of Texas had placed a constitutional amendment before the state legislature annually between 1935 and its final passage in 1954. Mrs. George Boller to RSD, July 1, 1960, Goulston & Storrs Files. The resolution had passed the legislature in 1949 but had failed to be ratified by popular vote.

162. Rowland Watts to Raya Dreben, Jan. 13, 1961, American Civil Liberties Union of Florida, Papers, P. K. Yonge Library of Florida History, Department of Special Collections, George A. Smathers Libraries, University of Florida, Gainesville. On Watts's important career, see obituary in the New York *Times*, Feb. 8, 1995.

163. Pauli Murray, "A Proposal to Reexamine . . . ," typescript, p. 31, Dec. 1962, Doc. II-20, Papers of the President's Commission on the Status of Women, Schlesinger Library.

164. *Fay v. New York*, 332 U.S. 261 (1947). The "blue ribbon" jury was a device permitted in New York in counties whose population was at least one million,

when the court was persuaded that "by reason of the importance or the intricacy of the case a special jury is required." Members of such a panel had to meet the usual juror requirements, and also be "the owner or spouse of an owner of property of the value of $250," "intelligent," and "well-informed."

165. Dorothy Kenyon Papers, Sophia Smith Collection, Smith College, Northampton, Massachusetts. In 1939, she described her municipal court as "The Poor Man's Court": "For those little claims often represent everything that the litigant has. Or else they're the things that he cares most about in the world. . . . My court is truly the court of social significance, the court that touches the lives of more of the people more closely than [almost] any other court in the city."

When she was named by Joseph McCarthy as a member of Communist-front organizations Kenyon forthrightly acknowledged that she had supported many antifascist and liberal causes but denied that she was a fellow traveler or disloyal. Although she emerged from the Senate Foreign Relations Subcommittee hearings something of a media heroine, Kenyon received no further public appointments.

166. Speech at Albert Einstein College of Medicine, April 2, 1959; and ACLU Minutes, Board of Directors Meeting, Feb. 14, 1967, p. 3 (mimeo), Dorothy Kenyon Papers, Sophia Smith Collection, Smith College.

167. She chaired the League of Women Voters' Committee on the Legal Status of Women in the 1920s and she kept jury service high on the League's agenda for decades. See League of Women Voters Papers, Series III, Part A, reel 18, p. 404; Minutes, Legal Status Meeting, New York City, Feb. 25, 1927, ibid., pp. 432 ff.; Dorothy Kenyon to Margaret Hicks, Aug. 2, 1927, ibid., p. 467.

168. 1935. Subsequent ads for the play included women. Dorothy Kenyon Papers, Sophia Smith Collection, Smith College.

169. "First Women Put on Jury Lists Here," New York Times, Sept. 9, 1937. By December, she had served on a jury; see "Few Women Seek Jury Exemptions," New York Times, Dec. 26, 1937.

170. HBE to Rowland Watts, Sept. 26, 1961, Goulston & Storrs Files: "Your young ladies approached the subject in a considerably less legalistic manner than our own Brief. There was even a note of the old suffragette indignation which I, for one, entirely enjoyed." Kenyon caught the condescending tone and turned it right back: "Your words are infinitely subtler flattery than you know since I am doubtless considerably older than you are, having been admitted to the Bar in 1917. The 'old suffragette indignation' to which you refer is something which I must have distilled without meaning to." DK to HBE, Oct. 5, 1961, Goulston & Storrs Files.

171. Watts told the Florida ACLU chapter that New York would happily do all the work but asked for the name of a Florida attorney which could be placed on the brief. In that way the name of Phyllis Shampanier, a young attorney who worked with the Miami branch of the ACLU, appeared along with Kenyon's. Phyllis Shampanier's presence on the brief was strictly emblematic; she was spending her time bailing out students who were being arrested for participation in Fair Play for Cuba demonstrations. Watts to Tobias Simon, July 24, 1961; Watts to Phyllis Shampanier, Aug. 23, 1961; Watts to Phyllis Shampanier, Aug. 23, 1961; Watts to Kenyon, July 24, 1961, American Civil Liberties Union

of Florida Papers, P. K. Yonge Library of Florida History, Department of Special Collections, George A. Smathers Libraries, University of Florida, Gainesville. (Hereafter ACLU-Florida.) DK to HBE, Oct. 5, 1961, Goulston & Storrs Files. Telephone interview with Phyllis Shampanier, March 1994.

172. HBE to E. P. Cullinan, Clerk U.S. Supreme Court, Sept. 16, 1961; Cullinan to HBE, Sept. 18, 1961; *Hoyt v. Florida* Papers, U.S. Supreme Court Archives.

173. A few years later, Hardee would appear before the Supreme Court on his own, establishing a significant precedent in admiralty law. *Morayne v. States Marine Lines, Inc.*, 398 U.S. 375 (1970). He died in 1988.

174. Florence Allen in Ohio and Benita S. Matthews on the DC Circuit.

175. Valerie Kincade Oppenheimer, *The Female Labor Force in the United States: Demographic and Economic Factors Governing Its Growth and Changing Composition* (Berkeley: Institute of International Studies, University of California, 1970), ch. 3, esp. pp. 69–70.

176. Appellee Brief, FSC, pp. 27, 35.

177. Appellee Brief, FSC, p. 6; Appellee Brief, FSC, p. 5.

178. Appellee Brief, FSC, p. 13.

179. Appellee Brief, U.S. Supreme Court, pp. 11–12 (emphasis added).

180. Appellee Brief, FSC, pp. 15–16.

181. Appellant Brief, FSC, p. 4. C. J. Hardee knew something of the tensions in the Hoyt family; many years later his former wife, Pat Hardee, would observe that they had believed Clarence to be "a mean, abusive person." Interview with Pat Hardee, New Smyrna Beach, Florida, March 23, 1990.

182. The pathbreaking case is *State v. Wanrow*, 88 Wash. 2nd 221, 559 P. 2nd 548 (1977). A good entry into the extensive literature is Elizabeth M. Schneider, "The Dialectic of Rights and Politics: Perspectives from the Women's Movement," *New York University Law Review*, vol. 61 (1986), pp. 589–652, and a special issue of the *Women's Rights Law Reporter*, vol. 9 (Fall 1986). The psychological dynamics of households characterized by a high degree of domestic violence are only just beginning to be studied, and the definition of battering is controversial. Violence in the Hoyt household was mutual, but the fact of her response would not today necessarily disqualify Gwendolyn Hoyt from arguing that she was abused; the court today would want to know more about psychological power and control in the household.

By the 1980s, George Georgieff would have developed a reputation for his vigorous defense of the death penalty; his 1961 observations about home and mother are a striking contrast to his opinions of 1981: "I know [the death penalty] is a deterrent because many years ago I was having a spat, a physical fight, with one of my ex-wives, and I found myself choking her, and I saw her eyes start to pop out, and suddenly off to the left or the right I saw the electric chair. It deterred *me*." Stephen Adler, "Florida's Zealous Prosecutors: Death Specialists," *The American Lawyer*, Sept. 1981, p. 36.

183. Supreme Court Brief, p. 4; this sentence also appears in the Jurisdictional Statement, pp. 3–4. In the Jurisdictional Statement, Dreben had put the matter precisely, arguing that the case raised the question "Whether said Section 40.01 (1) Florida Statues [which required women to volunteer to serve on juries], because of its effect in largely and systematically excluding women from the jury which tried the Appellant, *a woman accused of a crime under the circumstances*

and raising issues in which the point of view of women was most important [emphasis mine], is, as applied to the Appellant, repugnant to and a violation of the Fourteenth Amendment to the Constitution of the United States?" Jurisdictional Statement, p. 3, Goulston & Storrs Files.

184. Oral Argument Tape, U.S. Supreme Court Archives. Jurisdictional Statement, Appendix B, p. 5.

185. Appellant Brief, U.S. Supreme Court, p. 20, citing Strodtbeck, *Sociometry*, vol. 19 (1956), pp. 3–11.

186. Martha Minow, "Foreword: Justice Engendered," *Harvard Law Review*, vol. 101 (1987); *Making All the Difference: Inclusion, Exclusion, and American Law* (Ithaca, NY: Cornell University Press, 1990), ch. 1.

187. See "Appellant's Brief in Opposition to Appellee's Motion to Dismiss or Affirm," p. 4.

188. Tape recording of oral argument, *Hoyt v. Florida*, U.S. Supreme Court Archives.

189. ACLU Amicus Brief, p. 26.

190. Kenyon, ACLU Amicus Brief, pp. 26–27; Dreben, Jurisdictional Statement, p. 7; *Ballard v. U.S.*, 329 U.S. 187 (1946).

191. Supplementary Memo, O.T. 61, no. 31, originally 1960 Term, #639, *Hoyt v. Florida*, Container 1268, William O. Douglas Papers, Manuscript Division, Library of Congress.

192. Timothy B. Dyk, Bench Memo, no. 31, 1961 Term, *Hoyt v. Florida*, Folder 219, Earl Warren Papers, Manuscript Division, Library of Congress.

193. Interview with Timothy B. Dyk, Washington, DC, Feb. 26, 1991.

194. *Goesaert v. Cleary*, 335 U.S. 464, 466 (1948).

195. My interpretation of these notes differs somewhat from the account in Bernard Schwartz's *Super Chief: Earl Warren and His Supreme Court—A Judicial Biography* (New York: New York University Press, 1983), pp. 400–1.

196. Schwartz, p. 441. Schwartz discusses the 1960 and 1961 terms, which included *Hoyt, Baker v. Carr*, and *Engel v. Vitale* in ch. 10.

197. Ruth Bader Ginsburg, "The Burger Court's Grapplings with Sex Discrimination," in Vincent Blasi, ed., *The Burger Court: The Counter-Revolution That Wasn't* (New Haven: Yale University Press, 1983), p. 132.

198. Harlan cited *Hernandez*: "Circumstances or chance may well dictate that no persons in a certain class will serve on a particular jury or during some particular period." He acknowledged that the proportion of women on the jury list to the total of registered women was less than 5 percent, not 27 percent, but he accepted Lockhart's exclusion of all but thirty-five on the grounds of "age," and insisted that the proportion of males on the jury lists should not be compared to the simple list of male electors, but to lists of voters explicitly qualified for jury service. There was no "unfortunate atmosphere of ethnic or racial prejudices"; it was impossible to "attribute to these administrative officials a deliberate design to exclude the very class whose eligibility for jury service the state legislature, after many years of contrary policy, had declared only a few years before." *Hoyt v. Florida*, 368 U.S. 57, 65, 68 (1961).

199. *Hoyt v. Florida*, 368 U.S. at, 61–62; as the Court had ruled in *Fay v. New York* in 1947, exemption from jury service was interpreted as a privilege.

200. CCHC Transcript, printed as footnote 11 to Harlan opinion.

201. Memo signed BEJ, Sept. 8, 1960, *Hoyt v. Florida*, 1960 term, no. 639, Container

1268, Papers of William O. Douglas, Manuscript Division, Library of Congress; *Hoyt v. Florida*, 368 U.S. 57, 69.

202. George A. Trowbridge to JMH, Nov. 25, 1961, in John Marshall Harlan Papers, Box 138, Seeley G. Mudd Manuscript Library, Princeton University, ACLU Archives, Princeton University Library. Published with permission.

203. HBE to Superintendent H. D. West, Lowell, FL [sic], Jan. 2, 1961, Goulston & Storrs Files.

204. Gunnar Myrdal, *An American Dilemma: The Negro Problem and Modern Democracy* (New York: Harper & Brothers, 1944), pp. 1073–78, included as an appendix to the ACLU Brief in *White v. Crook*.

205. Simone de Beauvoir, *The Second Sex*, trans. H. M. Parshley (New York: Alfred A. Knopf, 1953), pp. 297–98; see also comments on pp. 116 and 259.

206. Interview with Raya Dreben, Dec. 6, 1989. Dreben was appointed to the Massachusetts Court of Appeals in 1979; she retired in 1997.

207. Pauli Murray, *Song in a Weary Throat: An American Pilgrimage* (New York: Harper & Row, 1987), p. 271.

208. Morris Milgram, who investigated Florida's vagrancy practices for the Workers Defense League, was a loyal friend throughout her life; years later he would edit a collection of Murray's poetry and push it to publication. *Dark Testament and Other Poems* (Norwalk, CT: Silvermine Press, 1970); see *Song in a Weary Throat*, p. 378.

209. Murray reviews these years in detail in *Song in a Weary Throat*, chs. 8–16.

210. Murray and her friend took careful notes on the foul conditions in the segregated prison. They also persuaded the other black prisoners not to scorn them. "We did kind of an educational job in saying why we were there . . . we got back an apology and . . . an admission of 'we are proud of you' . . . from the male prisoners . . . consciousness raising could go on right in the middle of a jail. . . . Can you imagine what it might have been like if I had had the background and the training and understanding, let's say, of the 1960s[?]" Pauli Murray interview by Genna Rae McNeil, Feb. 13, 1976, Southern Oral History Program (SOHP), 4007 G-44, Southern Historical Collection, Wilson Library, University of North Carolina, Chapel Hill, pp. 53–58.

211. The progress of her effort can be followed in University of North Carolina Archives, General Administration/Consolidated University President's Office Records, Frank Porter Graham Files. Subgroup II: Consolidated UNC Campus Files; Series 2: UNC-Chapel Hill; Subseries 1: Office of the Chancellor. Race and Ethnic Relations: Negroes. Admissions. 1933–35; 1937–41. See especially Pauli Murray to Frank Porter Graham, Jan. 17, 1939; Frank Porter Graham to Pauli Murray, Feb. 3, 1939; Pauli Murray to Frank Porter Graham, Feb. 6, 1939. Graham, who unsuccessfully sought to persuade the legislature to pay out-of-state tuition for black students' professional education, stressed his fear of "a throwback to a darker time with losses all along the line"; Murray maintained that "we of the younger generation cannot compromise with our ideals of human equality." She asked the NAACP to undertake her case; she believed that it did not because of a fear that her left-wing associations in New York would make her vulnerable to attack should the case be tried in court. Pauli Murray interview, SOHP, pp. 45–50. For Murray's reproach to Franklin Roosevelt and the beginning of her long friendship with Eleanor Roosevelt, a

friendship in which the younger woman never let her admiration for the elder submerge her impatience and anger about maintenance of a Jim Crow South in an allegedly liberal polity, see *Song in a Weary Throat*, pp. 107–29.

212. Pauli Murray interview, SOHP, pp. 60–63; see also Richard P. Sherman, *The Case of Odell Waller and Virginia Justice* (Knoxville: University of Tennessee Press, 1992).

213. Pauli Murray interview, SOHP, p. 63. Murray remained on good terms with Frank Porter Graham; in 1941 he agreed to her request that he prepare an introduction for a fund-raising WDL pamphlet she had written on the Waller case. "P.S.," she wrote, "This might have been a thesis at the University of North Carolina." Pauli Murray to FPG, March 7, 1941, Frank Porter Graham Papers, Folder 145, Southern Historical Collection, University of North Carolina, Chapel Hill.

214. Pauli Murray interview, SOHP, pp. 65–66, 74.

215. Cynthia Harrison, *On Account of Sex: The Politics of Women's Issues 1945–1968* (Berkeley: University of California Press, 1988), p. 126.

216. Murray describes *States' Laws* in *Song in a Weary Throat*, pp. 284–89.

217. Pauli Murray, "Why Negro Girls Stay Single," *Negro Digest*, July 1947, pp. 4–8. "We desire that the Negro male accept the Negro female as his equal and treat her accordingly and that he cease his ruthless aggression upon her and his emotional exploitation of her made possible by her admittedly inferior position as a social human being in the United States."

218. Edith Green to PM, Aug. 11, 1962; PM to Edith Green, Aug. 19, 1962, Box 49, Folder 875, PM Papers, Schlesinger Library.

219. Pauli Murray, "A Proposal to Reexamine the Applicability of the Fourteenth Amendment to State Laws and Practices Which Discriminate on the Basis of Sex Per Se," Dec. 1962, Document II-20, Papers of the President's Commission on the Status of Women, Committee on Civil and Political Rights, Schlesinger Library.

220. PM to Gertrude Wilson, Aug. 29, 1962, Box 49, Folder 875, PM Papers, Schlesinger Library. She went on: "Have you ever taken a look at the list of Spingarn Medalists (an honor granted each year by the NAACP) and noted how few women have been cited for this honor? Surely this is not entirely accidental. It is dramatic because the racial factor is removed."

221. PM to [Mel Wulf], General Counsel, ACLU, Aug. 15, 1962; Mel Wulf to PM, Aug. 20, 1962, Box 49, Folder 875, PM Papers, Schlesinger Library.

222. DK to PM, Jan. 30, 1963, Box 49, Folder 878, PM Papers, Schlesinger Library.

223. "Proposal to Reexamine," pp. 4–5.

224. They discussed *Hoyt* in detail; see Caroline Ware to "Pixie" [PM] Oct. 12, 1962, PM to "Skipper" [Caroline Ware], Oct. 23, 1962, Box 49, Folder 878, PM Papers, Schlesinger Library.

225. "Proposal to Reexamine," pp. 12, 21; Blanche Crozier, "Constitutionality of Discrimination Based on Sex," *Boston University Law Review*, vol. 15 (1935), pp. 723–55.

226. "Proposal to Reexamine," p. 7.

227. "Proposal to Reexamine," p. 25; the second was equal access to education, p. 30.

228. "Proposal to Reexamine," pp. 35–36.

229. Harrison, pp. 126–27.
230. Esther Peterson to PM, Jan. 11, 1963, in Box 49, Folder 878, PM Papers, Schlesinger Library.
231. DK to PM, April 4, 1963, Box 49, Folder 878, PM Papers, Schlesinger Library. Kenyon also saw in Murray's arguments a way to hold pressures for an Equal Rights Amendment at arm's length somewhat longer. DK to Board of Directors, ACLU, March 28, 1963, mimeo typescript. See also Alan Reitman to PM, April 3, 1963, Box 49, Folder 878, PM Papers, Schlesinger Library.
232. Erwin N. Griswold to PM, Jan. 31, 1963, in Box 49, Folder 878, PM Papers, Schlesinger Library.
233. It was one of the seven accompanying committee reports. See also *American Women, 1963–1968*, Report of the Interdepartmental Committee on the Status of Women, and four accompanying Task Force Reports of the Citizens' Advisory Council (1968) and Pauli Murray, "The Rights of Women," *The Rights of Americans: What They Are, What They Should Be*, ed. Norman Dorsen (New York: Pantheon, 1971), pp. 521 ff.
234. Murray supported the inclusion of *sex* as well as *race* as protected categories, even at the cost of putting herself at odds with many of her closest allies. To some black activists, it looked as though white women were trying to ride the coattails of a movement in which black lives had been risked and spent; in this context, Murray's commitment to ending "Jane Crow" as well as "Jim Crow" was fraught with the suggestion that she had cast her lot with white feminists. At a moment when younger activists in the civil rights movement were beginning to develop the theme of Black Power and to stress racial difference, Murray made the ideology of equality developed in three decades of civil rights struggle applicable to the search for gender equality. She was being true to what she had learned in her own life as she had lived it, but the position would put at risk her relations with a younger generation of black activists.
235. Pauli Murray and Mary O. Eastwood, "Jane Crow and the Law: Sex Discrimination and Title VII," *George Washington Law Review*, vol. 34 (Dec. 1965), pp. 235–41; "Proposal to Reexamine," p. 10.
236. CJH to HBE, Dec. 18, 1961, Goulston & Storrs Files. Interview with Pat Hardee, March 23, 1990.
237. Hoyt was discharged from parole on July 20, 1969. Judy Lee to author, Office of the Sheriff, Hillsborough County, Tampa, Oct. 20, 1989.
238. Murray had proposed a "permanent Commission or Committee on the Status of Women" to continue the Committee's work, particularly to identify "cases coming to its attention that would present in clear-cut form the question [of the] legal validity of particular instances of discrimination against women, and to oversee any resulting litigation with a view to assuring that the courts are properly supplied with the relevant legal and sociological data." She quickly changed "oversee" to "cooperate with respect to," since no such commission could have actual power over the courts. The ongoing legal program suggested in this memo would be taken on by the ACLU. "Proposal to Reexamine."
239. Minutes, Equality Committee, ACLU, Nov. 30, 1967; Dec. 28, 1967; Feb. 21, 1[9]68, ACLU Archives, Princeton University.
240. Like Murray, McKissick had grown up in Durham; he had in effect finished work she had begun when, in 1950, the Legal Defense Fund, Inc., of the

NAACP helped him sue the University of North Carolina for excluding blacks from its law school. Greenberg, p. 90.

241. Minutes, Equality Committee, ACLU, Dec. 28, 1967, ACLU Archives, Princeton University.

242. Murray, *Song in a Weary Throat*, p. 363. Viola Liuzzo's murder is reported in the New York *Times*, March 26, 1965; *Time*, April 2, 1965, p. 22. She was thirty-nine; the wife of a Detroit teamster union official, she had a married daughter living in Georgia. News reports stressed that she was the mother of five children; her six-year-old daughter asked, "Why couldn't Mommy have just died from being old?" *Newsweek*, April 5, 1965. *The Ladies' Home Journal* conducted a national survey which found that an overwhelming majority of women respondents—a majority strongest in the South, but averaging 55 percent nationally—believed that Liuzzo did not have "a right to leave her five children to risk her life for a social cause." *Ladies' Home Journal*, July 1965, pp. 42, 44. The first trial of the accused murderer, Collie Leroy Wilkins, resulted in a hung jury; at his second he was found innocent. *Time*, May 14, 1965, p. 27; *Newsweek*, Nov. 1, 1965, p. 36.

The three defendants were, however, ultimately found guilty of a federal charge of conspiracy to violate a person's civil rights, an 1870 civil rights law which had not been invoked since 1915, and then in a voting rights issue, not physical brutality. *Newsweek*, Dec. 13, 1965. Presiding over the federal trial, Fifth Circuit judge Frank M. Johnson rigorously monitored the management of the jury. "In his Montgomery courtroom," wrote Adam Clymer for *The Reporter*, Dec. 30, 1965, pp. 25–26, "Judge Johnson demands jury panels that represent a cross section of the twenty-three counties in his district. Where Federal law requires at least three hundred names in the jury box from which the venire is picked, Johnson requires more than three thousand. His commissioners spend a lot of time on the road, seeking out what they call a "responsible cross section." Johnson himself questioned the venire, keeping the lawyers out of the show. Racial inquiries were few. All fifty-eight who were interrogated said they could try the case fairly . . . Johnson had the [all-white, twelve-man jury] . . . locked in a hotel every night; their television viewing was monitored, and all courtroom and racial news was cut out of their newspapers."

243. *Gardenia White et al. and the United States of America v. Bruce Crook et al.*, 1965, Plaintiff's Brief, vol. 1, p. 61, Dorothy Kenyon Papers, Sophia Smith Collection, Smith College.

244. New York *Times*, Nov. 27, 1965.

245. *White v. Crook*, 251 F. Supp. 401, 408–9 (M.D. Ala. 1966). The court made it clear that it was sympathetic to "women themselves who assert their right . . . not to be excluded from jury service solely because of their sex." That is, like Harlan and his colleagues, they focused on the claims of prospective women *jurors*, not defendants like Hoyt who claimed her jury had not been drawn from a fair cross section of the community.

246. Murray, *Song in a Weary Throat*, pp. 364–65. But *White v. Crook* referred only to complete exclusion from jury service; the precedent in *Hoyt* still held. The following year a claim modeled on *White* was turned down by the Supreme Court of Mississippi: when a woman wanted her indictment for murder quashed because jury service was voluntary for women, the court ruled: "The legislature

has the right to exclude women so they may continue their service as mothers, wives, and homemakers, and also to protect them (in some areas, they are still on a pedestal) from the filth, obscenity and noxious atmosphere that so often pervade a courtroom during a jury trial." Leaning on *Hoyt*, the court asked, "How can any classification of jurors by sex be unconstitutional, if *some* classification is constitutional?" Papers, *Mississippi v. Hall*, 187 So. 2nd 861 (1966), 863, 868.

247. Mildred Adams Kenyon draft biography, DK Papers, Smith College.
248. Interview with Ruth Bader Ginsburg, Feb. 4, 1991, Washington, DC.
249. Interview with Ruth Bader Ginsburg, Washington, DC, Feb. 26, 1991.
250. RBG interview, Feb. 26, 1991. That there was so narrow a generational gap between Dorothy Kenyon and Ruth Bader Ginsburg suggests something of the erratic history of feminism in the twentieth century, and how few women had been admitted to law schools between Dorothy Kenyon's entry in NYU in 1917 and Raya Dreben's and Ginsburg's admission to Harvard in the 1950s. Hostility to the professionally educated woman pervaded academic institutions. In 1968, a survey of law schools showed that of 2,550 faculty members, 2,500 were men; that of 2,886 people who were partners or on the partner track in a national sample of law firms, more than 2,700 were men. See D. Sassower, "The Legal Profession and Women's Rights," *Rutgers Law Review*, vol. 25 (1970), pp. 61 ff., and Ruth B. Cowan, "Women's Rights Through Litigation: An Examination of the American Civil Liberties Union Women's Rights Project, 1971–1976," *Columbia Human Rights Law Review*, vol. 8 (1976), pp. 373–412.
251. Interview with Ruth Bader Ginsburg, Feb. 26, 1991; also listed in "Draft, ACLU Women's Rights Project, Ruth Bader Ginsburg, August 1, 1972," Folder 67, Box 5, PM Papers, Schlesinger Library. This list of four was given a prominent role in the casebook which Ginsburg wrote with Kenneth Davidson and Herma Hill Kay in 1974; although the book was subsequently thoroughly revised, the quartet of cases remains the basic starting place: see Herma Hill Kay, *Text, Cases and Materials on Sex-Based Discrimination* (3rd ed.; St. Paul: West Publishing Co., 1988), pp. 6–9.

When Jack Greenberg prepared the first casebook which emphasized the role of advocacy organizations and litigation planning in accomplishing social change, he too started with *Bradwell*, *Muller*, *Goesaert*, and *Hoyt*. Jack Greenberg, ed., *Cases and Materials on Judicial Process and Social Change: Constitutional Litigation* (St. Paul: West Publishing, Co., 1977). *Bradwell v. Illinois* 83 U.S. 130 (1872) had denied a married woman the right to practice law; *Muller v. Oregon*, 208 U.S. 412 (1908) had justified protective labor legislation on the grounds of women's maternal function; and *Goesaert v. Cleary*, 335 U.S. 464 (1948) had upheld a state's exclusion of women entirely from a line of work.
252. Ginsburg interview by Ruth Cowan, June 25, 1975, reported in Cowan, p. 380.
253. Interview with RBG, Feb. 26, 1991.
254. Eugene Cavanaugh to Maude Matthews, May 16, 1966; Maude Matthews, "Nonattendance Report," c. 1966, Box 61, Folder 1027, PM Papers, Schlesinger Library. PM took a particular interest in this case; the original correspondence is in her own files.
255. Kenyon and Murray had long been urging the ACLU to accept a case that would test sex discrimination as a denial of equal protection under the law;

indeed, Kenyon had once suggested that the ACLU staff was so inexperienced they probably would botch the job if they *did* take it on, and that if anything did appear, it should be given to her or to Murray. Minutes, Equality Committee, Nov. 30, 1967, Box 54, Folder 943, PM Papers, Schlesinger Library.

256. The Idaho attorney who was handling it agreed to let the ACLU bring the case, with the understanding that he would conduct the actual argument before the Supreme Court. Ginsburg played only a minor role in the oral argument. Interview with Ginsburg, Feb. 26, 1991; see also Deborah L. Markowitz, "In Pursuit of Equality: One Woman's Work to Change the Law," *Women's Rights Law Reporter*, vol. 11 (1989), p. 78.

257. *Frontiero v. Richardson*, 411 U.S. 677 (1973). The Court ruled in favor of Frontiero; Justice William J. Brennan, Jr., prepared a historically based opinion explaining the distance American public opinion had traveled since the 1870s, and drawing analogies between discrimination on the basis of race, which the Court had long subjected to strict scrutiny, and discrimination on the basis of sex, of which he and only three other justices were prepared to be equally skeptical.

258. Interview with RBG, Feb. 26, 1991. Kenneth M. Davidson, Ruth Bader Ginsburg, and Herma Hill Kay, *Text, Cases and Materials on Sex-Based Discrimination* (St. Paul: West Pubublishing Co., 1974).

259. Following the decision in *White v. Crook*, advocates for equality in jury service regularly stressed exclusions on gender as well as racial grounds; see, for example, Docket Reports, 1969, NAACP Legal Defense Fund Papers, Library of Congress. I am grateful to Jack Greenberg for sharing this with me.

260. *Alexander v. Louisiana*, 405 U.S. 625 (1972).

261. Interview with Atina Grossmann, New York City, March 12, 1991; interview with Richard Christie, New York City, March 11–12, 1991.

262. Quoted by Alschuler, "The Supreme Court and the Jury," p. 210.

263. Interview with Richard Christie, New York City, March 13, 1991. Not long after, a team of sociologists headed by Jerome Skolnick of UC-Berkeley did a similar study of the black community of the San Francisco Bay area, and advised the defense counsel in the Angela Davis trial *not* to call for a change of venue and said that working-class blacks were likely *not* to be sympathetic to her defense. A jury whose selection was guided in part by these principles found Davis not guilty. "We saved her life," Skolnick observed years later. Interview with Skolnick, July 1991.

264. The Jury Service Act of 1968 had given defendants who claimed that the jury was imbalanced the right to examine the questionnaires filled out by prospective jurors. Preparing to argue that race discrimination had entered jury selection in *U.S. v. Briggs*, 366 F. Supp. 1356, 1361. (N.D. Fla. 1973), Shulman and Copelon looked at the questionnaires of women as well as of African-American men. The court held that a jury selection plan that provides an automatic hardship excuse to women with children under ten was constitutionally permissible. As they packed up to leave, defeated, the court clerk told them privately that at least *he* had been persuaded; the day before two African-American women had come into the courthouse to claim their automatic exemption as caregivers. When one told him that she was a teacher, he convinced her not to claim the exemption. Copelon interview, March 9, 1991. *Laws of Florida*, ch. 67–154.

265. Interview with RBG, Feb. 26, 1991. Jurisdictional Statement, *Edna Stubblefield v. Tennessee*, U.S. Supreme Court, October Term, 1973. On appeal from the Tennessee Court of Criminal Appeals, p. 5A. 420 U.S. 903 (1975).

266. Tenn. Code Ann. Sec. 22-101; cited in Jurisdictional Statement, *Stubblefield*, p. 3. The history of the fight for women's jury service in Tennessee—and the compromise that resulted in making it fully optional in 1951—is splendidly detailed in Ruth A. Thompson, "Full Citizenship and Jury Service for Women: The Passage of Tennessee's Women Jurors Law, 1951" (unpublished M.A. thesis, History, Vanderbilt University, 1991). See especially pp. 25–33.

267. Jurisdictional Statement, p. 6. Thompson reports that "a survey of two Tennessee counties between 1961 and 1972 shows that less than 4 percent of women served [as jurors] in areas where women were over one-half of the population." Thompson, p. 32.

268. Jurisdictional Statement, pp. 4, 10a–11a. Judge Charles Galbreath's colleagues on the Criminal Court of Appeals shrugged off the claim that Edna Stubblefield had been heard by unfairly selected grand and petit juries; trial judge Dick Jerman observed, "I feel like we should have more women serve, but . . . I know [the jury commissioners] have trouble getting women to serve, because I can't get them to serve, and I give them my best civic lecture. It doesn't do a bit of good" (p. 5).

269. Jurisdictional Statement, p. 10.

270. *Healy v. Edwards*, 363 F. Supp. at 1111.

271. Brief for Defendants, *Healy v. Edwards*, p. 26.

272. Interview with Rhonda Copelon, March 1991. The Center for Constitutional Rights was founded in 1966 by attorneys Arthur Kinoy, William Kunstler, Morton Stavis and others who represented the more radical activists in the civil rights movement; they created CCR to be a legal arm of activists and movements for progressive legal change.

273. Brief for Amicus Curiae, Center for Constitutional Rights, *Edwards v. Healy*, No. 73-759, 1974.

274. The precedent had been refreshed and recently upheld in *Alexander v. Louisiana*, 405 U.S. 625 (1972).

275. *Healy v. Edwards*, 363 F. Supp. at 1117. "Rubin wrote an unusual decision because it was breaking a Supreme Court decision. . . . I know that Burger was displeased with Rubin. Instead of saying, 'This decision is obsolete and it's up to the Court to change it,' Rubin himself basically said it's obsolete and has been effectively overruled by changing times and later decisions . . . Rubin was *such* a good judge." Ruth Bader Ginsburg interview, Feb. 28, 1991.

276. *Healy v. Edwards*, 363 F. Supp. at 1115.

277. Interview with Charles J. Hardee III, New Smyrna Beach, Florida, March 1990.

278. *Taylor v. Louisiana*, 419 U.S. 522, 537 (1975). The decision in *Taylor* would be reinforced when, in *Duren v. Missouri*, 439 U.S. 357 (1979), Ruth Bader Ginsburg argued the case of a black man charged with crime in a state in which women had multiple opportunities to claim exemption from jury service on the grounds of sex. *Taylor* overturned "opt in" systems; *Duren* overturned "opt out" systems.

279. Interview with Carl Durrance, Feb. 11, 1991.

280. *Taylor v. Louisiana*, 419 U.S. at 541–42.

281. Interview with Elizabeth Schneider, Cambridge, Massachusetts, March 1991. The gradual development of this line of thinking can be followed in Rhonda Copelon, Elizabeth M. Schneider, and Nancy Stearns, "Constitutional Perspectives on Sex Discrimination in Jury Selection," *Women's Rights Law Reporter* II (1975, 3-12).

282. *State v. Wanrow*, 88 Wash. 2nd 221, 559 P. 2nd 548 (1977); see also Elizabeth M. Schneider, "Equal Rights to Trial for Women: Sex Bias in the Law of Self-Defense," *Harvard Civil Rights-Civil Liberties Law Review*, vol. 15 (1980), pp. 623–47.

283. Mrs. Elizabeth Snyder to John Marshall Harlan, November 29, 1961, and enclosure, Box 138, John Marshall Harlan Papers, Seeley G. Mudd Library, ACLU Archives, Princeton University Library. Published with permission.

284. See Alschuler, "The Supreme Court and the Jury," p. 166.

285. St. Petersburg *Times*, Dec. 17, 1957.

286. Clifford Geertz, *Local Knowledge: Further Essays in Interpretive Anthropology* (New York: Basic Books, 1983), p. 84.

287. See, for example, Alschuler, "The Supreme Court and the Jury," pp. 210–11.

288. *Swain v. Alabama*, 380 U.S. 202 (1965). Albert Alschuler has extensively and shrewdly examined the contradiction between the alleged American faith in the mystical properties of juries and the extraordinary efforts of lawyers to protect their clients against being judged by a random sample of the community, either by plea bargaining or by the use of peremptory challenges to reinforce stereotypes. See Alschuler, "The Supreme Court and the Jury," pp. 157–65, where he quotes Thurgood Marshall in *Batson v. Kentucky* to the effect that the Equal Protection Clause and the peremptory challenge are incompatible.

289. Susan L. McCoin, "Sex Discrimination in the *Voir Dire* Process: The Rights of Prospective Female Jurors," *Southern California Law Review*, vol. 58 (1985), p. 1234.

290. *Batson v. Kentucky*, 476 U.S. 79 (1986).

291. In *Powers v. Ohio*, 499 U.S. 400 (1991), from which Justices Scalia and Rehnquist vehemently dissented.

292. *Bobb v. Municipal Court*, 143 Cal. App. 3rd 860, 192 *Cal. Rptr.* 270 (1983); Carolyn Bobb won on appeal. McCoin, p. 1227.

293. Linda Greenhouse, "High Court Bars Sex as Standard in Picking Jurors," New York *Times*, April 20, 1994.

294. *Congressional Record*, Aug. 1, 1966, p. 17,769, vol. 112, part 13, 89th Cong., 2nd sess. Three decades earlier Celler had introduced a bill which would have permitted women to serve on federal juries; New York *Times*, April 12, 1935.

295. The process is described in Lawrence Schiller and James Willwerth, *American Tragedy: The Uncensored Story of the Simpson Defense* (New York: Avon Books, 1996, 1997), pp. 243–45, 274–76, 321–24, 535, 804–5. For a widely read popularization, see John Grisham, *The Runaway Jury* (New York: Doubleday, 1996). A vast array of publications now seek to instruct attorneys in the fine points; see, for example, James Rasicot, *Jury Selection, Body Language, and the Visual Trial* (Minneapolis: AB Publications, 1983); Jeffrey T. Frederick, *Mastering Voir Dire and Jury Selection: Gaining an Edge in Questioning and Selecting a Jury* (Chicago: American Bar Association, 1995).

296. Lawrence M. Friedman, *A History of American Law* (New York: Simon & Schuster, 1973), p. 254.
297. Alschuler, "The Supreme Court and the Jury," p. 167.

5. "A CONSTITUTIONAL RIGHT TO BE TREATED LIKE AMERICAN LADIES"

1. All direct quotations in this section come from an interview with Helen Feeney, North Andover, Massachusetts, March 6, 1993. See also Boston *Globe*, June 6, 1979. During his oral argument before the U.S. Supreme Court, Massachusetts Assistant Attorney General Thomas R. Kiley emphasized that Feeney had turned twenty-one in 1943 and she *could* have enlisted; "her peers," he said reproachfully, "were either volunteering or faced conscription." Oral Argument, p. 7.

    Feeney's mother's sentiments were not uncommon. See Mattie Treadwell, *The Women's Army Corps* (Washington, DC: Government Printing Office, 1954), pp. 206–7, 212–13: Much wartime morale building among troops was centered on the theme of protecting women at home; the theme lost its force if women went to a theater of war. See D'Ann Campbell, "The Regimented Women of World War II," in Jean Bethke Elshtain and Sheila Tobias, eds., *Women, Militarism, and War: Essays in History, Politics, and Social Theory* (Totowa, NJ: Rowman & Littlefield, 1990), particularly pp. 115–16, and remarks of Representative Beverly Vincent during House debate on forming WACs, *Congressional Record*, May 27, 1943, pp. 4994–95.
2. Theda Skocpol, *Protecting Soldiers and Mothers: The Political Origins of Social Policy in the United States* (Cambridge, MA: Harvard University Press, 1992), esp. ch. 2.
3. New York *Times*, June 6, 1979, p. A17. The first veterans' *benefit* enacted in this country may have been a pension provided by the Plymouth Colony in 1636. See John P. Resch, "Federal Welfare for Revolutionary War Veterans," *Social Service Review*, 1982, pp. 171–95, and Grace Blumberg, "De Facto and De Jure Sex Discrimination Under the Equal Protection Clause: A Reconsideration of the Veterans' Preference in Public Employment," *Buffalo Law Review*, vol. 26 (1976–77), pp. 3, 9.
4. *Congressional Record*, May 27, 1943, p. 5000.
5. For a summary account of the 1944 statute, see Steven Lim, "The Effect of Veterans' Reemployment Rights, Veterans Preference Laws, and the Protective Labor Laws on the Status of Women Workers in the World War II Period," *Hofstra Labor Law Journal*, vol. 2 (1985), pp. 301–54.
6. Hearing Before the Committee on Post Office and Civil Service, House of Representatives, 86th Cong., 2nd sess., H.R. 1907, Amending the Veterans Preference Act of 1944 to Redefine the Term Mother, April 6, 1960.
7. John H. Fleming and Charles A. Shanor, "Veterans' Preferences in Public Employment: Unconstitutional Gender Discrimination?" *Emory Law Journal*, vol. 26 (1977), pp. 13–64.
8. In 1895 Massachusetts had granted preference to veterans even if they *failed* the examination, but this was quickly invalidated by the state courts. See Aviam Soifer, "The Supreme Judicial Court of Massachusetts and the 1780 Constitution," *History of the Law in Massachusetts: The Supreme Judicial Court 1692–*

1992 (Boston: Supreme Judicial Court Historical Society, 1992), pp. 223–26; Fleming and Shanor, p. 18 n. 15. An extended history appears in Brief of the Plaintiffs, *Carol A. Anthony et al. v. Commonwealth of Massachusetts*, Civil Action No. 74-5061-T, and *Helen B. Feeney v. Commonwealth of Massachusetts*, Civil Action No. 75-1991-T, U.S. District Court for the District of Massachusetts, pp. 53–81. Archives of the Civil Liberties Union of Massachusetts, Box 000025. Hereafter CLUM Archives.

9. "Veterans' Preference in Employment," memo by Peter R. Gregware to ACLU Equality Committee, Dec. 28, 1971, Box 55, Folder 949, Pauli Murray Papers, Schlesinger Library, Radcliffe College.

10. In 1975, jobs in federal, state, county, and municipal governments accounted for nearly 20 percent of all employed persons. Blumberg, p. 5, citing Department of Commerce, *Statistical Abstracts of the United States* [1975], p. 272.

11. Memorandum, Judy Coburn to Mary Rhymes and Peggy Scarrow, Aug. 31, 1973, Internal Law Enforcement Assistance Administration Memo, Box 25, CLUM Archives. They emerged from their study with "a greater appreciation of the magnitude of the barrier posed by the absolute preference for veterans," but encouraged by the decision in *Frontiero* and by the expanding "judicial concern for women's equal protection rights."

12. *Esther L. Feinerman v. C. Herschel Jones et al.*, 356 F. Supp. 252 (M.D. Pa. 1973). The court required that she show "some irrational basis for granting a veterans' preference"; since the basis was rational, the state could do what seemed, in its judgment, best.

13. *Koelfgen v. Jackson*, 355 F. Supp. 243 (D. Minn. 1972), affirmed 410 U.S. 976 (1973). The plaintiffs included male nonveterans and female nonveterans; the Court treated all the plaintiffs as a single class, thus avoiding contemplation of the issue of gender discrimination.

14. Feeney took a total of nine examinations, and would have taken more had she not "felt that any such efforts would be futile." Brief for Plaintiffs, p. 9.

15. *Frontiero v. Richardson*, 411 U.S. 677 (1973).

16. Interview with Richard Ward, March 6, 1991; Memorandum for Mr. O'Donnell, Feb. 20, 1974, Box 25, CLUM Archives.

17. Interview with Carol Anthony, Boston, March 6, 1991.

18. "Brief of the Plaintiffs" (Statement of Facts, pp. 5–25, *Carol A. Anthony et al. v. Commonwealth of Massachusetts*, Civil Action No. 74-5061-T, U.S. District Court for the District of Massachusetts, Box 25, CLUM Archives.

19. The lawyers were removed from the civil service list on April 17, 1975; the rest of veterans' preference was sustained on April 22, 1975.

20. Interview with Betty Gittes, Brookline, Massachusetts, March 6, 1991. Betty Gittes had herself tied for the second-highest score; only two points lower than the top score, she was ranked 103rd, behind 76 male veterans, 64 of whom received lower grades than she. For an example of her inquiries, see Betty A. Gittes to Nancy Beecher, Chairperson, Massachusetts Civil Service Commission, July 11, 1974, Box 25, CLUM Archives.

21. Interview with HBF, March 6, 1993.

22. Interview with Richard Ward, Brookline, March 1991.

23. See *Anthony v. Commonwealth*, 415 F. Supp 485, 493 (1976). A good calendar is provided in Bellotti, et al. Brief for the Defendants.

24. *Anthony v. Commonwealth*, 415 F. Supp., at 489–90. The statutory limitation on women with children varied between the services; it was extended in the Army, the largest service, until 1976. Women have always been ineligible for the draft; until the initiation of the All-Volunteer Force in 1973, most men entered the Army involuntarily and no women entered involuntarily.

25. Brief of the Plaintiffs, *Carol A. Anthony et al. v. Commonwealth of Massachusetts*, Civil Action No. 74-5061-T, and *Helen B. Feeney v. Commonwealth of Massachusetts*, Civil Action No. 75-1991-T, pp. 156, 208–13. Note that this is a single brief for the two combined cases. Box 25, CLUM Archives.

26. *Anthony v. Commonwealth*, 415 F. Supp. at 488. See also unsigned "Case Comments: Veterans' Public Employment Preference as Sex Discrimination: *Anthony v. Massachusetts* and *Branch v. Du Bois*," *Harvard Law Review*, vol. 90 (1977), p. 805. Writing for a 2–1 majority, Judge Tauro noted at the outset that the veterans' preference statute did not draw a sex-based classification and found that it had not been enacted for the purpose of disqualifying women from civil service appointments. Nonetheless, it was neither "impartial" nor "neutral," and its impact on women was "much more than incidental."

27. Fleming and Shanor, p. 64. Shanor sent a copy to John Reinstein, "with the hope that our article . . . may be of some use to you." Charles Shanor to John Reinstein, Oct. 18, 1977, in Box 24, CLUM Files.

28. Jack Doucette, American Legion Post 159, to Lowell *Sun*, June 6, 1979.

29. Robert C. Hagopian, Disabled American Veterans, to Boston *Herald-American*, June 24, 1976.

30. Susan Jeffords, *The Remasculinization of America: Gender and the Vietnam War* (Bloomington: Indiana University Press, 1989), p. 116. See particularly chs. 4 and 6.

31. Christian G. Appy, *Working-Class War: American Combat Soldiers and Vietnam* (Chapel Hill: University of North Carolina Press, 1993), p. 309, citing Robert Jay Lifton, *Home from the War* (1973).

32. Interview with Paul Hunt, Quincy, Massachusetts, March 1994. For reflections on the metaphor of spitting and its actual frequency, see Appy, pp. 303–4.

33. As Hunt tells the story of lobbying to sustain veterans' preference, he also testifies to the important difference the GI Bill made in his own life: a working-class boy who served on Guam and Iwo Jima, Hunt contracted dengue fever and hookworm. His health was restored thanks to the care he received at Harvard's teaching hospital; he graduated from Harvard College and Harvard Law School thanks to the GI Bill.

34. In 1975, the Disabled American Veterans, the Veterans of Foreign Wars, the Jewish War Veterans, and the American Legion all tried to get the suits dismissed. They were granted permission to file amici curiae briefs; it was the American Legion that filed one with the Supreme Court. See ms. Brief for Plaintiffs, CLUM Archives. Paul Hunt had worked hard to persuade the Legion's Finance Committee to retain the prestigious Boston law firm of Bingham, Dana & Gould. "I had to go before the Finance Committee of the Legion. The Finance Committee were misers about spending the Legion's money . . . I went before them and told them what's the sense of being the American Legion if we couldn't do anything about veterans' preference, we represent vets, and they should put up the money. I almost had them in tears. I knew we had

the money; this was the time to spend it." Ultimately they spent $35,000 on the effort and felt vindicated by the Supreme Court decision. Interview with Paul Hunt, March 1994. For reflections on the return of the veterans, see Appy, ch. 9.

35. [Catherine P. Harris, Dedham] to HBF, June 6, 1979, in HBF's possession.

36. March 3, 1979, in HBF's possession.

37. Interview with HBF, March 6, 1993.

38. Sarah Livingston Jay, Paris [after Sept. 3, 1783], in Richard B. Morris, ed., *John Jay: The Winning of the Peace: Unpublished Papers 1780–1784* (New York: Harper & Row, 1980), vol. 2, p. 581.

39. Peter Riesenberg, *Citizenship in the Western Tradition: Plato to Rousseau* (Chapel Hill: University of North Carolina Press, 1992), pp. 7–9.

40. Riesenberg, pp. 20–21, and Aristotle, *Politics*, Book 3.

41. Riesenberg, p. 30. For the persistence of the argument that women are nothing but a burden to the state in time of war, see Part I.

42. Hanna Fenichel Pitkin, *Fortune Is a Woman: Gender and Politics in the Thought of Niccolò Machiavelli* (Berkeley: University of California Press, 1984), emphasizes Machiavelli's comment that "Fortune is a woman, and it is necessary, in order to keep her under, to cuff and maul her" (p. 152). See also Riesenberg, pp. 195 ff.

43. James Burgh, *Political Disquisitions: Or, An Enquiry into Public Errors, Defects, and Abuses*, 1774–75, cited in J. G. A. Pocock, *The Machiavellian Moment: Florentine Political Thought and the Atlantic Republican Tradition* (Princeton, NJ: Princeton University Press, 1975), pp. 84, 90.

44. This strain flourished in England; see Pocock. But arms-bearing was not so tightly linked on the Continent; see Riesenberg, ch. 5, and Charlotte Wells, *Law and Citizenship in Early Modern France* (Baltimore: Johns Hopkins University Press, 1995).

45. Joyce Lee Malcolm, *To Keep and Bear Arms: The Origins of an Anglo-American Right* (Cambridge, MA: Harvard University Press, 1994), pp. 2–3.

46. John Murrin, "From Liberties to Rights: The Struggle in Colonial Massachusetts," in Patrick T. Conley and John P. Kaminski, eds., *The Bill of Rights and the States: The Colonial and Revolutionary Origins of American Liberties* (Madison: Madison House, 1992), p. 73.

47. Thomas More, *Utopia*, ed. Robert M. Adams (New York: W. W. Norton, 1975), pp. 71–75; Malcolm, p. 9.

48. Malcolm, pp. 17 ff. In the reign of Charles II, the Game Act of 1671 effectively disarmed the countryside by establishing "the property qualification needed to hunt [as] . . . fifty times the amount needed to permit a man to vote." Malcolm, p. 71.

49. Blackstone, vol. 2, quoted in Malcolm, p. 130; see also pp. 119, 134. Elaine Scarry links the right to bear arms to the constitutional protections of the population's direct authorization of war, because the guns "must be carried onto the field by persons, the leaders must address the population and persuade them to carry those guns. With nuclear weapons, this requirement disappears." Elaine Scarry, "War and the Social Contract: Nuclear Policy, Distribution, and the Right to Bear Arms," *University of Pennsylvania Law Review*, vol. 139 (1991), p. 1266.

50. See the thoughtful review of Malcolm by Robert Cottrell and Raymond Diamond, "The Fifth Auxiliary Right," *Yale Law Journal*, vol. 104 (1995), esp. p. 1014 n. 83.
51. Malcolm, p. ix.
52. In Annapolis, Maryland, in 1776, Chilton Williamson reports, men who drilled in the militia took it for granted "that everyone who bore arms should be allowed to vote, although they were aware that the 'whole company was not worth 40 pounds sterling.' " Chilton Williamson, *American Suffrage: From Property to Democracy 1760–1860*, (Princeton: Princeton University Press, 1960), pp. 108–9.
53. In the early nineteenth century, the Connecticut Democratic-Republican Party grew in strength by positioning itself as the defender of suffrage for all men who served in the militia. Richard J. Purcell, *Connecticut in Transition, 1775–1818* (Washington, DC: American Historical Association, 1918), pp. 222–23. Note, however, that eighteen-year-olds were drafted in the Vietnam War long before 1971, when they were enabled to vote.
54. Tom Paine, *Collected Writings* (New York: Library of America, 1995): "The American Crisis, III," p. 122; "Common Sense," p. 27. Women could not pledge their honor in defense of the republic, since honor, like fame, was psychologically male. The Renaissance concept which Hanna Pitkin has so well described retained its vigor: women "are invested with *other* men's sense of honor." Pitkin, p. 118.
55. Riesenberg, pp. 125–26. These debates are described in some detail in James Kettner, *The Development of American Citizenship, 1608–1870* (Chapel Hill: University of North Carolina Press, 1978), chs. 7 and 8.
56. See Sanford Levinson, "The Embarrassing Second Amendment," *Yale Law Journal*, vol. 99 (1989), p. 651.
57. Pocock, p. 544.
58. For recent discussions of this point, see Mary E. Becker, "The Politics of Women's Wrongs and the Bill of 'Rights': A Bicentennial Perspective," *University of Chicago Law Review*, vol. 59 (1992), esp. pp. 494–501; Kenneth Karst, "The Pursuit of Manhood and the Desegregation of the Armed Forces," *UCLA Law Review*, vol. 38 (1991), pp. 499–581.
59. Joseph Story, *Commentaries on the Constitution* (1833), Book III, ch. 44 (1858 ed., vol. 2, p. 677).
60. June 14, 1788, cited in Levinson, p. 647.
61. Daniel Webster speech, Dec. 9, 1814, reprinted in John Chambers, ed., *Draftees or Volunteers* (New York: Garland, 1975), pp. 108–20; see also James M. Banner, *To the Hartford Convention: The Federalists and the Origins of Party Politics in Massachusetts 1789–1815* (New York: Alfred A. Knopf, 1970), p. 339.
62. *Report of the Decision of the Supreme Court of the United States, and the Opinions of the Judges Thereof, in the Case of Dred Scott versus John F. A. Sandford, December Term, 1856*, ed. Benjamin C. Howard (Washington, DC: Cornelius Wendell, Printer, 1857; New York: Da Capo, 1970), p. 17.
63. Ibid., p. 193.
64. Alien men who had declared their intention to become citizens were subject to the Civil War draft; see John Whiteclay Chambers II, *To Raise an Army: The Draft Comes to Modern America* (New York: Free Press, 1987), pp. 51, 59.

65. Quoted in *Woman's Journal*, April 2, 1870, with response by HBB (Henry B. Blackwell).

66. See HBB, in *Woman's Journal*, March 12, 1870. New evidence from the Parthenon suggests that in ancient Greek myth, men sacrificed themselves as soldiers, but women—like Iphigenia—were themselves the sacrifice. John Noble Wilford, "New Analysis of the Parthenon's Frieze Finds It Depicts a Horrifying Legend," New York *Times*, July 4, 1995, p. 11.

67. Box 10, Folder 1. See also Box 4, Folder 15, ch. 24, "A Fight Against Evil," 1871, and "Our New York Letter" in *Woman's Journal*, June 21, 1894: Lillie Devereux Blake Papers, Missouri Historical Society. Blake made military service a repeated theme in her speeches and newspaper columns.

68. "The Subjection of Women," in John Gray, ed., *John Stuart Mill: On Liberty and Other Essays* (Oxford: Oxford University Press, 1991), p. 484.

69. In Elizabeth Cady Stanton, Susan B. Anthony, and Matilda Joslyn Gage, eds., *History of Woman Suffrage* (Rochester, NY: Susan B. Anthony, 1886), vol. 3, pp. 7–8. On Mary Smith, who dressed as a man and fought with the 24th (Iowa) Infantry throughout the entire war, see vol. 3, pp. 631–32. World War I suffragists made much of Boadicea and Joan of Arc: see Bettina Friedl, ed., *On to Victory: Propaganda Plays of the Woman Suffrage Movement* (Boston: Northeastern University Press, 1987), and Kimberly Jensen, "Minerva on the Field of Mars: American Women, Citizenship, and Military Service in the First World War" (unpublished Ph.D. dissertation, University of Iowa, 1992).

70. "The ballot is the inseparable concomitant of the bayonet. Those who practice the one must be prepared to exercise the other. To introduce woman at the polls is to enroll her in the militia." *History of Woman Suffrage*, vol. 2, pp. 563–64; May 28, 1875. See also the comments of Henry Selden during Susan B. Anthony's trial for voting, in *History of Woman Suffrage*, vol. 2, p. 671.

71. William Ingersoll Bowditch, *Taxation of Women in Massachusetts* (Cambridge, MA: Press of J. Wilson & Son, 1875), p. 32.

72. Bowditch, pp. 31–32. See also Sarah Knowles Bolton, "Women Versus Women: A Protest," *The Revolution*, April 21, 1870.

73. In *History of Woman Suffrage*, vol. 3, p. 163. Order of sentences reversed.

74. The basic study is Harriet Hyman Alonzo, *Peace as a Women's Issue: A History of the U.S. Movement for World Peace and Women's Rights* (Syracuse: Syracuse University Press, 1993).

75. Mary Beard to Elsie Hill, July 10, 1921, in Nancy Cott, ed., *A Woman Making History: Mary Beard Through Her Letters* (New Haven: Yale University Press, 1991), p. 100.

76. *Selective Draft Law Cases*, 245 U.S. 366, 368, 378–80, 390 (1918).

77. *The Selective Service Act: Its Legislative History, Amendments, Appropriations, Cognates and Prior Instruments of Security*, Special Monograph no. 2 (Washington, DC: Government Printing Office, 1954), vol. 1, pp. 7, 79.

78. For an example, see J. K. Huddle, Chief of the Passport Division to Roger Baldwin, Oct. 22, 1926, quoted in National Council for Prevention of War, Washington, DC, *News Bulletin* no. 1, July 1929, and Washington *Post*, July 14, 1929, clipping in Citizenship and Conscience Collection, Box 1, Swarthmore College Peace Collection (hereafter SCPC).

79. Dorothy Dunbar Bromley, "The Pacifist Bogey," *Harper's Monthly Magazine*,

Oct. 1930, p. 555. By the 1940s Bromley would be the Women's Page editor of the New York *Herald Tribune* and an associate of Eleanor Roosevelt. See also Brief for Respondent, *U.S. v. Rosika Schwimmer*, U.S. Supreme Court, October Term, 1928, no. 484. Subject Files, Citizenship and Conscience Collection, SCPC, and pamphlet, *The Case of Rosika Schwimmer: Alien Pacifists Not Wanted!* (June 1929), SCPC.

80. *U.S. v. Schwimmer*, 279 U.S. 644, 653–54 (1929). Justice Brandeis joined with Holmes in dissent; Sanford agreed with the Court of Appeals. The vote was 6–3.

81. *U.S. v. Schwimmer*, 279 U.S. at 648, 650.

82. "An Adventure in Citizenship," July 30, 1930, Box 2, Rosika Schwimmer Papers, Hoover Institution on War, Revolution and Peace, Stanford University.

83. The New York *Times* pointed out the anomaly; see Alpheus Thomas Mason, *Harlan Fiske Stone: Pillar of the Law* (New York: Viking Press, 1956), pp. 520–21.

84. Mimeographed statement, April 9, 1929. Subject Files, Conscience and Citizenship, Box 1, SCPC. Freda Kirchwey also supported this work.

85. Typescript statement, July 1938. Dorothea Zukierelli was denied citizenship on the basis of the *Schwimmer* decision. Subject Files, Conscience and Citizenship, Box 1, SCPC.

86. Douglas C. MacIntosh, a minister who taught theology at Yale Divinity School, and Marie Averill Bland, a nurse, had served in noncombat roles in the Great War and were willing to again if called upon.

87. Naturalization of Alien Conscientious Objectors, Hearings Before a Subcommittee of the Committee on Immigration of the U.S. Senate, 72nd Cong., 1st sess., March 22 and 26, 1932, pp. 41–42, in SCPC. Representing the Immigration Restriction League and several fraternal orders, James H. Patten said, "The question is not whether Congress will actually require that supreme sacrifice on her part, but whether, if Congress should, would she, the alien applicant for all the privileges, immunities, and protection of citizenship our Army and Navy may be called upon to afford . . . in turn be willing to make such an effort to save our Government, our Constitution, our ideals, and, yes, even our Christian civilization?" (p. 93).

88. New York *Times*, June 20, 1931, p. 4. Bill to Permit Oath of Allegiance by Candidates for Citizenship to Be Made with Certain Reservations, Hearings Before the Committee on Immigration and Naturalization, House of Representatives, 71st Cong., 2nd sess., May 8–9, 1930. See esp. pp. 13–19, 46–52. See also Naturalization of Alien Conscientious Objectors, Hearings Before a Subcommittee of the Committee on Immigration of U.S. Senate, 72nd Cong., 1st sess., March 22 and 26, 1932, pp. 29–31. The bill was rejected May 2, 1932. Bland and MacIntosh managed to persuade Harlan Fiske Stone, who had received severe criticism from people he admired for his decision in *Schwimmer*, and who also was disposed to support religiously based conscientious objection. But the vote only shifted from 6–3 in *Schwimmer* to 5–4 in *Bland*; they could not command a majority. See Mason.

89. *Girouard v. U.S.*, 328 U.S. 61 (1946). Writing for the majority, William O. Douglas observed: "The oath required of aliens does not in terms require that they promise to bear arms. Nor has Congress expressly made any such finding

a prerequisite to citizenship. . . . The effort of war is indivisible; and those whose religious scruples prevent them from killing are no less patriots than those whose special traits or handicaps result in their assignment to duties far behind the fighting front. . . . Article VI, Clause 3 of the Constitution provides that . . . 'no religious Test shall ever be required as a Qualification to any . . . public Trust under the United States.' " See also McCarran Act, 64 Stat. 987, Internal Security Act, 1950, and also 1952 McCarran Act, 66 Stat. 163.

90. Public Law ch. 720, Sept. 16, 1940, 54 Stat., 76th Cong., 3rd sess., p. 885. The draft statute had been more capacious still: "every person enjoying the privileges of a citizen of the United States has therewith the duty of contributing military service in the common defense . . ." *The Selective Service Act*, vol. 1, p. 79; vol. 2, p. 271.

91. D'Ann Campbell, *Women at War with America: Private Lives in a Patriotic Era* (Cambridge, MA: Harvard University Press, 1984), pp. 38–39.

92. Margaret Hope Bacon, *One Woman's Passion for Peace and Freedom: The Life of Mildred Scott Olmsted* (Syracuse: Syracuse University Press, 1993), p. 229. The longest and most successful campaign of the Women's Committee to Oppose Conscription (WCOC) was against the bill to draft nurses, introduced into Congress in March 1945.

93. Text of the National War Service Act of 1943, *Congressional Record*, Feb. 8, 1943, pp. 666–71.

94. Testimony on National War Service Bill, S666, March 2–June 9, 1943, U.S. Senate Committee on Military Affairs, 78th Cong., 1st sess., pp. 406–7.

95. Mildred Scott Olmsted, "The Drafting of Women for the Armed Forces," Transcript, Town Meeting of the Air, Feb. 3, 1944, WCOC Papers, SCPC. I am grateful to Wendy Chmielewski, Curator of the Swarthmore College Peace Collection, for this reference.

96. Pamphlets: Frances Witherspoon, *Four Good Reasons*, 1943, and one by Witherspoon's longtime companion, Tracy Mygatt, *Keep the Home Fires Burning*, WCOC Papers, Series A, Box 1, SCPC. I am grateful to Wendy Chmielewski for this reference.

97. U.S. Senate, Committee on Military Affairs, Hearings on Manpower, National War Service Bill, March 25, 1943, p. 91, and Witherspoon, *Four Good Reasons*.

98. U.S. Senate, Committee on Military Affairs, Hearings on Manpower . . . March 25, 1943, pp. 88–91.

99. Hearings on Manpower, U.S. Senate Committee on Military Affairs, testimony of Colonel Lewis Sanders, Chief of the Reemployment Division, Selective Service System of the War Manpower Commission, pp. 1281–84.

100. For a subtle cultural analysis of the meaning of military obligation, see Robert Westbrook, " 'I Want a Girl Just Like the Girl That Married Harry James': Women and the Problem of Political Obligation in World War II," *American Quarterly*, vol. 42 (Dec. 1990), pp. 587–614.

101. *Congressional Record*, House of Representatives, June 2, 1948, pp. 6967–70; see also House of Representatives, April 21, 1948, p. 4717.

102. For reflections on the connection of military service and civic obligation, see Morris Janowitz, *The Reconstruction of Patriotism: Education for Civic Consciousness* (Chicago: University of Chicago Press, 1983), and Janowitz testimony on the All-Volunteer Force, Hearings Before the Subcommittee on Manpower and

Personnel of the Committee on Armed Services, U.S. Senate, 95th Cong., 1st sess., March 2, 1977.

103. One example: In 1970, when Women's International League for Peace and Freedom's national board considered the ERA, Olmsted opposed it, arguing that they should refuse until they had eliminated conscription; otherwise an ERA would give the government "power to control at least 50% more of the population." She was, however, outvoted. See Bacon, p. 327.

104. Riesenberg, p. 24.

105. John C. Dann, *The Revolution Remembered: Eyewitness Accounts of the War for Independence* (Chicago: University of Chicago Press, 1980), pp. xv–xvii, and John P. Resch, "Federal Welfare for Revolutionary War Veterans," *Social Service Review*, 1982, pp. 171–95.

106. Theda Skocpol, *Protecting Soldiers and Mothers: The Political Origins of Social Policy in the United States* (Cambridge, MA: Harvard University Press, 1992), ch. 2; quotations come from p. 151.

107. 1884 *Mass Acts*, c. 320. When the practice of veterans' preference was challenged by male nonveterans, courts upheld it. For a review of statutes and cases in Massachusetts, see Brief of the Plaintiffs, *Carol A. Anthony et al. v. Commonwealth of Massachusetts*, Civil Action No. 74-5061-T, and *Helen B. Feeney v. Commonwealth of Massachusetts*, Civil Action No. 75-1991-T, U.S. District Court for the District of Massachusetts, pp. 53–81, CLUM Archives, and Blumberg, pp. 10–14.

108. Lim, "The Effect of Veterans' Reemployment Rights," esp. pp. 310–15.

109. *Anthony v. Commonwealth* and *Feeney v. Personnel Administrator of the Commonwealth of Massachusetts*, 415 F. Supp. 485, 495, 499 (D. Mass. 1976).

110. Jean Cole, "U.S. Court Voids State Veterans' Preference Law," Boston *Herald-American*, March 30, 1976.

111. Edward Powers, quoted in Boston *Globe*, March 31, 1976: "it will open up positions to women, and it will have a very positive effect on the caliber of public employees generally."

112. See the good calendar of events in *Feeney v. Commonwealth*, 366 N.E. 2nd, 1262, 1264 (Mass. 1977).

113. Boston *Herald-American*, March 31, 1976.

114. Helen Feeney personal papers, n.p., n.d.

115. William Hogan of Everett, quoted in Boston *Globe*, April 14, 1976. The American Legion held a meeting in Peabody, attended by seventy-five "agitated American Legion officials."

116. John Swift, quoted in the story on the American Legion in Lowell *Sun*, April 3, 1976.

117. Boston *Globe*, April 14, 1976.

118. Boston *Herald-American*, April 1, 1976.

119. Kiley now practices law in Quincy.

120. Boston *Globe*, April 1, Apr. 8, 1976; Boston *Herald-American*, June 25, 1976.

121. Brief Amicus Curiae of Michael S. Dukakis, *Commonwealth of Massachusetts v. Helen B. Feeney*, Supreme Judicial Court, No. 817, March 1977, p. 3.

122. *Feeney v. Commonwealth*, 366 N.E. 2nd, at 1262 (Mass. 1977).

123. *Feeney v. Personnel Administrator of the Commonwealth of Massachusetts*, 451 F. Supp. 143, 150–52 (D. Mass. 1976). The decision was *Washington v. Davis*, 426

U.S. 229 (1976), which held that an official action which had a racially disproportionate impact but no discriminatory *motivation* does not violate the equal protection guarantee. The District Court did not change its mind.

124. New York *Times*, July 15, 1978, p. 16.

125. Interview with HBF, March 1994.

126. Lowell *Sun*, Oct. 13, 1977.

127. Lowell *Sun*, Jan. 22, 1978. Ignoring the 2 percent quotas, the *Sun*, like many of those who attacked Feeney, asserted: "[Women] have not been denied the same opportunity as men ever since the United States entered World War II in 1941."

128. Robert C. Hagopian, Disabled American Veterans, to Boston *Herald-American*, June 24, 1976.

129. Concurring when the case was sent back for reconsideration in light of *Washington v. Davis*; quoted in Bellotti, Kiley, et al., Jurisdictional Statement to Supreme Court, p. 19a; cited in Oral Argument, p. 11.

130. Ruth Bader Ginsburg to John Reinstein, Aug. 15, 1978, CLUM Archives.

131. It was widely reported that Easterbrook had written the draft.

132. Brief for the United States as Amicus Curiae, pp. 7–8.

133. Editorial, Boston *Globe*, Feb. 1, 1979, p. 14.

134. Office of Personnel Management (Margery Waxman); Department of Defense (Deanne Siemer); Carin Ann Clauss (Department of Labor), Issie L. Jenkins (Equal Employment Opportunity Commission), Brief, Amici Curiae, p. 14.

135. Transcript of Oral Argument, pp. 13–14.

136. Transcript of Oral Argument, p. 14.

137. Transcript of Oral Argument, pp. 19, 25, 31.

138. *Personnel Administrator v. Feeney*, 442 U.S. 256, 283 (1979).

139. June 1979 (in personal collection of Helen B. Feeney).

140. Editorial, Boston *Globe*, June 7, 1979, p. 16.

141. Quoted in Boston *Globe*, June 10, 1979, p. 42.

142. Phone interview with HBF.

143. New York *Times*, June 6, 1979, p. A17.

144. Transcript of Oral Argument, p. 16.

145. Samuel P. Huntington, *The Soldier and the State* (Cambridge, MA: Harvard University Press, 1957), p. 157. Cited in Sheila Tobias, "Shifting Heroisms: The Uses of Military Service in Politics," in Elshtain and Tobias, pp. 163–85.

146. Tobias, p. 180. In what Tobias calls the "war-related generational struggle" after World War II, one of the few women incumbents who won reelection was Edith Nourse Rogers, who had co-sponsored and led the legislative campaign for the creation of the Women's Army Auxiliary Corps.

147. I have discussed this matter in *Women of the Republic: Intellect and Ideology in the Revolutionary Era* (Chapel Hill: University of North Carolina Press, for the Institute of Early American History and Culture, 1980), ch. 2, and " 'History Will Do It No Justice': Women and the Reinterpretation of the American Revolution," in Ronald Hoffman and Peter J. Albert, eds., *Women in the Age of the American Revolution* (Charlottesville, University Press of Virginia, 1989), pp. 3–42.

148. Barton Hacker, "Women and Military Institutions in Early Modern Europe: A Reconnaissance, *Signs*, vol. 6 (1981), pp. 643–71.

149. Walter Hart Blumenthal, *Women Camp Followers of the American Revolution* (Philadelphia: G.S. MacManus Co., 1952), pp. 38–39, and "Return of . . . Men, Women and Children of the British and Foreign Regiments," in New-York Historical Society *Collections*, vol. 49 (1916), pp. 84–89.

150. Sarah Osborn's is the most poignant account of the surrender at Yorktown that we have. It is reprinted in John C. Dann, ed., *The Revolution Remembered: Eyewitness Accounts of the American Revolution* (Chicago: University of Chicago Press, 1980), pp. 240–50.

151. Alfred F. Young, *Masquerade: The Adventures of Deborah Sampson Gannett* (New York: Alfred A. Knopf, forthcoming).

152. A fine introduction to this problem is Lauren Cook Burgess, ed., *An Uncommon Soldier: The Civil War Letters of Sarah Rosetta Wakeman, Alias Private Lyons Wakeman, 153rd Regiment, New York State Volunteers* (Pasadena, MD: The Minerva Center, 1994). Mary Livermore of the U.S. Sanitary Commission estimated that more than 400 women bore arms; Burgess reports that documentation is now available for 135 (p. 15 n. 15). See Emily Young's insightful essay, "Confederate Counterfeit: The Case of the Cross-Dressed Civil War Soldier," in Elaine K. Ginsberg, ed., *Passing and the Fictions of Identity*, (Durham: Duke University Press, 1996), pp. 181–217.

153. Jane E. Schultz, "The Inhospitable Hospital: Gender and Professionalism in Civil War Medicine," *Signs*, vol. 17 (1992), pp. 363–92, and "Women at the Front: Gender and Genre in the Civil War" (unpublished Ph.D. dissertation, University of Michigan, 1988).

154. Jensen, p. 312 et passim.

155. Hearings Before the Committee on World War Veterans' Legislation, House of Representatives, Jan. 22, 1926, *Congressional Record*, pp. 396–410. See also Treadwell, *Women's Army Corps*, p. 14.

156. Jensen, pp. 361–98.

157. Susan M. Hartmann, *The Home Front and Beyond: American Women in the 1940s* (Boston: Twayne, 1982), p. 31; Darlene Clark Hine, *Black Women in White: Racial Conflict and Cooperation in the Nursing Profession, 1890–1950* (Bloomington: Indiana University Press, 1989). Four African-American WACs were court-martialed when they refused to perform menial hospital tasks instead of the medical technology for which they were trained; the sentence of a court-martial to one year at hard labor was overturned only after an outcry from citizens' groups, including the NAACP. General Court-Martial of Frances A. Futrell et al., Fort Des Moines, Iowa, Jan. 8–10, 1945 (CM274866).

158. Treadwell, pp. 11–12; 48; Michael Rustad, *Women in Khaki: The American Enlisted Woman* (New York: Praeger, 1982), pp. 28–29.

159. *Congressional Record*, House of Representatives, June 2, 1948, pp. 6967–70. Mr. Van Zandt: "There is not a member of the House Committee on Armed Services who has not received a telephone call or a call in person from enlisted men objecting to the idea of having to take orders from a WAVE officer. Put yourself in the position of an enlisted man and I am sure you will agree with them."

160. Hartmann, p. 46.

161. Hartmann, p. 38. Emphasis mine.

162. Campbell, *Women at War with America*, p. 45.

163. *Frontiero v. Richardson*, 411 U.S. 677 (1973), tested the rules for those in service.
164. Not until 1977, after a major lobbying campaign, and in a different political climate, would this be changed.
165. Hearings on S1614 Before the Subcommittee on Organization and Mobilization of the House Committee on Armed Services, 80th Cong., 2nd sess., No. 238 at 5563-64, 1948. See also *Congressional Record*, House of Representatives, April 21, 1948, pp. 4694, 4717.
166. See President's Task Force on Manpower Conservation, *One-Third of a Nation: A Report on Young Men Found Unqualified for Military Service* (Jan. 1, 1964).
167. U.S. Air Force. *Personnel Force Composition Study: an Analysis of the Effects of Varying Male and Female Force Levels.* Prepared for the House Committee on Armed Services by the USAF Special Study Team. March 1985, vol. I, Appendix I, pp. 1–4. Until 1974, the Air Force required enlisting women to provide, in addition to what was required of men, a picture, an interview, and a special screening test.
168. Morris Janowitz, *The U.S. Forces and the Zero Draft*, Adelphi Papers no. 94 (London: International Institute for Strategic Studies, 1973), pp. 2–3.
169. Forty-nine percent of the recruits to the Army Reserve in 1975 were women. See Women in the Military, Hearings Before the Military Personnel Subcommittee of the Committee on Armed Services, House of Representatives, 96th Cong., 1st and 2nd sess., Nov. 13–16, 1979, and Feb. 11, 1980, comment of Congressman Gillespie V. Montgomery, p. 24.
170. U.S. Department of Defense, Central All-Volunteer Force Task Force, Washington, DC, "Utilization of Military Women" (A Report of Increased Utilization of Military Women, FY 1973–1977), AD-764 510. See also Janowitz, *U.S. Forces and the Zero Draft*, pp. 9–10.
171. See, for example, some of the early discussions of the role of women in an All-Volunteer Force: U.S. General Accounting Office, Report to the Congress, *Problems in Meeting Military Manpower Needs in the All-Volunteer Force*, Department of Defense, 1973.
172. D'Ann Campbell, "Women in Combat: The World War II Experience in the United States, Great Britain, Germany, and the Soviet Union," *Journal of Military History*, vol. 57 (1993), pp. 301–23.
173. WACs were given no arms training during World War II. During World War II, women could not, by law, be assigned to any sea duty except on hospital ships; in 1979 the law was changed to permit women to be assigned to other ships so long as they were not in combat. See Office of the Assistant Secretary of Defense (Manpower, Reserve Affairs, and Logistics), *Women in the Military: Background Review*, Oct. 1981, p. 38. For expansion of occupations open to enlisted women, see pp. 32–33.

   By 1981 the Department of Defense was writing: "The Army has accepted the fact that women will be deployed in combat zones as an inevitable consequence of their assignment, but does not assign women to units where they would regularly be engaged in close combat as part of their primary duties. . . . women are assigned to combat support and combat service support units."
174. Quoted in Karst, p. 531. See also Judith Stiehm, *Arms and the Enlisted Woman* (Philadelphia: Temple University Press, 1989), pp. 198–205. The governing principle, Karst argues, is that "women can be in positions in which they will

be targets, but cannot deliver violence in line-of-sight firing" (p. 532). See also testimony of Major General Jeanne Holm, USAF, ret., Women in the Military, Hearings Before the Military Personnel Subcommittee of the Committee on Armed Services, House of Representatives, 96th Cong., 1st and 2nd sess., Nov. 13–16, 1979, and Feb. 11, 1980.

175. David Sitman to Linda K. Kerber, E-mail, Dec. 28, 1994.

176. *Rowland v. Tarr*, 341 F. Supp. 339 (E.D. Pa. 1972), Civil Action 71-1480, item 1: Complaint—Class Action June 16, 1971. Andrew Rowland was eighteen on May 20, 1971. Philadelphia *Inquirer*, July 19, 1980.

177. Telephone interview with Stuart Savett, Sept. 17, 1992. Sitman thinks it was Philadelphia Resistance that made the contact with Kohn, Savett.

178. Interview with Joanna Weinberg, April 1993.

179. Donald Weinberg graduated from the University of Chicago in three years, and then, in 1966–67, spent a year of graduate school in political science before entering Harvard Law School in 1967. Sometime during his first year of law school, 1967–68, Congress lifted all deferments, but if you were already in graduate school with a student deferment, you kept it. There was some confusion; Weinberg was treated as having left graduate school and not reentered it, he was reclassified 1-A, and passed the physical in 1968. When the lottery was held he was still 1-A and his lottery number was low; Joanna Weinberg remembers that *hers* was 360. Their son Paul was born in August 1969. Donald Weinberg challenged his classification on procedural grounds; had he remained in a continuous course of study he would have been eligible for a fatherhood deferment. The backlog of cases slowed the process of litigation. When Weinberg turned twenty-six the issue faded, and they celebrated the likely end of his draft eligibility. Interview with Joanna Weinberg, Oakland, April 1993; see also story in *National Law Journal*, Aug. 11, 1980.

180. Weinberg had graduated from Harvard Law School in 1970 and joined the firm after clerking for Judge Abraham Freedman of the Third Circuit.

181. The ACLU Foundation endowed a Donald L. Weinberg Fellowship Fund awarded annually to a law student or graduate for an internship to assist in the legal research work of the ACLU Foundation of Pennsylvania.

182. *Rowland v. Tarr*, 71-1480, item 1: Complaint—Class Action June 16, 1971. Signed only by Harold E. Kohn. Telephone interview with Joanna Weinberg, February 1993.

183. Charles C. Moskos and John Whiteclay Chambers II, "The Secularization of Conscience," in Moskos and Chambers, eds., *The New Conscientious Objection: From Sacred to Secular Resistance* (New York: Oxford University Press, 1993), pp. 3–14.

184. Quoted in Jervis Anderson, *A. Philip Randolph: A Biographical Portrait* (New York: Harcourt Brace Jovanovich, 1973), p. 275. I am indebted to Gerald Gill for this reference.

185. *United States v. Seeger*, 380 U.S. 163, 176 (1965).

186. *Welch v. U.S.*, 398 U.S. 333, 340 (1970), added "ethical and moral beliefs."

187. Moskos and Chambers, p. 41. See also Charles Chatfield, *The American Peace Movement: Ideals and Activism* (New York: Twayne, 1992), pp. 127–28.

188. Moskos and Chambers, p. 226 n. 4 and p. 41; U.S. Selective Service System, *Semiannual Report of the Director of Selective Service for the Period January 1 to*

June 30, 1973 (Washington, DC: Government Printing Office, 1973), p. 55.

189. They also had technical reasons: the plaintiffs had failed "to state a claim for which relief can be granted." The complaint was grounded in the jurisdictional statute for the Civil Rights Act, which applied only to individuals acting under state law, not federal officials acting under federal law.

190. *Suskin v. Nixon*, 304 F. Supp. 71 (N.D. Ill. 1969). Among other losing challenges to the Vietnam War draft were *U.S. v. Fallon*, 407 F. 2nd 621 (7th Cir. 1969); *Suskin v. Nixon*, 304 F. Supp. 71 (N.D. Ill. 1969); *U.S. v. Dorris*, 319 F. Supp. 1306 (W.D. Pa. 1970); *U.S. v. Baechler*, 509 F. 2nd 13 (4th Cir. 1974).

191. *U.S. v. St. Clair*, 291 F. Supp. 122, 125 (S.D. N.Y. 1968); New York *Times*, July 17, 1968, p. 37.

192. Item 6: Response of defendants, U.S. Attorney Louis C. Bechtle and Assistant U.S. Attorney Warren D. Mulloy.

193. Docket item 10, p. 25. "This suit *does not* seek a judicially imposed end to the Indochina War."

194. As one Louisiana judge put it: "Congressional chivalry in drafting men only to comprise any army has a sufficiently rational basis to avoid constitutional condemnation." *U.S. v. Clinton*, 310 F. Supp. 333 (E.D. La. 1970) (item 11).

195. *U.S. v. Cook*, 311 F. Supp. 618, 622 (W.D. Pa. 1970) (item 12). They also cited *Massachusetts v. Laird*, 400 U.S. 886 (1970), on selective objection, which was dismissed despite the dissent of Justice Douglas.

196. Weinberg tried one other gambit—that the Rowland case be consolidated with another civil action, *Atlee v. Laird*, 339 F. Supp. 1347 (E.D. Pa. March 28, 1972), in which a group of taxpaying citizens challenged the war on the grounds that it was undeclared and that the conduct of the United States violated both international treaties and the U.S. Army's own regulations, especially "saturation bombing of civilian population" and the use of napalm. Chief Judge Joseph Lord III denied the move to consolidate (May 24, 1972).

197. Item 17, on April 27, 1972 (*Goldberg v. Tarr*, 510 F. Supp. 292, 293 ([E.D. Pa. 1980]).

198. See item 23 on docket. *Andrew Rowland v. Curtis Tarr*, 480 F. 2nd 545 (3rd Cir. 1973), U.S. Court of Appeals, decided May 11, 1973.

199. Item 32, April 24, 1974.

200. *Rowland v. Tarr*, 378 F. Supp. 766 (E.D. Pa. 1974). See Rosenn dissent, on the grounds that federal courts had already refused the argument of nonstudents that student deferments are unfair; therefore the argument of men that women's deferments are unfair is not logical. See item 34 on docket. Rosenn said new information in 1980 made him change his judgment. Telephone interview November 1994.

201. Item 48, July 22, 1975. E-mail from David Sitman to Linda K. Kerber, July 1995.

202. Telephone interview with Robert Goldberg, March 20, 1993. Interview with Joanna Weinberg, Berkeley, California, April 1993. On June 25, 1975, Goldberg "was permitted to intervene as a party plaintiff," the title of case was changed, and all the others except Sitman dropped out. *Goldberg v. Tarr*, 510 F. Supp. at 292 n. 1 (E.D. Pa. 1980).

203. Information from Item 81, Case Records. Pretrial Examination of Robert Goldberg, June 10, 1976, the day before his graduation from Jefferson Medical Col-

lege. Goldberg had filed for CO status five days before his eighteenth birthday.
204. Interview with Robert Goldberg, March 1993.
205. Actually, he remembered it wrong; he remembered it as 300. The number comes from his Pretrial Examination, June 10, 1976, item 81 on docket.
206. In 71-1480 Exhibits, dated Oct. 8, 1971; filed Oct. 12, 1971.
207. Item 45, May 29, 1975, Motion for Robert L. Goldberg to intervene as plaintiff. Note that this is the category Weinberg emphasized in persuading the three-judge panel that the case was not moot.
208. Interview with Robert Goldberg, March 20, 1993. Getting Goldberg into this case came perilously close to soliciting; see Goldberg's Pretrial Examination, Item 81, June 10, 1976, pp. 49–50.
209. *Kennedy v. Mendoza-Martinez*, 372 U.S. 144, 159–60 (1963).
210. *Schlesinger v. Ballard*, 419 U.S. 498 (1975), Jan. 15, 1975, sustaining 10 U.S.C. $6382. This in defendants' memo 44. May 28, 1975.
211. *U.S. v. St. Clair*, 291 F. Supp. 122, 124 (S.D. N.Y. 1968) at 124, citing *Hoyt v. Florida*, 368 U.S. 57, 62 (1961), and also *White v. Crook*, 251 F. Supp. 401 (M.D. Ala. 1966).
212. Interview with Ruth Bader Ginsburg, Washington, DC, Feb. 1990. These cases remained central to the way Justice Ginsburg understood her work and her place in history; see, for example, Jeffrey Rosen, "The New Look of Liberalism on the Court," *New York Times Magazine*, Oct. 5, 1997, pp. 60–65, 86, 90, 96–97.
213. *U.S. v. Reiser*, 394 F. Supp. 1060, 1062–63, 1069 (D. Mont. 1975). This decision will be overturned: 532 F. 2nd 673 (9th Circuit 1976).
214. Item 61, May 5, 1976; item 90, June 7, 1977, asking for extension of time. For defendants' memos, see item 57, Dec. 23, 1975; item 64, May 13, 1976, defendants' answers; item 71, June 3, 1976.
215. The hostages were taken on Nov. 4, 1979; the Soviet Union invaded Afghanistan on Dec. 27–28, 1979. The Military Selective Service Act permitted the President to reinstitute registration simply by proclamation. But because Carter wanted also to register women, he needed congressional authorization. Carter's proposal was accompanied by a long report to Congress, "Presidential Recommendations for Selective Service Reform," Feb. 11, 1980.
216. The Carter administration sought to establish a ten-year limit on the length of time veterans could claim an additional ten points on civil service examinations; congressional committees extended it to fifteen years. New York *Times*, July 15, 1978, p. 16. Women's rights groups supported Carter's efforts and shared his disappointment when he failed to limit extensive veterans' preference programs in the federal government and elsewhere.
217. Selective Service Registration, Hearings Before the Task Force on Defense and International Affairs of the Committee on the Budget, House of Representatives, 96th Cong., 2nd sess., Feb. 20, 1980, pp. 2–4.
218. See Costs of the All-Volunteer Force, Hearings Before the Subcommittee on Manpower and Personnel of the Committee on Armed Services, U.S. Senate, 95th Cong., 2nd sess., Feb. 6, 1978.
219. Interview with Richard Danzig, Washington, DC, May 1991.
220. See testimony of Robert B. Pirie, Jr., Assistant Secretary of Defense for Manpower, and M. Kathleen Carpenter, Deputy Assistant Secretary of Defense for

Equal Employment Opportunity, Nov. 13, 1979, Hearings Before the Military Personnel Subcommittee of the Committee on Armed Services, House of Representatives, 96th Cong., 1st and 2nd sess., Nov. 13–16, 1979, and Feb. 11, 1980. See esp. pp. 21–22. See also Karst, p. 577 nn. 284 and 285.

221. Office of the Deputy Chief of Staff for Personnel, *Women in the Army Policy Review* (Washington, DC: Department of the Army, Nov. 12, 1982). The Reagan administration established a "womanpause" in 1982, holding women's enlistment constant for one year before the numbers were allowed to climb again.

222. Unless otherwise noted, all direct quotations from Danzig, Rostker, and Pirie come from interview, March 29, 1995, Washington, DC. Danzig, Rostker, and Pirie believe that Lloyd Cutler was the President's adviser most in favor of registration; Stuart Eizenstat and John White most opposed. For Pat Schroeder's comments, see her testimony cited in note 217.

223. Early Monday morning, Rostker "got a phone call about eight o'clock from John White, who was Deputy Director of OMB—and had been in a sense a mentor to all of us, he had been my mentor at Rand, actually we had been in graduate school together—that said stop everything you're doing, come over here, don't tell anybody where you're going. And I came to his office, and he said, 'I need you to start writing paragraphs [about] why this is a bad idea.' And he stuck me into somebody's office, and I sat there scribbling, sending pieces of paper out" until the afternoon. "And then about four o'clock he came back and said it's lost, stick around here and the President's going to announce it." See Senate Subcommittee on Manpower Personnel, Hearings March 13, 1979. For Pirie's doubts that in the case of a draft men would insist on combat duty for women, see Hearings Before the Military Personnel Subcommittee of the Committee on Armed Services, House of Representatives, 96th Cong., 1st and 2nd sess., Nov. 13–16, 1979, and Feb. 11, 1980; Pirie testimony, Nov. 13, 1979, pp. 24–25.

224. 96th Cong., 2nd Sess. U.S. House. Committee on Armed Services. Subcommittee on Military Personnel. "Hearings on Military Posture and H.R. 6495 . . . Department. of Defense Authorization for Appropriations for Fiscal Year 1981 and H.R. 7266 Armed Forces Educational Assistance Act of 1980 . . . Feb 8, 13, 19, 21, 25–29, May 7, 1980. Washington DC, Government Printing Office, 1980. (1988 CIS microfiche H201-35.8, p. 135. Presidential message inserted in testimony.)

225. Pirie: "During the congressional campaign to reinstitute registration two years before, we had been beaten up one side and down the other by prodraft forces without the appearance of any congressional allies whatsoever. However, when the tables turned, and the President wanted to reinstitute registration, the antidraft forces in Congress came out of the woodwork, and *they* beat us up. So we got it coming and going."

226. Interview with Richard Danzig, May 1991, Washington, DC.

227. When both House and Senate committees rejected registering women, Senator Nancy Kassebaum introduced a resolution on the floor of the Senate that "would have prevented the President from registering men unless he also registered women." Herma Hill Kay, *Text, Cases and Materials on Sex-Based Discrimination* (St. Paul, MN: West Pubublishing Company, 1981), pp. 20–21 ff.

228. Jane J. Mansbridge, *Why We Lost the ERA* (Chicago: University of Chicago

Press, 1986), pp. 67–89; Donald R. Mathews and Jane Sherron De Hart, *Sex, Gender and the Politics of the ERA: A State and a Nation* (New York: Oxford University Press, 1990), pp. 138–40.

229. Mathews and De Hart, pp. 162–63; on the cultural bases of resistance to the ERA, see ch. 6.

230. Hearings on National Service Legislation Before the Military Personnel Subcommittee of the Committee on Armed Services, House of Representatives, 96th Cong., 2nd sess., March 4, 1980, pp. 101 ff.

231. H201-35.8, p. 151. In 1980, six out of seven men were in noncombat positions; 5 percent of all Army occupational classifications were "combat"-related, but they accounted for 43 percent of all Army job titles.

232. Jean Bethke Elshtain, *Commonweal*, vol. 109 (June 5, 1981), p. 331, in response to *Rostker v. Goldberg*.

233. *The Phyllis Schlafly Report*, Aug. 1981, pp. 1–3.

234. In Selective Service Registration, Hearings Before the Task Force on Defense and International Affairs of the Committee on the Budget, House of Representatives, 96th Cong., 2nd sess., Feb. 20, 1980.

235. They did urge their members to set up a "Register for Peace" booth at local post offices and offered "Register for Peace" cards for members to distribute, but the announcements were buried deep in the inner pages of *Peace and Freedom*. See issues of March 1980, p. 12; June–July 1980, p. 12; and "On Women and the Draft," Oct. 1980, p. 3.

236. Selective Service Registration, Hearings Before the Task Force on Defense and International Affairs of the Committee on the Budget, House of Representatives, 96th Cong., 2nd sess., Feb. 20, 1980, esp. Pat Schroeder, p. 4: "It has become patently clear that we are not really buying into defense, but rather into symbols."

237. See, for example, John M. Swomley, Jr., "Too Many Blacks? The All-Volunteer Force," *Christian Century*, vol. 97 (Oct. 1, 1980), pp. 902–3. Acknowledging that black leadership was divided on the subject, Manning Marable attacked Carter's proposal as one whose goal was "primarily to obtain conservative and anti-communist support in his drive toward reelection." They were suspicious; "in the final analysis, black and brown youth will still be placed in disproportionate numbers in combat or 'high risk' units. . . . the initiation of the draft means the perpetuation, not the abandonment, of racism within the military." *Black Scholar*, Jan.–Feb. 1981, pp. 13–14.

238. March 1980, pp. 38–42.

239. Selective Service Registration, Hearings Before the Task Force on Defense and International Affairs of the Committee on the Budget, House of Representatives, 96th Cong., 2nd sess., Feb. 20, 1980, p. 22.

240. Chicago *Tribune*, March 3, 1980, sect. 5, p. 6. See also Chicago *Defender*, Feb. 18, 1980, p. 5; Feb. 26, 1980, p. 13; Washington *Post*, March 3, 1980, p. 43. Was it a snide comment that led the Chicago *Defender* to accompany the article of Feb. 26 with a photograph of a grinning white woman posing with an attack gun?

241. Hearings Before the Armed Services Committee, House of Representatives, 96th Cong., 2nd sess., March 1980, p. 40.

242. Ibid., p. 82.

243. Ibid., pp. 41–42.

244. Ibid., p. 71.

245. "Our young women have a constitutional right to be treated like American ladies, with the respect and the chivalry that ladies are accorded in the Judeo-Christian culture." Ibid., p. 105.

246. Ibid., p. 7.

247. Ibid., p. 104.

248. Ibid., p. 105.

249. This argument is close to the one made by Orthodox Jewish men on behalf of Orthodox women. Jews have not traditionally been conscientious objectors, and Jewish women would not be able to make a traditional claim. "Orthodox Judaism seeks to inculcate a sense of modesty, self-discipline and family purity in relations between the sexes, and it militates against the wanton permissiveness so prevalent in many segments of our society. Drafting women and having them occupy the same barracks as men . . . and fight in isolated posts over extended periods creates tensions and temptations which are morally unwholesome." Bernard Rosensweig, president of the Rabbinical Council of America, and Julius Berman, president of the Union of Orthodox Jewish Congregations of America, letter to New York *Times*, Feb. 13, 1980. Also see Amicus Curiae brief filed in *Rostker v. Goldberg* by the Orthodox Jewish Coalition on the Draft, 453 U.S. 57 (1981) (No. 80-251).

250. Hearings, House Armed Services Committee, March 1980, p. 105.

251. 510 F. Supp. 292, 294. Docket item 92. DW responds June 8, 1979.

252. Telephone interview with Joanna Weinberg, Feb. 1993.

253. See item 143. Pinzler also tried to add two more nineteen-year-olds, Carter Faust and Steven Goldberg, but failed.

254. The room holds less than 100.

255. Rosenn, Trial Transcript, p. 20.

256. Trial Transcript, pp. 25–28.

257. Trial Transcript, p. 44.

258. Trial Transcript, pp. 47–48.

259. Trial Transcript, pp. 74–88.

260. Trial Transcript, p. 88.

261. Affidavit of Bernard Rostker, director of the Selective Service system, July 15, 1980.

262. Trial Transcript, p. 28.

263. Trial Transcript, Goldberg v. Rostker (E.D. Pa. 1980), 509 F. Supp. 586, 593.

264. *Goldberg v. Rostker*, 509 F. Supp. 586, 594, 596, 603.

265. Docket item 170: Hearing Re: Government's Application for a Stay, Friday, July 18, 1980, transcript, p. 3.

266. Philadelphia *Journal*, July 19, 1980: "Federal judges sitting in Philadelphia put a double whammy on the draft yesterday by holding it unconstitutional." Philadelphia *Inquirer*, July 19, 1980: "Male-Only Draft Ruled Illegal; Court Bars New Registration." *National Law Journal*, Aug. 11, 1980.

267. Interview with Joanna Weinberg, November 1992.

268. Interview with Judge Louis Pollak, Oct. 18, 1994, Federal Courthouse, Philadelphia.

269. Perhaps predictably, a flurry of activist organizations offered their help at this

point. "There was some conflict," Joanna Weinberg recalls, "some resentment, some protection of turf." But ultimately Weinberg and his colleagues were grateful for the assistance, particularly that of Isabelle Pinzler, Barbara Brown, and Lawrence Tribe of Harvard, who called to offer his help and that of his students.

270. Docket item 158: Supreme Court of the United States, No. A-70, "On application for stay." Brennan believed that the President's order was "a deliberate response to developments overseas"; suspending it "might frustrate coordinate branches in shaping foreign policy." Rostker himself did not believe this; interview, March 1995.

271. Amicus Curiae Brief of Congressman Lawrence P. McDonald et al., *Rostker v. Goldberg*, 453 U.S. 57 (1981) (No. 80-251). They emphasized that "the judiciary would be in the position of directing how our armed forces should prepare for national defense. This is contrary to the express intent of the Constitution and clearly not in the best interests of our national security."

272. Rosensweig, letter to New York *Times*, Feb. 13, 1980. Also see brief filed in *Rostker v. Goldberg*: "The Coalition believes the conscription of women would rend our society as perhaps no other issue could. On an individual level, it would promote rootlessness and the dissolution of the family unit which has long served as a stabilizing element in society. Socially, it would create conflict and disharmony between the majority of our society and substantial minority groups who could not conscientiously cooperate with it. . . . It would undermine national unity, subvert our national resolve, and introduce irrelevant and divisive elements into our defense efforts." Pp. 351–52.

273. Amicus Curiae Brief of Stacey Acker et al., *Rostker v. Goldberg*, 453 U.S. 57 (1981) (No. 80-251). See also *The Phyllis Schlafly Report*, XIV, No. 6, Aug. 1981 (1–3); includes photographs of the women.

274. Amicus Curiae Brief of the Women's Equity Action League Educational and Legal Defense Fund, *Rostker v. Goldberg*, 453 U.S. 57 (1981) (No. 80-251).

275. Senator Carl Levin and Congressmen Don Edwards and Robert Kastenmeier.

276. Rostker, March 29, 1995. Had they moved more efficiently, the case would have been named for Rostker's successor, Tom Turnage, who would have had less ambivalence than Rostker about the terms in which the case was set; we would know it now as *Turnage v. Goldberg*.

277. *The Phyllis Schlafly Report*, XIV, No. 6, Aug. 1981.

278. Telephone interview with Robert Goldberg, March 20, 1993.

279. Interview with Stuart Savett, Sept. 17, 1992.

280. In the possession of Joanna Weinberg. Owen Jones, who joined the suit in the final stages and was a freshman at Oberlin, came.

281. *National Law Journal*, April 6, 1981, pp. 15–16.

282. *Craig v. Boren*, 429 U.S. 190, 197 (1976).

283. Interview with Joanna Weinberg, Nov. 1992.

284. *Landmark Briefs and Arguments of the Supreme Court of the United States* (Washington DC: Government Printing Office, 1981), vol. 170, pp. 398–430.

285. All quotations from Folder 4, Box 545, William Brennan Papers, Manuscripts Division, Library of Congress.

286. *Rostker v. Goldberg* 453 U.S. at 77–79.

287. See Mary E. Becker, "The Politics of Women's Wrongs and the Bill of 'Rights':

A Bicentennial Perspective," *University of Chicago Law Review*, vol. 59, (1992), 453–517. For a bitter attack on the failure to address domestic violence forcefully in Northern Ireland, see Ailbhe Smyth, "Paying Our Disrespects to the Bloody States We're In: Women, Violence, Culture and the State," *Journal of Women's History*, Special Double Issue, vol. 6, no. 4/vol. 7, no. 1 (1994–95), pp. 190–215.

288. D'Ann Campbell quotes an Army marching song:
The WACs and WAVEs are winning the war, parley vous
The WACs and WAVEs are winning the war, parley vous
The WACs and WAVEs are winning the war
So what the hell are we?
"The Regimented Women of WWII," in Elshtain and Tobias, p. 116.

289. For thoughtful reflections on the associations of race, sex, and violence, see George L. Mosse, *Nationalism and Sexuality: Middle-Class Morality and Sexual Norms in Modern Europe* (Madison: University of Wisconsin Press, 1985).

290. Robert J. Cottrol and Raymond T. Diamond, "The Second Amendment: Toward an Afro-Americanist Reconsideration," *Georgetown Law Journal*, vol. 80 (1991), p. 359.

291. Robert Gross, "Public and Private in the Third Amendment," *Valparaiso Law Review*, vol. 26 (Fall 1991), pp. 215–21; Elizabeth Schneider, "The Violence of Privacy," *University of Connecticut Law Review*, vol. 23 (1991), pp. 973–99; Susan Schechter, *Women and Male Violence: The Vision and Struggles of the Battered Women's Movement* (Boston: South End Press, 1982).

292. Wendy Brown, "Guns, Cowboys, Philadelphia Mayors and Civic Republicanism: On Sanford Levinson's 'The Embarrassing Second Amendment,'" *Yale Law Journal*, vol. 99 (1989), p. 665.

EPILOGUE

1. Hendrik Hartog, "The Constitution of Aspiration and 'The Rights That Belong to Us All,'" *Journal of American History*, vol. 74 (1987), p. 1014.

2. Jean Bethke Elshtain, *Democracy on Trial* (New York: Basic Books/Harper-Collins, 1995), p. 29.

3. Georgie Anne Geyer, *Americans No More* (New York: Atlantic Monthly Press, 1996), p. 32.

4. "Statue of Liberty or Statue of Sham?" in Folder 455, Box 46, Dorothy Kenyon Papers, Sophia Smith Collection, Smith College, Northampton, Massachusetts.

5. For example, some of the most forceful Supreme Court decisions sustaining the power of husbands over their wives well into the twentieth century—*Thompson v. Thompson* (1910), which denied a wife damages against violent beating by her husband on the grounds that to do so would undermine "the peace of the household"; or *Breedlove v. Suttles* (1937), which rewarded women for not voting; or *Mackenzie v. Hare* (1915), which removed citizenship from American-born women who married foreign men—do not appear at all in otherwise admirable standard histories.

6. *Planned Parenthood of Pennsylvania v. Casey* 112 S.Ct. 2791 (1992): "Women do not lose their constitutionally protected liberty when they marry."

7. Robert H. Bork, *Slouching Towards Gomorrah: Modern Liberalism and American Decline* (New York: HarperCollins, 1996), p. 195.

8. Until 1986, the childless widow in Iowa would discover only after her husband died without writing a will that after $50,000 of their property was reserved for her, the rest would return to his next of kin—his parents, his siblings, his nieces and nephews.

9. This important connection is key to the argument made by Garry Wills, *Lincoln at Gettysburg: The Words that Remade America* (New York: Simon & Schuster, 1992).

A NOTE ON SOURCES

Few historians have dealt with political obligation, but many political philosophers have. I am most deeply indebted to Carole Pateman, *The Sexual Contract* (Stanford: Stanford University Press, 1988), Michael Walzer, *Obligations: Essays on Disobedience, War, and Citizenship* (Cambridge, MA: Harvard University Press, 1970), and Gabriel A. Almond and Sidney Verba's now classic *The Civic Culture: Political Attitudes and Democracy in Five Nations* (Princeton: Princeton University Press, 1963). I've also relied on J. Roland Pennock and John W. Chapman, eds., *Political and Legal Obligation* (New York: Atherton Press, 1970), and Peter Riesenberg, *Citizenship in the Western Tradition: Plato to Rousseau* (Chapel Hill: University of North Carolina Press, 1992).

A rich historical literature on the making of American constitutional and legal thought is often instructive about Americans' changing understanding of obligation. Basic are James H. Kettner, *The Development of American Citizenship, 1608–1870* (Chapel Hill: University of North Carolina Press, 1978), and Michael Grossberg, *Governing the Hearth: Law and the Family in Nineteenth Century America* (Chapel Hill: University of North Carolina Press, 1985). Important recent books on citizenship in American history and practice are David Thelen, ed., *The Constitution and American Life* (Ithaca: Cornell University Press, 1988)—a reprint of the Constitutional Bicentennial issue of the *Journal of American History*, vol. 74 (Dec. 1987); and Candice Lewis Bredbenner, *A Nationality of Her Own: Woman, Marriage, and the Law of Citizenship* (Berkeley: University of California Press, 1998). Rogers M. Smith, *Civic Ideals: Conflicting Visions of Citizenship in U.S. History* (New Haven: Yale University Press, 1997) is a magisterial examination of the anomalies and contradictions at the heart of American concepts of citizenship.

Classic essays are Blanche Crozier, "Constitutionality of Discrimination Based on Sex," *Boston University Law Review*, vol. 15 (1935), pp. 723–55; Pauli Murray and Mary O. Eastwood, "Jane Crow and the Law: Sex Discrimination and Title VII," *George Washington Law Review*, vol. 34 (Dec. 1965); Kenneth Karst, "The Pursuit of Manhood and the Desegregation of the Armed Forces," *UCLA Law Review*, vol. 38 (1991), pp. 499–581; and Rogers M. Smith, " 'One United People': Second-Class Female Citizenship and the American Quest for Community," *Yale Journal of Law and the Humanities*, vol. 1 (1989).

The last great periods of attentiveness to citizenship in the United States occurred amid the massive immigration of the turn of the century and again in the late 1930s, when the flood of refugees from Nazi Germany challenged the residents of democracies to decide whom they would accept as fellow citizens. At the end of the Cold War, we again find ourselves in a time of extraordinary political fluidity; a fresh wave of scholarship seeks to offer grounding for new ruminations about the status of citizen. Recent studies that have challenged me to think about these matters include: Rogers Brubaker, *Citizenship and Nationhood in France and Germany* (Cambridge, MA: Harvard University Press, 1992); Yasemin Nuhoglu Soysal, *Limits of Citizenship: Migrants and Postnational Membership in Europe* (Chicago: University of Chicago Press, 1994); Arjun Appadurai, *Modernity at Large: Cultural Dimensions of Globalization* (Minneapolis: University of Minnesota Press, 1996); and Gerald L. Neuman, *Strangers to the Constitution: Immigrants, Borders, and Fundamental Law* (Princeton: Princeton University Press, 1996). Jean Bethke Elshtain has been ruminating on the relationship between individuals and the state for many years; see *Private Man, Private Woman: Women in Social and Political Thought* (Princeton: Princeton University Press, 1981); *Women and War* (New York: Basic Books, 1987); and *Democracy on Trial* (New York: Basic Books, 1995). Robert D. Putman offers fresh perceptions in "Bowling Alone: America's Declining Social Capital," *Journal of Democracy*, vol. 6 (Jan. 1995), and *Making Democracy Work: Civic Traditions in Modern Italy* (Princeton: Princeton University Press, 1993). David A. Hollinger's *Postethnic America: Beyond Multiculturalism* (New York: Basic Books, 1995) is a wise and original contemplation of the challenges the U.S. faces.

1. "NO POLITICAL RELATION TO THE STATE"

The records of the Supreme Judicial Court of Massachusetts are housed in the Archives of the Commonwealth of Massachusetts, at Columbia Point, Boston; they can be supplemented by Papers of Francis Dana, James Sullivan, Theodore Sedgwick, and Robert Treat Paine at the Massachusetts Historical Society. The work of Maeva Marcus and her colleagues as editors of the *Documentary History of the Supreme Court of the United States, 1789–1800* (New York: Columbia University Press, 1985–) clarifies much that otherwise seems impenetrable. The standard legal treatises of the period include Zephaniah Swift, *A System of the Laws of the State of Connecticut* (Windham: John Byrne, 1795); Tapping Reeve, *The Law of Baron and Femme, Parent and Child, Guardian and Ward, Master and Servant, and of the Powers of the Courts of Chancery* (1816; Burlington: Chauney Goodrich, 1846); Joseph Story, *Commentaries on the Constitution of the United States* (1833; Boston: Little, Brown, 1858). For general treatments of early American legal history, with attention to a full range of obligations, see William E. Nelson, *Americanization of the Common Law: The Impact of Legal Change on Massachusetts Society, 1760–1830* (Cambridge, MA: Harvard University Press, 1975), and Morton J. Horwitz, *The Transformation of American Law 1780–1860* (Cambridge, MA: Harvard University Press, 1977). Martha McNamara, "Disciplining Justice: Massachusetts Courthouses and the Legal Profession" (unpublished Ph.D. dissertation, Boston University, 1995), has much to say about the legal culture of the early republic and the architectural spaces lawyers and judges occupied.

2. "I AM JUST AS FREE AND JUST AS GOOD AS YOU ARE"

Like everyone who seeks to understand the history of Reconstruction, I am indebted to the volumes that have thus far been published in *Freedom: A Documentary History of Emancipation 1861–1867* (Cambridge: Cambridge University Press, 1990), a stunning sampling of the millions of documents held in the Freedmen's Bureau collections of the National Archives, edited by Ira Berlin and Leslie Rowland. Chapter 2 rests on a small but significant selection from the as yet unpublished manuscripts of this great documentary project. Books that I have found indispensable in trying to understand the Reconstruction in Texas are Eric Foner, *Reconstruction: America's Unfinished Revolution 1863–1877* (New York: Harper & Row, 1988), William L. Richter, *Overreached on All Sides: The Freedmen's Bureau Administrators in Texas, 1865–1868* (College Station: Texas A&M University Press, 1991), and William Cohen, *At Freedom's Edge: Black Mobility and the Southern White Quest for Racial Control 1861–1915* (Baton Rouge: Louisiana State University Press, 1991). I have been greatly instructed by the work of Robert J. Steinfeld, notably *The Invention of Free Labor: The Employment Relation in English and American Law and Culture, 1350–1870* (Chapel Hill: University of North Carolina Press, 1991), and Christopher Tomlins, notably "Subordination, Authority, Law: Subjects in Labor History," *International Labor and Working Class History*, no. 47 (Spring 1995), pp. 56–90. Both build on the classic work of Richard B. Morris, *Government and Labor in Early America* (New York: Columbia University Press, 1946).

3. "WHEREVER YOU FIND TAXEY THERE VOTEY WILL BE ALSO"

The basic collection of documents from the Smith sisters' struggle is Julia E. Smith, *Abby Smith and her Cows, With a Report of the Law Case Decided Contrary to Law* (Hartford, 1877), reprinted Arno Press, 1972. For biographical information in this chapter, I have relied on Kathleen L. Housley, *The Letter Kills But the Spirit Gives Life: The Smiths—Abolitionists, Suffragists, Bible Translators* (Glastonbury: Historical Society of Glastonbury, Connecticut, 1993). Like every other student of the nineteenth-century women's movement, I am deeply indebted to the magisterial collection edited by Elizabeth Cady Stanton, Susan B. Anthony, and Matilda Joslyn Gage, *History of Woman Suffrage* (Rochester, NY: published by Susan B. Anthony, 1886), especially vols. 2 and 3. Legal treatises in wide use at the time include James Schouler, *A Treatise on the Law of the Domestic Relations; Embracing Husband and Wife, Parent and Child, Guardian and Ward, Infancy, and Master and Servant* (Boston: Little, Brown, 1870); Thomas M. Cooley, *A Treatise on the Law of Taxation, including the Law of Local Assessments* (Chicago: Callaghan and Company, 1876), and Cooley's *A*

Treatise on the Constitutional Limitations Which Rest upon the Legislative Power of the States of the American Union (Boston: Little, Brown, 1868; 4th ed., 1878).

Ellen Carol Du Bois's analyses of the history of women and politics are indispensable; see "Outgrowing the Compact of the Fathers: Equal Rights, Woman Suffrage, and the United States Constitution, 1820–1878," *Journal of American History*, vol. 74 (1987), pp. 836–62, and her older volume *Feminism and Suffrage: The Emergence of an Independent Women's Movement in America, 1848–1869* (Ithaca: Cornell University Press, 1978). Carolyn C. Jones's essays "Dollars and Selves: Women's Tax Criticism and Resistance in the 1870s," *University of Illinois Law Review*, vol. 1994, pp. 265–309, and "Split Income and Separate Spheres: Tax Law and Gender Roles in the 1940s," *Law and History Review*, vol. 6 (1988), pp. 259–310, are key contributions to the developing history of women and taxation in the United States, as is Edward J. McCaffery, *Taxing Women* (Chicago: University of Chicago Press, 1997).

4. "WOMAN IS THE CENTER OF HOME AND FAMILY LIFE"

Transcripts and other materials related to the trials described in this chapter are housed in the Florida State Archives and the National Archives. The national records of the American Civil Liberties Union—recently made accessible thanks to an index funded by the National Historic Records and Publication Commission—are housed at the Seeley G. Mudd Manuscript Library Department of Rare Books and Special Collections, Princeton University. The ACLU of Florida Papers are at the P. K. Yonge Library of Florida History, Department of Special Collections, George A. Smathers Libraries, University of Florida, Gainesville; the Civil Liberties Union of Massachusetts Files are at the CLUM offices in Boston. The *Papers of the League of Women Voters 1918–1974* are available on 98 reels of microfilm with a three-volume guide (Frederick, MD: University Publications of America, 1985). The papers of a number of the state chapters, including that of Florida, are in the Manuscript Division of the Library of Congress. Supreme Court Justices Earl Warren, William O. Douglas, Thurgood Marshall, and William Brennan have placed their papers in the Manuscript Division of the Library of Congress.

There is a substantial literature on the history of juries in Anglo-American law and practice. For the English background, see Thomas A. Green, *Verdict According to Conscience: Perspectives on the English Criminal Trial Jury, 1200–1800* (Chicago: University of Chicago Press, 1985). For early American legal history, see J. P. Reid, *Constitutional History of the American Revolution, vol. 1: The Authority of Rights* (Madison: University of Wisconsin Press, 1986); Shannon Stimson, *The American Revolution in the Law: Anglo-American Jurisprudence before John Marshall* (Princeton, NJ: Princeton University Press, 1990); and the books by Nelson and Horwitz listed under Chapter 1.

On modern jury practice, the place to begin is the classic Harry Kalven and Hans Zeisel, *The American Jury* (Boston: Little, Brown, 1966). Albert W. Alschuler's work is indispensable: see "Implementing the Criminal Defendant's Right to Trial: Alternatives to the Plea Bargaining System," *University of Chicago Law Review*, vol. 50 (1983), pp. 931–1011; "The Supreme Court and the Jury: Voir Dire, Peremptory Challenges and the Review of Jury Verdicts," *University of Chicago Law Review*, vol. 56 (1989), pp. 153–233; and, with Andrew G. Deiss, "A Brief History of the Criminal Jury in the United States," *University of Chicago Law Review*, vol. 61 (1994), pp. 867–928. See also Carol Weisbrod, "Images of the Woman Juror," *Harvard Women's Law Journal* IX (1986), pp. 59–82, and Barbara Allen Babcock, "A Place in the Palladium: Women's Rights and Jury Service," *University of Cincinnati Law Review*, vol. 61 (1993), pp. 1139–68.

Pauli Murray's autobiography, *Song in a Weary Throat: An American Pilgrimage* (New York: Harper & Row, 1987), was brought into print after her death by devoted friends and editors. She told her life history in an extended interview with historian Genna Rae MacNeil, part of the Southern Oral History Program at the Southern Historical Collection of the University of North Carolina, where the transcript and tapes are housed. Her personal papers are at the Schlesinger Library, Radcliffe College, Harvard University. Herbert Ehrmann left a manuscript autobiography, "The Education of a Liberal," among his papers, housed at the Harvard Law School Library. Dorothy Kenyon did not write an autobiography, but her sister-in-law Mildred Adams Kenyon began to draft one, which is now part of the splendid collection of the Dorothy Kenyon Papers in the Sophia Smith Collection at Smith College, Northampton, Massachusetts.

5. "A CONSTITUTIONAL RIGHT TO BE TREATED LIKE AMERICAN LADIES"

The papers of Mildred Scott Olmsted, the Women's Committee to Oppose Conscription, and the Conscience and Citizenship Subject Files are in the Swarthmore College Peace Collection.

We lack a fully researched scholarly history of the women in the U.S. armed forces. The classic essay on the Revolutionary period is still Barton Hacker, "Women and Military Institutions in Early Modern Europe: A Reconnaissance, *Signs*, vol. 6 (1981), pp. 643–71. For the mid-nineteenth century, see Jane E. Schultz, "Women at the Front: Gender and Genre in American Civil War Literature" (unpublished Ph.D. dissertation, University of Michigan, 1988). For World War I, see Kimberly Jensen, "Minerva on the Field of Mars: American Women, Citizenship, and Military Service in the First World War" (unpublished Ph.D. dissertation, University of Iowa, 1992). A good deal more is available on World War II; see the informative Mattie Treadwell, *The Women's Army Corps* (Washington, DC: Government Printing Office, 1954), and the analytical Leisa D. Meyer, *Creating GI Jane: Sexuality and Power in the Women's Army Corps During World War I* (New York: Columbia University Press, 1996). For a subtle cultural analysis of the meaning of military obligation, see Robert Westbrook, " 'I Want a Girl Just Like the Girl That Married Harry James': Women and the Problem of Political Obligation in World War II," *American Quarterly*, vol. 42 (Dec. 1990), pp. 587–614. Jean Bethke Elshtain and Sheila Tobias, eds., *Women, Militarism, and War: Essays in History, Politics, and Social Theory* (Totowa, NJ: Rowman & Littlefield, 1990), suggests the potential of new scholarship; see particularly Sheila Tobias, "Shifting Heroisms: The Uses of Military Service in Politics," pp. 163–85. D'Ann Campbell's recent essays, "The Regimented Women of World War II," in Elshtain and Tobias, and "Women in Combat: The World War II Experience in the United States, Great Britain, Germany, and the Soviet Union," *Journal of Military History*, vol. 57 (1993), pp. 301–23, are helpful.

On resistance to conscription, good places to begin are John Whiteclay Chambers and Charles Moskos, eds., *The New Conscientious Objection: From Sacred to Secular Resistance* (New York: Oxford University Press, 1993), and John Whiteclay Chambers, ed., *Draftees or Volunteers: A Documentary History of the Debate over Military Conscription in the United States, 1787–1973* (New York: Garland, 1975).

INDEX

Aberdeen sexual harassment scandals, 300
abolitionists, 85, 98, 184
Abzug, Bella, 285
Acker, Stacey, 295
Adams, Abigail, 10, 12, 23
Adams, John, 21, 23–24, 94, 319*n58*
Adams, John Quincy, 20, 85
Adams, Richard Frank, 45–46, 324*n118*
Adams, Sam, 319*n58*
Addams, Jane, 299
Adkins v. Children's Hospital (1923), 169
Aeschylus, 238
Afghanistan, Soviet invasion of, xxiv, 278, 288, 293, 375*n215*
African-Americans, 184; jury service by, 133–34, 139–40, 160, 197–98, 204, 358*n263, n264*; and military service, 243, 249, 263–64, 269, 284–85, 371*n157*, 377*n237*; naturalization of, 36; political rights for, 88, 93; segregation of, 161; vagrancy laws and, xxiii, 47–52, 55–80; voting rights

for, 96–98, 100, 119; *see also* civil rights movement; slavery
agricultural workers, 73, 74, 78
Aid to Dependent Children (ADC), 75
Aid to Families of Dependent Children (AFDC), 76
Air Force, U.S., 229, 265, 267, 300, 372*n167*
Alabama Court of Appeals, 198
Albritton, Dallas, 154–55, 163
Alcott, Louisa May, 107
Allen, Nancy R., 334–35*n55*
All-Volunteer Force, xxii, 250, 256, 265–66, 273, 275, 278–79, 281, 284–85, 288, 299, 300, 363*n24*
Alschuler, Albert, 360*n288*
American Association of University Women, 168, 295
American Bar Association, 168
American Civil Liberties Union (ACLU), 119, 169–70, 185, 189–90, 192, 194–97, 199, 208, 210, 229, 247, 254, 280, 296, 358*n256*; Equality Committee, 194–95, 227,